THE BRITISH REVOLUTION
VOLUME TWO

Lord Randolph Churchill
An Introduction to the House of Commons
Rosebery
Gallipoli
Chips: The Diaries of Sir Henry Channon
Memoirs of a Conservative: J. C. C. Davidson's Memoirs and Papers
Churchill: A Study in Failure 1900–39
Ambitions and Realities: British Politics 1964–70
The Complete Speeches of Sir Winston Churchill 1897–1963
Victor Cazalet: A Portrait
The British Revolution, Vol. 1

ROBERT RHODES JAMES

THE BRITISH REVOLUTION

BRITISH POLITICS, 1880–1939

VOLUME TWO
FROM ASQUITH TO CHAMBERLAIN
1914-1939

HAMISH HAMILTON
LONDON

First published in Great Britain 1977
by Hamish Hamilton Ltd.
90 Great Russell Street, London WC1B 3PT
Copyright © 1977 by Robert Rhodes James
SBN 241 89460 3

Printed in Great Britain by
Western Printing Services Ltd., Bristol

Oh, why not sing anew the songs
We sang in Yesteryear?
And, why not laugh the laughter once again
That, in Yesteryear, we knew so well?
And, why not shed the tears again
That once we shed together,
And mourn again with bitter grief
The years and friends we lost?

What point in that? What point?
Why laugh, or sing, or weep again?
We, who travelled so hard, so long, so cruelly,
Are now tear-spent, songless, and with bruiséd hearts.
Let gentle silence fall across our puny hills.
Let others laugh, or weep, or mourn;
Let others praise, and raise, and lower their sad flags.
Because, God knows, we did enough of that, and more, in Yesteryear.

And, as God also knows, we shall conquer
Tomorrow, as you, my love, triumphed in Yesteryear.

CONTENTS

ILLUSTRATIONS

Nos. 1, 2, 3, 6, 9 and 16 are reproduced by permission of the Mansell Collection, and no. 16 by permission also of *Punch*; no. 5 by permission of Glasgow Art Gallery.

Cartoons by Sir David Low are reproduced by permission of the *Evening Standard*.

PREFACE

THE FIRST VOLUME of this work presented a narrative of British politics from the formation of Mr. Gladstone's second Administration in April 1880 until the outbreak of the Great War in August 1914. This one continues that account from August 1914 to the beginning of the Second World War in September 1939. These volumes are designed as a continuous narrative of a political system and society subjected to substantial changes and formidable challenges over a period of nearly sixty years, and in which I have endeavoured to give emphasis to those individuals, episodes, and developments that seem to me to have been the most central and significant.

In the first volume I devoted particular attention to what I described as 'London Politics', with special concentration upon the House of Commons. It will be seen that as this volume develops the overwhelming significance of Parliament, and, indeed, of the British Cabinet, declines. Both continue to assert themselves, but their dominant place in the British Revolution had passed. They increasingly reacted to, rather than initiated, the most significant features of that revolution. The movement towards a full democracy was achieved by 1929, and the advent of a mass electorate required new methods and techniques. It was also to provide new priorities and new political imperatives. Radio broadcasting, to take only one development, transformed the technique of political communication even more dramatically than the new mass circulation newspapers. But the real changes lay in Britain's new position in the world, a position that in November 1918 seemed to be one of infinite power, and yet which was, within twenty years, exposed as one of desperate peril. This volume endeavours to relate how the British political system was affected first by the events of the Great War and then by the internal and external tides that buffeted it so brutally in the inter-war period.

The historian must always be afflicted by the haunting realisation of what he has omitted, whether deliberately or through his own ignorance or limitations, and also oppressed by the knowledge that the strength and failings of a nation lie principally in the contributions of those individuals whose names are not to be found in histories such as this. Thus, in dedicating this volume to the memory of my Father, I recall the many others who, by their service, their agitation, their toil, their disappointments and their sacrifices, played their individual vital roles in the vicissitudes and achievements of this remarkable nation, and who were the crucial elements in the British Revolution.

*

In the course of my researches on this and on the first volume I am indebted to so many people for assistance and advice, and to so many historians and commentators for providing the raw material of my narrative, that I can only record a general expression of my profound gratitude. With that, I hope they will be content. My gratitude to my friends and colleagues of All Souls College, Oxford, is impossible to express with adequacy, as is my thankfulness to my patient wife and family. Miss Dina Simon and Mrs. Wendy Coleman have endured the agony of typing my drafts, and have done so with infinite forbearance and great skill. I am particularly grateful to Mr. A. F. Thompson, Professor Max Beloff, the late Professor David Potter of Stanford University, California, and the late Earl Swinton for much help and encouragement over the years.

As in the first volume, I have included in the Index brief biographies of the principal individuals referred to, and have attempted to keep all footnotes to the irreducible minimum. I am once again indebted to Mr. F. T. Dunn for his most skilful preparation of the Index, and to Christopher Sinclair-Stevenson and Raleigh Trevelyan for a multitude of kindnesses.

ROBERT RHODES JAMES

CHAPTER ONE

WAR AND COALITION, 1914–1915

FROM 1870 UNTIL July 1914 the principal preoccupations of British politicians had been domestic, with Imperial interludes. After a visit to Britain in 1899, von Bülow wrote that:

British politicians know little of the Continent. They do not know much more of Continental conditions than we do of those of Peru or Siam. To our ideas they are rather naïve. They are naïve in their candid self-seeking and again in the way in which they give their confidence. They believe with difficulty that others have bad motives. They are very calm, very easy-going, very optimistic.

This domestic preoccupation was not surprising, and was particularly evident in the years 1906–14. The Tariff Reform–Free Trade battles of 1903–5 had been followed by the long drawn-out struggle between the Conservative-dominated House of Lords and the Liberal Government that had not been resolved until August 1911; this, in turn, was followed immediately by the Home Rule crisis, which opened at the beginning of 1912 and was not resolved by August 1914. Other matters of concern, such as the serious industrial unrest of 1911 and 1912, the suffragette movement, and the controversies over the implementation of the social programme of the Liberal Government, ensured that the domestic political scene was heated, time-consuming, and absorbing—and irrelevant to the new challenges from abroad.

In retrospect, it is evident that by at least 1909 a definite change had occurred in Britain's relationship with Europe. It was not so evident to contemporaries. The established principle of British foreign policy since the 1870s had been non-commitment to foreign alliances, and particularly European alliances, while at the same time preserving British interests and keeping a wary eye on the ambitions of the major European powers. But by 1909 this principle had been slowly and irreversibly eroded. Three times between 1898 and 1901 there were serious attempts to build an Anglo-German Alliance, to which the unmistakable response was the Second Navy Law of 1900 and the threat of a German battle fleet of thirty-four battleships and fifty-two cruisers within sixteen years. The German assumption that the British could not find allies elsewhere in Europe seemed well-founded in 1900; all over the world there seemed unlimited possibilities for serious clashes between the British on the one hand and the French and the Russians on the other. Thus, Joseph Chamberlain's threat that the British, if spurned, would turn elsewhere was not taken seriously in Berlin.

Von Bülow would have been well advised to have read the wise remark of the French historian Sorel, written in 1893, upon the British:

Their history is full of alternations between indifference which makes people think them decadent, and a rage which baffles their foes. They are seen, in turn, abandoning or dominating Europe, neglecting the greatest continental matters and claiming to control even the smallest, turning from peace at any price to war to the death.

The British emergence from European isolation had not been a planned operation. It was a slow dawning of recognition that a new peril lay close. The Anglo-Japanese Treaty of 1902, the entente with France in 1904, and the convention with Russia in 1907, were not connected parts of a coherent strategy, but were separate, individual, *ad hoc* defensive arrangements. But, when assembled together, they represented a very important change from the situation that had existed when Salisbury had ceased to be Prime Minister. The very fact that the major differences between Britain and Russia and France had been resolved was in itself of very considerable importance, and signified that the British, after a long absence, were now concerned with European power politics.

The Algeciras Crisis at the beginning of 1906—which occurred almost immediately after Sir Edward Grey came to the Foreign Office—had been an important demonstration that the new entente with France was not to be easily fractured. It also gave impetus to the secret Anglo-French military, and subsequently naval, conversations. Furthermore, Russia had supported the French, and the international recognition of the mandates of France and Spain in Morocco was manifestly the result of British and Russian support for the French. The Anglo-Russian Convention of 1907 may not have been popular in Britain—particularly in the Liberal Party—but it, too, marked another important development of what was to become called the Triple Entente. Europe was moving slowly and uneasily into two armed camps and Britain was clearly showing her preferences.

The character and capacity of Edward Grey remain subjects of deep controversy. He enjoyed to a very exceptional extent the trust of his colleagues and the respect of his political opponents. The warmth and kindliness of his character glow down the years; he was not regarded as partisan; his social radicalism—which was genuine—won him admiration among the Liberals, and his record of sympathy towards Imperialism and British interests evoked strong support among the Conservatives.[1] But it is difficult to believe that Grey fully appreciated the direction in which British foreign policy was now moving. He believed in the Concert of Europe. He believed in the preservation of peace. He had little understanding of the brutal realities of European power-politics. He lacked Rosebery's or Salisbury's intuitive knowledge of how nations saw their futures or sought their aspirations. He viewed Europe from afar. Furthermore, he was under pressure from all sides. The Liberals loathed expenditure on armaments, the overwhelming mood of the Liberal Party was pacific, and French and Russian ambitions were viewed by many with no less suspicion than those of Germany. He followed Rosebery's tactic of secrecy in his conduct of foreign affairs, and his colleagues were in general very inadequately informed of his actions, and of their implications. Thus, when the crisis came at the end of July 1914 few Ministers had any realisation of the trap in which they had been caught. But in the Services, and in the Foreign Office itself, where the powerful personality of Sir Eyre Crowe was dominant, there was strong pressure to convert loose entente agreements into precise and binding alliances. Grey, while aware of the strength of these arguments, did not or would not carry them out. He achieved the worst of all possible situations, in which there was no clear understanding by the European powers of what the

---

[1] The title of 'the Unionist Party', first suggested by Lord Randolph Churchill in 1886 to cover the Conservatives and those Liberals who opposed Irish Home Rule, lasted until 1921, and the party still calls itself 'the Conservative and Unionist Party'. But in this volume it will be described as the Conservative Party throughout.

British would or would not do in the event of a serious crisis, and yet had permitted commitments which severely reduced the freedom of manoeuvre which had been the key element of British European policy. Of these facts the majority of the British Cabinet were wholly unaware. Thus, Britain drifted along, while war-fever began to mount.

On this latter point, a digression may be permitted. One of the most interesting aspects of popular literature in Europe from 1900 onwards was the considerable preoccupation with future wars. In 1900 a German writer, Karl Eisenhart, described a war against Britain; an English author, Colonel Maude, published in the same year *The New Battle of Dorking* which envisaged a French invasion of Britain. In *The Invaders* (1900), Louis Tracy related the fortunes of a secret Franco-German invasion. In Max Pemberton's *Pro Patria* (1901) a secret Channel Tunnel from which Britain was to be invaded by the French was opportunely discovered by a British officer. In March 1900—at the height of the Boer War—*Le Monde Illustré* devoted an entire issue to an illustrated account of a Franco-British war; a 'Capitaine Danrit' (whose real name was Driant, and who was killed at Verdun) described a swift invasion and total defeat of Britain, proving that 'Britain is really a colossus with feet of clay'.

Such publications had been intermittent since the 1870s, and the first authentic example was probably Sir George Chesney's *The Battle of Dorking*, first published in the May issue of *Blackwood's Magazine* in 1871. The interesting features of the publications at the beginning of the century were their quantity and their choice of enemies. Until the early 1900s, British authors usually chose France as the enemy, and the French were divided between Germany and Britain; after 1904 Germany held the field. In Germany itself there was little interest in this *genre* until about 1904, but subsequently it was as popular in that country as elsewhere; on the whole, England had the edge over France as the likely foe.

Perhaps the most sensational single work—and unquestionably the only example of real and lasting literature—was Erskine Childers' classic *The Riddle of the Sands* (1903), which described how a young and rather pompous amateur yachtsman cruising with a friend in the Friesland Islands blundered across a German rehearsal for a full-scale invasion of England. No less a person than the Kaiser himself appeared, and it was not surprising that in Germany copies were confiscated. In England it had a spectacular success, and several hundred thousand copies of the cheap edition were sold. More was to be heard later of the author, at that time a clerk in the House of Commons.

Few could rise to this standard, but William Le Queux and Guy du Maurier—whose play, *An Englishman's Home*, opened in 1908 and ran for eighteen months—approached it. In 1906 Le Queux serialised in the *Daily Mail* an account of a German invasion of England that sold a million copies when published in book form, and was translated into twenty-seven languages; in the German edition the ending—a total German defeat—was tactfully omitted. The work was specially commissioned by Harmsworth, and Le Queux not only spent four months in the probable invasion area but had worked out with Lord Roberts the most likely German tactics. For sales reasons, the final account involved battles up and down the country, and *Daily Mail* sandwich men, dressed in Prussian uniforms and helmets, stalked the streets. The success was phenomenal. Lord Roberts wrote an introduction to the book version:

> The catastrophe that may happen if we still remain in our present state of unpreparedness is vividly and forcibly illustrated in Mr. Le Queux's new book which I recommend to the perusal of every one who has the welfare of the British Empire at heart.

Humour was, alas, rarely seen, although the opening chapter in *The Riddle of the Sands* is a very notable exception. Another was the young P. G. Wodehouse's *The Swoop! Or How Clarence Saved England*, a sadly neglected work of this brilliant writer, which relates how nine invasion armies stormed wildly across the country, wholly ignored by the inhabitants. Russians, Germans, Swiss, Chinese, Young Turks, Moroccan brigands, the Mad Mullah and the Prince of Monaco were actively involved. In these irritating excitements cricket, golf, and normal life continued unperturbed; Londoners complained of the noise; the news of the invasion was given in the Stop Press between the racing results and the cricket scores. Eventually the locals became annoyed, the invaders fell into severe disputes with each other, and went home. The book was not a commercial success.

Another interesting point about this literature—which had become very voluminous by 1914—was the fact that very few of the authors foretold the future with any accuracy. There were, however, some notable exceptions. A Captain Guggisberg in 1903 described a German invasion of Belgium and a consequent British involvement in a European war. H. G. Wells anticipated the tank in his short story 'The Land Ironclads', and, astonishingly, the atomic bomb—by name—in *The World Set Free*, giving the year 1959 when every Power 'went to war in a delirium of panic, in order to use their bombs first', and describing the consequent 'unquenchable crimson conflagration of the atomic bombs'. This, also, was a commercial failure. When Conan Doyle, in the July issue of the *Strand Magazine* in 1914, anticipated the defeat of Britain as a result of a naval blockade by enemy submarines he was formally, officially, and majestically censured for alarmism by responsible naval opinion.[1]

These works have much more than a mere antiquarian interest. Their volume and popularity give at least some measure of the alarm and interest in war matters that existed in Europe from 1900 onwards. Henry Newbolt has written of his generation that 'we spent all our lives among warring nations, and in grave anticipation of the supreme danger which broke upon us at last'. The popular reaction to the Dreadnought crisis in 1908 and the vehemence of the popular Press undoubtedly played its part. Writing in the *Nineteenth Century* in August 1911, General Sir Reginald Hart declared that 'War represents motion and life, whereas a too prolonged peace heralds in stagnation, decay, and death'. Certainly in the Services, there was little doubt of who the future enemy was to be.

Their view was given strong support by the actions of the German Government. The British made many mistakes in this period, but their recognition of the essential belligerence and expansionism of Germany was well-founded. France, although with an immense army, was weak at sea. The large and rambling Austrian-Hungarian Empire was in clear decomposition, and the deposition of the Sultanate in Turkey and the accession of a group of arrogant, brutal, and ambitious officers under the evil genius of Enver Pasha had done nothing to reverse the relentless disintegration of the Ottoman Empire. Here, too, the Germans were eager and active. Wherever one looked in Europe during these years, the presence of German interest and ambition was evident, and it was not at all fanciful to see the very real possibility of a Europe—and even a Middle East—dominated by Germany. It was

---

[1] See I. F. Clark: *The Tale of the Future* (1961). Quoted in A. J. Marder: *From the Dreadnought to Scapa Flow* (vol. I, 1961), p. 3.

this prospect that so concerned the Foreign Office, and it was based upon the new stern realities of the situation.

But—and this was particularly true of the public awakening to the softly developing crisis—it was the building of a modern North Sea Fleet which provided a direct challenge that could not be ignored. All attempts to end the naval race by negotiation failed; the last ones were in 1912, when Haldane proposed to the Kaiser a lowering of the British superiority rate, and in March 1913, when Churchill proposed a 'naval holiday' in battleship construction. The German Government proceeded relentlessly on its course. The Cabinet decided to retain a sixty per cent superiority of Dreadnought strength and build two keels to one; it was also decided to increase the association with the Dominions for Imperial defence and to withdraw from the Mediterranean, leaving that area to the French, and concentrating on the North Sea and the Channel. It was this decision which, perhaps almost more than the military conversations, put the British in really close association with the French. Formal letters between Grey and the French Ambassador on November 22nd 1912 stated that these arrangements did not bind either Government; but each also agreed that, if danger threatened either, the two Governments would consult. Remorselessly, the freedom to manoeuvre independently, which was at the heart of late-Victorian foreign policy, was disappearing.

This became grimly evident in the Agadir crisis of 1911. The Germans had a real grievance that the French were not honouring the Algeciras agreements of 1906, but the German methods—the dispatch of a warship to Agadir, a closed port, and demands for French concessions in the Congo—compromised their case. As Asquith pointed out to the King on July 4th:

> The sudden discovery of German 'subjects' and 'threatened interests' in the immediate neighbourhood of the only harbour on the western coast of Morocco which can be developed into a naval and commercial base, facing the Atlantic, is an interesting illustration of 'Real-Politik'.

The crisis was important for another reason. It drew Lloyd George out of his marked pacifist stage. 'I think *au fond* he has a strong element of Jingoism in his nature', Winston Churchill had written to Rosebery in 1905. 'I should not be surprised to see that develop with the exercise of power.'[1] His Mansion House speech of July 21st was a personal and national turning-point:

> I would make great sacrifices to preserve peace. I conceive that nothing would justify a disturbance of international goodwill except questions of the gravest national moment. But if a situation were to be forced upon us, in which peace could only be preserved by the surrender of the great and beneficent position Britain has won by centuries of heroism and achievement, by allowing Britain to be treated, where her interests were vitally affected, as if she were of no account in the Cabinet of Nations, then I say emphatically that peace at that price would be a humiliation intolerable for a great country like ours to endure.

This was a very serious crisis, at which, at one point, war seemed more probable than peace. But although it was resolved, it had momentous consequences. The revelation to the Cabinet of naval unpreparedness, furthermore, resulted in Winston Churchill replacing Reginald McKenna at the Admiralty. Churchill's period as First Lord was to be tumultuous and controversial, but the advantages far outweighed the errors that he committed. Churchill's sense of the melodramatic, his overwhelming egotism and lack of tact in dealing with men older and more experienced than himself, made him many enemies in the Navy, and not all his actions proved to be wise. But he injected into naval affairs an energy and a decisiveness which had been lacking under McKenna, and which were to ensure that the Royal Navy remained, by 1914, the greatest sea power in the world. Since they had first met in 1906, Churchill had held a high regard for the opinions of the former First Sea Lord, Lord Fisher, now in retirement but still intensely active and vehement. Between 1911 and 1914 they were in constant communication and in substantial agreement about what must be done. The conversion of Churchill and Lloyd George, the two most vigorous opponents of the Dreadnought programme of 1907–8, was a most significant event. Although they were at loggerheads over the issue of the Naval Estimates early in 1914, this was a formidable combination.

The general deterioration in Anglo-German relations, and in particular the potentially perilous situation in the Balkans, combined to edge Britain towards total European involvement. From this Grey

[1] Rosebery Papers (Churchill to Rosebery, May 9th, 1905).

and the Cabinet shrank, yet the actions of the British Government between 1907 and 1914, taken collectively, presented it with less and less opportunity for disengagement. All plans for the part to be played by a British Expeditionary Force were based on the assumption of joining with the French Army against Germany, and British naval dispositions were also based on the same premise.

The inflexibility of the plans of all the Great Powers has been constantly emphasised by historians of the pre-war period, and this emphasis is fully merited. The concept of 'contingency plans' did not exist. The German military plan was for a bold sweep through Belgium to envelop the French defences; this presupposed British neutrality. The German *naval* plans, however, assumed hostile British participation. The French plan was for an immediate assault upon the lost provinces of Alsace-Lorraine, with the British Army protecting their left flank and the Navy guarding the Channel and the North Sea. Russian support, to divert and hold down substantial German forces, was also assumed. The British position did not mean automatic participation in a Franco-German war, but the distinction was somewhat unrealistic. The plans themselves were dangerous enough— the assumptions were even more perilous. Until something happened, no one really knew what would happen.

The pacific element in the Cabinet, the Liberal Party, and particularly in the Labour Party, was powerful. To this group, prospect of involvement in a European war was anathema, and was rarely considered probable. Two leading Liberal dailies, the *Daily News* (edited by A. G. Gardiner) and the *Manchester Guardian* (edited by C. P. Scott), and the weekly *Nation* (edited by H. W. Massingham), were strongly opposed to any British intervention in any European war. It had been with considerable difficulty, and at the cost of a Cabinet crisis, that Churchill had been able to get his Estimates for 1914–15 agreed, and then only on the understanding that those for 1915–16 would show substantial reductions. At the height of the debates in the Cabinet at the end of July 1914, Asquith noted of the strongly anti-interventionist views of Lord Morley (Lord President of the Council) and Sir John Simon (Attorney-General) that 'This no doubt is the view for the moment of the bulk of the party', and all the available evidence strongly supports this conclusion. Up to August 3rd Ministers were being vigorously urged by Liberal and Labour associations throughout the country to keep Britain out of the European crisis.

This crisis, when it came on July 24th, was wholly unexpected. Between January 29th and July 24th the Cabinet discussed foreign affairs only twice—on May 14th (when the suggestion that military conversations with Russia should be opened was turned down, although naval co-operation should be extended) and on May 21st when the deportation of a Turkish officer at Durazzo by Austria and Italy without consultation was raised by Grey; in addition, on June 26th it was agreed to grant £100,000 to Persia 'to keep the gendarmeries going', and on July 2nd a possible British base in the Persian Gulf was discussed. There was no general discussion on foreign affairs before July 24th. The British and German Governments had come to an agreement concerning the Baghdad–Berlin Railway in June; relations with Russia over Persia had reached a low point.

All politicians were obsessed by the Irish Question, and the real possibility of civil war. The European situation seemed calm. There was, accordingly, no immediate appreciation of the seriousness of the situation when the assassination of the Archduke Prince Ferdinand of Austria in Sarajevo set in motion immense forces. The successfully resolved crises in the Balkans in 1912 and 1913 had lulled apprehensions. Thus, it was only very slowly that the magnitude of the new crisis impressed itself vigorously upon Ministers. On July 24th, after hearing of the brutal Austrian ultimatum to Serbia, Asquith noted that 'Happily there seems to be no reason why we should be anything more than spectators.' Morley's account records that after Grey's statement about the developing situation on the Continent and the need for a fundamental decision about Britain's role, 'the Cabinet seemed to heave a sort of sigh, and a moment or two of breathless silence fell upon us'.

When it became apparent that this was a real war-crisis, the Cabinet broke apart. By July 28th it was evident that, out of twenty Ministers, there was a potential 'peace party' of ten, of whom Lloyd George, Morley, Burns, and Harcourt were the most significant. It is very doubtful that a positive declaration by the British Government at this stage would have stopped the ponderous war-machines that were now heaving laboriously into action all over Europe; but the British Government was in no condition to deliver such a declaration. On July 29th it proceeded cautiously towards the heart of the matter, the threatened neutrality of Belgium. Morley described the discussion as 'thin and perfunctory', and Asquith reported to the King that:

After much discussion it was agreed that Sir E. Grey should be authorised to inform the German and French Ambassadors that at this stage we were unable to pledge ourselves in advance either under all conditions to stand aside, or in any conditions to join in.

Asquith, Grey, Churchill—'with his best daemonic energy', in Morley's words—and Haldane were the most vigorous advocates of intervention, and certainly Churchill was the most vehement, demanding immediate mobilisation. Asquith, although in basic agreement with Grey, was cool. His main preoccupation was to keep the Cabinet united during what Churchill called 'this flaming week'. Although Asquith supported Grey, his attitude on the main question strengthened only gradually. As late as August 1st he was writing that 'I am still *not quite* hopeless about peace, tho' far from hopeful'.

'The Cabinet', as Churchill has written, 'was overwhelmingly pacific.' On the 28th it approved his decision—actually taken in the first place by Prince Louis of Battenberg, the First Sea Lord—to postpone the dispersal of the First and Second Fleets after manoeuvres. But the dissensions were acute. 'Had it not been for Asquith', Grey has written, 'the outbreak of war might have found us with a Cabinet in disorder or dissolution, impotent to take any decision.' But resolution of the crisis needed time. The French expostulated, the European war-machines were in motion. On July 31st Grey informed the French that he was still unable to 'give any pledge at the present time'. He also asked the French and German Ambassadors whether their Governments would respect Belgian neutrality, and asked the Belgian Government whether it would fight if invaded. The French and Belgians replied affirmatively; the Germans refused to make any statement one way or the other. On July 30th Austria declared war on Serbia, and Grey's proposal for another London conference to settle the Balkans dispute was abortive.

On August 1st the British Cabinet was on the point of disintegration, and the City of London was strongly pacific. That evening Germany and Russia were at war. Anti-war demonstrations were hurriedly planned in London. On August 2nd Burns resigned when it was agreed that the German Fleet would not be permitted to enter the Channel. Other resignations loomed. On the same day the Unionist leaders sent a letter urging support of France and Russia but making no reference to Belgium. Burns was adamant against involvement,

Morley and Beauchamp were close behind him, and it was evident that Lewis Harcourt (Colonial Secretary) and Sir John Simon were on the verge of resignation. 'We came, every now and again, near to the parting of the ways', Asquith recorded. But Lloyd George was beginning to move in the direction of the interventionists. When the Cabinet met on August 3rd Burns, Morley, Simon and Lord Beauchamp had resigned. Churchill had made overtures to the Conservative leader Bonar Law for a possible Coalition Government, but he was acting alone and Law did not respond. With this exception, there was no consultation at all between the principal party leaders on a matter of such momentous importance for the nation. But the news of the German ultimatum to Belgium and its rejection earlier that morning had transformed the situation, and it was Lloyd George who success-fully appealed to the four Ministers to postpone their resignations and to sit on the Treasury Bench.

Grey's statement in the Commons that afternoon is often cited as one of those rare occasions when a speech swings the House of Com-mons. It can now be seen that its principal legal point—British commitment to Belgium—was dubious, and that Grey's claim that 'if we are engaged in war we shall suffer but little more than we shall suffer if we stand aside' should have been more thoroughly ques-tioned. But that extraordinary phenomenon, which we can only call war-fever, had gripped the House of Commons as avidly as it had Europe. When the Cabinet met on August 4th, only Burns and Morley had resigned, Redmond had declared the support of Ireland, and only a fragment of the Labour Party had expressed its opposition to war. The only business was to approve the issue of an ultimatum to Germany to withdraw from Belgium, to expire at 11 p.m.

Outside Parliament, the movements to oppose the war had been overtaken by events. The attitude of the Labour Party was somewhat confused, and it, also, had serious divisions. On Sunday, August 2nd, there had been a demonstration against the war in Trafalgar Square, addressed by Keir Hardie, H. M. Hyndman, George Lansbury and Arthur Henderson. But at a meeting on the following morning of Labour MPs it was clear that they were seriously divided. In the event, only Ramsay MacDonald and the Independent Labour Party members opposed the war. After Grey's triumph, only MacDonald had asked the fundamental question, Was Britain in danger? On August 5th he resigned as leader, and was replaced by Arthur

Henderson. He was at the time, and for many years, most cruelly excoriated. But this courageous action was to begin the process whereby he was to rise to be the first Labour Prime Minister of Britain.

But he and his tiny band were a minority indeed. Other bodies, such as the hastily formed Neutrality Committee and the Neutrality League, had hardly begun activity before war was declared. A full-page appeal by the League against the war was published in the *Daily News* on August 5th, a pathetic memento of a movement that never had time to plead its cause. The violation of Belgium had united the Cabinet, the Liberals, and the country. The carefully prepared plans of the War Office and the Admiralty were now put into operation. Europe marched joyously, and with ardent expectations, into catastrophe.

*

Britain went to war in a glow of national unity. The German invasion of Belgium seemed to sweep away the disputes and controversies that had occupied the nation for the previous decade. Home Rule was to be postponed until the end of the war, and Irishmen from north and south enlisted in the British Army. The struggle between the Conservative Opposition and the Liberal Government was covered by a display of all-party concord. The Liberal Party and the trade unions pledged their support. In the Commons on August 3rd Ramsay MacDonald had courageously declared that 'whatever may be said about us, we will take the action . . . of saying that this country ought to have remained neutral, because in the deepest parts of our hearts we believe that that was right and that that alone was consistent with the honour of our country and the traditions of the Party that are now in office.' But MacDonald's was almost a lone voice raised in protest, and after his replacement as chairman of the Parliamentary Labour Party by Arthur Henderson opposition to the war, to all practical purposes, did not exist. It was this unity which, although sorely tried, was to bring Britain through a war whose magnitude was undreamed of in August 1914.

But the events that had preceded the war in British domestic politics could not be swept aside. No Act of Oblivion could be passed. The circumstances of the political struggle had been drastically changed, and were to be even more drastically changed before the end of the war, but the struggle itself could not for long be suppressed.

As Mr. A. J. P. Taylor has emphasised,[1] the Englishman in 1914 was a very free agent. Since 1905, State expenditure on the social services had roughly doubled, but the impact was small. The State now protected the very needy to a modest extent, and rather less than eight per cent of the national income went on taxes. There was no compulsory military service, no limitations on the freedom of the law-abiding citizen to go where he liked, do what he liked, and buy what he liked. The apparatus of the State, familiar in France and Germany, and to an even greater extent in Russia, barely existed at all in the England of 1914. Unemployment stood at just over three per cent. On the debit side, however, was the fact that although income tax did not start until a man's income exceeded £160 per annum there were less than one and a quarter million taxpayers —or less than seven per cent of the occupied population. Some two and a half per cent of the population owned two-thirds of the nation's wealth. The average annual wage of the industrial worker was £75 per annum; that of the salaried middle class was £340. As Charles Masterman has written, 'the rich despise the Working Class; the Middle Class fear them'. But although this situation was potentially dangerous, there seemed to be no problems that could not, eventually, be solved without any untoward disturbances. Britain was still a very rich nation. Her navy had an immense reputation, and, numerically, an overwhelming preponderance over any possible rival. The Empire was united. It was perhaps in this self-assurance and confidence that Britain presented to superficial observers her most formidable and impressive characteristics.

*

The opening six weeks of the war constituted in many respects the most dramatic and exciting period of all. Europe surged to the colours. There was never a more popular war. The generals and the admirals were at last able to put in motion, and test in action, their long-prepared plans. The Russian steamroller started to move purposefully westwards. The Schlieffen Plan progressed smoothly. The French marched ardently into Alsace-Lorraine. The British Expeditionary Force was conveyed swiftly and efficiently across the Channel in conditions of deep secrecy to take up its allotted position on the

[1] *English History, 1914–45*, 1.

French left flank. The Navy at once initiated the blockade of Germany, and one of its first actions was to cut the Germans' Transatlantic cable.

In a sense, everything was going to plan and nothing was going to plan. The most striking feature of these opening manoeuvres was their remarkable lack of mutual relevance. Europe was marching and counter-marching, immense armies were deploying into well-rehearsed positions, but the relationship between these formidable movements was, initially, difficult to determine. Indeed, were it not for the very hugeness of these forces, one has the feeling that they might have marched indefinitely without making serious collision.

The first month of the war saw the plans of every belligerent go bitterly agley. The Germans had not expected a Russian invasion of East Prussia, and were temporarily thrown off balance. Then, the Russians were brought to a shattering halt at Tannenberg. The French were bundled ignominiously out of Alsace-Lorraine. The Belgian resistance was more severe than the Germans had antici-pated; the massive German bombardments of the Belgian fortresses were infinitely more severe than anyone had expected. The Schlieffen Plan then went forward after this temporary setback with an ease which the Germans had never expected. The German armies marched through militarily deserted countryside while their lines of com-munication became dangerously extended. On August 22nd two British divisions of the B.E.F. blundered into six divisions of the German 1st Army at Mons. It is difficult to say which side was the more surprised; probably the Germans. If the dramatic appearance of the British in Belgium was a shock to the Germans, the vigour and efficiency of their fighting was even greater. Since the Boer War the British Army had laid great emphasis upon musketry, and the devastating effect of the British rifle-fire at Mons passed into legend. But it was impossible to hold the position when the French 5th Army on the British right fell back, and the retreat from Mons began. On August 26th the IInd Corps, under Smith-Dorrien, fought a brilliant but costly rearguard action at Le Cateau. After this the British retreat could continue undisturbed. They marched 200 miles in thirteen days, almost due south. The bewilderment and exhaustion of the troops were alike considerable. Unmolested, the German 1st Army continued its sweeping movement to the south-west.

Britain had gone to war in a somewhat magisterial manner. At 10.30 p.m. on the evening of August 4th the King held a Privy Council which was attended by only one Minister—ironically, Beauchamp, the First Commissioner of Works, who succeeded Morley as Lord President of the Council on the following day—which sanctioned the proclamation of the declaration of war with Germany. The Cabinet was not involved. The Empire was not consulted. Each Governor-General, as the King's representative, issued the royal proclamation. No objection was necessary. The Empire was solidly for the war.

Asquith did not consider that the emergency justified any major changes in the Government. No consideration was given to the possibility of a Coalition. Relations between the two parties were so bad that it would have been difficult for either side to work harmoniously with the other, and there was, in addition, the antipathy between Asquith and Bonar Law. Had Arthur Balfour still been the Conservative leader, it might possibly have been different. Asquith always showed Balfour particular favour, and he had retained his position on the Committee of Imperial Defence.

There was, however, one notable change in the Cabinet. Lord Kitchener, the conqueror of the Sudan, the (eventual) victor in South Africa, and also the victor over Curzon in India, and, since 1911, 'British representative' in Egypt, was regarded as a great capture as Secretary of State for War. Kitchener's prestige was enormous, and this widespread confidence was not wholly misplaced. Kitchener was not as great a man as his contemporaries generally believed, but he was a far greater one than his many subsequent detractors have alleged. On all the big issues he was right. When everyone said that the war would be brief, Kitchener startled the Cabinet when he sombrely retorted that it would be long. Enormous new armies had to be created and equipped. He took on his shoulders all the burdens of the Army. The officers of the General Staff, so laboriously created by Haldane, were bundled off to the war and their places filled by nonentities. Kitchener's achievements were astounding, and, for a time, the Cabinet was awed. 'All-powerful, imperturbable, reserved, he dominated absolutely our counsels at this time', as Churchill has recorded. But Kitchener did too much; the burden was too great. Edward Grey's estimate of Kitchener is perhaps the most fair:

> His conception of work was that it must be a one man job. He shouldered the responsibility, and did the work of a Titan; but he did not realize that general responsibility must be shared with the

Cabinet, and strategic responsibility with the most independent
and expert military brains, organized in a General Staff; he abided
loyally by this decision, which he accepted; but he seemed to regard
it rather as a supersession of himself than as an addition of strength.
Nor did he realize that for an Army such as he was raising, the
whole industries of the country must be organized for war, and that
this could not be done inside the War Office.

Yet no one but Kitchener measured the dimensions of the war
with such prescience; no one but he foresaw how great would be
the need for men, and from the first moment he prepared accordingly. He inspired the country with the magnitude of the military
need, and gave it confidence. It may be that before his end came all
that was in his power to contribute to winning the war had been
given. But without that contribution the war might have been lost,
or victory rendered impossible.[1]

There was a considerable gulf between Kitchener and the rest of
the Cabinet. Kitchener, like most soldiers, was a Conservative. He
regarded his political colleagues with, at best, distaste. To Rosebery
he remarked that the Cabinet merited the Victoria Cross for declaring
war with such inadequate resources. He was dismayed by the paucity
of the British military capacity. 'Did they (the Government) consider
when they went headlong into a war like this, that they were without
an army, and without any preparations to equip one?' he enquired
with justification. He also remarked that 'my colleagues tell military
secrets to their wives, except X who tells them to other people's
wives'. Kitchener's taciturnity and lack of confidence in his colleagues
was both distressing and disconcerting to them. Lloyd George subsequently compared him to 'one of those revolving lighthouses which
radiate momentary gleams of revealing light far out into the surround-
ing gloom and then suddenly relapse into complete darkness'. Matters
were complicated further by the bad relations that existed between
Kitchener and Sir John French, commanding the B.E.F. French, at
least for the first six months of the war, had the full confidence of
Asquith, and was also close to Churchill. Again, Kitchener was right.

Asquith's decision to invite Kitchener to join the Cabinet does not
appear to have been thought out in advance. Kitchener had been
about to return to Egypt on August 3rd, and had reached Dover when

[1] Grey: *Twenty-Five Years*, 246.

he was recalled to London and asked to hold himself ready for consultation. When, on August 5th, Asquith invited him to become Secretary for War, the Prime Minister did so apparently on the grounds that no member of the Cabinet was suitable, and he himself described it as a 'hazardous experiment'. It was an enormously popular decision, and henceforth, whether they liked it or not, Ministers were tied to Kitchener. If his reputation with the Cabinet steadily declined, that with the public steadily rose, to the point that removing him became a political impossibility.

The structure of government was unaltered by the outbreak of war. Parliament dispersed for the summer recess on August 10th. There were some important measures—including the closing of military areas to aliens, the forbidding of trade with the enemy, and the requisitioning of merchant ships—taken by proclamation. But the theme was, as Churchill declared, 'business as usual'. It was to be a long time before the fatal inadequacy of this approach was appreciated. The first War Budget, in November, raised the 9d income tax paid by those with an income between £160 and £500 a year to 1s 6d. The duty on tea was raised from 3d to 8d per pound, and that on beer raised by a penny. That was all. *The Economist* described the measures as constituting 'an unprecedented sacrifice'. 'No government action', the President of the Board of Trade informed the Commons, 'could overcome economic laws, and any interference with those laws must end in disaster.'

When the war broke out, Britain had less than 250,000 men in the Regular Army, scattered around the world. Expenditure on the Army before the war was running at less than £30 millions, whereas that on the Navy was over £50 millions. The effect of this order of priorities was quickly apparent. The British Army was admirably trained and proficient with the rifle. But it was too small. Each Division had only twenty-four machine-guns, or two per battalion. It had virtually no hand grenades, entrenching tools or howitzers. There was almost no mechanisation; the British Army had a total stock of eighty motor vehicles, whereas each Division had 5,600 horses. There were no field telephones or wireless equipment. Haldane had done a great deal, but his widely praised economies now began to reveal their serious impact on the efficiency of the Army.

But the main problem was simply one of size. On August 6th Parliament authorised an increase of half a million men; on September 15th it authorised another half-million. In November another million was added, and then, in December, a third and fourth million. Over two and a half million men had enlisted before voluntary recruitment came to an end in March 1916. Such an enormously increased Army had to be based upon the existing cadres, and to rely heavily upon the officers and non-commissioned officers of the Regular Army. But, by the end of 1914, this vital experienced material had been decimated in France. Unlike any other army in Europe, therefore, the British had to start from the beginning in creating their new armies. The combination of old or failed officers and raw troops was not an efficient one. This citizens' army did wonders, but it was, from the very outset operating under grievous limitations.

This was, furthermore, to be a volunteer army. Of all the major belligerents Britain was the only one that put its faith in voluntary recruitment. The pre-war Liberal hostility to the idea of conscription was firmly retained and, as the volunteers poured in at a rate that overwhelmed the arrangements for coping with them, they seemed to be justified. The long-term social perils of this policy were not perceived in 1914, nor even in 1915.

The doctrine of 'Business as Usual' also applied to the central government. The Cabinet, which met irregularly, remained the private gathering of His Majesty's Ministers under the chairmanship of the Prime Minister. No records were kept, except for the formal letter written by the Prime Minister to the Sovereign, which remained a private communication. This method was not often very illuminating, even to the King, and Asquith's reports—which compare very unfavourably in content with those of Salisbury and Balfour during the Boer War—frequently contained such statements as this in 1916:

Considerable discussion took place, without any definite conclusion being reached, on a number of miscellaneous topics.

The imperfections of this arrangement had been evident long before 1914, and had been at least partly responsible for the confusion in the Balfour Government in 1903 over the corn duties.[1] Nothing, however, had been done. No knowledge of Cabinet decisions was disseminated, and no positive instructions given to Departments. As Curzon subsequently wrote:

[1] See Volume I, p. 208.

The Cabinet often had the haziest notion as to what its decisions were. . . . Cases frequently arose when the matter was left so much in doubt that a Minister went away and acted upon what he thought was a decision, which subsequently turned out to be no decision at all, or was repudiated by his colleagues.

A good example of the remoteness of the Cabinet from the really important decisions concerned the deployment of the B.E.F. On August 6th a Council of War, consisting of sixteen men—'most entirely ignorant of their subject' as General Sir Henry Wilson tartly commented—debated the matter; only four Ministers—Asquith, Churchill, Grey and Haldane—attended. The meeting had to accept Wilson's brusque statement that the B.E.F. had no choice, and must go to Maubeuge, on the French left. On the following day the Cabinet insisted that, of these seven divisions, two must stay at home. Kitchener persuaded them to change the destination from Maubeuge to Amiens. Under pressures from Wilson and the French, Kitchener changed his mind on August 12th. On September 1st he sent French one of the remaining divisions. Thus, without the Cabinet having any real say in the matter at all, the B.E.F. was committed as part of the French Army, tied irrevocably to the decisions and actions of the French commanders.

Attempts to improve this slipshod organisation were unimpressive. In November a War Council was set up, in which all the deficiencies of the Cabinet system were repeated and a few new ones added for good measure. The War Council consisted of Asquith, Grey, Lloyd George, Churchill, Kitchener, Sir Archibald Wolfe Murray (Chief of the Imperial General Staff), Fisher[1] and Balfour. McKenna, Lewis Harcourt and Admiral Sir Arthur Wilson were subsequently added. The War Council met irregularly, and only when the Prime Minister deemed it necessary. It did not work to an agenda. It did not forward its conclusions to the Cabinet. Its proceedings were kept by the secretary of the Committee of Imperial Defence, Maurice Hankey, in manuscript. It received very few departmental memoranda. In no sense did it superintend the day-to-day operation of the war. There was, furthermore, a fatal misunderstanding about the role of the Service members. The atmosphere of Council meetings was that of a

[1] Fisher had replaced Battenberg as First Sea Lord after a scurrilous Press campaign against the latter's alleged German connections.

Cabinet meeting to which Service advisers had been invited, to speak when spoken to. 'It is a mistake to call us members of the War Council', Fisher subsequently stated: 'it was no such thing. We were the experts there who were to open our mouths when told to.' The awesome presence of the taciturn and glowering Kitchener effected the total silence of Wolfe Murray. This new organisation was not a success; indeed, it did little more than to add a committee to the government structure and take up the time of busy men.

But the problem went far deeper than one of organisation. Men and attitudes are always more important than organisation.

With the exception of Kitchener and Churchill, there was not a single member of the Government or the War Council with any practical military experience of any kind. Virtually none had hitherto shown any interest in the subject. The majority, indeed, regarded it with repugnance. Some—notably Lloyd George—picked up the essentials in due course; the majority did not. Virtually from the beginning of the war there was a mutual antipathy between the military and the politicians, which was to develop into a wide and bitter gulf. There was no individual comparable to General Ismay in the Second World War, who had the confidence of all. Kitchener could have played such a role, but chose not to, and in any event was unsuited to it. The soldiers played politics—notably French and Sir Douglas Haig—and the politicians played at war. Churchill initially, and then closely challenged by Lloyd George, hungered for active and personal control over military matters. Each side cultivated the Press and was not reticent in its complaints about the other. What began as an uneasy entente gradually degenerated into a ferocious, squalid, and implacable enmity.

Furthermore, the Government lacked leadership. In a revealing self-portrait, Asquith once wrote that:

> Some people, sadly wanting in perspective, went so far as to call you 'chivalrous'; it would be nearer the truth to say that you had, or acquired, a rather specialised faculty of insight and manipulation in dealing with diversities of character and temperament.[1]

This was no longer enough. Asquith's techniques of managing a Cabinet had worked well in peacetime, although in both the Constitutional Crisis of 1909–11 and the Home Rule Crisis of 1912–14 its

[1] Roy Jenkins: *Asquith*, 336.

limitations had been apparent. They were grievously inadequate for wartime leadership. The preservation of Cabinet unity was important, but not as important as the reaching of quick decisions and following a policy. As Churchill commented in a 1915 Cabinet memorandum:

> Nothing leads more surely to disaster than that a military plan should be pursued with crippled steps and in a lukewarm spirit in the face of continued nagging within the executive circle. Unity ought not to mean that a number of gentlemen are willing to sit together on condition either that the evil day of decision is postponed, or that not more than a half-decision should be provisionally adopted. . . . The soldiers who are ordered to their deaths have a right to a plan, as well as a cause.

Asquith had been Prime Minister for six and a half years by August 1914. He was in his sixty-third year. It has been frequently emphasised that he had never, since his second marriage, been averse to the pleasures of the table, and he was the first Prime Minister in modern times to appear in public evidently the worse for drink. But although his mind remained clear, cool, and logical, and he dominated his colleagues, close observers were concerned at his lassitude, his casualness save when aroused, and intellectual arrogance. He was at this time conducting an extraordinarily voluminous, and rather pathetic, correspondence with a young lady of twenty-one, Miss Venetia Stanley. Perhaps too much has been made of this. Asquith was not the first, nor assuredly the last, Prime Minister who needed an emotional outlet which he could not obtain from his marriage, family, or colleagues. But although he had always firmly drawn the line between 'shop' and relaxation, it seemed to some of his colleagues that the latter was becoming too prominent in his life. This may have been unfair, but it can hardly be contested that Asquith's bland and often dilatory methods of conducting political business were totally unsuited to the conduct of a major war.

He still enjoyed very considerable prestige, and his air of calm and magisterial wisdom continued to dominate men who had worked with him for so long, and who had developed not only respect but personal affection for him. But, if at this early stage doubts began to arise about the suitability of his talents for this situation, they were only doubts. At the time, only Churchill and Lloyd George were seriously critical of the manner in which the war was being conducted, and both were careful not to criticise Asquith personally. Later, it was different. As Lloyd George was subsequently to write: 'There was no co-ordination of effort. There was no connected plan of action. There was no sense of the importance of time.' Churchill, characteristically, favoured leadership of a decisive, semi-authoritarian, nature: 'No man', he wrote afterwards, 'had the power to give clear, brutal orders which would command unquestioning respect. Power was widely disseminated among the many important personages who in this period formed the governing instrument.'

By September the war plans of every belligerent were in even greater disarray. The Germans, with Paris seemingly at their mercy, swung eastwards. A vital gap opened between the German armies. Joffre stood and fought on the Marne, and the Germans began to fall back. The pursuit was not—indeed could not—be swift enough. On September 14th the Germans stopped on the River Aisne and dug in. The British and French forces were checked, some 200 miles from the sea. There then followed the celebrated 'race to the sea', which was in fact a series of attempts by each side to outflank the other before the Channel was reached. By October the opposing trench-lines writhed savagely from the Channel to the borders of Switzerland, and the first real lessons in trench warfare were being painfully learned. A melodramatic, if militarily justifiable, attempt by Churchill—in person—to hold Antwerp had ended in disaster, although it is probable that the few days gained were vital to the saving of the Channel ports. At the time, the sacrifice of the untrained marines of the Royal Naval Division—Churchill's own creation—brought him much obloquy. Subsequently, he was credited —not least by himself—with having won for the Allies 'the race to the sea'. Both censure and praise were exaggerated; the latter, certainly, ignores the fact that the brunt of the resistance was borne by the Belgians.

To this point, the B.E.F. had not been fully engaged, and its role —although important—had been peripheral to the main battles; it took virtually no part in the Battle of the Marne. Its first major battle, the so-called First Battle of Ypres (October 12th–November 11th), was a victory of sorts, but at appalling cost. More than half the original B.E.F. had now become casualties; one-tenth had been killed.

All this had been a considerable shock to the British public. In all, over a million men had been killed in the first fury of the war, and the

British losses, although small in comparison with those of the Russians, French, Austrians and Germans, were, in relation to the numbers engaged, very heavy. But it was the series of reverses at sea that caused the greater dismay.

In this respect it can be argued that the British public had expected too much. Certainly they had never expected what actually happened. The *Goeben* and *Breslau* evaded British and French warships in the Mediterranean and reached Constantinople, the first decisive step in the series of events that was to bring Turkey into the war, at the beginning of November, on the German side. On September 22nd three British cruisers were sunk by a single German submarine in the North Sea with the loss of nearly 1,500 officers and men. In the South Atlantic and Pacific a German squadron under Admiral von Spee roamed almost at will, completely destroying a small British force under Admiral Cradock at Coronel. In the Indian Ocean the cruiser *Emden* almost completely paralysed the movement of British vessels. In December a German cruiser force shelled the Hartlepools, Whitby and Scarborough, killing 137 people and injuring 592.

Of much greater seriousness, although it was not yet perceived, was the German superiority in submarines, a matter on which Churchill's judgement had proved to be seriously at fault. The British attitude to submarine warfare was a mixture of the moralistic and pragmatic. Merchant ships were armed, *ordered* to paint over their names and port of registry, and to fly the flags of neutral nations when in British waters. Some were converted into 'mystery' or 'Q' ships, heavily armed and manned by naval crews, and initially had considerable success.

At this stage, the so-called Cruiser Rules were accepted by all maritime nations. Under these, an unarmed merchant ship could be stopped, searched, and if a neutral unharmed and if a belligerent sunk, after the crew had been permitted to take to the boats. This practice was in general scrupulously observed by the Germans in the early stages of the war, and it placed their boats frequently in peril.

Churchill's approach was aggressive. Merchant captains were forbidden to obey a U-boat's command to stop, and ordered to counter-attack. The purpose was deliberate—to compel the Germans to abandon the Cruiser Rules and to take the risk of sinking a neutral ship, 'and thus', in Churchill's own words, 'embroiling Germany with *other* Great Powers'. Much, meanwhile, was made of the bestiality of

this new form of warfare, and there was still little recognition in the
Admiralty of the threat which the U-boats constituted to British naval
superiority.

The early British reverses at sea were embarrassments rather than
a dire threat to British naval supremacy, but they had a disconcerting
effect. Battenberg was hounded from office by a vicious Press campaign, but was sacrificed readily enough by Churchill; his replacement
by the aged Fisher had, initially, excellent results. A gigantic shipbuilding programme was put urgently in hand. The *Emden* was
hunted down and sunk. Von Spee's squadron was destroyed at the
Falkland Islands. The blockade proceeded efficiently. The German
High Seas Fleet did not emerge in force, and the two fleets sparred
uneasily with each other at a distance in the grey expanses of the
North Sea, the monotony only varied by isolated actions such as that
at the Dogger Bank, hailed as a great British victory but in reality only
a relatively minor German reverse. In retrospect, it is clear that the
British were winning the sea war; at the time it did not appear thus.
When, at the end of October, the new battleship *Audacious* was sunk,
the Cabinet decided that the news should be rigidly suppressed. In
September it passed what was in effect a formal vote of censure on the
officers of the Royal Navy. From general criticism of the Navy it was
only a very short step to personal criticism of the ebullient Churchill.

Thus, everything had gone differently to what everyone had
expected. The Western Front was established, and the machine-gun,
the spade, and barbed wire were the masters. As French subsequently
lamented:

No previous experience, no conclusions I had been able to draw
from campaigns in which I had taken part, or from a close study
of the new conditions in which the war of today is waged, had led
me to anticipate a war of positions. All my thoughts, all my prospective plans, all my possible alternative of action, were concentrated
upon a war of movement and manoeuvre.

It was evident that some serious re-thinking would have to be done.
The Germans, advancing in massed close formation, had been shot
down by the British and French in rows with contemptuous ease. The
Russians had been out-generalled and out-fought. The French doctrine—more a religion than a tactic of war—of attack *à l'outrance* had
resulted in dreadful casualties and the first blunting of the ardour

with which the French army and nation had gone to war. Both the French and the Germans had used their young officer cadets, the St. Cyr cadets at the Marne and the German officer-cadets on the Aisne; in each case it had been a massacre of the innocents. The ponderous German artillery had proved unsuitable for open warfare; the French seventy-five, the finest field gun in the world, was of little use against trenches. The British had virtually no artillery at all, and very few shells. The British had lost their army, and now had to fight a type of warfare for which they had no training and for which they had no equipment. But the predicament of the Russians was perhaps the worst of all. By the end of 1914 they had lost over a million men, more than a million precious rifles, had barely a week's reserve of shells, and, since the Turks closed the Dardanelles in November, had lost their warm-water outlet to the West.

It was also becoming evident that this was to be a different war in other respects. The rigour of the German repression of civilians in Belgium was equalled by the Russian ferocity in East Prussia. This was going to be a brutal war, and it was already apparent that it was one in which few distinctions were going to be made between civilian and military in culpability and suffering. The peoples of Europe began to understand the full implications of 'Total War'. These implications had not yet, however, been appreciated in Britain.

*

From August 1914 until the end of 1915 the two dominant problems for the British were *how* the war was to be fought and *where* it was to be fought.

The question of 'how' was not merely technical, although that aspect was of great importance. The conflict between laissez-faire methods and the concept of 'the nation in arms' was fundamental, and it should not be seen in party political terms. There were those in the Liberal Government—notably Lloyd George and Churchill—who gradually leaned towards the 'nation in arms' concept; there were Unionists who shrank instinctively from the prospect of military and industrial conscription. But the movement against the Asquith Government was based on the growing conviction that pre-war methods were fatally inappropriate. Unhappily, the conviction took a long time to develop.

The dilemma of 'how' and 'where' came together when the strategy of the war was being considered. The British had entered the war with very little in the way of strategical concepts, and they, like every other belligerent, had been trapped by events and chance. The fact that the British Army in France was in effect part of the French Army had at once eliminated any freedom of manoeuvre or disposition that it might have possessed; the losses sustained in the B.E.F. had finally confirmed that situation.[1] As the events of 1915 were to emphasise, the British Army was barely capable of acting in an effective subsidiary capacity in France.

The fact that the Army was in France, however, was of crucial importance. Beyond strategical and tactical arguments there were other ones. As Eyre Crowe had written to Grey on July 31st:

> The Entente has been made, strengthened, put to the test and celebrated in a manner justifying the belief that a moral bond was being forged. The whole policy of the Entente can have no meaning if it does not signify that in a just quarrel England would stand by her friends. This honourable expectation has been raised. We cannot repudiate it without exposing our good name to grave criticism.

The subsequent debate between 'Westerners' and 'Easterners' cannot be interpreted in purely rational terms. The British had incurred a strong moral and military burden in France, which many were determined to honour. But of greater importance was that defeat in France would mean, militarily, the end of the war. The guns could be heard in Kent. The enemy, it seemed indeed, was hammering at the door. In the face of such indisputable facts, the argument that the war could best be won elsewhere seemed lunatic.

Furthermore, how was the German Army—the principal enemy—to be defeated if troops and equipment were to be taken away from this decisive theatre and employed elsewhere? From these arguments —many of which were incontrovertible—there stemmed a passionate commitment by many soldiers and politicians that everything must be subordinated to the war in Flanders. No one, at the beginning of 1915, had any real concept of the magnitude of what that war was to

---

[1] British casualties up to the end of November 1914 were 842 officers and 8,631 other ranks killed; 2,097 officers and 37,264 other ranks had been wounded; 688 officers and 40,432 other ranks were listed as missing, making a total of 3,627 officers and 86,327 men who had been killed, wounded, or missing in the first four months of the war, of whom the majority had fallen in the First Battle of Ypres.

involve. In January 1915 the War Office submitted to the Cabinet a memorandum that declared that 'Germany can do no more in the way of increasing her armies, and will, a very few months hence, begin to feel the want of resources in men to keep her existing armies up to strength.'

The argument of the 'Westerners' was, however, made suspect by certain discomfiting facts. The first of these was that although the trench systems of the opposing armies were nothing to what they were to become, they already presented a very severe obstacle to any attacking force. The losses already suffered by troops, even with supporting artillery, assaulting well-trained soldiers in good positions had been unimaginably horrific. The survivors of Pickett's Charge at the Battle of Gettysburg could have borne testimony to these perils. The commanders blamed their lack of success on various factors, of which, for Sir John French, the lack of adequate shells was already becoming the most important. But, even with the trench system as it was early in 1915, the only way in which the deadlock could be broken was by the frontal assault and breakthrough. There was no alternative, no way round. It was already becoming apparent that this could only be achieved after the introduction of entirely new methods, of which the first was the use of gas by the Germans at Ypres in April 1915. Gas was, however, a perilous weapon, subject to the vagaries of the wind, and as likely to inflict equal injuries on the assailant. Its initial shock value was very great, but it was not the answer to the impasse. The commanders on both sides became obsessed by the havoc that could be rendered by artillery, if only the guns were more accurate and the shells more lethal. After which, the infantry would advance. It is easy to deride these commanders, but they were confronted by an unparalleled situation in which the only gift that modern technology appeared to offer was the skill of the artilleryman. And at this point that skill was notoriously deficient. The politicians, and Kitchener, viewed with dismay the prospect of incurring losses on the scale of First Ypres and of sending troops to 'chew barbed wire in Flanders', in Churchill's words, but they were to a considerable extent dependent upon the opinions of the officers on the spot and of French policies.

The other point that reduced the impact of the 'Westerner' argument was the simple fact that this was a war that did not merely concern France. The Russians were in dire straits. The Balkan States and Italy were hovering on the verge of intervention—but on which side? Turkey posed a continuing threat to the British position in Egypt—a fact dramatically emphasised by a daring attack on the Suez Canal in January 1915—and in Persia, and, most of all, to the Russians' south-eastern flank. Meanwhile, in Africa, an entirely separate war was being fought.

Thus, the dilemma of 'how' and 'where' was a very real one, and it was one, furthermore, to which there was no real answer. The truth of Kitchener's sombre dictum that 'we must fight war not as we would but as we must' was being fully justified within five months of the outbreak of hostilities.

The result of the debate between the 'Westerners' and the 'Easterners' throughout 1915 was a series of disastrous compromises. The British fought everywhere, and achieved nothing save further appalling casualties. No real order of priorities was agreed. With resources that were barely sufficient for one military campaign, the British were eventually running four—in France, Gallipoli, Salonika and Mesopotamia. The deficiencies of the pre-war system of Ministerial responsibility were well shown up by this situation. As General Sir William Robertson subsequently wrote:

> The Secretary of State for War was aiming at decisive results on the Western Front; the First Lord of the Admiralty was advocating a military expedition to the Dardanelles; the Secretary of State for India was devoting his attention to a campaign in Mesopotamia; the Secretary of State for the Colonies was occupying himself with several small wars in Africa; and the Chancellor of the Exchequer was attempting to secure the removal of a large part of the British Army from France to some Eastern Mediterranean theatre.

The debates on the conduct of the war were not confined to Ministerial circles. The Opposition had agreed to the suspension of normal party warfare, but the announcement that the Government proposed to put certain Home Rule measures through created a violent Parliamentary storm. Bonar Law compared the action of the Government with the German invasion of Belgium, and led a mass walk-out of his party from the Commons, which Asquith derided as 'a lot of prosaic and for the most part middle-aged gentlemen, trying to look like early French revolutionaries in the tennis court'. Asquith viewed alliance with the Conservatives with profound repugnance. When, in May 1915, it was inevitable, he did so with barely concealed

distaste. 'To seem to welcome into the intimacy of the political house-
hold, strange alien, hitherto hostile figures', he wrote, was a 'most
intolerable task.' Until then, with the exception of Balfour's membership of the War Council, no Conservative had any part in the conduct
of the war. Bonar Law was invited to one meeting of the War Council
in March 1915; it was not a successful experiment, and was not
repeated. The less seen of Mr. Bonar Law and his associates, it was
felt in Liberal circles, the better. This was politically and nationally
unwise. For the first nine months of the war, the Liberals bore complete responsibility for its conduct.

It was ironical, but very understandable, that it should be against
Churchill, who favoured Coalition, that the bulk of the Conservative
hostility was directed. His pre-war record had not endeared this
brilliant, arrogant, impulsive, egocentric and flamboyant personality
to the Opposition. Bonar Law openly detested him. Now there were
the apparent fiascos of the 'Dunkirk circus'—where Churchill had
directed a demonstration in September—and Antwerp. Fisher's
honeymoon with Churchill had been short-lived, and he was reopening
his contacts with the Opposition. Admiral Beatty put his finger on the
basic problem: 'The situation is curious, two very strong and clever
men, one old, wily and of vast experience, one young, self-assertive,
with a great self-satisfaction, but unstable. They cannot work together,
they cannot both run the show.' Churchill's own Director of Operations regarded him as 'a shouting amateur', and there was mounting
criticism within the Admiralty of the First Lord's personality and
methods, and not least his frequent absences and involvement in
matters beyond his official position. These criticisms were echoed in
the Navy, in the newspapers, and in the Opposition ranks. Churchill's
friend, Lord Beaverbrook, has described his position:

> His attitude from August 1914 was a noble one, too noble to be
> wise. He cared for the success of the British arms, especially in so far
> as they could be achieved by the Admiralty, and for nothing else.
> His passion for this aim was pure, self-devoted, and all-devouring.
> He failed to remember that he was a politician and as such treading
> a slippery path; he forgot his political tactics. . . . As he worked
> devotedly at his own job, the currents of political opinion slipped
> by him unnoticed.[1]

[1] Beaverbrook: *Politicians and the War*, 125.

This was a kindly judgement. Churchill was obsessed by the war and by his position in its conduct. To his colleagues he seemed to be everywhere, eager, intrusive, voluble and often hectoring, and always seeking the limelight. He began to bore and irritate them, and confidence in his judgement and capacity was being eroded. He was being, like his father, a young man in a hurry, and Ministers and important elements in the Navy increasingly put down to vaulting personal ambition what he genuinely regarded as his intense patriotism and passion to win the war. And so he crashed along, arousing mistrust and active dislike, but heedless of the resentment he caused.

The peril of Churchill's position was greatly increased by the fact that he had never struck deep roots in the Liberal Party. His strength had lain in the confidence and respect—sometimes amused and often exasperated—with which the Liberal leaders, and particularly Asquith, regarded him. By the beginning of 1915, however, much of this confidence had begun to falter. In particular, Asquith's opinion of his judgement and reliability had been undermined. 'To speak with the tongue of men and angels', he noted at this time of Churchill, 'and to spend laborious days and nights in administration, is no good if a man does not inspire trust.' Ths hostility of the Conservative Press was unrelenting, led by *The Times* and the *Morning Post*.

Churchill's dismay at the events of the war at sea had been manifest since the autumn of 1914. From the outset his attitudes had been belligerent. He had wanted to chase the *Goeben* and *Breslau* to Constantinople. He had armed the British merchant marine and ordered it to adopt aggressive manoeuvres against U-boats. He had authorised the bombardment of the Dardanelles' outer defences on November 3rd before war with Turkey had been declared. At the first meeting of the War Council early in November he had urged an attack on the Dardanelles. He was playing with a scheme to send old battleships up the Elbe. His eager, questing, original mind chafed at opportunities forsaken and others ignored. Churchill's mind, Lord Halifax subsequently commented with truth, was 'a most curious mixture of a child's emotion and a man's reason'. The historian, reading his letters, memoranda, and comments, can easily understand why he in turn baffled, impressed, bewildered, and enraged those with whom he had public business. Hankey later wrote that Churchill 'had a real zest for war. If war there must needs be, he at least could enjoy it.' 'He is a wonderful creature', Asquith wrote of him in October, 'with a curious dash of schoolboy simplicity (quite unlike Edward Grey's) and what someone said of genius—"a zigzag streak of lightning in the brain".' It was his extraordinary fluctuation between real wisdom and superficial folly which made him so uncomfortable and so dangerous a colleague and Minister. His judgement rested almost entirely upon intuition. Often it was right, but, in F. E. Smith's words, 'when he is wrong—My God!'

But by the end of 1914 two other important individuals had come to much the same conclusion as Churchill, that it was urgently necessary to look elsewhere than France for immediate results. Lloyd George and Hankey, acting entirely independently, produced memoranda at the end of December that urged investigation of other alternatives to the Western Front. These papers coincided with an appeal for assistance, if only a diversion, from Russia to reduce the Turkish pressure in the Caucasus. In fact, the threat to the Caucasus had disappeared by the time the Russian appeal was received in London, but this was not known until some time later.

It was this conjunction of events that gave Churchill his opportunity early in January to put a plan for a naval forcing of the Dardanelles to the War Council. Having obtained provisional assent, he used the replies of the Admiral at the Straits—Carden—to persuade the War Council of the soundness of a plan which had been regarded as impossible by responsible naval and military opinion as late as 1907 and by Churchill himself in a memorandum in 1911.[1] Churchill marshalled his arguments with great care and thoroughness; his colleagues were swept along by his infectious enthusiasm. Only Kitchener and Fisher were doubtful; Kitchener because he did not want another military commitment, and Fisher because he saw in the operation a possible diminution of the strength of the Grand Fleet. More fundamentally, they regarded the operation as irrelevant to the main purpose of the war—to defeat the Germans on land and sea. But neither, after the events of the past few months, had any clear policy by which this might be achieved, and the prospect of a swift, easy, and spectacular victory over one of Germany's principal allies enraptured the War Council. 'The idea caught on at once', Hankey has recorded of the vital Council meeting of January 13th. 'The War Council turned eagerly from the dreary vista of a "slogging match" on

---

[1] 'It should be remembered that it is no longer possible to force the Dardanelles, and nobody would expose a modern fleet to such peril.'

the Western Front to brighter prospects, as they seemed, in the Mediterranean. . . . Churchill unfolded his plans with the skill that might be expected of him, lucidly but quietly and without exaggerated optimism'. Fisher's recollection supported Hankey's: 'He was beautiful! He has got the brain of Moses and the voice of Aaron. He would talk a bird out of a tree, and they were all carried away with him. I was not, myself.' The Council resolved that 'the Admiralty should also prepare for a naval expedition in February to bombard and take the Gallipoli Peninsula, with Constantinople as its objective'.

Churchill had managed to persuade Fisher, but it was not long before the old man's doubts returned. The senior officers of the Admiralty, hardly involved at all in the strategical discussions, were even more doubtful, but Asquith—at Churchill's prompting—suppressed a memorandum to the War Council that spelt out these doubts. Of the Ministers, only Lloyd George expressed reservations, and Hankey, in a series of prescient memoranda, vainly appealed for a more thorough appraisal of the various factors involved. All doubts were swept aside, and it was with full War Council approval that the naval assault was launched on February 19th.

But it was not long before serious shadows began to darken the gleaming expectations held out by Churchill to his colleagues. Disputes arose with Kitchener about the availability of troops to follow up the successful forcing of the Straits. An attempt to make use of an offer of Greek troops was peremptorily vetoed by the Russians—a fact that has been over-emphasised in almost all accounts of the campaign, for it is very doubtful if Venizelos was in any position to provide the troops, and even more doubtful if they would have been of any decisive value.

The approval given by French to the expedition had been reluctant, and based entirely on the understanding that it was to be a solely naval attack, and that the War Council consented to further offensives in France. In fact, the military demands of the Dardanelles expedition became quickly apparent. After observing the situation, Lt. General Birdwood reported privately to Kitchener that there was no chance of the Navy getting through by itself, and an army that consisted mainly of an Australian and New Zealand (ANZAC) Army Corps and a French division was made available in Egypt. Units of the Royal Naval Division were ordered to the Middle East and, on March 10th after three weeks of haggling, the last Regular Division in Kitchener's possession, the 29th, was sent. The War Council records make clear that Churchill's argument was that the troops would not be used in the forcing of the Dardanelles, but were required 'to occupy Constantinople and to compel a surrender of all Turkish forces remaining in Europe after the fleet had obtained command of the Sea of Marmara. . . . The actual and definite object of the army would be to reap the fruits of the naval success'. The island of Lemnos was loaned by Greece—commandeered by the British would probably be a more apt description—and Admiral Wemyss was dispatched there to establish an advanced base. As he had no facilities whatever, Wemyss found his task difficult.

French was not the only commander who viewed these developments with concern. General Sir John Maxwell, the British commander in Egypt, considered that his position was difficult enough already, and he could obtain no clear account from London of the use to which troops were liable to be used in the Dardanelles offensive.

At the Dardanelles Admiral Carden was encountering serious difficulties. The weather, always bad in the Aegean at that time of the year (a point which might have been taken into account) was hindering him badly. His ships were old, and the crews mainly the residue from the Grand Fleet. His only minesweepers were East Coast fishing smacks crewed by civilians and commanded by a naval officer with no experience whatever of minesweeping. The Outer Defences were easily subdued, but when the warships entered the Straits their difficulties became serious. The minesweepers could make little headway against the fierce Dardanelles current, and were subjected to constant harassing fire. The mobile Turkish batteries were only a nuisance to the warships but unnerved the minesweeper crews. Turkish resistance to landing parties of marines became more resolute. By mid-March an impasse had been reached. Carden was subjected to a flow of admonitory telegrams from Churchill, but the fact remained that he could not advance until the minefields were cleared. He accordingly was forced to reverse his tactics; the suppression of the batteries would precede the clearing of the mines. On the eve of the attack on March 18th he collapsed, and was replaced by Rear-Admiral de Robeck.

Meanwhile, it had been decided to send out a senior officer to command the 70,000-odd British, French and Dominion troops made available for the operation. The choice—Kitchener's, with Churchill's warm support—had fallen upon General Sir Ian Hamilton, commanding the Central Force in England. Hamilton was sixty-two. He was a man of great physical courage, recommended thrice for the Victoria Cross. He also possessed much charm and political adroitness, and had been one of the most trenchant critics of Roberts' conscription campaign. Events were to prove him sadly inadequate to his responsibilities, but he hardly had a fair chance. He was appointed at twelve hours' notice, had to gather an improvised staff together, and hastily quit London on Friday, March 13th. As one of his staff subsequently wrote:

I shall never forget the dismay and foreboding with which I learnt that apart from Lord Kitchener's very brief instructions, a pre-war Admiralty report on the Dardanelles defences and an out-of-date map, Sir Ian had been given practically no information whatever.

He arrived, with his hotchpotch and bewildered staff, just in time to witness the celebrated débâcle of March 18th.

This famous attack has been the subject of many accounts. It opened propitiously, in perfect weather, but shortly before 2 p.m. the French battleship *Bouvet* was rocked by a giant explosion, spun over, and disappeared. The British battleships *Invincible* and *Ocean* were sunk, and *Inflexible* crippled. The French battleship *Gaulois* was also badly damaged. The minesweepers had not even reached the edge of the minefields. The Turks had shot away virtually all their heavy ammunition, but they still had sufficient ammunition to dominate the sweepers. The Turks had had forty men killed and seventy wounded. Out of 176 guns only eight had been hit, and four put out of action. The Allied losses were over seven hundred officers and men. The real lesson of March 18th was that the Dardanelles was impassable unless the sweeper force was drastically reorganised. This was realised by Roger Keyes, de Robeck's Chief of Staff, but even he admitted that to compose such a force would take three weeks.

A fact to which sufficient emphasis can hardly be given was that the soldiers were very keen to intervene. Birdwood had never believed that the Navy, by itself, could get through the Dardanelles; Hamilton had seen for himself what had happened on March 18th; Kitchener, by the dispatch of Hamilton, had gone a long way towards accepting Birdwood's arguments. On March 22nd, on board the battleship

Queen Elizabeth at Mudros, Hamilton and de Robeck agreed on a joint operation. Hamilton returned to Alexandria to reorganise his army, now scattered around the Eastern Mediterranean in spectacular confusion. Thus, without the knowledge or approval of the War Council or the Cabinet, the decision to open a major military campaign was taken in a matter of minutes by the senior naval and military officers on the spot. Churchill was eager to renew the naval attack, but was not able to convince his Service advisers. The action of Hamilton and de Robeck was decisive. 'The silent plunge into this vast military venture', Churchill later recorded, 'must be regarded as an extraordinary episode.' The War Council did not meet for ten weeks after its meeting of March 10th.

Meanwhile, French had launched his assault in France. The Battle of Neuve Chapelle (March 10th–13th) merely confirmed all previous lessons of trench warfare against entrenched positions. British casualties were 583 officers and 12,309 other ranks. In April the Germans hit back in the Second Battle of Ypres (April 22nd–May 31st) and nearly broke through. In May the British attacked at Aubers Ridge and Festubert. Vast casualties were suffered;[1] no gains were made. French claimed that the cause was a deficiency of shells. On April 21st, in the House of Commons, Lloyd George strongly defended Kitchener against these charges, reporting that there had been a nineteen-fold increase in shell production since September 1914. This temporarily only checked the allegations, which broke out with redoubled vigour after French's further setbacks in May.

By itself, what developed into the 'shells scandal' was not sufficient to topple the Government, although it shook it. For one thing, the issue involved personal criticism of Kitchener, the one Minister in whom the Opposition had confidence. Bonar Law had his followers under control over the issue of shells, but it represented another opportunity for criticisms of the general conduct of the war in the Conservative Party.

There was a strong tendency among some Ministers to regard this unrest in the Opposition and in the Press as factious and unpatriotic. Churchill's project to commandeer *The Times* was a case in point. There was certainly no comprehension of, nor sympathy with, the

---

[1] Losses at Aubers Ridge were 458 officers and 11,161 other ranks; at Festubert 710 officers and nearly 16,000 other ranks. In addition to these losses, the cost of the Second Battle of Ypres had been 2,150 officers and 57,125 other ranks.

problems of the Opposition, which were put succinctly by Curzon in a memorandum to Lansdowne in January 1915:

> We are expected to give a mute and almost unquestioning support to everything done by the Government; to maintain patriotic silence about the various blunders that have been committed in connexion with the War. . . . The Government are to have all the advantages, while we have all the drawbacks of a Coalition. They tell us nothing or next to nothing of their plans, and yet they pretend our leaders share their knowledge and their responsibility. . . . I do not think this state of affairs can continue indefinitely, both because the temper of our party will not long stand it, and because, in the interests of the nation, the position is both highly inexpedient and unfair.

*

Hamilton, after reorganising his forces in Egypt, launched his attack on the Gallipoli Peninsula on Sunday, April 25th. By the end of a tumultuous day the British and Dominion troops, at heavy loss, were hanging on to precarious positions. In the following two weeks they suffered further heavy casualties, had only succeeded in establishing their foothold on the Peninsula, and Hamilton was calling for reinforcements. In a period of less than two weeks, on two small fronts, the British, Dominion, and French forces suffered over 20,000 casualties out of a total strength of 70,000 men, and of whom 6,000 had been killed. At the tip of the peninsular they were definitely halted on the slopes of Achi Baba and, to the north, on the harsh cliffs of Sari Bair. The British had acquired another major campaign, but were not yet fully aware of the terrible sacrifices which that insatiable fragment of ground was to demand over the next months.

On May 7th there occurred a dramatic incident which was to play its part in the eventual entry of the United States into the war, and over which considerable mystery remains. The Cunard liner *Lusitania*, with a number of Americans aboard, was torpedoed and sunk by a German submarine off Kinsale, on the southern Irish coast. The great ship sank within minutes, and 1,201 persons lost their lives. There was intense outrage in Britain and America at this further example of German 'frightfulness', an emotion which was sedulously encouraged by British Intelligence and its agents abroad.

But there were certain aspects of this tragedy which were perplexing, if not downright suspicious, and recent research has raised certain questions which have not been adequately answered.[1] Above all is the suspicion that the sinking was deliberately calculated—or, at the least, was fervently hoped for—by the Admiralty. Even though this has not been proved, it is now clear that the *Lusitania* was carrying considerable quantities of war material, and it would appear almost certain that her sudden destruction—virtually a nose-dive into the sea—was the result of a massive internal explosion and could not have been wholly caused by a single torpedo, at a time when they were so notoriously ineffective that most German submarine commanders preferred to use their guns on the surface. The episode did not bring America into the war, and President Woodrow Wilson was to ride to an unexpected re-election a year later on the cry that 'he kept us out of the war'. But official American–German relations, already cool, had suffered a major deterioration. And in Britain this event, coming at the moment it did, was not helpful to the rapidly declining position of the British Government.

The check at Gallipoli coincided with both the loss of the *Lusitania* and French's disastrous assault at Aubers Ridge. French then informed the military correspondent of *The Times* that the attack had failed as a result of a shortage of shells, and on May 14th *The Times* published his telegram that 'the want of an unlimited supply of high explosive shells was a fatal bar to our success', and commented in a leading article that 'British soldiers died in vain on Aubers Ridge . . . because more shells were needed. The Government, who have so seriously failed to organise adequately our national resources, must bear their share of the grave responsibility.'

The fact that *The Times*' attack was launched against Kitchener personally, however, reduced much of its impact, particularly on the Opposition. It was Fisher's dramatic resignation early on the following day that was the final factor that made the position of the Government impossible. Fisher's discontent with Churchill had preceded the Dardanelles operation, but had been mightily augmented by it. The almost universal judgement in the Admiralty was hostile to the campaign, and was burdened by recurring criticism of Churchill personally. These criticisms were conveyed to the Opposition, and by the end of April—two weeks before Fisher resigned—Law and his col-

---

[1] Colin Simpson: *The Lusitania* (1972) makes a very effective case for the argument that the ship was deliberately sacrificed, but it is not fully proven.

leagues were fully informed of the hostility of the bulk of the Board of Admiralty to the mercurial First Lord. Fisher's resignation, therefore, was not unexpected to them, and their profound antipathy to Churchill ensued that they would not look charitably upon his explanation. In the event, he was not given an opportunity to explain.

Asquith, having at first refused Churchill's offer to resign, now quickly realised that his own position was in serious danger. Law had seen Lloyd George, and had made it plain that the Conservatives could not support Churchill in a quarrel of such magnitude with Fisher. Lloyd George, whose sense of political possibilities was acute, eagerly accepted Law's statement and threatened resignation unless a Coalition was formed. Asquith had no wish to have a Coalition, but he acted with decision and celerity to preserve his own position. The Conservatives made it clear that Churchill would have to be sacrificed, and Haldane as well. Churchill fought desperately to survive, but to no avail. His bitterness at his downfall was intense, and he subsequently commented:

> Asquith did not hesitate to break his Cabinet up, demand the resignations of all Ministers, end the political lives of half his colleagues, throw Haldane to the wolves, leave me to bear the burden of the Dardanelles, and sail on victoriously at the head of a Coalition Government. Not 'all done by kindness'! Not all by rosewater! These were the convulsive struggles of a man of action and of ambition at death-grips with events.[1]

The Ministerial Crisis of May 1915 remains a somewhat mysterious episode, but its root cause was the pervasive feeling in the House of Commons—and not confined to the Opposition—that the Government was inadequate to meet the burdens of the war. The 'shells scandal' and the Fisher resignation brought to a head a judgement which had become very widespread, and which was not unjustified, that the Government was simply not equipped in procedures, personnel, or attitudes to wage the war competently. Unhappily, the cure was to prove at least as bad as the disease.

---

[1] Churchill: *Great Contemporaries*. See also Martin Gilbert: *Winston Churchill*, Volume III, Chapters 13 and 14.

CHAPTER TWO

THE FALL OF ASQUITH, 1915–1916

A POLITICAL COALITION is a loveless relationship, created only out of dire necessity and resented for that in itself, and in which the partners eye each other warily and not without hostility. Coalition is, of its very nature, contrary to the basic tenets of politics, and it is not surprising that most politicians abhor both the concept and the reality. Coalition means the abandonment of the deliciously enjoyable dramas of partisan politics. Coalition means co-operation with men against whom a politician has been in dispute for years. Coalition means the subordination of political dogmas and creeds to new and uncomfortable necessities. Coalition means that there are fewer positions available to the party faithful. Coalition, in short, means the sacrifice of almost everything that renders political life so stimulating and rewarding.

A successful Coalition requires a decent minimum of mutual confidence and respect between its leading members. It would be quite unreasonable to expect complete mutual confidence; human nature —and, above all, political nature—could hardly stand such a severe test. But the Asquith Coalition was remarkable in that even the minimum requirements were not met. A few months earlier Asquith had come across a statement of Bolingbroke's: 'Sir, I never wrestle with a chimney-sweep', and noted 'A good saying, which I sometimes call to mind when I am confronting Bonar Law'. In November 1915 Law wrote to Asquith:

> The criticism which is directed against the government and against yourself is chiefly based on this—that as Prime Minister you have not devoted yourself absolutely to co-ordinating all the moves of the war because so much of your time and energy has been devoted to control of the political machine.

At no point during the Asquith Coalition were relations between Asquith and Law anything but distant. For this situation both men were to blame, but the greater responsibility was Asquith's. He regarded Law's timidity and caution as signs of weakness, and, if anything, his contempt for the Conservative leader was increased by the experience of working with him. This was to be a fatal error, as Law had a genuine regard for Asquith and a profound mistrust of Lloyd George. If Asquith had made an ally of Law—as he could easily have done—his position would have been greatly strengthened by the Coalition. But he made no move. Asquith wrote to Law, 'My dear Bonar Law'; Law replied, 'Dear Mr. Asquith'. This mode of address adequately symbolised the gulf between the two men.

In the Coalition as a whole, feelings were even stronger. Many Liberals bitterly—and not unjustifiably—resented the imperative Conservative veto, based wholly upon personal prejudice, against Haldane. 'You cannot imagine', Augustine Birrell wrote to Redmond, 'how I loathe the idea of sitting cheek by jowl with these fellows.' The Conservatives regarded the Liberals with no greater enthusiasm. Walter Long wrote to Carson on May 25th that he did not expect the Coalition to work 'when it comes to daily administration. I loathe the very idea of our good fellows sitting with these double-dyed traitors.' The repugnance with which Asquith viewed his new colleagues was thinly disguised, and in many instances warmly returned.

The Coalition had been forced upon Asquith, but he was able to maintain the Liberal dominance in the new Cabinet. The Conservatives were emphatic about the exclusion of Haldane and Churchill's removal from the Admiralty, but were surprisingly docile on other appointments. Remarkably, even Churchill was retained, with the post of Chancellor of the Duchy of Lancaster, and with a seat on the new version of the War Council, called the Dardanelles Committee. And, almost immediately after the formation of the Coalition, Churchill was able to persuade the Committee and the Cabinet to send substantial reinforcements to Gallipoli.

Churchill had gone down fighting, but it had been impossible to keep him at the Admiralty. He had tried everything—even including a proposed rapprochement with Fisher, which had been indignantly rejected—but his position was hopeless. In later years Churchill convinced himself that he had been destroyed by Tory hostility and Asquith's weakness. Churchill had formidable powers of self-deception.

His loyalty to Asquith was now fatally undermined; his dislike of Bonar Law substantially augmented.

But in the difficult circumstances Asquith had done very well for Churchill and the Liberals. All the key posts remained in Liberal hands. Lloyd George went to the new Ministry of Munitions; Grey stayed at the Foreign Office; McKenna took the Treasury, and Simon the Home Office. Kitchener stayed at the War Office. Law went to the relative backwater of the Colonial Office; Curzon became Lord Privy Seal; Sir Edward Carson became Attorney-General, with a seat in the Cabinet; Walter Long became President of the Local Government Board. Of the Conservatives only Balfour (Admiralty) occupied a major Cabinet post. The Liberals held the twelve key positions, the Conservatives had eight minor posts, and Labour received one Cabinet office, Arthur Henderson taking the Board of Education. Asquith's only failure concerned Redmond, who declined an invitation to join.

This was a remarkable exercise in political legerdemain. It was, however, just a bit too clever. Asquith did not realise that his best chance of remaining Prime Minister was to be head of a genuine and strong Coalition. But the failure was deeper. Despite all the experience of the war, there were no changes in the manner in which the Government itself operated. The Dardanelles Committee did not differ in substance from the old War Council. It was replaced in November 1915 by a War Committee which faithfully reproduced all the weaknesses of the previous arrangements. The old failures of leadership and coherence remained; the internal discord and mistrust between Ministers added an additional element of weakness.

Although the Coalition brought into the Cabinet the dilemmas of how the war was to be fought and where it was to be fought, the Conservative impatience with the old attitudes was an instinctive rather than a logical one. They knew that something was wrong, but they had few practicable alternatives to offer. The idea of nationalising key industries or of the Government stifling private enterprise was as loathsome to them as it was to the Liberals. In military matters their resources were so slender that their response was to rely upon the military authorities to an even greater extent. In any serious dispute between the Services and the Government the Conservatives were almost certain to support the former.

Nevertheless, a fundamental change of outlook existed, and was to become even more marked in 1916. The Conservatives, in short, were moving, however irrationally, blunderingly and nervously, towards the 'nation in arms' concept from which the Liberals still shrank. Thus, a highly improbable alliance between the Conservatives and Lloyd George began slowly to develop. This process was gradual, and shadowed by old antipathies; indeed, up to the Ministerial Crisis of December 1916 Law distrusted Lloyd George to a far greater extent than he had lack of confidence in Asquith. But, as the war marched on its terrible course, the Conservative leaders found themselves in increasing, if reluctant, sympathy with Lloyd George's attitudes and objectives. They mistrusted and disliked him still, and knew him too well to be overwhelmed by the charm which he could use so effectively on others. They had good cause to hate him, and yet the exigencies of the situation created a slow but perceptible change in their attitudes.

A strange light still flickers around Lloyd George's personality and career. That he was an adventurer and an opportunist is evident enough, but he has succeeded well in obscuring the motives that drove him onwards, and has eluded his several biographers. Mere ambition cannot adequately explain it, although he was a profoundly ambitious man. Principle did not figure conspicuously at any stage in his long career, yet on several occasions—notably in the Boer War—he had courted political disaster for the sake of principle. He rose as the champion of the under-privileged; he was to become obsessed by the menace of organised labour and international communism. An ardent pacifist in the Boer War, initially a very reluctant supporter of intervention in 1914, he was to be the only Minister who served in high office throughout the war; was to attain international stature as a great war leader; and, in October 1918, was to advocate the continuance of the war until Germany had been totally overrun. The leading Radical of the early 1900s, he did more than anyone else to destroy the Liberal Party and to place his own fate in the hands of the Conservatives. The self-appointed spokesman for Welsh nonconformity, his own private life—in matters financial and sexual—left much to be desired. He followed no star save his own, dwelt on no philosophy save his own, and yet was, at his peak, one of the most powerful and persuasive speakers that British Radicalism has produced. His early speeches can still be read with excitement. Thus, on Joseph Chamberlain in 1903, at Oldham:

Mr. Chamberlain has appealed to the workmen, and there were very fine specimens of the British workmen on his platform. There were three Dukes, two Marquesses, three or four Earls. They had gone to help the workman to tax his own bread. The Corn Laws meant high rent for them, and when a statesman of Mr. Chamberlain's position comes forward and proposes a return to the old Corn Law days, Lords and Dukes and Earls and Squires all come clucking towards him like a flock of fowls when they hear the corn shaken in the bin.

But Lloyd George was at his best when he dwelt on deeper matters. Thus, at Swansea, in October 1908:

What is poverty? Have you felt it yourselves? If not, you ought to thank God for having been spared its sufferings and temptations. Have you ever seen others enduring it? Then pray God to forgive you, if you have not done your best to alleviate it. By poverty, I mean real poverty, not the cutting down of your establishment, not the limitation of your luxuries. I mean the poverty of the man who does not know how long he can keep a roof over his head, and where he will turn to find a meal for the pinched and hungry little children who look to him for sustenance and protection. That is what unemployment means.

Lloyd George was an instinctive politician. His reading was not extensive, and he always preferred an oral to a written argument. It was said of him with justice that when he was alone the room was empty. He was, unlike most politicians, an eager and excellent listener. He did not impose his views on his audiences, he reacted instinctively to what the audience wanted to hear. He drew into his mind and memory the views and experience of others; he was prone to make snap decisions on the basis of his impression of a man's capacity; he had an unfortunate tendency to making swift estimates, and he always preferred the colourful and articulate in mankind. The fact that he was not over-encumbered with principle or prejudice often gave him an air of cynicism and blatant opportunism; yet it was, particularly in war, a source of strength. Unlike Churchill, he did not attempt to impose things on people; he drew from people.

He could be a bully, and he personalised politics to an excessive extent. He was a good hater, and was relentless in his persecutions. His character was not devoid of cruelty, and he was not the kind of person to whom one would wish to be beholden on any matter affecting one's well-being or fortune. His energy was prodigious, and at this time in particular people felt in his presence a vitality which they could see in no other politician—all the more impressive because it lay in the man. Churchill had run around in a fever of activity that seemed juvenile and melodramatic, as if rushing around on the spur of the moment was synonymous with real action. Lloyd George gave the impression of tremendous mental and physical energy held on a leash, and with a much more impressive evidence of shrewdness and timing. And some, at least, detected in the small, vibrant, eager personality an element of cold ruthlessness which the sentimental, romantic, and warm-hearted Churchill did not possess, and which Asquith reserved for domestic political matters which closely affected himself.

His oratorical styles in Parliament and on a public platform were entirely different. In the House of Commons he adopted a deliberately low key, characterised by studied moderation and courtesy. On the platform a new man stood forth, brilliant, exciting, witty, provocative, and emotional. His Parliamentary speeches were devoid of remarkable and memorable phrases; his speeches outside Parliament were replete with them. For the platform the purple passage and the piercing personalities; for Parliament, calmness and sweet reason; for private conclave, a ready ear, a keen intelligence, and no claptrap. A most formidable combination!

Churchill has written of Lloyd George that 'he had the greatest capacity in the art of *getting things done* of any man in public life that I have known'. Lloyd George's record at the Board of Trade and at the Treasury certainly demonstrated the validity of this tribute. Lloyd George had perhaps the most acute and perceptive intelligence of any individual in public life. His charm has been commented on by all who knew him. It could be—or appear to be—a genuine, unforced charm, and few did not succumb to it, even those who knew him for what he was and were unimpressed by the Celtic extravaganzas. His private secretary once confessed that, after listening to Lloyd George singing Welsh hymns, he was almost persuaded of his religious convictions. He was, if nothing else, the most brilliant actor in British politics since Disraeli—and, like Disraeli, perhaps the actor was the real man.

From an early stage in the war, Lloyd George had prised the control of munitions away from the War Office and Kitchener. Kitchener, under pressure, set up an Armaments Output Committee on March 31st, 1915; it became independent of the War Office on April 28th. By May it was in virtual control of the material side of armaments. When the Coalition came in May 1915 Lloyd George took over the new Ministry of Munitions and hurled himself energetically into its development. His subsequent claims must be approached with caution; Kitchener had laid the foundations, and the proportion of 'duds' in British shells in the Battle of the Somme in 1916 revealed that complaints that quality had been sacrificed to quantity were not unjustified. Nevertheless, Lloyd George had been right. The production of war matériel required a separate Ministry and full-time devotion to the task. The Ministry of Munitions was to become one of the great success-stories of the wartime administration. Shell production in December 1914 was 871,700; in December 1915 it was 23,663,186; in December 1916 it was 128,460,113. Production of guns increased six-fold between June 1915 and June 1916.

This new creation, and the manner in which it was run, represented a very sharp departure from 'business as usual'. Lloyd George was now thrusting forward as the most vigorous and articulate exponent of 'the nation in arms'. Above all, he gave an impression of direction and confidence which was in marked contrast with the Government as a whole.

His position was not yet strong in the Government. The Conservative suspicions and resentments remained. Neither the King nor the Army viewed him with enthusiasm, and he was already trying the patience of the Liberal and Labour parties, who were beginning to detect in him a tendency to authoritarianism from which they instinctively rebelled. But Lloyd George bided his time, watched events carefully, and lost no opportunity for advertising his own achievements, to the point that some of his speeches in support of his colleagues sounded uncommonly like Motions of Censure upon them.

*

Throughout 1915 Ministers grappled earnestly but futilely with the deteriorating military situation. It was a year of virtually unrelieved disaster. In the battles of Neuve Chapelle (March), Second Ypres (April), Festubert (May) and Loos (September) the British suffered more than 150,000 casualties. The total Allied casualties in Gallipoli amounted to some 250,000, of whom nearly 200,000 were British and Dominion. In August, Ian Hamilton had made his supreme effort, and had bungled it. The decision to abandon this tragic venture was not an easy one, and Churchill fought bitterly for its continuation. But Churchill was now in eclipse. At the beginning of November the Dardanelles Committee was ended, and replaced by a War Committee consisting of Asquith, Balfour, Grey and Lloyd George; the Conservatives were incensed at the omission of Law, who joined it shortly afterwards with McKenna—four Liberals and two Conservatives. Churchill, for the first and last time in his career, resigned, and made a defiant speech in defence of the Dardanelles operation before placing himself 'unreservedly at the disposal of the military authorities'. Asquith—and, much more surprisingly, Law—expressed formal regrets at his departure; others were more critical of his description of the Dardanelles operation as 'a legitimate war gamble'. *The Times* commented that 'Nobody imagines that his disappearance from the political arena will be more than temporary'. To the regret of many, this forecast proved to be true. Churchill entered into his responsibilities on the Western Front with ardour and deep seriousness, but with his attention still concentrated upon political developments in London. In the maelstrom of events, Churchill's dramatic donning of khaki aroused little public or political interest. Churchill and his circle regarded his fortunes as central to the fate of the nation; but the nation had more immediate preoccupations than the fate of one egotistical and apparently failed middle-aged politician.

In Mesopotamia, a bold and foolish march into the desert towards Baghdad had ended in disaster. By the end of 1915 virtually no progress had been made on the Western Front; Gallipoli had had to be abandoned, the evacuation of the Allied troops being the only thoroughly successful and professional feature of the enterprise; Bulgaria had entered the war on the side of the Central Powers; Serbia had been totally defeated; a vast and absurd new commitment in Salonika had been undertaken. The only gleams of solace were the continued superiority of the British at sea; the accession of Italy on the Allied side; and the ever-increasing volume of fresh troops from the Dominions. But these were only flashes in the darkness. London was being bombed, which was not serious physically but unnerving psychologically; the condition of the Russians was grievous; the Turks were more firmly in control of the Straits than ever; the Western Front had now acquired its own hideous character.

In most wars it is possible to trace the success or failure of the combatants in territory gained, towns captured, casualties suffered. In the Great War the historian reads constantly of epic struggles to seize a shell-crater in what was once a farm, of major engagements to wrest a shattered patch of woodland, or of how Captain X or Sergeant Y died heroically in a raid on trench HK3. It was an unglamorous, beastly, vicious, and debilitating conflict, with much physical discomfort, boredom, and peril, but which was endured not merely with stoicism but often with enthusiasm. In spite of everything, the competing armies had faith and confidence. The real comradeship of the trenches bound them together, and the will to win was overpoweringly infectious. This is difficult to recapture, and for some impossible to comprehend, but it was the dominant element on both sides in that ghastly, unending, duel.

Amidst these misfortunes for the British, there was no financial or economic crisis. The British economy—assisted by the blockade of Germany—proved itself fully capable of meeting the financial demands of the war. McKenna's first Budget, in November 1915, imposed an excess-profits duty of fifty per cent—in 1917 raised to eighty per cent —on any increase in pre-war profits. It did nothing to reduce war-profiteering, but it provided the Treasury with a handsome income. But McKenna also imposed duties of thirty-three and one-third per cent on a number of 'luxury' items such as motor cars, clocks, and watches. One of the reasons Asquith had privately advanced for not sending Law to the Treasury had been because of his Protectionist views; in the eyes of many Liberals, McKenna had delivered a serious blow against Free Trade. Income tax rose to 3s 6d in the pound, and more War Loans were floated. Had it not been for heavy loans to her allies—£1,825 millions in all, met largely by American borrowings— the British could have handled their war with no serious losses, and, indeed, made a profit as well.

The dominating problem was not, in 1915–16, economic. It was one of manpower. By the end of 1915 the British had suffered casualties of 21,747 officers and 490,673 men, of whom about 200,000 were dead or missing. By the middle of 1915 the recruiting figures were already dipping drastically. The first enthusiasm was gone, and the ever-lengthening casualty lists cast a pall over the nation. The French,

Russian and German losses had been far greater than those of the British—by the end of 1915 the French had endured casualties amounting to over 50,000 officers and nearly two million other ranks of whom dead or missing totalled over one million—but conscription had to some extent spread the losses better.

Behind the issue of conscription there lay the broader issue of the attitude of the Government to the war, and, even more important, that of the nation itself towards the war.

Edward Grey has written that:

> Conscription in the early days of the war was impossible; public opinion was not ready for it; it would have been resisted. Voluntary enlistment gave the country a good start in good-will and enthusiasm; conscription would have given it a bad start. There would have been division of opinion, much resentment; the country might even have foundered in political difficulties.[1]

It is probable that this was an incorrect assessment, and it is arguable that in fact the beginning of the war had been the one moment when conscription would have been freely accepted. But the Liberal Government had never considered it, and the moment had passed.

The roots of the hostility to military conscription lay deep in British history, attitudes, and society. The case for conscription had been made before the war, but had made virtually no impact. Liberals in particular were instinctively opposed to the proposal; the Labour movement, fearing that it would be the first step towards industrial conscription, was adamantly hostile. But the hostility lay much deeper. The State, it was argued, was entitled to ask for the citizen's services; it was not entitled to demand it.

The attitude of Labour reflected this general attitude. Under the Defence of the Realm Act (D.O.R.A.) the Government had taken strong powers. The Munitions of War Act gave the Government authority to deal with industrial stoppages and to assume direct control of certain factories in which no normal trade union activities would be permitted. This was a blow to Labour's high opinion of Lloyd George—the first of many. A voluntary War Munitions Volunteer Scheme was put into operation; under the Act, the Government had the power to direct those workers who joined this scheme.

[1] Grey, op. cit., 72.

Joining, in short, was the only voluntary aspect of it. Munitions Tribunals were set up to deal with infringements of the Act. Most significant of all, a National Register of everyone between the ages of fifteen and sixty-five was initiated. These actions were viewed with considerable hostility by the Labour movement. When Lloyd George visited Glasgow on Christmas Day, 1915, he had a rough reception. The Socialist journal *Forward* was suppressed for a report that began:

> The best paid munitions worker in Britain, Mr. Lloyd George (almost £100 a week) visited the Clyde last week in search of adventure. He got it.

Greeted with cries of 'Get your hair cut' and other unfriendly observations, Lloyd George was virtually howled down. An official version of what occurred was issued, in which no mention was made of the disturbances, nor of the fact that Lloyd George's speech had never been delivered. No reference was made to David Kirkwood's statement that 'I can assure him that every word he says will be carefully weighed. We regard him with suspicion, because every action with which he is associated has the taint of slavery about it.' These were, of course, extreme attitudes, and Glasgow Socialism had a vivid character of its own. Labour now had a stake in the Coalition Government, and it recognised, however uneasily, the duty of the Government to harness the nation's industrial capacity. But military conscription, with the possibility of industrial conscription, was another matter.

Thus, even if the Government had been united on the need for conscription—which it certainly was not—it had to move circumspectly. In October 1915 the Earl of Derby was appointed Director-General of Recruiting, with instructions to find a way out of the dilemma. Derby's difficulties were not lessened by the fact that he had become convinced that conscription was essential. What emerged as 'the Derby Scheme' was a classic but ingenious compromise proposal. Adult males were to be persuaded to 'attest'—i.e. to give an undertaking to serve if and when called upon to do so. No married men would be called up so long as unmarried men were available—a qualification that had the result that might have been expected. Those men who had important skilled occupations or exceptional personal reasons would be exempted. Tribunals were to decide on the latter cases.

This was a very clever scheme, combining an adroit link between voluntary recruiting and compulsion. As has been remarked, it was 'a gigantic engine of fraud and moral blackmail, but, given that the Government had to find soldiers somehow, it was a very astute piece of political tactics. If it succeeded, well and good—the sanctity of voluntaryism had been maintained; if it failed, the case for conscription would be well-nigh irresistible.'[1]

The answer came soon. Within six weeks Derby reported that only half—just over a million—of the total number of single men of military age had attested; the same ratio existed for married men. The demands of the trenches could not be met in this way if the magical— and somewhat arbitrarily determined figure—of seventy divisions, with full support, laid down by Kitchener was to be met.

The next stage was the Military Service Act, hurriedly drafted and introduced in January 1916, which declared that all single men between eighteen and forty-one—including widowers without children —would be deemed to have enlisted and to have been transferred to the Reserve, whence they would be called up as required. One Liberal Minister—Simon—resigned in protest, and the Liberal and Labour parties and Press were deeply unhappy about the Bill. Henderson resigned on January 10th, and the two junior Labour Ministers followed his lead; on the next day Asquith addressed the Parliamentary Labour Party and persuaded the Labour Ministers to remain. The T.U.C. voted overwhelmingly against the Bill, but the Labour members of the Government stayed on the grounds that industrial conscription was not involved, but the Act was passed, although some fifty Liberals voted against it in the Commons. Two vigorous opponents in the Cabinet—Runciman and McKenna—did not carry their disagreement to resignation.

Whether it liked it or not, the Government was now fully embarked on the road to conscription, and the pressures on it to go further mounted, actively encouraged by Lloyd George. At one stage Asquith seriously considered resignation, and the Government seemed on the brink of collapse. A feeble compromise Bill was introduced on April 27th, which so disappointed both sides that it had to be ignominiously withdrawn. In May a second Military Service Bill was brought forward, that introduced at long last the principle of universal conscription. The Easter Rising in Dublin and the surrender of General

[1] A. J. Marwick: *The Deluge*, 77.

Townshend at Kut were the final factors that made the House of Commons act.

The conscription issue was of great political importance. It exposed the divergence of outlook between Liberals and Unionists in the Government and in the House of Commons; it became a symbol of two attitudes to the war—the vigorous and determined, the half-hearted and timorous. The actual effects of conscription on the armies were not great. Claims for exemption were nearly three-quarters of a million, and the Ministry of Munitions had already 'starred' a million and a half men in crucial war-work. In the first six months of conscription the average monthly enlistment was not much over 40,000—less than half under the voluntary system. Furthermore, the Act did not apply to Ireland. The manner in which conscription had come did Asquith no good politically,[1] although it is difficult to see what other course he could have followed.

But attitudes to the war were now definitely changing. Impatience with lack of success was becoming increasingly demonstrated. The war had become something less than a glittering adventure. One significant example of the degree to which the war now extended in the normally easy-going British society was shown in the changing attitude towards conscientious objectors. In December 1914 a No Conscription Fellowship had been set up for young men of military age; it had not received much custom hitherto, but by the end of 1915 it was active. It was as a result of their activities that the Derby Scheme considered appeals for exemption on grounds of conscientious objection—a new phrase in the English language.

The local tribunals did not always view such applications with sympathy. One classic exchange took place in Bradford.

Member: What would you do if a German came to you with a bayonet fixed?

Applicant: I shouldn't know what to do . . .

Member: If the only way to save your mother were to kill a German, would you still let him kill her?

Applicant: Yes.

Member: You ought to be shot.[2]

[1] As Hankey commented: 'The fact was that the people who wanted compulsory service did not want Asquith, and those who wanted Asquith did not want compulsory service.'

[2] John Rae: *Conscience and Politics*, 106

The Military Service Bill had been pushed through with such speed that there were bound to be difficulties and anomalies, and there was certainly hostility to conscientious objectors by the Boards and the Army, but, considering the passions of the time, they did not fare too badly. 2,919 men served in the Non-Combatant Corps, and 1,969 who refused to do so were court-martialled. Several were sentenced to death, but it is now clear that there was no real possibility of the sentences being carried out, and all were quickly commuted. Commanding officers who treated objectors badly were rigorously dealt with. Nonetheless, the legend of a military plot to send objectors to France, try them summarily for capital offences, and execute them has proved very enduring.[1] But although the objectors were turned over to the civilian authorities, their lot was not always easy.

The issue was subsequently evaded by various methods. Some 7,000 objectors agreed to perform non-combatant services, and another 3,000 went to labour camps. Tribunals often deemed an objector's occupation to be of national importance and exempted him on other grounds. There were, in all, less than two thousand who absolutely refused all compulsory service. Lloyd George, once the champion of the oppressed and the pacifist pro-Boer, was among the loudest in demanding severe treatment for such people. This attitude further improved Lloyd George's standing among all patriotic men and women who 'wanted to get on with the war', and, in particular, among the Conservatives. It was another step towards 10 Downing Street— and another away from the Radical support that had given Lloyd George his political opportunity.

At this point, the virtually forgotten Irish Question returned.

*

'This has taken everyone by surprise.' With these words James Stephens—a Registrar at the National Gallery of Ireland—opened his personal daily narrative of the Easter Rising in Dublin.[2] It was an exact statement of fact. 'The general state of Ireland, apart from recruiting, and apart from the activities of the pro-German Sinn Fein minority, is thoroughly satisfactory', the Director of Military Intelligence had reported to London two weeks before the Rising. 'The mass of the people are sound and loyal as regards the war, and the country

[1] Ibid.   [2] James Stephens: *The Insurrection in Dublin* (1916).

is in a very prosperous state and very free from ordinary crime.' There were a quarter of a million Irishmen—Northern and Southern— serving in the British Army or in associated forces such as the Royal Irish Constabulary. Even Patrick Pearse—who proclaimed the Republic in April 1916—wrote in 1915 that 'the last sixteen months have been the most glorious in the history of Europe. . . . The old heart of the earth needed to be warmed with the red wine of the battle-fields', which merited James Connolly's withering retort: 'No, we do not think that the old heart of the earth needs to be warmed with the red wine of millions of lives. We think anyone who does is a blithering idiot.'

Later, it was clear that the Rising did not come out of a clear blue sky. As Stephens wrote immediately afterwards: 'If freedom is to come to Ireland—as I believe it is—then the Easter Insurrection was the only thing that could have happened.' But, at the time, the sur-prise was total, and nowhere more than in Dublin, whose amazed citizens found themselves in the middle of street-fighting, and stood bemusedly watching Volunteers in Phoenix Park and British troops clattering down the streets. As Stephens wrote:

> None of these people were prepared for Insurrection. The thing had been sprung on them so suddenly that they were unable to take sides, and their feeling of detachment was still so complete that they would have betted on the business as if it had been a horse race or a dog fight.

The Easter Rising and its concomitant activities were, even by Irish standards, a spectacular shambles. After the outbreak of war the Irish Volunteers had not disbanded, and continued to drill. Birrell, the Irish Secretary, took the view that it would be unreasonable to disarm them without disarming the Ulster Volunteers; in this attitude expedience also played at least some part. The British had quite enough on their hands without taking on the Irish Volunteers—few in number and poorly armed—and Birrell was the last man to seek trouble.

Furthermore, Ireland was to all appearances patriotic and quies-cent. Redmond had given eloquent expression to his own patriotism in the House of Commons, and his son had been killed on the Western Front. As an issue, Home Rule was in the past. Ireland would receive her independence when the war ended and the Bill became law. Thus, it was widely believed, every attempt made by Irishmen to defeat Germany was a step towards the long-awaited independence.

But the Volunteers were planning for a rising with German assistance on Easter Sunday 1916. Their plans were elaborate, and involved a rising in Dublin itself, assaults on British garrisons, and a march on the capital. It was a bold attempt to effect a *coup d'état*. The British had ample warnings, but ignored them.

There were many fatal defects in the plan, of which the most conspicuous was the half-hearted attitude of the Germans. Sir Roger Casement, who had earned international recognition for his exposure of the methods employed by the Belgians in the Congo, had gone to Germany after a fund-raising visit to the United States in December 1914, but had found little practical support. An attempt by Casement to recruit an Irish Legion from among Irish prisoners of war had been a dismal failure. All that the Germans would do was to ship Casement and two associates to Ireland in a submarine and to send a shipload of arms and ammunition captured by them at Tannenberg in the steamship *Aud*.

The ensuing events had a high element of comedy in them. The *Aud* eluded the British Navy by adopting a number of obvious subterfuges which were for some time successful, but failed to keep a rendezvous. Casement and his companions were picked up, drenched and exhausted, within a few hours of staggering ashore. The captain of the *Aud* scuttled his ship when the suspicious British ordered it to berth under naval escort.

There was a crucial difference of outlook among the Volunteers' leaders. John MacNeill was the President and Chief of Staff of the Volunteers, and Patrick Pearse was Director of Organisation. The total force of the Volunteers was never more than 16,000. MacNeill had no knowledge of the *Aud* or of Casement's imminent arrival, and had always insisted that the Volunteers should not rise save in self-defence. Pearse was a member of the Irish Republican Brotherhood and it was the I.R.B. leaders who were determined to have their revolution. They accordingly published, on April 19th, a forged letter —the 'Castle Document'—purporting to show that the authorities proposed to arrest the Volunteers' leaders and dissolve the movement. This forced a decision from MacNeill, which he now rescinded on the evening of April 21st, in spite of Pearse's bitter protests. But the Military Council of the I.R.B.—Pearse, Connolly, MacDonagh,

Plunkett, Clarke, MacDermott, Ceannt—was determined to proclaim the Republic.

Easter Sunday passed peacefully. On Easter Monday, 1,200 Volunteers in Dublin, led by Pearse and acting quite independently, seized the General Post Office and other strategic points and declared the establishment of the Irish Republic. Dubliners returning from their Easter holiday in the country discovered their city in a state of insurrection. Throughout the events that followed they were either apathetic onlookers or vehement against the Volunteers; as Stephens noted, it was the women in particular who were the most angry and resentful.

The British, after their initial amazement—on the afternoon of Easter Monday an English officer walked into the General Post Office and tried to buy a book of stamps from the astounded Volunteers—reacted vigorously. Four days of severe fighting ensued, in which some 100 British soldiers and 450 Volunteers were killed. The total casualties on both sides were 1,351, and very substantial damage was done. Over 100,000 people had to be given public relief, and the centre of Dublin was in ruins. It seemed that it had been a gallant, futile venture, in the Irish tradition. As Stephens wrote:

> For being beaten does not greatly matter in Ireland, but not fighting does matter. 'They went forth always to the battle; and they always fell.' Indeed, the history of the Irish race is in that phrase.

The Rising was widely condemned in Ireland. The *Irish Catholic* denounced it 'as criminal as it was insane,' and 'traitorous and treacherous to our native land'. The Bishop of Ross described it as 'a senseless, meaningless debauch of blood'. Stephens noted that the Dubliners, and particularly the women, were 'actively and viciously hostile to the rising'. In essentials, Birrell and the Viceroy had been right. The I.R.B. was an impotent minority party; the Volunteers had no basis of popular support. The reactions of the British were entirely understandable. Ireland had been promised her freedom when the war ended, and had joined with the British in the war against Germany. Irishmen, no less than Englishmen, Scotsmen or Welshmen, owed allegiance to King and Country. Together they were falling in battle in terms of thousands. Here was a reckless minority which had traded with the enemy and raised arms against the ordered Government.

The Government handed the matter over to the military, and dispatched General Sir John Maxwell—former General Officer Commanding in Egypt and a persistent difficulty to Ian Hamilton—to Ireland to declare martial law and bring matters under control. This was swiftly done. Military justice then followed. Only the ringleaders would suffer. Sixteen were court-martialled and shot—not all at once, but over a period of days. Immediately, Irish opinion was transformed. The blundering incompetents became martyrs. Yeats, who a few years earlier had written contemptuously of Ireland as 'a little greasy huxtering nation groping for halfpence in a greasy till', now wrote that 'A terrible beauty is born'.

Out of many tragedies, one in particular should be recorded.

Francis Sheehy-Skeffington, the youthful biographer of Michael Davitt, was, like his admired subject, an individualist. A contemporary of James Joyce at University College, Dublin, he had taken up the causes of nationalism, pacifism, socialism and the emancipation of women with ardour and independence. His convictions about Irish Independence did not embrace the use of violence, and he was a vehement opponent not only of war but of the actions by his countrymen in the Rising. He tried to organise a citizens' force to prevent looting in Dublin, and was arrested by the British. Tragically, he fell into the hands of one Captain Bowen-Colthurst, himself an Irishman, who had him and two equally innocent men—Thomas Dickson and Patrick MacIntyre—shot without any form of trial. After repeated efforts by Dillon, Bowen-Colthurst was court-martialled and his conduct investigated by a Royal Commission of Inquiry. He was found guilty but insane. After a period in Broadmoor he emigrated to Canada, where he lived until 1965. To read Sheehy-Skeffington's study of Davitt—written before he was thirty—is to appreciate what was lost by the action of a mad officer.[1] Particular poignancy is provided in the cold record of Sergeant Aldridge, given to the official enquiry:

You told us that Captain Colthurst said he wanted the three men out to speak to them?—Yes.

[1] Sheehy-Skeffington's biography of Davitt was published in 1908, and reprinted, with an introduction by Professor F. S. L. Lyons, in 1967. Its concluding section, with its warnings against 'the Irish tendency to hero-worship', deserves to be remembered, including this phrase: 'It is only the commonplace man who grows cold and conservative with age; the rare spirits who have made the world worth living in widen their outlook and strengthen their faith in progress year by year.'

Did he speak to them?—Only to tell them to go to the wall.

Did he accuse them of anything?—No.

Did he ever explain to them that he was going to shoot them?—No.

Did he ever ask them if they had anything to say?—No.

Did you feel that you had no alternative but to obey his orders?—No. I did not understand that he was going to have them shot. It was a surprise to me, and the men themselves did not realise what was going to happen. When he asked for the seven men (for the firing party) I thought he wanted them as an escort.

Did anybody make any sort of protest at all?—No; there was no one there to do it.

It is easy to blame both the Government and Maxwell. Yet, by the lights of the times, they had been lenient. This was to be one of the last of a long, long series of examples of how little the British, after four hundred years, understood the Irish.

Yet, there was still hope. Asquith seriously considered the immediate granting of Home Rule. Lloyd George negotiated on his own with Carson and Redmond, and secured agreement whereby twenty-six counties would receive Home Rule at once, with the six Ulster Counties to remain British until after the war, when their position would be reviewed by an Imperial Conference. This was a solution that offered real chance of success. But, once again, Lansdowne was implacable. Compromises had to be made to meet Unionist demands, until Redmond refused to go further. The attempt to negotiate a settlement broke down. Ireland was ruled by Dublin Castle, as before. The Irish Nationalist Party at Westminster was virtually destroyed by this final failure. The dead Volunteers became martyrs. The extremists made spectacular gains. Sinn Fein, which had in fact played no part in the Rising, became a force and no longer a minority voice. Its amended Constitution in 1917 declared that 'Sinn Fein aims at securing the international recognition of Ireland as an independent Irish Republic', and drew into it all the principal elements of the revivified Irish nationalism. The relative political importance of Redmond's party and Sinn Fein were exactly reversed. The subsequent proposal to impose conscription upon Ireland was the final stroke. The Irish Question now entered a new, and decisively terrible, period, 'Death answering to Death like the clerks answering one another at the Mass', in the tragic words of Lady Gregory. Stephens concluded his account of the Easter Rising with the words: 'The Volunteers are dead, and the call is now for Volunteers.' And still the English did not understand. They had crushed a small rebellion. They had created an immense revolution.

There remained the embarrassing question of what to do with Casement. On June 29th he was convicted of high treason and sentenced to death. His appeal was rejected, and the Attorney-General, F. E. Smith (now Sir Frederick Smith), refused to give leave for a further appeal to the House of Lords. The only hope for Casement lay with the Home Secretary's prerogative of mercy.

Exceptionally, but justifiably, Herbert Samuel referred the matter to the Cabinet. On July 19th it decided unanimously that Casement should be hanged, and on August 2nd stood by this decision in spite of urgent appeals from abroad, notably from the United States. Casement was duly executed on August 3rd. Another incompetent revolutionary had become a martyr, and the manner in which his homosexual diaries were shown to individuals who had been disposed in his favour added a peculiarly nauseating touch to the macabre business. Asquith, Grey, and Lansdowne had originally wanted him declared insane, but after a professional report that he was 'abnormal but not certifiably insane' they bowed to the majority feeling in the Cabinet. After the Maxwell executions they perhaps had no alternative, but the effects were disastrous. As the British Ambassador in Washington reported of the Irish-Americans, 'there is blood in their eyes whenever they look at us'.

Mr. Taylor has written that 'This was the only national rebellion in any European country during the first world war—an ironical comment on the British claim to be fighting for freedom'.[1] The Easter Rising was not, in the first instance, a 'national rebellion'. The actions of the British Government and General Maxwell turned it into one. Some six months before his death Pearse had written:

The lawyers have sat in council, the men with the keen, long faces
And said, 'This man is a fool', and others have said, 'He blasphemeth';
And the wise have pitied the fool that hath striven to give a life
In the world of time and space among the bulk of actual things
To a dream that was dreamed in the heart, and that only the heart
    could hold.

[1] Taylor, *English History 1914–1945*, 56.

O wise men, riddle me this: what if the dream come true?
What if the dream come true? and if millions unborn shall dwell
In the house that I shaped in my heart?

The Easter Rising and its sequel cast long and dark shadows. Birrell
clearly had to go, although Asquith accepted his resignation with
reluctance. The Under-Secretary, Sir Matthew Nathan, was also
removed, although he had had a better understanding of Irish affairs
than most of his predecessors. But he had made several very fundamental errors. He over-valued the role of Casement, and assumed
that, when Casement was captured, the moment of peril was past.
On April 10th he had told Birrell that he did not believe that the
Volunteers meant insurrection, nor that they had the means. On
Easter Sunday, April 22nd, he had written to Birrell that 'I see no
indication of a rising'. Most damning of all was the evidence that the
Viceroy, Lord Wimborne, had wanted the known leaders of the
Volunteers arrested on the Sunday, and that Nathan had hesitated.
Nathan had been exceptionally unlucky, another in the long and
uncompleted list of those destroyed by the Irish Question.

Birrell's loss was not a serious one. Sixteen years after the Rising,
when its full effects were plain for all to see, he wrote blandly in
reminiscence:

> It was a supreme act of criminal folly on the part of those who were
> responsible for it, for it never had a chance, and was really nothing
> more than a Dublin row.

Of much greater significance was the fact that Redmond's political
fate was sealed by 'the Dublin row'. He had condemned the Rising,
and had said that 'the overwhelming mass of the Irish people' regarded
it, as he did, 'with a feeling of horror and detestation'. On May 3rd,
when the executions were in full swing, he issued a statement condemning the Rising as a blow against Home Rule and declaring that
'Germany plotted it, Germany organised it, Germany paid for it'.
That statement ended his career as an Irish leader. As John Dillon
wrote to T. P. O'Connor in the autumn of 1916, 'enthusiasm and trust
in Redmond *is dead*, so far as the mass of the people is concerned'.

Dillon had been in Dublin throughout the Rising. On April 30th
he wrote to Redmond to impress upon the Government 'the *extreme*
unwisdom of any wholesale shootings of prisoners. The wisest course

is to execute *no one* for the present. This is *the most urgent* matter for the moment . . . *So far* the feeling of the population in Dublin is *against* the Sinn Feiners. But a reaction might very easily be created. . . .' Redmond did see Asquith about the executions, but with no success: 'He said some few were necessary, but they would be very few. I protested.' Redmond then issued his statement condemning the Rising and blaming it upon German influence.

Dillon might have saved the Nationalist Party. On May 11th and 12th in the House of Commons he spoke of the Volunteers in warm terms, and cried to the Government:

> We have risked our lives a hundred times to bring about this result [Anglo-Irish union]. We are held up to odium as traitors by the men who made this rebellion . . . and you are washing out our whole life-work in a sea of blood.

The breakdown of the Lloyd George negotiations, and, above all, the disclosure that the Nationalist leaders were prepared to omit the six Ulster counties from Home Rule, finished the Nationalist cause in Ireland. The Irish leaders themselves considered that Lloyd George had double-crossed them, and it was several months before Redmond would have any dealings whatever with Lloyd George. Already, he could dimly see the truth of the words spoken by Pearse at the court-martial which was described as a trial: 'We seem to have lost: we have not lost.'

*

The end of 1915 had seen the formal abandonment of 'side-shows' and the concentration on the Western Front. General Sir Douglas Haig had replaced Sir John French as Commander-in-Chief in France; Sir William Robertson had become Chief of the Imperial General Staff, and had re-created the General Staff. When Kitchener returned from his visit to the Middle East in November he found these two men in their positions, and his powers drastically curtailed. These two determined, obstinate men henceforth dominated British strategy. Kitchener's star was in the descendant. He contemplated resignation, but was persuaded to stay. The politicians regarded him as a useless but crucial ornament, a kind of national talisman, but little more. Their over-estimation of Kitchener in 1914 was hardly less reasonable than their under-estimation of him in 1916.

The first effects of the Haig-Robertson combination were seen in the Battle of the Somme, which opened on July 1st. Haig had originally wanted to attack further in the north, but the agreement to have an Anglo-French offensive dictated that it should be in the Somme. Already, the French were heavily engaged at Verdun, first attacked in February, with the result that the Somme battle became more irrelevant than ever. But it had acquired its own momentum, and Haig was no longer troubled by its locale. It was a catastrophic British defeat. On the first day the British suffered 57,000 casualties, of whom 19,000 were killed.[1] On one day! But, undeterred, Haig hung on, and the battle raged until November, by which time the British had suffered 420,000 casualties and the French 194,000; the German losses were also heavy, 465,000. The secret to success in trench warfare—the tank—had arrived, but the few available were used in small groups. Two days after their first use—on September 15th—Haig asked for a thousand. Although they were as yet unaware of the fact, the British had at last a weapon that could win the war. The Somme was a bitter battle, and something more than a bitter disappointment.

It was not the only one. On May 31st the Battle of Jutland had been fought. The British lost three battle-cruisers, three cruisers, and eight destroyers; the Germans lost one battleship, one battle-cruiser, four light cruisers and five destroyers. The Germans issued a statement on June 1st which was in effect a claim of a great victory; the Kaiser declared a national holiday and bestowed the Ordre Pour Le Mérite on Admirals Scheer and Hipper. The Admiralty asked Jellicoe for his comments on the German communiqué; these had not been received by the 2nd, by which time the news was beginning to reach the country through the foreign press. The Admiralty accordingly issued the German statement without any comment. The effect of this upon British morale was severe, and in New York British stocks fell sharply. To make matters worse, Balfour put out a factual statement on June 3rd that concentrated on the British losses and seemed to confirm the German claims. It was as if Nelson had been defeated at Trafalgar. The true facts came out later; at the time public confidence was grievously, and unnecessarily, shaken. An optimistic article by Churchill—sponsored by the Admiralty—could not correct the first impressions.

---

[1] Over 1,000 officers and 20,000 men killed, fatally wounded, or missing; over 1,300 officers and 34,000 other ranks wounded.

The Times, indeed, commented tartly that 'this use of Mr. Churchill—who has no association whatever with the Government, who apparently aspires at this moment to lead an Opposition, and whose strategical utterances during the war have hardly been models of accuracy—was the most amazing confession of weakness on the part of the Admiralty'. It was certainly an odd tactic.

The Germans, realising that they had only just escaped complete defeat, turned to the submarine offensive. Scheer's official despatch of July 4th, indeed, stated bluntly that 'a victorious termination of the war within measurable time can only be attained by destroying the economic existence of Great Britain, namely, by the employment of submarines against British commerce'. The results were soon apparent. In November the President of the Board of Trade, Runciman, circulated a memorandum which stated that, if present shipping losses continued, Britain would collapse by the summer of 1917. He had no suggestions to offer, and his contribution has been described, not unjustly, by Christopher Addison as 'the most invertebrate and hopeless of any memoranda presented to the Government during the war by a responsible head of a department on a great issue'.

But Runciman's dilemma was acute. The obvious answers—control and regulation—were anathema. The alternative to a controlled economy was a negotiated peace. In November Lansdowne circulated a memorandum to the Cabinet seeking specification of British war aims and, by implication, a settlement on the pre-war status quo. It received short shrift.

Asquith's troubles were now piling heavily upon him and his Government. Everywhere the war was going badly. The Kitchener Armies were being destroyed on the Somme, and on June 5th Kitchener himself had perished as well, in the cruiser *Hampshire* en route for Russia. It is difficult to say whether the British were more shaken by this event than by the failures at Jutland and the Somme. But the political consequences were profound.

A month elapsed between Kitchener's death and the assumption of office by his successor. Asquith proposed to take his time over the matter. What actually occurred has become the object of considerable controversy. One account has it that Asquith, faced by the alternative of Bonar Law or Lloyd George, procrastinated and hoped to put in Derby, but that Law and Lloyd George delivered a joint ultimatum which he had to accept. Mr. Jenkins has, however, raised some pertinent questions about this version.[1] The King, and the generals, did not view the prospect of Lloyd George with much satisfaction, but Asquith seems to have recognised that he was clearly the best man for the job. In the event, Lloyd George succeeded Kitchener at the end of June. Margot Asquith later considered that this was the beginning of the end of Asquith's Premiership. Certainly, Lloyd George began to act more boldly. He publicly advocated the doctrine of the 'knock-out blow' and spoke belligerently of fighting to 'a decisive finish'. The Northcliffe Press, unsparing in its criticism of Asquith, began to call for new leadership and to use Lloyd George's name frequently in this connection. *The Observer*—an Astor paper—joined the opposition to Asquith. The decision of the Government to permit Royal Commissions to enquire into the Dardanelles and Mesopotamia campaigns was a serious blunder, and particularly affected relations within the Cabinet, never good at the best of times. And these were not the best of times.

But Asquith's position was still a strong one. The Unionists may have been increasingly admiring of Lloyd George's energy and capacities and increasingly impatient of Asquith, but their mistrust of Lloyd George remained. Law considered that Lloyd George was 'a self-seeker and a man who considered no interest except his own', and who wanted merely 'to put Asquith out and to put himself in'. It was neither an uncommon nor a wholly unfair judgement. There was still a Liberal majority in the House of Commons and in the Government, and remarkably many Conservatives still regarded Asquith as indispensable. Even those who did not feared the effects on national unity of division and discord in the Government. Bonar Law's attitude has been described by his friend Max Aitken, shortly to become Lord Beaverbrook:

> Since the formation of the Coalition Government, no one had been a more loyal member of the Cabinet in the face of much provocation, and the appeal to loyalty was to the Prime Minister's hand. At the same time, a kind of scepticism about strong emotions and distrust of ardent passions or sharp measures, mixed with a contempt for personal ambition, made him by instinct, if not by reason, regard the rise of Lloyd George to supreme power as a dangerous portent in politics.[2]

[1] Jenkins, op. cit., 406–9.   [2] Beaverbrook: *Politicians and the War*, 353.

Asquith was, however, fighting a mood rather than an effective political combination at this stage. The pent-up frustrations of two years of war, in which no gains could be counted and only hideous losses incurred, required a scapegoat. This was a natural feeling, even if it was unfair. Similar emotions were evident in France, Russia, and even in Germany. Beaverbrook's words admirably sum up the mood against Asquith in the early winter of 1916:

His complete detachment from the spirit of the struggle; his instability of purpose; his refusal to make up his mind on grave and urgent issues of policy; his balancing of one adviser against another till the net result was nil; his fundamental desire to have a peaceful tenure of office in the midst of war, could in the long run have only one result. The men who were in tune with the atmosphere of the war—the bold, the eager, the decisive spirits—first fell away from him and then combined against him. And while all this was going on, he was immersed in his own social circle and engaged in responding to the devotion of his friends.'[1]

By the end of November a Ministerial crisis was imminent.

*

The position of a Prime Minister is always a strong one. He has in his hands the political careers of his colleagues. He has the weapon of Dissolution. He controls patronage and preferment. If he resigns, he can take his Government with him. He can divide his opponents by raising some and lowering others. He has the power—implicit and explicit—of the Party Machine. Asquith, in November 1916, did not possess all these advantages; it would be difficult, in wartime, to justify a general election, and such a course could only have been taken either in concert with his Conservative and Labour allies or as a result of breaking up the Coalition. Nevertheless, the inherent advantages possessed by a Prime Minister were with him.

Asquith had been Prime Minister since 1908. In that period he had presided in peacetime over a Cabinet of exceptional ability and also exceptional divisive potentiality. He had survived the Ministerial Crisis of May 1915, since then had kept the Coalition together, and had brought it through the crises of the Dardanelles evacuation, the

[1] Beaverbrook, op. cit., 226.

divisions over Conscription, and even that in Ireland. It cannot be pretended that it was a harmonious Cabinet, but it had held together.

The question was how long Asquith could maintain this delicate balance. Hankey's comments are of particular interest:

> The machinery of the War Committee was at this time working smoothly. An Agenda paper was issued before each meeting. Full records were as before kept in manuscript. The conclusions after being approved and initialled by the Prime Minister—in this matter Asquith was prompt and punctilious—were circulated to the Cabinet whose members were thus kept fully abreast of what was going on.

It was Hankey's opinion that 'with a loyal and united team' this system might have been adapted to meet the problems of the latter part of the war.

> But, with a Government composed of members of opposite political parties who had never been able entirely to forget their differences and in an atmosphere poisoned by the Dardanelles and Mesopotamia Commissions, this proved impossible even under so patient and experienced a leader as Asquith.[1]

The autumn meetings of the War Committee had been long, exhausting, and usually inconclusive. On November 8th, in a debate on the disposal of assets in Nigeria, Bonar Law had had a very rough passage in the House of Commons, and the Government had been nearly defeated. As in the celebrated 'Three Acres and a Cow' debate of January 1886,[2] the issue of Nigeria itself was irrelevant. It provided an issue on which the greatest number of Conservatives could be gathered to vote against the Government, and which would provide Carson with a suitable opportunity to attack Law personally.

The old alliance between Carson and Law had been broken since the former had resigned from the Government in November 1915. Carson invariably injected into his political and forensic life a strain of personal bitterness and animosity that made him a very formidable opponent but which also often poisoned his personal relationships. It is difficult to categorise or explain the causes of his resentment against

---

[1] Hankey, op. cit., II, 543-4.

[2] See Volume I, 96. The Norway Debate of May 1940 was another comparable occasion.

Law—a resentment that was not returned. Those Conservatives who wanted to topple Asquith knew that the weak point in the edifice was Law's position. Law was indispensable to Asquith; he had also made it plain when he took office that he did so on the condition that he retained the support and confidence of his party. At that time he had said:

> I say quite plainly that if I found that in this new position I had lost the confidence of our party I should feel I was of no further use to the Government. Certainly, so long as I myself believe that, whatever its defects, I can see no better way of carrying on this war, I should not oppose it, but if the party to which I belong had lost confidence in me I should not for a moment dream of continuing to be a member of the Government.

Thus, in striking at Law, the Conservative opponents of the Government were striking at Asquith. Added force was given to their attack by Carson's personal hostility towards Law.

In the event, the Government just survived; most important, Law had a small majority—seventy-three to sixty-five—of the Unionists who voted; but 148 did not. Among those who voted against the Government was Churchill, now definitely returned to the political front, clearly out to make trouble, and deeply discontented with his lot. One significant absentee was at once noted: Lloyd George had not voted. Indeed, he had that evening been dining at the home of Lord Lee of Fareham—the former Arthur Lee—with Carson and Milner. It is not quite clear whether Lloyd George, as he claimed to Bonar Law on the following morning, had been paired; it is very probable that he was not, and that his absence was deliberate. It was certainly interpreted as such at the time, and awoke politicians and political commentators to the interesting fact that the Government was now being attacked from front and rear.

It had survived, but only barely. Law rejected Aitken's proposal that he resign and force the issue. His loyalty to Asquith was strong. So was his mistrust of Lloyd George. As a party leader himself, he had an instinctive distaste for rebels, and at least part of his support for Asquith was based on the 'dog don't eat dog' principle. These feelings were considerably strengthened by a discussion with Churchill at Cherkley on November 12th, vividly described by Beaverbrook.[1] Law

---

[1] Beaverbrook, op. cit., 105–6.

disliked Churchill very strongly, and after he had endured a characteristic Churchillian harangue he threatened him with a general election. With Law in this mood, and with Asquith showing no inclination whatever to resign, the possibilities of a successful coup against the Prime Minister seemed to suffer a serious setback. The malcontents—Liberal and Unionist—were once again confronted by the realities of the political situation and the strength of the position enjoyed by a Prime Minister determined not to be pushed out.

The Lansdowne Memorandum[1] gave them another opportunity for attacking the Government. Asquith did not support Lansdowne's pessimistic view of the situation, but the Memorandum was immediately leaked to the Press, and the impression was quickly gained that Asquith himself was not opposed to the views it contained. It was ironical that Lansdowne, who had so often deliberately harmed Asquith in the past, should now unwittingly deliver this severe blow.

Before he left with Asquith to attend an Allied conference in Paris on November 14th, Lloyd George used Aitken to sound out Bonar Law on the possibility of their urging the creation of a small War Committee, to be independent of the Cabinet, and without the Prime Minister at its head. Lloyd George's principal preoccupation at this point was not Asquith, but Sir William Robertson. When Aitken put the idea to Law, the Unionist leader was 'desperately "sticky"'. Law's dislike and distrust of Lloyd George were as great as ever, and he was, moreover, oppressed by his own problems as Conservative leader. When he heard that Carson agreed with Lloyd George on the matter he felt that he would have at least to give consideration to the proposal, although he was clearly unenthusiastic. When Lloyd George got back from Paris,[2] he invited Law to dine with him alone, but Law refused. On the following day Law told Asquith of what was in the wind.

Asquith did not express surprise, and commented that he could not believe that Lloyd George's ambitions would be content with chairmanship of such a body. In this he struck a receptive chord in Law.

[1] See p. 63.

[2] This conference had exposed the differences in attitudes towards the military shown by Asquith and Lloyd George. Lloyd George wanted Ministers to meet before the military conference was held; in the event he did not get his way, and the Ministers accepted the decisions of the generals. Lloyd George returned from Paris even more convinced than ever that the generals, if left to themselves, would lose the war.

A FORLORN APPEAL.

Mr. Asquith. "COALITION, ERE WE PART, GIVE, O GIVE ME BACK MY—ER—PARTY!"

1   Asquith by Ravenhill in *Punch*, 1918

2   A Young Man in a Hurry. Winston Churchill by Bert Thomas
in the *World*, 1919

THE NEW CONDUCTOR.

OPENING OF THE 1917 OVERTURE.

3 Lloyd George by Ravenhill in *Punch*, 1916

Lord Oxford.

LOW

4   Asquith by Low in *The New Statesman*, February 1926

He also expressed doubts about including Carson on the basis of his previous performance as a member of the Government.

On November 20th Lloyd George, Carson and Bonar Law met at the Hyde Park Hotel. Law's attitude remained one of scepticism and suspicion of Lloyd George's motives. Nevertheless, he did see the advantages of getting Carson on to the Committee. This was the first meeting of the 'Triumvirate', and its results were to be momentous.

There were further meetings on the following three days, in which Law became increasingly attracted by the War Committee idea. By Saturday, November 25th, he was ready to accept a written agreement, prepared by Aitken, which was in the form of a public announcement by Asquith, and to submit it to the Prime Minister. It would announce the creation of 'a civilian General Staff' of which Asquith would be president, and Lloyd George the actual chairman. The members would be Lloyd George, Carson and Bonar Law himself. It was a skilfully worded document, designed to placate Law's suspicions of Lloyd George's motives and to give Carson and Lloyd George what they wanted.

On the next day (Sunday, November 26th), Law presented this paper to Asquith. The Prime Minister had, on Thursday 23rd, been alerted by the curious fact that the *Morning Post*, an old ally of Carson's but never enthusiastic about Lloyd George, came out for a Lloyd George premiership and styled him the 'saviour of society'.

In his reply to Law's missive, Asquith wrote that, after due reflection, he was not taken by the idea of the small War Committee, and put forward some very reasonable and acute criticisms of the proposal. It was a measured, calm, precise response. Again, one has the impression of a great judge giving mature consideration to a project, analysing it, and returning a fully considered and unanswerable opinion. And there was a sting in the tail, when the judge came to deal with the plaintiff Lloyd George:

> He has many qualities that would fit him for the first place, but he lacks the one thing needful—he does not inspire trust. . . . Here, again, there is one construction, and one only, that could be put on the new arrangement, that it has been engineered by him with the purpose, not perhaps at the moment, but as soon as a fitting pretext could be found, of his displacing me. In short, the plan could not, in my opinion, be carried out without impairing the

confidence of loyal and valued colleagues, and undermining my own authority.

This flung the 'Triumvirate' into some confusion. Carson was all for fighting Asquith, but Law had not yet reached this point, and Lloyd George, although quite untroubled by the severe comments on himself, began to back-pedal.

Carson and Aitken had no doubts or hesitations, and began to use their formidable newspaper contacts to good purpose. A Ministerial Crisis is difficult to create by Press agitation, but a Little Ministerial Crisis can be built up into a Big Ministerial Crisis with judicious fire and brimstone applied at the right moment. Aitken, who was convinced that Asquith must go, was particularly active. On November 29th the *Daily Chronicle*, an influential Liberal newspaper, came out with strong criticism of the manner in which the war was being conducted. The *Daily Express, Daily Mail, Morning Post* and *Times* echoed these charges, and they constituted a formidable coverage of the national Press. All week the barrage against the Government was maintained.

On the Thursday (November 30th), Bonar Law told his Conservative colleagues in the Government what had transpired. Not unnaturally, they were affronted by the fact that they had not been consulted; none of them liked the proposals themselves, and particularly the elevation of Lloyd George. Lord Robert Cecil, in fact, openly accused Law of 'dragging the Conservative Party at the coat-tails of Lloyd George'. The Ministers favoured a reorganisation of the present War Committee but would not support the 'Triumvirate's' proposals. Law stood by them, and the meeting broke up in disagreement.

On the next day (Friday, December 1st) Lloyd George in effect told Asquith that unless he accepted the terms of the Triumvirate, he would resign. In reply Asquith admitted that the system needed revision, but insisted that the Prime Minister must remain head of any reorganised War Committee. Lloyd George considered this 'entirely unsatisfactory'.

The key to the situation was Bonar Law. If he backed Lloyd George, Asquith's position would be extremely serious. If he did not, Lloyd George would have either to suffer a serious humiliation or resign alone. There are moments in politics when a man needs friends. Lloyd George had none in the Coalition Cabinet. He was fighting alone, and had reached a crisis-point.

If Bonar Law was to be moved, his close friend Aitken was the only person who could achieve this. On the evening of December 1st he dined alone with Law at the Hyde Park Hotel, and pressed Lloyd George's case upon him. At length Law decided to see Lloyd George at once, and they went in a taxi to the Berkeley Hotel, where Lloyd George was dining with the Governor of the Bank of England, Lord Cunliffe.[1] Lloyd George joined Aitken and Law—patiently waiting in the taxi—and returned to the Hyde Park. Lloyd George handled Bonar Law dexterously and sympathetically. On the following morning he sent Law a copy of Asquith's letter to him and a brief note that read: 'The life of the country depends on resolute action by you now.'

Bonar Law called a meeting of his Conservative ministerial colleagues for the Sunday (December 3rd) morning. Balfour and Lansdowne were not present. The Ministers came in a passion, having read or been told about an article in *Reynolds' News* that morning which gave the full story from Lloyd George's angle. It was, as Beaverbrook subsequently commented, 'like an interview with Lloyd George written in the third person'. The Ministers were deeply chagrined, and instructed Law to transmit to Asquith a resolution recommending the resignation of the Government; if this were not done, they authorised Law to tender their resignations.

Some historians have accepted Beaverbrook's opinion that this was a purely anti-Lloyd George move, designed to expose Lloyd George's isolation, and bring Asquith back on the Conservatives' terms. This interpretation seems both too naïve and too subtle; it imposes clarity of thought and action upon an angry and confused meeting; it does not credit the Conservative Ministers with much intelligence or competence. This was an ultimatum to Asquith that a major reconstruction from the top was necessary, and on the Conservatives' terms. Curzon, who wrote an account for Lansdowne, took a strong anti-Asquith line, and said that the object of the resolution was to bring Lloyd George face to face with the fact of political responsibility: 'His Government will be dictated to him by others, not shaped exclusively by himself.'

Law saw Asquith—who had been urgently summoned back from

[1] 'I had the means of finding Lloyd George at that time at any hour of the day or night', Beaverbrook has recorded.

his weekend in Kent—after lunch with Aitken. Aitken had tried to persuade Law not to show Asquith a passage from the Conservative resolution which rebuked Lloyd George for his disclosures to the *Daily Chronicle*, *Daily Express*—Aitken's own work—and *Reynolds*. At the meeting with Asquith, Law did not give him the resolution. Law's account is that he forgot to show him the actual paper, although he described its contents. In any event, Asquith took Law's message to be that all the Conservative Ministers were in complete hostility to him.

Much heat has been engendered about this meeting, and of Law's failure to give a copy of the resolution to Asquith.[1] Law's explanation is so simple and human that it sounds very authentic, but, given Aitken's urgings to him at luncheon, this commentator is sceptical. It is difficult to determine whether it had any real consequence on the eventual result, but it certainly complicated matters. And it must have determined Asquith on his next move, which was to see Lloyd George and virtually give him everything he had asked for. Law joined this meeting at the end, and they decided that all Ministers other than Asquith should resign and the Government be reconstructed on the basis of the new arrangement. It seemed an admirable compromise. Lloyd George would get his War Committee; Asquith would remain Prime Minister, and with 'supreme and effective control of War Policy'. Asquith was not unjustified when he wrote that evening:

> The 'Crisis' shows every sign of following its many predecessors to an early and unhonoured grave. But there were many wigs very nearly on the green.

On the following morning (Monday, December 4th) the wigs were back on the green.

The cause was a leading article in *The Times*, which attacked Asquith personally. Furthermore, it showed clear signs of having been written by someone with very good inside information indeed, and implied that Asquith had made a complete surrender of his powers to Lloyd George. Asquith assumed at once that Lloyd George was the informant. He did not know that Lloyd George had been seeing Northcliffe regularly during the previous weeks, and that there had been three meetings in the previous three days, but his assumption

[1] See Robert Blake, *The Unknown Prime Minister*, 317–25; Beaverbrook, op. cit., 419–36; Jenkins, op. cit., 438–40.

that Lloyd George had been up to his old tricks was not surprising. Some confusion exists about Lloyd George's part in the *Times* article, which was written by the editor, Geoffrey Dawson. It has also been alleged that the sole purpose of Northcliffe's discussions with Lloyd George was to offer him a post on his newspapers. It requires considerable credulity to accept this version implicitly; in any event, it is doubtful whether these conversations about Lloyd George's future career did not include some chance observations on the current political situation. The last of these conversations took place on the Sunday evening. Dawson's claim—supported by Mr. Taylor[1] and Dawson's biographer—that his sole informants were Waldorf Astor and Carson does not wholly exonerate Lloyd George. From whom else would Carson get his information? Asquith's conclusions may not have been correct, but they certainly were not unjustified.

Asquith at once wrote a curt letter to Lloyd George, reminding him of their arrangement. Lloyd George replied that he had not read *The Times*, and advised Asquith to take no notice of what Northcliffe said. Asquith, at 12.30 told the King that the Cabinet had resigned, and that the Government would be reconstructed. That afternoon there were two inconclusive but significant meetings with Law, at which Asquith made it clear that he was reconsidering the War Committee arrangement, and that other ex-Ministers—Liberal and Conservative—were hostile to it. Law emphasised that it was vital to keep to the arrangement. Later Asquith wrote to Lloyd George in effect throwing over the arrangement, and making it quite clear that this was to be a reconstruction on his, and not on Lloyd George's, terms.

Thus, Asquith had determined to fight. Lloyd George was determined to fight as well. On the following morning, as soon as he had read Asquith's letter, he withdrew from the arrangement. This was expected. What was not expected was a letter from Balfour, who had been unwell for several days, which in effect supported Lloyd George. But Asquith, heavily pressed, does not seem to have grasped the implications. Balfour, with characteristic feline subtlety, was on the move.

At one o'clock on that fateful Tuesday, December 5th, the Liberal ex-Ministers met to consider the situation created by Lloyd George's

[1] Taylor: *Beaverbrook*, 118.

withdrawal, and concluded that Asquith could best meet the challenge by resigning himself.

Asquith hoped that the Conservative ex-Ministers would support him, even if the new Government did not include Law or Lloyd George. Their answer was that they could not, and that the arrangement over the War Committee must stand. Balfour had meanwhile sent another letter from his sick-bed at Carlton Gardens, which made his movement even clearer. Later in the afternoon Asquith told his Liberal colleagues that he would resign, and at 7 p.m. he did so, still believing that he would win his struggle. The King summoned Bonar Law and, at the end of a somewhat chaotic interview, invited him to form a Government.

Thus matters stood on the evening of December 5th. Through a series of events, not all of which his critics controlled, Asquith had resigned after eight years and 241 days as Prime Minister, and Bonar Law had been invited to form an Administration.

It has been often alleged that Asquith's resignation was a manoeuvre to expose and crush his critics. It is difficult to accept this sweeping conclusion. Asquith had chosen to reconstruct his Government on his own terms, and not those of Bonar Law and Lloyd George. He thought he could do it. He could not. Continuance in the premiership in these conditions had become impossible. There was no alternative to resignation once the Liberal and Conservative ex-Ministers—for different reasons—had advised such a course.

All that remained was aftermath. There was a conference of the leading politicians at Buckingham Palace on the afternoon of December 6th, attended by Asquith, the recovered Balfour, Lloyd George, Bonar Law and Arthur Henderson, and with the King in the chair. Lloyd George later alleged that everyone was ready to serve under Balfour, and that Asquith dramatically declared that 'What is the proposal? That I who have held first place for eight years should be asked to take a secondary position.' There is no reference to this in the accounts of Balfour or Stamfordham, and it would seem to be another example of Lloyd George's dramatic inventiveness that make his *War Memoirs* occasionally interesting. What is uncontested is that Balfour urged Asquith to serve under Law, and that Asquith refused.

The conference only emphasised the political realities of the situation, which were well summed up by Balfour. Asquith could not form a Government. Lloyd George was indispensable. If Asquith would not serve under Bonar Law, then a Government would have to be formed either by Law or Lloyd George. After again consulting his colleagues, Asquith wrote to Law to reiterate that he would not serve under him. At seven o'clock Law went to Buckingham Palace to decline the King's Commission; at 7.30 Lloyd George was invited to form a Government, and accepted.

Thus, almost soundlessly, Asquith fell. Churchill subsequently expressed the opinion that if Asquith had taken the battle to the House of Commons he would have won a vote of confidence, instead of fighting what Churchill called 'secret, obscure, internal processes'. This seems highly improbable. Certainly, it would have been a bitter debate, and matters had gone too far already to be thus retrieved.

Tactically, Asquith made many errors. He fought hard to keep the premiership, but although he was consistently out-manoeuvred by Lloyd George and was over-influenced by the *Times* article of December 4th, it was not really tactics that ended his premiership. The fact was that he no longer possessed the confidence in the House of Commons or in the Cabinet that was required to beat off such a major challenge to his leadership. That authority had gone; it was a matter of how and when the attack was mounted. When it came, Asquith was utterly defeated. But he still had many friends in the Liberal Party who were incensed by Lloyd George's activities, and who remained loyal. Although Lloyd George had won, he had done so with Conservative support. It was in fact a major Conservative victory, and the wounds inflicted on the Liberal Party by the events of December 1st–7th were never to be healed.

Asquith had been brought down by his own inadequacies. The feeling against him was well expressed at the time by Haldane:

> Asquith is a first-class head of a deliberative council. He is versed in precedents, acts on principle, and knows how and when to compromise. Lloyd George cares nothing for precedents and knows no principles, but he has fire in his belly and that is what we want.

CHAPTER THREE

A NATION AT WAR, 1916-1918

THE GREAT WAR illuminated the strengths, and also the deficiencies, of the British society that had been developing for the previous half-century. It is a baffling feature of the British character that it responds to major challenges and crises with exhilaration, and demonstrates depth of courage and initiative that lie dormant in quiet times. It is the element that has brought the British to remarkable heights and has brought them also to the edge of disaster. It is also the factor that makes them such an enigma to their foes and so infuriating an ally to their friends.

The effects of the war on British society were highly complex, and were not to be seen clearly for several years. At the time, it was a period of confusion, excitement, tragedy and disillusionment.

The most remarkable immediate revolutions were technological. The disparity in quality between British and German steel emphasised the fact that Britain had been overtaken in what had been her principal product both in quantity and quality. In 1914 Britain did not possess a chemical industry. The National Physical Laboratory—founded in 1902—limped along on a government grant (in 1914) of £7,000 a year. The Imperial College of Science and Technology had not been established until 1907. The war exposed these, and many other, painful deficiencies in a modern industrial nation. These were seen in many areas. Wireless telegraphy had hardly been exploited; in the manufacture and use of the internal combustion engine Britain lagged behind her Continental rivals; the demand for new munitions of war revealed that the country was seriously deficient in such matters as the production of optical glass, dye-stuffs, magnets, drugs, tungsten and zinc that were vital for the war effort. They emphasised what had been only dimly apparent to contemporaries before the war, that Britain from being a great industrial nation had become a great trading nation.

Some of these weaknesses could be cured—in time. In August 1915 the Government announced the establishment of an Advisory Council to a Committee of the Privy Council devoted to scientific and industrial research. It received a grant of £25,000 for the first year, and £40,000 for the second. As from December 1st, 1916, it was reorganised as a separate Government Department of Scientific and Industrial Research (D.S.I.R.) with, at last, substantial funds behind it. But its contribution could only be fragmentary and limited in the immediate crisis.

The technological contributions that were made by the British owed more to individual enthusiasms and private enterprise than to Government sponsorship or encouragement. The tank was a case in point. The idea itself had been mooted before—notably by Ian Hamilton in somewhat vague terms in his evidence to the Royal Commission on the Boer War—and it began to make progress shortly after the outbreak of war, principally as a result of the keen interest shown by Churchill. In August 1915 the project was transferred to the Ministry of Munitions, and the firm of William Foster and Co. produced the first prototype, called 'Little Willie'. It was succeeded in turn by 'Big Willie', eventually rechristened 'Mother', which was ready for tests in January 1916. By the autumn of 1916 a number were available for action at the Somme. Very little interest had been shown in the project by the War Office, and the Western Front generals were at best unenthusiastic. There was no attempt to examine the tactical and strategical implications of the new weapons, which were frittered away at the Somme in 'penny packets'. Nevertheless, Haig was impressed enough to order a thousand of the cumbersome, fearful new invention, but no further study was made of how it was to be employed, with the result that at Cambrai (November 20th, 1917) the tanks tore a gaping hole in the German lines which could not be exploited. The British had in fact found the answer to the perennial problem of the Western Front.

It is easy to criticise the reaction of the soldiers. They had not yet realised—nor, indeed, had anyone—the one gleaming lesson of twentieth-century warfare; that strategy follows, and does not precede, the scientist and the technician.

Much more success had been achieved in the air. At the outbreak of war the Army and the Navy had their own flying services, the Royal Flying Corps and the Royal Naval Air Service, with a Joint Air

Committee of the Committee of Imperial Defence to secure co-operation. Service aviation thus got off to a bad start, and the mutual jealousies and animosities between the army and naval aviators was to plague British aviation up to the eve of the Second World War. The attempts to concentrate the services under one Air Council were poisoned by personal antipathies and the interventions of Northcliffe, Rothermere, and others who flung themselves into the political and personal problems with greater enthusiasm than they demonstrated for the technical and operational ones.

But the technical performance was remarkable. In 1914 the British possessed 272 machines, and were heavily dependent on other countries for aero-engines. By the end of the war the new Royal Air Force had over 22,000 effective machines; most impressive of all, the British aero-engines were the best in the world. The reconnaissance aircraft possessed by the B.E.F. in 1914 had a maximum speed of 80 m.p.h., a rate of climb from ground level of between 300 and 400 feet a minute, and were equipped with engines of between 60 and 100 horse-power. In 1918 the fastest fighter-aircraft could reach 140 m.p.h. and had a rate of climb from ground level of 2,000 feet per minute. By 1918 the British had developed the first heavy bomber, the Handley Page V/1500, which had a maximum flying height of 25,000 feet and was capable of bombing Berlin from French airfields. Other new bombers—notably the Vickers Vimy, which achieved the first transatlantic flight in 1919—were also available by the end of the war. Many of the technical innovations were German, but in many cases the British developed them more efficiently; the synchronised machine-gun firing through the propellor was a case in point.

In wireless, also, the British had had a bad start. Supplies of radio valves from the pioneer companies—Marconi, Edison, Swan and Cossor—were inadequate, and contracts were given to the principal producers of electric light bulbs, thus bringing firms of the experience of General Electric, British Thompson-Houston, and British Westing-house into this new field. These companies were to bring strong pressure to bear after the war for the official encouragement of national broadcasting, and to create in effect a new industry of enormous potentiality. For these advances the war was entirely responsible.

The war had no responsibility for the one spectacular scientific contribution—the artificial disintegration of the atom by Rutherford at Manchester in 1918. The revolution this gave to British physics needs no emphasis. The Cavendish at Cambridge and the Clarendon at Oxford became the best physics laboratories in the world. The man who developed the latter was Professor F. A. Lindemann, whose main contribution in the war had been in the highly dangerous techniques of obviating the effects of aircraft spins, which until then were almost invariably fatal. We shall hear more of this curious man.

In a sense, Britain was so backward technically and scientifically in 1914 when compared with Germany and even France, that any advance would have been notable. But the outstanding feature of the period 1914–18 was that the strange pause in industrial and technical inventiveness in Britain that had existed since the 1870s came to an end. Until 1916 there were few official organisations that could harness and exploit these developments, and the pressures to create such organisations grew, and were the vital background to the burst of government sponsorship of the war effort in the last two years. But, typically, the gains were to be thrown away. The central organisations were to be swiftly dismantled; the supply of Government funds was to be cut off, few of the great advances made were to be properly exploited. The old traditions of laissez-faire and Free Trade were to prove more durable than the new technology created by the war. In 1919 the British lapsed into the pre-1914 system with an audible sigh of relief, and all the advantages of the war were needlessly thrown away. Most tragic of all was the virtual abandonment of the new aircraft industry, which by 1919 was producing the best aircraft in the world and was eager for new advances. Not until 1935 was it to be given another opportunity to demonstrate its quality.

*

Thus, before the fall of the Asquith Coalition in December 1915, British industry and society had already changed to meet the new challenges of wartime conditions. One remarkable feature was the changed status and responsibilities of women. The statistics tell only part of the story. It was subsequently estimated that, in July 1914, there were 23,721,000 women in Britain, of whom 4,809,000 were under ten years of age. The total in occupations or professions was 5,966,000, of whom 2,178,000 were in industry. By July 1918 the total in occupations or professions was 7,311,000 (an increase of 1,345,000). The number of women in commerce increased from 505,000 to

934,000; in transport from 18,000 to 117,000, and in national and local government (including education) from 262,000 to 460,000. The number of women over the age of ten not in occupations fell by 450,000; the only profession in which numbers fell was domestic service. In July 1914 these totalled 1,658,000; in July 1918, 1,258,000 —a fall of exactly 400,000.

The importance of women's work was recognised at the outset of the war. A 'Central Committee for the Prevention and Relief of Distress', headed by the President of the Board of Trade, was set up on August 4th, and asked local authorities to set up similar bodies at the local level. The Board of Education asked local education authorities at least to consider providing instruction in new industries or under-developed ones, in areas where unemployment would be caused by the war. The Board of Agriculture was made responsible for instruction for women over school-leaving age. On August 20th the Central Committee for Women's Employment, headed by Queen Mary, was set up, 'to consider, and from time to time report upon, schemes for the provision of work for women and girls unemployed on account of the war'.

These organisations were basically relief projects; this relief was certainly needed, as a substantial proportion of the women employed by the outbreak of war were in luxury trades. By September 1914, forty-four per cent of the total number of women in industry were either unemployed or on short time, as opposed to twenty-seven per cent of men.[1]

The Central Committee for Women's Employment attempted to increase the number of firms and workers participating in government work, and in some cases through its Contracts Department actually intervened to spread the work on large orders as widely as possible among small firms. It also interested itself in the development of new trades for women and even on occasion provided loans on wages which were to be repaid out of profits. Emergency workshops, in which women could be trained either from scratch or to move into other work, were set up; experimental schemes in training in domestic economy and home help were also initiated.

Most useful of all was the work done by the local committees for the Prevention and Relief of Distress. By January 1915 there were

[1] I. O. Andrews and M. A. Hobbs: *Economic Effects of the War Upon Women and Children in Great Britain*, 23.

approximately seventy workrooms and training centres administered by these local bodies, and they had enrolled 8,963 women.

By the end of 1914 the 'relief' side of this work had become of lesser importance. The problem had changed from there being a surplus of labour to an acute shortage. Early in 1915 the Government began to campaign for women workers, and urged them to register for war service in industry at the Labour Exchanges. By April 1915, 47,000 women had registered, but only 440 had been placed.[1]

The Munitions of War Act, 1915, created a Labour Regulation Department and Labour Supply Department in the new Ministry of Munitions. The country was divided into forty-three districts, with three Commissioners in each district. A Central Labour Supply Committee was also set up to advise the Minister on the most productive use of available labour. Women also had to register under the National Registration Act. This was a long stride in the direction of government direction of labour, although the main weapons of the government ramained, to the end, those of persuasion rather than of compulsion. The Ministry embarked upon a substantial programme urging employers to bring schemes of 'dilution' of women into industry, issuing pamphlets and bulletins to industrialists, while at the same time fostering the local authorities' interest and organisation in persuading women to work in industry.

All this aroused strong opposition in the trade unions. Women were reluctant to attempt agricultural work, and the National Federation of Women Workers was severe in its criticism of the recruiting of women for rough, dirty and sometimes dangerous work without proper safeguards; they were also concerned—and rightly—by the considerable possibility of exploitation of cheap labour by certain industrialists. The invasion of industry by women, however, caused a minor revolution in attitudes to working conditions, the provision of canteens and washing facilities. At the end of 1915 the staff of the Director of Welfare for Controlled Factories had inspected the 1,396 controlled factories employing 198,661 women, and reported that 31 per cent of the factories merited an A rating; 49 per cent B; and 20 per cent C. This new interest by the Government in factory conditions constituted, in itself, a considerable development.

Politically, the war had abruptly ended the Suffragette Movement's

---

[1] *Hansard*, April 27th, 1915, 563.

activities. There was a split between the majority, which was prepared to drop the matter of female suffrage for the duration, and the determined activists. The movement fragmented, but the war gave it the victory so long denied to it. Not that it was a total victory, and its origins were curious. The 1918 Representation of the People Act started its life in 1916 as a measure to provide for the registration of voters who had moved as a result of war work. This led to the proposal to enfranchise soldiers over twenty-one, which, in turn, led to a demand that women should not be excluded. A conference, presided over by the Speaker, recommended a six months' residence qualification for males, instead of occupancy. It also recommended (by a majority) that women over thirty should have the vote if they themselves, or their husbands, could meet the *former* property qualifications. Thus, the division between the sexes was carefully maintained.

The Representation of the People Act, 1918, was the most dramatic single advance towards a full democracy. With one stroke it added two million women and six million men to the electorate. It established the principle of 'one man, one vote', the only exceptions being the University seats and a vote for business premises; the second exception seems, in retrospect, even more astonishing than the first. The women had won a victory, but perhaps it was, in relation to their contribution to the war effort, a somewhat meagre one.

*

The full extent of the new political situation on the accession of Lloyd George was swiftly seen. Not a single Liberal member of the 1915–16 Cabinet was retained, and only a few lesser Liberals took office under the new Prime Minister. Edwin Montagu (India) and Churchill (Munitions) were brought in some six months later—the latter to the dismay and fierce opposition of the Unionists. Bonar Law did not exaggerate when he told a Conservative gathering in November 1918:

> By our own action we have made Mr. Lloyd George the flag-bearer of the very principles upon which we should appeal to the country. It is not his Liberal friends, it is the Unionist Party which has made him Prime Minister, and made it possible for him to do the great work that has been done by this government.

Lloyd George's personal influence was, however, initially overwhelming. The old Cabinet system was swept away, and replaced by a small War Cabinet of five—subsequently increased to seven—Ministers, of whom only one (Bonar Law) had any departmental responsibilities. The Ministers were Lloyd George, Curzon, Law, Lord Milner and Henderson. Smuts joined in June 1917, and Carson in July. This reorganisation of function and personnel was accompanied with a transformation of the machinery of the Cabinet. In this, Hankey's views and Lloyd George's coincided almost exactly. Cabinet meetings were to an agenda; minutes were taken, printed, and circulated; departments were informed of decisions concerning their operations, and the Cabinet Secretariat followed up to ensure that the decisions were in fact being carried out. These changes resulted in much more efficient control at the top and a far more practical and businesslike approach. From December 1916 to October 1919 the War Cabinet met more than 650 times, and much of the work previously done in full Cabinet—or not done at all—was delegated to committees. Other Ministers were only summoned to Cabinet meetings when their departments were involved.

All this was certainly to the good, and the effects were permanent. Other innovations did not survive Lloyd George. The creation of a personal Secretariat in St. James' Park—the 'Garden Suburb'—was viewed with suspicion in some quarters. In part, this new organisation pandered to a particular aspect of Lloyd George's character—'of secretaries', Thomas Jones (one of them) has related, 'Lloyd George never could have enough'—but it also represented his reaction to the fact that the Prime Minister has no department. The Garden Suburb became in effect Lloyd George's private army, and was accordingly increasingly regarded with the mixed feelings that accompany private armies in politics as elsewhere. Subsequently there tended to be a confusion between the official Secretariat and the Garden Suburb in the popular comprehension. 'Hankey and his Secretariat was essential', Sir Henry Wilson has written, 'whereas Philip Kerr, Ned Grigg,[1] etc., are poisonous.'[2] By 1922 the Civil Estimates, under the item 'Cabinet Office', recorded a staff of 129 persons and a cost of over £38,000.

Another important innovation that did not survive the war was the creation of 'functional' Ministries on the same lines as the Ministry of Munitions. Labour, Shipping, Food, National Service and Food

[1] Later Lord Lothian and Sir Edward Grigg, respectively.
[2] C. E. Callwell: *Wilson*, II, 343–4.

Production now became matters that merited separate departments, and new men. They had substantial powers, but these were seldom used; the new system, like the old, relied upon co-operation of industry and labour for success.

It would be dangerous and inaccurate to see in these changes any detailed plan of action brought by the new Prime Minister. As Professor Marwick has rightly commented, 'Lloyd George was nothing of a theorist, very little of a planner; his concern was to get things done, his strength that he would give a hearing and a trial to all suggested means towards this end'.[1] Indeed, Lloyd George's genius as a war leader lay in his immediate reactions to problems with immediate—virtually instinctive—solutions. The results were not always successful, but there was, from the outset, a sense of pace and urgency in the Lloyd George regime that was in marked contrast with his predecessor. The crisis had brought the politicians and the industrialists reluctantly—and in some cases without fully realising it—to the situation of accepting the 'nation in arms' concept to an extent that had been unthinkable in 1914 or even 1915. There were still pockets of resistance, and many of the changes were accepted on the explicit understanding that there was to be no permanence in them. Circumstances impelled changes which might have been far-reaching upon British industry and society, but which in fact were not.

In one vital respect there was little change. Lloyd George was never in a position to control the conduct of the war in a Napoleonic, or even in a Churchillian, sense. 'Of all the civilians I have known', John Buchan wrote, 'Lloyd George seems to have possessed in the highest degree the capacity for becoming a great soldier. But he might have lost several armies while he was learning his trade.' Lloyd George certainly possessed drive, imagination, and single-minded pursuit of the enemy, and his scepticism of the capacities of the senior British commanders—notably Haig and Robertson—was not ill-founded. But his lack of knowledge of military matters meant that his contribution tended to be a negative one; whenever driven to suggest alternatives they were usually even more disastrous than the disease they were meant to cure.

Ironically, the change in Government had actually increased the independence of the Service Departments. Carson, now at the

---

[1] Marwick, op. cit., 252.

Admiralty, accepted everything from his advisers and became an implacable opponent of anything that did not appeal to them. Derby, who had become Secretary of State for War, was completely under the influence of Robertson and Haig. Haig was a match for Lloyd George in intrigue, and cultivated powerful allies with the King and in the Conservative Party. This created a very serious situation, whose military implications were not fully seen until early in 1918. The relationship between Asquith and the senior commanders had been bad in that the latter were in complete control, and civilian control was virtually non-existent. Now, the control was retained, but a strong reciprocal mistrust and suspicion developed between the Prime Minister and the senior military advisers, to the point that Robertson described the Cabinet as 'the enemy' and the Prime Minister as 'the wrong 'un'. Thus, from the beginning, Lloyd George had to handle the military with caution.

The situation at the outset of 1917 has been described with characteristic sharpness by Beaverbrook:

The politicians gave little credit to the generals.

The generals denounced the politicians.

The soldiers and sailors serving in the forces had little confidence in either.

The public had no heroes.[1]

Lloyd George's position was complicated further by the fact that Northcliffe—who controlled not only *The Times* but half the daily papers sold in London—was a strong supporter of the military, and was described by Lloyd George (later) as 'the mere kettledrum of Sir Douglas Haig and the mouth-organ of Sir William Robertson'. This particular obstruction was neatly—but only temporarily—removed in May 1917 when Lloyd George appointed Northcliffe to head a British mission to the United States over the strong objections of the Foreign Secretary (Balfour), the British Ambassador in Washington, the President of the United States, and the American Secretary of State. But Northcliffe remained an implacable critic of Lloyd George, and his newspapers consistently supported the soldiers against the politicians.[2] It is to Churchill that we owe the best account of the picture that was conveyed:

[1] Beaverbrook: Introduction, *Men and Power*, 1917–18.

[2] Nonetheless, Northcliffe's star was fading. On his return in November he publicly refused to take the Air Ministry and abused the Government. In Beaverbrook's

The feeble or presumptuous politician is portrayed cowering in his office, intent in the crash of the world on Party intrigues or personal glorification, fearful of responsibility, incapable of aught save shallow phrase-making. To him enters the calm, noble, resolute figure of the great Commander by land or sea, resplendent in uniform, glittering with decorations, irradiated with the lustre of the hero, shod with the science and armed with the panoply of war. This stately figure, devoid of the slightest thought of self, offers his clear far-sighted guidance and counsel for vehement action or wise delay. But his advice is rejected; his sound plans put aside; his courageous initiative baffled by political chatterboxes and incompetents. As well, it was suggested, might a great surgeon, about to operate with science and the study of a lifetime upon a desperate case, have his arm jogged or his hand impeded, or even his lancet snatched away from him, by some agitated relation of the patient. Such was the picture presented to the public, and such was the mood which ruled.[1]

Nonetheless, although the Service commanders were still firmly in control, now, for the first time, their actions were under scrutiny and had to be justified. And Lloyd George could get results by untraditional methods. His action in going behind the backs of the Board of Admiralty to discover the views of junior officers on the convoy system would have been unthinkable to Asquith; but the results were admirable.

The fairest summary comes in a letter from Balfour to Lord Robert Cecil on September 12th, 1917. Balfour had few illusions about Lloyd George; indeed, he had few illusions about any politician. He considered that Lloyd George was 'impulsive', and went on:

> . . . he had never given a thought before the war to military matters; he does not perhaps adequately gauge the depths of his own ignorance; and he has certain peculiarities which no doubt make him, now and then, difficult to work with. But I am clearly of the opinion that military matters are much better managed now than

---

words: 'Night of gloom closed in upon Northcliffe. His gaiety and high spirits were memories of the past. Although he gave much attention to his newspapers, his shadow was no longer lengthening across the land' (op. cit., 89–90). He died insane, in 1922.

[1] Churchill: *The World Crisis 1916–18*, Part I, 244.

they were in the time of his predecessor . . . [Asquith] never seriously
attempted to co-ordinate in one homogeneous whole the efforts of
soldiers, sailors, and diplomatists, and the result was disaster. . . . Is
there any one of his colleagues in the present War Cabinet you
would like to see in his place? Is there any member of the late
government you would like to see in his place?

By the middle of 1917 all the major steps had been taken at last to
put Britain on a war footing. If the results—particularly in industry—
had been a series of compromises between laissez-faire and government control, the Government now possessed the powers at least to
direct industry. It had the power to conscript young men and to
influence the deployment of labour; it could, to a substantial degree,
control prices. Towards the end of 1917, for example, flour and potato
subsidies were introduced, and food prices controlled by what
Beveridge called a mixture of 'costings, conference, and compromise'.
Farmers had a minimum guaranteed price, and agricultural workmen
a guaranteed minimum wage. Bulk purchasing of raw commodities
from abroad became the rule rather than the exception. Compared
with the situation in 1914 and 1915, this cumulatively represented a
real economic revolution. The machinery of State interference, virtually non-existent in 1914, had been created, and was working with—
on the whole—remarkable absence of serious friction. The emphasis
upon co-operation rather than compulsion was probably the right one;
it was certainly the only one that had a chance of substantial success.
'As the war continued', wrote Evelyn Wrench, 'we became increasingly
accustomed to restrictions of every sort. When the fourth anniversary
came, government control was so much part of our lives that we found
it difficult to jump back in our minds to the pre-war world in which
we lived in July 1914.'[1]

One of the most impressive features of the war had been the manner
in which the Dominions had rallied to the British cause. The per-
formances of the Canadian, Australian, New Zealand and Indian
armies had been such as to arouse the admiration and enthusiasm of
all observers. This revived high hopes among the Imperialists of the
Milner school—particularly now that Milner had made a remarkable
renaissance and was in the War Cabinet. In short, might not the old
dream of Imperial Federation be turned into actuality as a result of

[1] E. Wrench: *Struggle 1914–20*, 333.

the experiences of the war? Certainly, enthusiasm for the Empire had never been greater. Unfortunately, as the meeting of the Dominion Premiers in 1917 demonstrated, these national achievements actually worked *against* federation. Lloyd George's plan of creating a real Imperial War Cabinet was largely based on the hope that it would increase civilian control over the military. Both his hopes and those of the Imperialists were dashed. The self-governing Dominions were to remain emphatically self-governing, and they gave no support to Lloyd George's schemes.

It was ironical that the unity of the Empire in the war was, in the long run, a step towards further independence of the self-governing Dominions. Furthermore, in the greatest British possession of all—India—there were indications of stirrings against the British supremacy. British policy towards India from 1905 onwards was one of 'gradualness', but at so slow a pace that the final grantings of genuine self-government on the Australia-Canada-New Zealand-South Africa pattern was scarcely envisaged at all. All reforms were based on increasing Indian consultation and participation without sacrificing the reality of British rule. The Morley–Minto Reforms of 1909 were based on this premise; so were the Montagu–Chelmsford proposals of 1917, eventually embodied in the Government of India Act of 1919. Under the Act, Indian membership of the Viceroy's Executive Council was increased; an elective majority in the legislative assembly would be Indian; and in the Provinces the system of 'Dyarchy' was created, whereby the Governor-in-Council had special reserved powers and Indian ministers were responsible for the administration of certain areas of responsibility—education, health, and local government. The 'reserved' powers were, of course, the real powers.

Seen through British eyes, these were substantial concessions to Indian nationalist feeling; indeed, they were opposed by F. E. Smith as going much too far. In the pre-1914 context, they represented a considerable step forward. But in the post-1914 context they were inadequate. Thus, the war that seemed to demonstrate the vast strength and unity of the British Empire struck a mortal blow at the edifice.

*

1917 proved nearly disastrous for the Allies. It opened with the renewal of unrestricted submarine warfare by the Germans, which had immediate success, and very nearly ended the war. By April one out of four ships leaving British ports was sunk. In February the total shipping losses—British, Allied, and neutral—were 540,000 tons; in March, 593,841 tons; in April the total was 881,027 tons, of which 542,282 tons were British. Between February and June some 3·3 million tons of shipping were lost to the submarine campaign, of which almost two million were British. This came on top of the very real success of the 'restricted' submarine campaign; in the last month— January 1917—of restricted submarine activity the Germans sank nearly 370,000 tons of British and foreign shipping. Jellicoe was not being alarmist when he wrote late in October 1916 that this rate of loss might compel the Allies to make peace in the summer of 1917.

The Admiralty had no answer to this menacing situation except to search and destroy the submarines by various methods. By February 1917 there were some three thousand vessels engaged in this work, and operating with an alarming lack of success. In February the British sank three submarines and a fourth was blown up by a mine; in March another four were sunk; in April only two. The Germans had one hundred and eleven submarines available for active service in February, of which about a third were on operations at a given time. Thus, in spite of massive anti-submarine activity by the British, the rate of destruction was less than the rate of new building. Meanwhile, the total of merchant losses rose to crisis level.

The obvious answer was to revert to the older system of convoy, but the Admiralty produced formidable arguments against adopting this policy. The total of arrivals and departures from British ports was 2,500 a week, and it would be impossible to organise this vast number into protected convoys. Furthermore, it was argued, the convoy system required a high standard of sea discipline of which most merchant captains were incapable. The faster ships would have to go at the pace of the slowest, and would present a much easier target.

Lloyd George doubted these arguments on the first occasion that he heard them in October 1916. As the months passed his doubts had increased. He sought advice from junior officers, who were whole-heartedly in favour of the convoy system. Coal convoys to the French ports were operating efficiently and safely, the Grand Fleet, of course, moved in convoy, and the figure of 2,500 included *all* sailings, including ships of all nationalities, and coastal trade.

On April 25th Lloyd George received the approval of the War

Cabinet to visit the Admiralty in person on the 30th to discover the situation. But by this stage the balance of Admiralty opinion had already changed. An experimental convoy left Gibraltar early in May and arrived without mishap. At the end of May the first convoy from America—curiously enough, the American naval authorities also opposed the convoy system—sailed across the Atlantic in safety. By the end of September the convoy system was in full operation with complete success. British shipping losses fell from over 365,000 tons in July to about 200,000 tons in September. This was the turning-point.

The battle of the seas was not won by the convoy system; but it was saved by it. It was not until July 1918 that the tonnage of new shipping was greater than the amount lost, but the tide had been turned in the autumn of 1917 when the convoys began in earnest. The early Admiralty calculations had proved wrong, and the amateur civilian politicians and junior naval officers had been proved right. Lloyd George's personal intervention—although it has been over-dramatised —had been decisive.

The German adoption of unrestricted submarine warfare had nearly ended the war, but its consequences were disastrous. The attitude of the Germans to the United States is difficult to comprehend. The sinking of ships such as the *Lusitania* and the *Arabic* in May 1915 had outraged American opinion, but calmer reflections could only lead to the conclusion that neutrals who travelled in wartime on British, French or German ships could not expect immunity from enemy attack. But the new methods were different. Even in the period of restricted submarine warfare, a German submarine went across the Atlantic; after calling at Newport, Rhode Island, it proceeded to sink five ships off Nantucket Island. When an American destroyer attempted to pick up survivors it was ordered to move out of the way so that the submarine could torpedo another ship. An American ship was sunk off Cape St. Vincent in the same month. The resumption of unrestricted submarine warfare included permission for *one* American ship a week to cross the North Atlantic, which was in itself a declaration that other American ships would be sunk on sight. Wilson broke off diplomatic relations on February 3rd. On March 1st the Zimmerman Telegram,[1] offering Mexico an offensive alliance against the

[1] For the best account of this episode see Barbara Tuchman: *The Zimmerman Telegram.*

United States, and which had been intercepted by the British, was published. This was in itself 'an unfriendly act' in the full sense of the phrase. Three American ships were sunk with great loss of life on March 18th. On April 2nd Wilson made his historic speech to Congress; by the afternoon of April 6th the United States was at war.

This massive new ally could not be of much direct help in 1917. As Wilson's confidant Colonel House noted on December 16th after an alarming talk with the Secretary of the Navy: 'We have no large guns; if we had them we have no trained men who would understand how to handle them. We have no air service, nor men to exploit it; and so it is down the list.' The situation was not quite so disastrous as this, but it would be some time before the presence of the United States in the war could be fully felt.

Joffre had at last been relieved of his command of the French forces at the end of 1916, and had been replaced by a dashing and heroic new personality. General Nivelle was sixty in 1916, and he seemed to have the secret to the impasse on the Western Front. The terrible Battle of Verdun, in which more than a million casualties were suffered by the opposing armies, had ended in a French victory of sorts. The German strategy of 'bleeding France white' at Verdun had boomeranged badly, and, together with their losses at the Somme, 1916 had been as bitter a year for the Germans in the West as it had been for the Allies. Verdun had become for the French a symbol of their resistance to the enemy, and the battle had been fought with barbaric fury by both sides. On October 24th General Nivelle had electrified France with the recapture of Forts Douaumont and Vaux and advanced over nearly two miles of ground which had taken the Germans almost eight months of furious fighting to capture. On December 15th Nivelle launched another attack, which was even more successful.

Nivelle's 'answer' to the Western Front situation was simply a more sophisticated use of artillery. The enemy lines would be overwhelmed with a tremendous surprise bombardment, while the advancing troops would proceed behind a 'creeping' barrage which was far deeper than those previously attempted. Exhilarated by his successes on a small front against an exhausted enemy in poor positions, Nivelle now expounded his faith in these methods on any front in any circumstances.

Nivelle's plan was to concentrate a 'mass of manoeuvre' of twenty-seven divisions. This would mean that the British should keep the Germans fully stretched on their part of the front and should also take over part of the French line to allow the concentration of the mass of manoeuvre. Haig was impressed, but was also anxious to drive forward to the north to secure the Belgian ports and drive the Germans out of western Belgium. He eventually settled on a major offensive at Ypres. Nivelle was not interested, but agreed that if his own offensive failed Haig could have his troops back and could deliver his Ypres attack. Nivelle did not expect to fail.

Lloyd George, who was keenly interested in British support to the Italians at this point, and who was more sceptical than ever of Haig, was suddenly and dramatically converted to Nivelle's plans. It was a curious reversal of the usual situation. Haig was cautious in his estimates of Nivelle's chances, whereas Lloyd George was now Nivelle's most enthusiastic champion. So enthusiastic was he that he proposed to the French that Haig should be subordinated to Nivelle. The French, not surprisingly, were quick to accept this proposal. Briand proposed to Lloyd George that, in effect, the French Commander-in-Chief should have total authority over the British forces, so that Haig would be reduced, for all practical purposes, to 'an Adjutant-General in charge only of discipline and personnel'.[1] On February 24th the War Cabinet agreed that Lloyd George should take measures to ensure the unity of command on the Western Front, but it is doubtful whether they had a full realisation of what Lloyd George was up to; they did know, however, that all this was being done without the knowledge of Haig or Robertson.

Haig and Robertson reacted violently. Haig and Nivelle agreed that Haig would be under Nivelle's orders in the coming battle but would be free to determine his own actions in his own sector. Haig also alerted the King to the situation, which was timely, for Lloyd George had characteristically kept the King wholly uninformed of what was going on. Derby and Curzon backed Haig strongly, and the War Cabinet hastily passed a vote of confidence in him. The result was to make Haig's position stronger than ever, but relations between himself and Robertson, on the one hand, and Lloyd George, on the other, were lastingly damaged.

[1] Woodward, *Short Journey*, 263.

It was an odd, but illuminating, episode. Lloyd George's total lack of confidence in Haig had occasioned this attempt to strip him of his powers, but the methods he used to achieve this were admirably qualified to bring Haig strong support in the Government and in the Press. Lloyd George never seems to have considered the public outcry that must surely have followed the publication of the news. Haig and Robertson had won this round, but Lloyd George was ever a determined man.

The much-heralded Nivelle Offensive virtually eliminated France from the war. Ludendorff had already begun the construction of a new line of defences in September 1916 which was built with immense skill and ingenuity, with much of the work done by prisoners of war and pressed civilians. It was originally intended as a precautionary measure, but Ludendorff became increasingly attracted by the opportunity of shortening his line, moving his men back to a greatly improved position, and thereby to save some thirteen divisions. The area evacuated would be utterly devastated, and it is an interesting commentary on the humanitarian feelings that still remained that the Crown Prince of Bavaria protested strongly against this devastation and that the French and British troops were shocked and embittered by the cutting down of fruit trees and the pollution of wells. Across the former main street of a flattened village an unknown German left the message: 'Do not be angered; only wonder.'

This withdrawal, which began on March 16th, destroyed the whole point of Nivelle's offensive. Furthermore, the Germans knew all about it, having captured the complete plans in a trench raid. The results were what might have been expected. The Canadians and British seized Vimy Ridge, but the British did not exploit this fine victory.[1] This battle cost 158,000 casualties, of whom nearly 30,000 were killed, but the British could point to a significant success, which was more than the hapless French Army could. The Nivelle attack opened on April 16th; after five days virtually no progress had been made and terrible losses had been suffered. In spite of increasing doubts by the French Government—shared by Haig—that there was no point in continuing the offensive, Nivelle persisted until sections of his army were in mutiny and the Government removed him. His successor was Pétain, who described his policy as 'Aggressive-Defensive'. Haig noted

---

[1] The best account of this battle is Edward Spears: *Prelude to Victory*.

in his diary that 'doubtless in his mind he figures the British Army doing the aggressive work, while the French Army "squats" on the defensive'. This was indeed what happened, but Haig was not an unwilling ally. He still assumed that victory could be achieved in 1917.

This was the background to the Flanders offensive that opened on July 31st. Lloyd George fought a stubborn action to hinder Haig in going forward. In the Cabinet, only Milner supported him. As Haig knew full well, the French were in no condition to support him with adequate attacks as they had originally promised. He withheld this information from the War Cabinet, which unhappily approved his offensive. Its unhappiness continued as Haig's attacks secured no notable gain in August, by which time the British casualties amounted to 3,424 officers and 64,586 men. The second stage opened on September 20th after the special Committee on War Policy appointed by the Cabinet had approved it by a majority. The subsequent fighting around Passchendaele acquired a terrible quality of its own. The British gained their principal objective, but at a cost of 244,987 casualties; all these gains were to be lost in the following March.

*

Most understandably, morale at home now began to cause serious concern. The new machinery of controls did not begin to make its real impact until towards the end of the year, by which time the British were beginning to see the consequences on their daily lives of the submarine campaign and the drain of the war to an extent that they had not before. The Russian Revolution of March 1917 was eagerly welcomed in the Labour Party, and it gave a new impetus to those who advocated peace by negotiation. The Independent Labour Party and the British Socialist Council, which was a Marxist body, set up a United Socialist Council, which in June summoned a convention at Leeds which endorsed the Russian peace programme for a peace with 'no annexations and no indemnities' and called for the setting up of workers' and soldiers' councils. Eleven hundred delegates assembled and MacDonald and Snowden attended.

It was at this point that Lloyd George made a political error that was to have far-reaching consequences.

Arthur Henderson had been a loyal and important member of the Government since May 1915. The division in the Labour Party between himself and the minority of opponents of the war had never been serious, and party co-operation had been retained to a certain extent. In May 1917 a conference on war aims was called by the Petrograd Soviet with the formal approval of the Provisional Government (which itself was replaced by a new coalition on May 20th). The Petrograd Soviet then issued invitations to an International Socialist Congress on War Aims at Stockholm in order that 'the work for peace started by the Russian Revolution [might] be brought to a conclusion by the efforts of the international proletariat'. The Executive of the Labour Party voted to send three representatives to visit Petrograd to determine Soviet intentions, and chose George Roberts, a right-wing personality, William Carter of the miners, and Ramsay MacDonald. The new Russian Foreign Minister asked that MacDonald be given permission to go to Petrograd. The Government were in a difficult position, and decided to send Henderson to report on the situation. Henderson was not in favour of the Stockholm Conference nor of the re-institution of the International, and his mission was attacked by Snowden and others on the grounds that he did not represent Labour opinion.

Six weeks in Petrograd convinced Henderson that if Russia were to be kept in the war the British Labour Party should accept the Russian peace programme and send delegates to the Stockholm Conference. The War Cabinet was hostile to these arguments when Henderson presented them—Lloyd George was absent—on July 26th. On the next day Henderson, MacDonald and G. H. Wardle (acting Chairman of the Parliamentary Party) went to Paris to attend a meeting called by the French United Socialists to discuss the method of proceeding at the Stockholm Conference.

It was this visit that started the storm. *The Times* on August 1st launched a sharp attack on Henderson:

It is plain that no man harbouring such ideas and endeavouring to realise them by furtive co-operation with persons like Mr. Mac-Donald is fit to keep in a War Cabinet. His action is indefensible, and, if his colleagues are wise, they will renounce all further attempts to defend it.

The kernel of the difficulty was that Henderson considered it essential that German delegates should attend Stockholm; Lloyd George initially agreed and then, at French insistence, changed his mind.

On the afternoon of August 1st the Cabinet discussed Henderson's position, with Henderson himself waiting outside for an hour 'on the doormat', at the end of which he was, in Lloyd George's words, 'in a highly resentful frame of mind'. Henderson in effect challenged the Cabinet to demand his resignation. Lloyd George persuaded him to explain his position in the Commons that evening, which he did. Lloyd George's own speech was a dexterous affair, in which he spoke principally of the value of Labour participation in the Government. By the evening of August 1st Henderson was an angry man. The events of the next two weeks made him angrier still.

A Party Conference had been called for August 10th to consider the Stockholm invitation. Lloyd George claims that at a meeting of the Cabinet on August 8th Henderson gave his colleagues the impression that the motion would be defeated 'by a fair majority', a statement denied by Henderson and his biographer. In any event, on the 10th Henderson spoke vigorously for British representation at Stockholm, and the motion was carried by 1,846,000 votes to 550,000. A long wrangle on representation then followed, and it was with some difficulty that Henderson persuaded the conference to defer a decision until August 21st.

This caused consternation in the Cabinet; *The Times* declared that 'the hand of Germany is discernible throughout', and Henderson resigned in a dignified letter on the following day. Lloyd George's reply was anything but dignified, and was released to the Press before Henderson had had any chance to respond. In no uncertain terms Lloyd George accused Henderson of not informing the Conference of a telegram he had received on the 9th to the effect that the new Kerensky Coalition, formed on the 6th, had changed its attitude to Stockholm. The implication that Henderson had misled both his Cabinet colleagues and the Conference was plain enough, and was made even more plain by a violent attack on Henderson that Lloyd George delivered in the Commons on August 13th. It was now that Henderson revealed the 'doormat incident' on August 1st. The effect on the Labour Party was considerable. As Snowden wrote in the *Labour Leader* on the 16th:

This incident shows plainly that while Mr. Henderson was in the Cabinet he was never of it, and that the Prime Minister regarded him as useful only for the purpose of deluding democracy into the belief that it was exercising an influence upon the policy of the Government.

Labour was by no means united on the wisdom of the Stockholm Conference. Indeed, when the Party Conference resumed on August 21st, a motion to reaffirm its previous decision was carried by only 3,000 votes after the miners reversed their vote. The miners also carried a motion on representation that in effect barred the Socialists. Nevertheless, the consequences of the doormat incident and its sequel were very considerable. Henderson was bitterly personally estranged from Lloyd George, and resolved that he would never join a government in which Labour did not predominate. Lloyd George assumed that Henderson's successor in the Cabinet, G. N. Barnes, would also be his successor in the party leadership. This assumption was incorrect. Henderson, without really meaning to, had at last created some unity of outlook in the Parliamentary Party towards the war.

His energies were now devoted exclusively to the party's problems and its future. The Labour Memorandum on War Aims, drawn up at the end of 1917, was a significant step that caught the attention of President Wilson among others. The American Ambassador, Walter Hines Page, wrote to Wilson in January 1918 that 'the Labour Party is already playing for supremacy'. It would have been more accurate to have said 'working for political independence'.

In September Henderson submitted a memorandum to the National Executive that proposed 'the reorganisation of the Party with a view to a wider extension of membership, the strengthening and development of local parties in the constituencies, together with the promotion of a larger number of candidates, and the suggestion that a Party programme be adopted'. This was referred to a sub-committee, of which MacDonald and Sidney Webb were members, and which produced a draft constitution. It contained few novelties, except in the section relating to the party's objectives, and particularly the celebrated Clause IV, originally drafted by Henderson in standard cautious trade union language, but subsequently amended—almost certainly principally by Sidney Webb—to read:

To secure for the producers by hand and brain the full fruits of their industry, and the most equitable distribution thereof that may be possible upon the basis of the common ownership of the means of production and the best obtainable system of popular administration and control of each industry or service.

In June 1918 the Party conference adopted a policy statement also compiled by Webb called *Labour and the New Social Order* that incorporated the concept of the national minimum wage and standard working conditions with a maximum working week of forty-eight hours; it urged the democratic control of industry; the subsidisation of social services by heavy taxation of large incomes; and The Surplus for the Common Good, whereby the balance of the national wealth would be devoted to increasing the opportunities in education and culture for the people. This distillation of previous resolutions was certainly not an extreme manifesto. The debates within the Party on the draft constitution emphasised the dislike of the trade union leaders for socialist theory, and their clear intention to make the Party, in the words of one unionist leader, 'our political arm'.

But this programme—coupled with the decision in November 1918 to withdraw from the Coalition and fight alone—gave Labour the opportunity to project itself for the first time as a separate party and as a positive alternative to Liberalism and Conservatism. In the second 1910 election Labour had fielded 78 candidates, fighting upon the Liberal programme; in the 1918 election it was to sponsor over 360 candidates, fighting on its own programme. All this might have happened in any event; but the alienation of Henderson gave immense impetus to the movement towards separation. The consequences of the doormat incident remain with us to this day.

Labour was not the only element that was questioning the value of the war. On November 29th Lansdowne published in the *Daily Telegraph* a letter on war aims which aroused even more excitement and controversy than his leaked memorandum of a year before. It was condemned in violent terms from the usual quarters, Northcliffe describing it publicly as 'the stupid, senile manifestation of an old man who has lost control of himself', and both the *Daily Mail* and the *Morning Post* described it as an offer of surrender. The Liberal papers, however, and particularly the *Daily News* and the *Manchester Guardian*, warmly welcomed Lansdowne's initiative, and Gardiner described it as 'a torch in the darkness' which 'has made it respectable and even patriotic to think'; from Labour, George Lansbury welcomed the letter and wrote that 'we are not going, because of old quarrels, to

belittle the great word he has spoken now'. The Conservatives would
have no part of his action, which was strongly condemned by his
former close colleague Bonar Law at a meeting of the National
Unionist Association on November 30th. As Lloyd George commented: 'The direction in which [his sword] was waveringly pointed
was no longer heeded by the exclusive regiment he once led.' It did,
however, force Lloyd George to make a belated and generalised
declaration on British War Aims to the Trades Union Conference on
January 5th, 1918.

But these protests against the war had little substantial political
impact. War-weariness had not yet reached the point when alternatives were seriously considered. Clemenceau's dictum that 'the war
aims for which we are fighting are victory' echoed the dominant
feeling in Britain and also in Germany. But, for all the major belligerents, 1917 had been the worst year of the war. Russia had crumbled
and was out of the conflict. The Italians had been swept back at
Caporetto. The French armies had survived mutiny, but were on the
defensive. On the other side, although Austria-Hungary and the
Ottoman Empire were virtually *in extremis*, the Germans were massively formidable. For the Allies the best hope lay in the Americans;
for the Germans, a decisive blow on the Western Front before the
Americans arrived. When 1918 dawned, the surviving belligerents
were still fighting for victory.

*

Lloyd George was a Prime Minister without a Party. He had now
moved too far from Labour to have any substantial hope of future
support from that quarter. The Liberals who had remained faithful
to Asquith—estimated at over 100—regarded Lloyd George with
even greater animosity than did Asquith himself. Thus, Lloyd George
was wholly dependent upon the Conservatives and those Liberals who
had followed him for his retention of power. In these circumstances
his room for manoeuvre was limited, and everything depended upon
the skill with which he managed the forces on which he relied. For a
man who had always lived by his wits, and whose political antennae
were exceptionally sensitive, this situation was admirably suited to his
character. As he once wrote: 'I never believed in costly frontal attacks
either in war or politics, if there were a way round.' Furthermore, his

fundamental opportunism gave priority in his calculations to the retention of power; as Beaverbrook[1] has observed, his object was to remain in the driver's seat, and the direction in which he was travelling was of less concern to him. Anything served his purpose. All was grist to his mill. He had colleagues, supporters and admirers, but no friends. The maxim that there are no friendships at the top in political life was certainly true when Lloyd George was Prime Minister.

But it was this ruthlessness, guile and pragmatism that made him a great War Minister. He himself has described the ideal:

> But a War Minister must also have vision, imagination, and initiative—he must show untiring assiduity, must exercise constant over-sight and supervision of every sphere of war activity, must possess driving force to energise this activity, must be in constant consultation with experts, official and unofficial, as to the best means of utilising the resources of the country in conjunction with Allies for the achievement of victory. If to this can be added a flair for conducting a great fight, then you have an ideal War Minister.[2]

Judged by these dazzling standards, Lloyd George was deficient in certain respects, but no qualification can be entered against his energy, imagination and enterprise. The reorganisation of the Cabinet had resulted in vastly more efficient control at the top, the dissemination of decisions among departments, and an infinitely greater practical and businesslike approach. The creation of 'functional' Ministries and the introduction of professional businessmen to run them marked the end of the former laissez-faire attitude to the running of the war. As has been emphasised, all this did not form part of a grand overall plan of government control and direction, and the changes were made on a pragmatic basis; but the cumulative effect was that, by the beginning of 1918, Britain was at long last geared for the tests of total war. But it was Lloyd George's continued attempts to seize control of the direction of the war from Robertson and Haig that brought the last major crisis faced by the Lloyd George Coalition.

By the end of 1917, after the dreadful cost of the Passchendaele offensive, relations between Lloyd George, on the one hand, and Haig and Robertson on the other were at their nadir. It may have been true that

---

[1] Max Aitken had become Lord Beaverbrook on the formation of the Lloyd George Government.
[2] Lloyd George: *War Memoirs*, I, 602.

Lloyd George knew little about military matters, but he had learned a great deal about the military mind the hard way since August 1914. He had been sceptical about Gallipoli, but ignored. He had been bewitched by Nivelle, and deceived. He had been reluctantly persuaded to go along with the disastrous British summer and autumn campaign of 1917. He had rightly over-ruled naval advice on the convoy system. If he viewed the military experts of the nation, from Kitchener and French to Haig and Robertson, without awe it was not altogether surprising. But he was serving as head of a government which had not reached his conclusions, was dependent upon a party whose instinctive reaction was to support soldiers against politicians, a Press that was overwhelmingly pro-military, and in an uneasy relationship with a monarch who was in close touch with Haig and had views of his own. The principle of civilian control over the military continued to exist in theory rather than fact. Lloyd George had to move warily. He could not act frontally, and his attempts to undermine Haig's position had failed, at the cost of creating a profound mutual mistrust.

The faults were by no means all on one side. Lloyd George had a marked tendency—not uncommon in men who had risen by methods he had employed—of seeing conspiracies against him on all sides. He came to believe that there were intrigues afoot in the army against the government and—more importantly—against him personally, and he told Lord Esher—who passed on the information to Haig—that 'his means of information are varied and go deep into the camp of his opponents. Of this there was ample proof from what he said to me. Conversations with pressmen, communications with critics and wreckers of the Government, all brought to him by agents who have a footing in what he calls "both camps".' In his War Memoirs he was subsequently to write that there had been a cabal to 'enthrone a Government which would be practically the nominee and menial of the military party'. No evidence that such a cabal existed, or that there was ever a 'military party' as such, has emerged. In his later account Lloyd George no doubt deliberately dressed up the grumbling of the military commanders into the garb of a deep-rooted campaign against him; it is very possible that he believed this lurid portrait.

By the end of 1917, Lloyd George had no confidence in Haig and Robertson, and Haig and Robertson had none in Lloyd George. Robertson wrote to Haig on December 8th, 1917, of 'the impossibility of honestly working with such a man'. Haig warmly agreed: 'How unfortunate the country seems to be to have such an unreliable man at the head of affairs in this crisis', he noted in his diary on September 24th. Haig, like Kitchener in his duel with Curzon, had powerful allies whom he carefully cultivated. He could count upon Conservative and Royal support in the event of a crisis, and the military reverses of 1917 had not seriously affected his national position. Haig could adopt as devious and pragmatic methods as Lloyd George himself, and had some understanding of the dark arts of propaganda and influence-peddling. Robertson, however, did not possess Haig's connections or guile. He emerges from all accounts—including his own, which is unusual in soldiers' memoirs—as an attractive and bloody-minded professional of limited but clear perspectives. His celebrated retort, 'I've 'eard different', to eloquent analyses was unlikely to attract politicians—and particularly Lloyd George—but gave confidence to others. Nonetheless, his taciturn contempt for politicians and other amateurs was not conducive to the successful prosecution of the war; his judgements were not often justified by events; and, as he was about to discover to his cost, he had no powerful allies, not even Haig.

In spite of the American declaration of war, whose effects were only slowly beginning to be felt, the military situation at the end of 1917 was not good, and was obviously not going to get any better after the collapse of Russia. In December Haig issued instructions on defensive measures on the Western Front. This was indeed necessary. For two years all British plans had been for the attack, and the British defensive positions were at no point remotely comparable to those of the Germans. The British calculated that by the end of February 1918 the Germans would have 185 divisions on the Western Front, giving them a superiority over the British and French of some 200,000 men. This disparity was not, in itself, of critical importance; in the great assaults of 1916–17 the Allied superiority over the Germans had been considerably greater. What was serious was the condition of the Allied lines and the enormous amount of work necessary to put them into reasonable shape. The new lines gained in the Passchendaele offensive were the worst of all, providing little effective defence and unspeakable living conditions, and there was a chronic shortage of men and equipment to make them capable of withstanding the major German attack that was now expected.

The question of manpower was clearly crucial. In December the

War Cabinet set up a special committee to consider the problem, consisting of Lloyd George, Curzon, Barnes, Carson and Smuts. It had to consider the whole question of manpower—industrial as well as military—and its conclusions were sobering. In short, the barrel had nearly been scooped dry. Haig and Robertson asked for 615,000 new men, and pointed to the two million troops in the Middle and Near East. The Cabinet came to the conclusion that only 100,000 new men in the 'A' class could be available for the Army, and Lloyd George was adamantly opposed to withdrawing men from the Middle East.

Indeed, it was in this area that the British had made their most substantial advances. The army of Mesopotamia was in Baghdad, and General Allenby—atoning for a somewhat undistinguished performance as an Army Commander on the Western Front—had entered Jerusalem on Christmas Day. Militarily, the Turks were being pushed back relentlessly; politically, the rich pickings of the Ottoman Empire were falling into British hands. Arab support for the British was extending dramatically, while, by the Balfour Declaration of November 8th declaring British support for a Jewish National Home in Palestine, it was hoped that Jewish support for the Allies—particularly in the United States—would be substantially gained. The fatal clash between reconciling Arab ambitions and creating a national home for the Jews in Palestine had not been appreciated. In the case of Salonika, Lloyd George was equally adamant. This vast Allied force—amounting to over a million men— had remained on the defensive since the end of 1915, but there were solid political reasons for retaining a large British presence in this area. Emotional considerations also played their part in Lloyd George's feelings towards this theatre.

The Italian front was even less appropriate for a substantial withdrawal of British forces in the aftermath of Caporetto, although one division was brought back. This meant that the reinforcements would have to come from England. Some 130,000 'A' men were sent to the Western Front between January 1st and March 21st and, on the advice of the General Staff, 120,000 troops were kept in England. Lloyd George subsequently made much of this in his War Memoirs, but there were sound military reasons for doing so, not the least of which was the fact that these men could be moved to France in the eighteen days for which Haig said his existing forces could hold an enemy attack.

Much harsh controversy subsequently raged over these actions and attitudes. The essential fact was that, as Lloyd George bluntly said, 'I don't trust Haig with men'. With good reason, given recent experience, he feared another futile offensive, whereas in fact Haig's principal interest was to maintain his existing positions. The result stemmed less from the situation itself than from the poisoned relations between the British commanders and the British Prime Minister. Both were grievously at fault, but Haig's case is marginally the better one. When the German attack began on March 21st, the British forces were well below the minimum level deemed by Haig to be essential.

Haig was beyond Lloyd George's reach, and the Prime Minister had to move cautiously. In November 1917, at his urging, a Supreme War Council, consisting of the Allied Prime Ministers and specially appointed military advisers, was set up at Versailles. It proved effective and valuable in all save military co-ordination. Robertson refused to work with the Council and when, at his promptings, the Liberal Opposition raised the matter in the House of Commons, Lloyd George hastily retreated. The Council, he explained, had only advisory powers, and he was 'utterly opposed' to the suggestion of an Allied Commander-in-Chief.

In February 1918 he tried again, and with more success. The Supreme Council decided to set up a general reserve of Allied forces, under the control of its own military advisers. Robertson refused to have anything to do with this, or even go to Versailles. The King and Asquith supported him, as did Derby, Lord Robert Cecil, Walter Long and Curzon. This time Lloyd George felt strong enough to deliver an ultimatum to his colleagues and to the King. Robertson's supporters swiftly vanished. Haig at once said that he would accept the view of the Cabinet, and gave practical demonstration of his willingness to assist the Supreme Council by accepting Marshal Foch as president of the Executive Committee. On February 18th the abandoned Robertson read in the newspapers that he had resigned, and had been replaced by Sir Henry Wilson. Wilson's slipperiness would have awed an eel, but he had a real understanding of the need for military and political agreement, particularly on his own terms. Robertson fell sheer. He did not even subsequently receive the comparable handsome financial rewards given to senior commanders after the war, although he was not wholly forgotten.

This was rough, but in Beaverbrook's memorable phrase, 'he had taken a pot-shot at Santa Claus—and missed'.

On March 21st the German attack fell upon the British Third and Fifth Armies, of which the greater part—some forty miles—was held by the Fifth Army under General Sir Hubert Gough. Haig was not convinced that it would fall on the Fifth Army, and he viewed the prospect of a major German attack with some confidence; indeed, on February 28th, he told the army commanders that he was 'only afraid that the enemy would find our front so very strong that he will hesitate to commit his army to the attack with the almost certainty of losing very heavily'. Perhaps this was partly to boost morale; he was still far short of the numbers of troops he had asked for in December.

The Fifth Army was swept aside, and by the afternoon of March 22nd Gough was ordering a general withdrawal. Within a few days the Germans advanced forty miles.

At the outset of the war the British were trained for open warfare, and had been totally unprepared for trench warfare; now they were professionals at trench warfare, and totally unprepared for the new conditions of open warfare. The Germans swept on.

Lloyd George now repeated what he had done in the previous April over the convoy crisis; he took over the direction of the War Office from Derby, discovered that nearly 90,000 troops were home on leave, and returned them and the reserve to Haig. It may be argued that it was Lloyd George's fault that Haig did not have enough troops in the first place, but he certainly acted energetically to meet the crisis. Like Julius Caesar, he was at his best when recovering from his own errors. On March 28th, without consulting Balfour, he asked President Wilson for the immediate use of all available American troops; Wilson agreed, and over-ruled the irascible and difficult General Pershing. This was leadership of a kind that would never have occurred to Asquith.

The Allies now faced a really grave crisis. Haig proposed to fall back on the Channel ports; Pétain had orders from the French Government to cover Paris at all costs. Furthermore, Pétain's defeatism was such that Haig was convinced that his replacement was essential; he asked on March 25th that Wilson and the Secretary of State for War should arrange that 'General Foch or some other determined general who would fight, should be given supreme control in France'. Lloyd George sent Milner, whom he appointed Secretary for War in Derby's place on April 19th.

It was quite evident that Pétain, whose nerve had been broken at Verdun, and who regarded the battle and the war as lost, could not remain in charge of the French effort, and there could be no question of Haig being subordinate to such a commander. Haig was now anxious that Foch should become supreme commander in order that he should keep Pétain in control. Foch accordingly was appointed to co-ordinate the British and French armies; on April 3rd—with Haig's full approval —he was given the 'strategic direction of military operations'. On April 14th Foch was named 'Commander-in-Chief of the Allied Armies'. This was somewhat grandiloquent; in his own phrase, he was merely a conductor who beat time well. It was, however, a very different beat to that which Pétain would have struck.

Before the German campaign eventually ran out of steam, it had serious effects on the course of British politics. The first affected Ireland. Protests in England against the calling-up of men had been accompanied with complaints that Ireland still enjoyed freedom from conscription, and Lloyd George thought he saw the solution— conscription would be extended to Ireland in return for Home Rule.

This maladroit manoeuvre, intended to placate the Conservatives and the Irish with one move, completed the work that General Sir John Maxwell had put in hand. The Irish M.P.s left the House of Commons in a body, and joined with Sinn Fein. Eamonn de Valera, a survivor of the Easter Rising, led the opposition, strongly supported by the Roman Catholic hierarchy, hitherto independent of the recent nationalist movements. On April 23rd there was a twenty-four-hour general strike. The Government reacted with a heavy hand. French was made Viceroy, his mandate to rule by force; the Sinn Fein leaders were arrested—many for the second time in two years—and imprisoned in England. Lloyd George dropped Home Rule. He also dropped conscription in Ireland, but the mortal damage had been done.

The German offensive also led to the most serious challenge yet to the Government. When Milner went to the War Office in succession to Derby he promptly removed Robertson's Director of Military Operations, General Sir Frederick Maurice. On May 7th Maurice, in a sensational public letter, brought out into the open charges that had been hitherto circulating privately in military and official circles. The allegation that Lloyd George had deliberately withheld troops from Haig to compel him to remain on the defensive had been denied by Lloyd George on April 9th in the Commons: 'Notwithstanding the heavy casualties in 1917', he said, 'the army in France was considerably stronger on January 1st 1918 than on January 1st 1917.' Now, Maurice in effect said that Lloyd George—abetted by Bonar Law— was a liar. There is now strong evidence to the effect that Maurice's charges were well founded, but the manner in which he made his revelations was intolerable. And the matter of whether Maurice's charges were justified is of less importance than the political consequences.[1] On May 7th, in answer to questions in the House from Asquith and others, Law foolishly agreed to set up a judicial enquiry into Maurice's charges; Asquith insisted on a debate first, which was fortunate for the Government, which hurriedly withdrew the offer of an enquiry.

On May 9th the famous Maurice Debate took place. Asquith spoke in a low key, and did not speak as though he were launching a Vote of Censure. But Lloyd George replied with a devastating counter-attack. He produced two defences; the first was that he made his statement of April 9th on the basis of figures supplied by Maurice himself; the second—rather less impressive—was that he had not included the non-combatant troops, and would have been justified in doing so.

But the real impact of Lloyd George's speech was personal. Here, he emphasised, was a Prime Minister, at a critical moment in the nation's fortunes, being forced to meet a fractious, disloyal, partisan attack. The self-portrait was irresistible. Perhaps Lloyd George really did believe—as he later stated in his memoirs—that this was all part of a plot to 'blow up the Government'; in any event, he emphatically pinned the badge of lack of judgement and patriotism upon Maurice and Asquith.

When the division was held, 100 Liberals—including two tellers— voted against the Government, supported by 6 Labour, 1 Unionist and 1 Irish Nationalist; 293 M.P.s supported the Government, of whom 71 were Liberals. This division marked the end of the Liberal Party as a unified force. The schism already created by the events

---

[1] See Jenkins, op. cit., 470–1, and A. J. P. Taylor: *English History 1914–1945*, 104–5.

of December 1916 was now substantially increased by the bitterness of the Maurice Debate.[1]

*

It was Lloyd George's last serious test. The German offensive congealed. The British and French forces held. The Americans were present in force. On July 15th the French withstood the last German offensive; on August 8th the British attacked north of Amiens, using 456 tanks in massed formation—the 'battering-ram' so long argued for by the tank experts. Haig checked the advance after two days, and attacked elsewhere. The Germans began to fall back. In September the new tactics were employed all along the line. There was no great break-through or triumph, and Allied casualties exceeded German when the attack was launched, particularly among the Americans.

But now, the Central Powers began to crumble. The last Turkish army was defeated by Allenby; the long immobile Salonika force at last advanced, and the Bulgarians hastily signed an Armistice. Ludendorff considered that the war was lost. And so it was. Apart from the British and the French, now pressing forward with renewed vigour and at last scenting victory, the impact of the fresh American divisions was psychologically overwhelming. On October 4th the German Government appealed to President Wilson for an immediate armistice and the opening of peace negotiations. Wilson eagerly accepted the opening to force the Fourteen Points upon both the Germans and the Allies. The principal Points were 'Open covenants of peace, openly arrived at'; absolute freedom of navigation on the seas in peace and war; the removal, so far as possible, of all economic barriers and equality of trade conditions; guarantees for arms reduction to the lowest point consistent with domestic safety; a free, open-minded, and absolutely impartial adjustment of all colonial claims, the interests of the population involved to have equal weight with the

---

[1] Not content with trouncing Maurice—whose military career was ended—Lloyd George returned to him with relish in his *War Memoirs*. The index references give a good indication of Lloyd George's ferocity:

'*Maurice, Sir Frederick*: comfortably placed as any politician . . . subservient and unbalanced . . . his astonishing arithmetical calculations . . . the instrument by which the Government was to be thrown out . . . intrigues against the Government, his mind being apparently unhinged . . . tool of astuter men . . . his double-dealing denounced by Lloyd George . . . his grave breach of discipline condoned by Asquith . . . dismissed.'

claims of the government making the claim; the evacuation of all Russian, French, and Belgian territory by the Germans; autonomous development for the peoples of Austria, Hungary and the Ottoman Empire; the creation of an independent Poland with a free and secure access to the sea; 'A general association of nations must be formed under specific covenants for the purpose of affording mutual guarantees of political independence and territorial integrity to great and small states alike.'

On October 23rd the Germans accepted the Points, and then, on November 4th, the Supreme War Council followed suit, with reservations by both the French and the British. On October 30th the Turks signed an armistice of surrender; on November 3rd the Austro-Hungarians concluded a similar armistice with the Italians. Morale in the German army was low, except in a few elite divisions; the fleet mutinied when ordered to sea; on November 9th the Kaiser fled to Holland and a Republic was proclaimed. At 5 a.m. on November 11th the Germans signed the armistice, which came into force at 11 a.m. For many, the delight at victory was tempered by other thoughts, not least of the joyous crusade that had ended in calamity for so many, and of the gay volunteer armies that were lost forever. In Siegfried Sassoon's words:

> And through some mooned Valhalla there will pass
> Battalions and battalions, scarred from Hell.
> The unreturning army that was youth;
> The legions that have suffered, and are dust.

*

Nations may weep or celebrate, but politics must continue. There had not been a General Election since 1910, and at the beginning of November Law and Lloyd George agreed to maintain the Coalition and to have an immediate election. Lloyd George had been planning for this eventuality for some time. After the events of December 1916 Asquith had taken much of the Liberal machine with him; Lloyd George had accordingly set up his own Liberal organisation and had started to create his personal political fund. Thomas Jones states[1] that 'During the summer of 1918, and indeed earlier, Lloyd George was planning an election which would give him a mandate from a

[1] T. J. Jones: *Lloyd George*, 158.

united nation not only to lead it to victory but to negotiate the peace'. At Manchester, in September, he made what was in effect the first election speech of the new campaign. Before the Armistice was signed the plans were ready. In the euphoria of victory, the doubts which Law had had about Lloyd George had now vanished. To Archibald Salvidge, boss of the Conservative organisation in Liverpool, he said emotionally: 'Salvidge, I tell you we must never let the little man go. His way and ours lie side by side in the future.'

Lloyd George, after an unconvincing attempt to bring Asquith—as Lord Chancellor—and Labour into the Coalition, fought the election as the head of the Government. His most violent diatribes were, however, directed against the Liberals who had tried 'to overthrow a Government that was in the midst of a crisis whilst wrestling for victory'; those who had repented were compared to Germans who cried 'Kamerad!' Such statements were not designed to heal the gaping wounds in the old Liberal Party. The position of the Asquithian Liberals in any event was a very difficult one. They were caught in the open between the Coalition and Labour. Only 159 Liberals were spared Coalition opposition and received the joint letter of commendation from Lloyd George and Bonar Law, derided by Asquith as 'the coupon'.

Contrary to Asquith's allegation—accepted by many subsequent historians—the Maurice Debate voting was not the decisive test for the bestowal of the 'coupon'. The choice of the favoured 159 was done on strange and arbitrary causes, but the effects were devastating. Only 18 Liberals survived opposition from a sponsored Coalition candidate. When the election dust cleared, the Coalition had 484 Members—338 Conservatives, 136 Lloyd George Liberals, and 10 other supporters; opposed to them were 59 Labour and 26 Asquithian Liberals. Asquith himself, although his opponent did not receive the 'coupon', was defeated; so were Henderson, MacDonald and Philip Snowden. MacDonald had not expected to be re-elected in Leicester, anticipating 'an . . . combination against everyone who has thought and acted independently upon the war'. He was swept away by 20,570 votes to 6,347, but in 1920 was adopted for Aberavon. In the meanwhile he was to keep the flame of the Labour nascence alive and vehement. He fell in good company. Only 229 members of the new Parliament had not received the 'coupon'. 541 'coupons' were issued; 478 'couponed' candidates were returned.

The 1918 General Election was remarkable for other reasons. It was a dirty fight. Lloyd George, in *The Truth About the Peace Treaties*, subsequently cited a speech at Bristol in which he had gone into the whole question of German reparations. This defence has been destroyed by Jones,[1] who comments that 'he was inclined to shout the popular demands and to whisper the qualifications'. On the matter of the treatment of the Kaiser, one commentator[2] claims that Lloyd George referred to 'hanging the Kaiser' on twenty separate occasions. One example of Lloyd George's style (December 6th) is sufficient:

> The Kaiser must be prosecuted. The war was a crime . . . a hideous, abominable crime, a crime which has sent millions of the best young men of Europe to death and mutilation, and which has plunged myriads of homes into desolation. Is no one responsible? Is no one to be called to account? Is there to be no punishment? Surely that is neither God's justice nor man's. The men responsible for this outrage on the human race must not be let off because their heads were crowned when they perpetrated the deed.

A statement to the Press on the eve of the election put prosecution of the Kaiser first, and reparations second, as the election issues; 'rehabilitation of those broken in the war' and 'domestic reform in all spheres' were bottom of the list of priorities. Apart from the speechifying about 'hanging the Kaiser' and 'squeezing Germany until the pips squeak', the real issue was whether the country wanted the victorious Lloyd George Coalition to continue. To this question the answer seemed to be overwhelming.

But there were some significant portents. The Labour national executive sponsored 363 candidates, and in fact a total of 447 Labour candidates (of whom 36 supported the Coalition) stood, and polled 2,374,385 votes. The Irish Nationalist Party had vanished, a remnant of seven returning to Westminster. Seventy-three Sinn Feiners had been elected—including the first woman M.P., the flamboyant Countess Markiewicz—but refused to take their seats in the English Parliament; 36, indeed, were in no position to do so, being in prison at the time. Most interesting of all, in the first General Election in British history

[1] Jones, op. cit., 161–3.
[2] S. Lauzanne: *Le Diable Aux Yeux Bleu.* Churchill, also, joined in the cry for punishing the Kaiser and harsh reparations.

that could truly claim to be such, with seventy-eight per cent of the adult population now entitled to the vote, only some fifty-six per cent actually voted. So far as could be seen, the women's vote had no impact whatever.

The election was, above all, a triumph for the Conservative Party and a catastrophe for the Liberals. Each had entered the war with approximately the same number of seats—260; now, the Conservatives had 338, and the Liberals were fatally split in twain. In 1914, the United Liberal Party had enjoyed Irish Nationalist and Labour support; by the end of 1918 the Irish Nationalists had disappeared, and Labour was an independent, hostile, party.

Thus, the Great War had not only changed the face of Europe; it had also transformed the features of British politics. For the time being, Lloyd George reigned supreme and unchallenged, hailed as 'the man who won the war'. But there were others who described him as 'a fire-brand scattering hate across England', and Augustine Birrell wrote to Asquith: 'You surely are better out of it for the time, than watching Ll.G. lead apes to Hell.' Lloyd George still remained in 10 Downing Street so long as the Conservatives were content to leave him there. He believed that they owed their victory to his leadership; for a time, many of them believed it as well.

*

The physical wounds of the Great War on Britain were not severe as they had been on other belligerents, although they seemed appalling at the time. The British economy had not been severely harmed, and in many fields—notably technological—her industries had advanced dramatically. The British people had withstood, and conquered, the perils and hardships of the war, and it had been for many a liberating experience. Thus, for those who had gone through the war and had emerged unscathed, there were high expectations for the future. But the desire to return to 'normalcy' now assumed the proportions of a cult. The war-time system of government direction and control was enthusiastically dismembered, as were many of the industries—notably the aircraft industry—that the war had in fact created. As Sir Llewellyn Woodward has written:

> The Brigade of Guards got back into Scarlet, and the Treasury set about restoring Treasury Control. After the march of armies, the

wrigglings of martinets. . . . Mr. Austen Chamberlain returned to
the Treasury to which he had first been appointed in 1903; Lord
Curzon presided over the Foreign Office, and Mr. Arthur Balfour,
fresh from the Congress of Berlin, exchanged reminiscences with
M. Clemenceau, whose memories stopped short at 1870. No
wonder that no one knew . . . whether we were going on or going
back.

And, in 1927, a group of young Conservatives that included Harold
Macmillan and Robert Boothby commented that:

The war period shattered preconceived economic notions, proved
possible theoretic impossibilities, removed irremovable barriers,
created new and undreamt-of solutions. Yet by far the greater part
of the legislation which today governs trade and industry dates from
before that period. We are surely entitled to ask whether it is now
adequate to meet the vastly changed conditions of the modern
economic era.

The question was well-based, and it was not to be answered. And
thus the victors returned to the problems of Ireland, of Empire, and
of how to administer a Free Trade economy. Men reared in Victorian
politics resumed their old, inconveniently interrupted, activities with
pleasure. They did not hesitate to dwell movingly on the mighty
sacrifices that had been made, insensitive to the surly anger of those
who had suffered. To quote Woodward again:

Laurence Binyon's noble words 'they shall not grow old as we who
are left grow old' took on an ironic meaning in the mouths of
speakers who were well content to grow old and fat, and who had
never asked the dead whether they had chosen to die young in
order to avoid old age. As time went on, I began to dislike more and
more the celebration of Armistice Day. I wished that all the formal
ceremonies might be abandoned, and that this commemoration
of the dead could be left to those for whom it had some personal
meaning. Darkness is not better than light, death is not better than
life; no praise from comfortable men can bring the dead back to
the sun they loved.

The war did not, in itself, make men disillusioned; it was the peace
that achieved this, which four bitter years of war had failed to do. In

the 1922 General Election Lord Winterton—a Conservative M.P. since 1904, who had served in the war at Gallipoli and in Mesopotamia—was 'shocked' to hear the following exchange at an election meeting:

> *The Chairman*: Our candidate fought most gallantly in the war.
> *A Voice*: More bloody fool he (Cheers and laughter).[1]

That exchange would have been unthinkable in 1918. But much occurred between then and 1922.

[1] Lord Winterton: *Orders of the Day*, 118.

CHAPTER FOUR

POST-WAR, 1919–1922

The world's great age begins anew,
The golden years return,
The earth doth like a snake renew
Her winter weeds outworn;
Heaven smiles, and faiths and empires gleam,
Like wrecks of a dissolving dream.[1]

BRITAIN WAS STILL a very rich nation in 1914, and, had it not been for the substantial loans to her Allies, would have been even richer by 1918. The most significant feature of the British economy at the end of the nineteenth and beginning of the twentieth centuries was the change from an industrial to a trading nation; as R. C. K. Ensor has said, 'If she was no longer so much as formerly the world's workshop, she was more than ever its warehouseman, its banker, and its commission agent. And these were relatively the better-paid functions'.[2] These changes had not materially affected the nation's overall prosperity, but they were the essential background to the rise of the trade union movement in the 1890s and 1900s, and the serious industrial disputes of 1910–11. This industrial situation, coupled as it was with bad housing and urban conditions, did not lead directly to the emergence of the Labour Party, but it was the combination of industrial stagnation with doubts over the legal position of the Unions that had led to the movement to have working-class representation at Westminster. From the 'new Unionism' of the 1890s —given its greatest impetus by the success of the 1889 dock strike— the Labour Representation Committee of 1900 was an indirect growth; it was, in time, to be its most significant political consequence. The rise of the Labour Party up to the Great War was

[1] Shelley, *Hellas*, quoted by Curzon in the House of Lords, November 18th 1918, in moving an Address to the King.
[2] Ensor: *England 1870–1914*, 507.

something less than meteoric, but the groundwork had been laid for the subsequent edifice, and the first Labour leaders—Henderson, MacDonald, Clynes, and Snowden—had received their political apprenticeship. It is hypothetical to consider whether Labour would have grown into a separate party had it not been for the war and for the Liberal schisms, but the nature of the post-war Labour Party was largely shaped in the pre-war decade.

The emergence of Labour as a distinct—if not separate—political group was one of the most significant features of the pre-war period. It owed much in the first instance to the Liberal obsession with Irish Home Rule and schisms over Imperialism from 1886 to 1894, and to its consequent political impotence and divisions; its survival was ensured by the Taff Vale Judgement, the increased trade union financial support, and the MacDonald–Gladstone Pact of 1903. Nevertheless, up to 1914, it was essentially an appendage of the Liberal Party, without distinct leadership, policy, or philosophy. These only emerged in 1917–18.

Perhaps the most significant political fact of all in this period had been the dramatic extension of the electorate. In 1886 it had stood at just over one million; in 1883 it was 2·6 million; in 1886, after the 1885 Reform Act, it was some 4·4 million; by 1900 it had grown, by natural increase, to 6·7 million, or some 27 per cent of the total adult population; in 1910 it was just under 7·7 million, some 28 per cent of the total adult population; in 1918 it had swollen dramatically to 21,755,583, or 78 per cent of the adult population. This was not yet full adult suffrage, which was to come ten years later, but it was very nearly that. In these years Britain had come close to becoming a true democracy for the first time in her history.

This revolution—for such it was—had been much more considerable in local government before 1914. The Municipal Corporations Act of 1882 and the creation of the elective County and Borough Councils in 1888 had removed local government from a privileged minority and established a system which, with all its inadequacies, was a vast improvement on its predecessor.

But although Members of Parliament now received a small salary, national politics remained the privilege of a very small proportion of the nation until 1918. For those without private means or a substantial alternative income public service involved considerable sacrifices and careful husbandry of very limited resources. The early Labour M.P.s had to live frugally, and formed no part of the highly political and small world of London society. Politics remained remarkably central-ised. The great and lesser men might sally forth into the country, but their base was London. The modern idea that a Member of Parliament should live in his constituency, or have some personal connection with it, was not widespread, in spite of the example given by those notable exceptions, the Chamberlains. The control exercised by Lord Derby over Lancashire Conservatism—which was to continue until his death—demonstrated that the days of the great territorial mag-nates had not wholly passed, but the influence and control of the Conservative Central Office were developing rapidly. The Liberal central dominance was less, but reflected the same tendency to draw political power and influence into a small central core of active London politicians. The powers of the central party machine, although perhaps exaggerated at the time, had substantially increased, and were moving political parties into nationally organised entities to a degree which had not been dreamed of in the early 1880s. The Primrose League proved to be a much clearer portent than the Birmingham Caucus, and Captain Middleton a more significant individual than Schnadhorst. Even in the Labour Party, the move-ment towards central direction was evident.

It was still not difficult for a rich man to buy his way into Par-liament, but the Corrupt Practices Acts gave the advantage to central organisation rather than to the individual. Many constituency organ-isations in the Liberal and Conservative parties remained fiercely independent, but in the majority it was the voice of London which mattered. When Joseph Chamberlain first heard F. E. Smith speak he arranged for him to have a more hopeful constituency in Liverpool. It was not the Oldham Unionist Association which sought the candidature of Winston Churchill, but one of its M.P.s, an admirer of Lord Randolph Churchill. When Churchill made his political debut at Bath in 1897, it was arranged by Central Office. Politics remained a national pastime, but increasingly orchestrated from London.

Thus, it would be unwise to exaggerate the changes—considerable though they were—in the structure of British society and government between 1880 and 1914. Money and power were limited to a very small minority. The first steps towards a national education policy tended to emphasise further the vast gulf which separated the pros-perous few and the many poor. The men and women who managed to bridge this gulf did so through intense application and self-education in very difficult circumstances. The much-hailed social reforms of the period 1880–1914 did not seriously affect the structure of a society in which the accident of birth remained the most crucial of all factors in one's prospects. The resilience and strength of the top element in this society lay in its willingness to accept new recruits and to instil in them the precepts of success and wealth, trinkets and honours. And these trinkets were highly attractive and very seductive.

London Society may have been vulgar in many respects between the 1890s and the outbreak of the war, but its outward appearances were glittering. The great country houses were run on a scale which had changed little over the years. King Edward VII, in his style, priorities, and standards, was not an unrepresentative monarch of this small but immensely powerful fragment of his realm.

The war did not wholly destroy this situation, but it aroused a new awareness—and not only among the deprived—of the perils and inequities of this society. The war itself had removed some of them, of which the greatly expanded franchise was the most portentous. The class structures remained, but the old assurances and acceptances had been altered. All classes had suffered in the war, and the rolls of honour of the public schools and universities testify to how heavy were the losses of the pre-1914 elite. There was a new militancy and expectation among those who had previously been poor but acquiescent to their fate. It was to be some time before these new attitudes became apparent in political terms, but the most perceptive commentators had the sensation of real, deep, social movement.

The façade remained largely unchanged, and the established institutions unaltered. The monarchy, certainly, emerged from the war more popular than ever.

The 'powers' of the monarchy had been recognised as limited to advice and influence by the middle of the reign of Queen Victoria; if King George V was a very different monarch to her, this owed more to the differences in character and experience than to a profound alteration in the position of the monarchy. King Edward VII and King George V lacked Queen Victoria's unique experience of politics, and their prejudices were less deep. But, after a difficult start, King George developed a style and technique of his own that gave him eventually a very considerable influence as well as much popularity. The 'powers' of the monarchy in reality were gone before the death of the Prince Consort, who had done more than any other individual to put it on the constitutional lines that have been followed ever since; the influence of the monarch still remained, could be important on occasions, and varied with the personality and experience of each sovereign. There were no indications before 1914 that the public respect for the monarchy had seriously waned, although, had King George accepted the advice urged on him by one of his advisers in the first crisis of his reign in 1911 and been seen to have been taking sides,[1] the situation might have been very different.

One really marked change had concerned the position of the House of Lords. Between 1868 and 1905 it was usual for the Foreign Secretary to be a peer; Lord Clarendon from 1868 to 1870; Granville from 1870 to 1874 and 1880 to 1885; Salisbury in 1885-6; Rosebery and Iddesleigh in 1886; Salisbury 1887-92; Rosebery 1892-4; Kimberley 1894-5; Salisbury, 1895-1900; Lansdowne 1900-5. Salisbury had been Prime Minister for over thirteen years between 1885 and 1902, and Rosebery for over a year in the same period. After 1886, the Lords became even more than in the past a Conservative stronghold. The Liberal campaigns against the peers in 1883-4 and 1892-5 did not have substantial immediate effect, but they were the first shots in the battle that developed fully between 1906 and 1909, and which reached its culmination in the constitutional crisis of 1910-11. The Liberal objections to Rosebery in 1894 were not principally the result of his being a peer, but after that disaster it was highly improbable that the Liberals would ever consider a member of the Lords as leader again. And in 1911 one of the arguments which had a strong influence with Asquith in appointing Churchill to the Admiralty over Haldane's claims was the belief that an office of that importance must be held by a member of the House of Commons. Thus, although the 1911 Parliament Act did not, in itself, grievously diminish the powers of the House of Lords, the accumulation of events leading up to it had shown that in the last analysis the Lords could no longer withstand a determined Government with a Commons majority and public support. The latter remained the key factor, as the examples of 1893 and 1906-9 had demonstrated.

But the blatant partisanship of the Lords had destroyed its influence. So long as the hereditary principle lasted, it could count upon a regular intake of young men interested in politics, but for

[1] See Volume I, 251.

those who were more fortunate the Commons was the centre of ambition. The Lords declined into the Valhalla of failed or ageing politicians, generals, and officials, addressed by fading titans of the past or undistinguished junior Ministers. The Salisbury–Rosebery debates had been the last occasion on which the party leaders had combated in the Lords, and after Salisbury's death the declined status of the Lords became increasingly evident. It still had its great days and great orators—Milner and Curzon, Birkenhead and Carson, Hailsham and Swinton. But the reality of power now lay elsewhere.

This had been the lesson of 1830–2, but it was not fully applied until 1911. Ministers still sat in the House of Lords, but the balance had now swung sharply towards the Commons. It subsequently became very uncommon for a peer even to be Foreign Secretary, the exceptions in the inter-war period being Curzon (1919–23), Reading (for three months in 1931) and Halifax (1938–40); in May 1923, when Law's succession was discussed, the fact that Curzon was a peer was held to be a significant objection. There *might* have been a peer as Prime Minister in May 1940 (Halifax), but this would have been seen as a major change in accepted practice, justified only by very exceptional circumstances. The Lords could still be a nuisance to a radical government, but little more.

Although the apparatus of the central Government affected the ordinary citizen very little in 1914, there had been a very considerable increase in the size and scope of government since the early 1880s. In 1880 there were over 50,000 civil servants of all categories, including those engaged in postal and telegraph services; by 1914 the figure had risen to 280,000. The creation of the Board of Agriculture (1889) and the Board of Education (1899) had been the first, rather timorous, steps in the direction of 'functional' Ministries. The operation of the National Insurance Act of 1911 required new organisation, which was created in the form of four linked commissions, represented by the Treasury in Parliament. This was an example—of which others were to come later—of government legislation leading directly to the creation of new organisation outside the existing government structure. The Labour Exchanges, on the other hand, were created within the structure of the Board of Trade. The non-contributory old age pensions scheme enacted in 1909 similarly did not merit a new department of State.

The volume of public expenditure was in itself an indication of what had happened. In 1901 the Civil Estimates were £23·6 million, and the Service Estimates were £60·9. By 1914 the Civil Estimates had risen to £57·6 million, and the Service Estimates to £80.39. The marked disparity between military and civil expenditure still remained, but the sharp increase in civil expenditure was a significant trend. This jump in public expenditure at home—principally on education and social remedial legislation—demonstrated a real movement away from the mid-Victorian philosophies of 'self-help'.

The dictum of Disraeli that 'the vicissitudes of politics are inexhaustible' had been demonstrated frequently in the years 1886–1918. The period opened with the thunderbolt of Gladstone's espousal of Home Rule, and the subsequent split in the Liberal Party that had taken Joseph Chamberlain and Hartington and ninety-one other Liberals into the Conservative lobby in June 1886, and that eventually resulted in the Unionist Alliance. Then, shortly after their victory in the 1886 General Election, the Conservatives had been shaken by the unexpected resignation of Lord Randolph Churchill: the policy of 'killing Home Rule by kindness', coupled with that of 'twenty years of resolute government' personified by Balfour, led to a revival of the Irish cause, a revival given enormous impetus by the Pigott forgeries, only to be temporarily crushed by the Parnell divorce case and the subsequent internecine feuds among the Irish Nationalists.

The Liberal victory of 1892 had been, accordingly, a barren one, and, particularly after the resignation of Gladstone, subsided feebly towards defeat. Between 1866 and 1886 the Liberals were in office for a total of eleven and a half years; in the twenty years following, they were in office, and only with the support of the Irish vote, for under three years.

The Liberal revival of 1903–5 was the result less of Liberal advances in thinking or activity than the collapse of the Unionist Alliance, and a startling swing of circumstances in their favour. But from December 1905 until May 1915 the Liberals were in office, and it was the Unionists who seemed to be doomed to perpetual opposition. It was this fact that imparted to the political crises of 1906–14 much of their bitterness.

This period also saw the decisive movement towards full Irish independence. After the setbacks of the 1890s, and the slow rebuilding of the Irish Nationalist Party by Redmond, Home Rule seemed very near in 1914, its proximity only shadowed—now that the absolute

veto of the House of Lords had been destroyed by the Parliament Act
—by the refusal of Ulster to be coerced into a Home Rule Parliament.
But the aftermath to the Easter Rising of April 1916 and the attempt
to impose conscription in 1918 had transformed the emphasis of the
movement away from limited Home Rule to full independence.
Between 1880 and 1916 the separatists had always been in a minority;
now they were, as the General Election of 1918 decisively demonstrated, the majority. The Irish Question was to torture the British
domestic political scene for another three years, and then to disappear,
but not permanently.

In the Empire, there had been a subtle but very significant development since 1880. By 1918 the Empire seemed more secure, united, and
confident than ever. Its members had rallied to the British cause, and
had shared the British sacrifice. The unhappy saga of British relations
with the Boer Republics had resulted in the fulfilment of Bartle
Frere's old dream of the South African Federation. Canada, Australia,
New Zealand and South Africa now enjoyed full self-government. In
India, a policy of 'gradualness' was slowly incorporating Indians into
the process of consultation—although not that of government. There
were, in 1918, few indications in London of the storm that was about
to break.

The years following the Boer War, and the Great War itself, far
from destroying the Empire, had apparently strengthened its cor-
porate sense and had certainly seen a substantial increase in its size.
The new possessions in the Middle East, and the acquisition of the
former German colonies, represented a very considerable accession of
British territorial possessions. These developments were of great
encouragement to what might be loosely described as the 'idealistic
imperialists' of the Milner school. They had, however, failed to learn
the real lessons of 1900–18. Every attempt to bring the Empire into
a closer federation—economic or military—had merely emphasised
the increasing sense of independence of its members. These attitudes
were to be formally enacted in the Statute of Westminster in 1931, and
their full implications were to be seen at the Imperial Conference of
1937 and in the Munich Crisis in 1938.

So far as the Colonies were concerned, British power and influence
remained strong. But the acceptance by Lloyd George of Woodrow
Wilson's concept of 'self-determination', and the fact that Britain had
gone to war ostensibly to preserve Belgian independence, provided

critics of British rule with formidable new weapons. And, by the Balfour Declaration of November 1917, the British had ensured that their occupancy of the Middle East was to be a difficult one. The dominant attitude of the British towards the Colonies remained that of Milner's conclusion on self-government in Egypt: 'The people neither comprehend it nor desire it. They would come to singular grief if they had it. And nobody, except a few silly theorists, thinks of giving it to them'.[1] But now, it was becoming less a question of giving than surrendering. It was to be many years before British politicians comprehended the vast aspirations to which their own rhetoric had contributed. Hobson had exaggerated—but not greatly—when he had written in 1902 that 'not five per cent of the population of our Empire are possessed of the political and civil liberties which are the basis of British civilisation'.[2] The blatant absence of these liberties was now beginning to arouse resistance and hostility which had little to do with theorists, silly or otherwise.

Thus, the war that had demonstrated so dramatically the cohesion of the Empire, was also to open large fissures in that cohesion. Ireland was to provide the first example.

*

But Britain emerged from the Great War militarily triumphant and seemingly more powerful than ever. The war had swept away all the other familiar landmarks in Europe. Germany and Russia, crushed by military defeat and internal collapse, had ceased to exist as great powers. The Austro-Hungarian and Ottoman Empires had literally vanished. France, although a nominal victor, was exhausted by her prodigious sacrifices—even more exhausted than was realised at the time. The German High Seas Fleet lay in sullen docility in Scapa Flow. The German colonies had been expropriated. Everywhere the British armies rested on their arms, with vast new areas of conquest to their name. The Empire revelled in the splendour of total victory. The Prime Minister of Britain, at the zenith of his fame, journeyed to Versailles to dictate terms to the defeated and to parley from a position of power to his allies. President Wilson journeyed across the Atlantic to build a new World Order, but in fact to meet and be vanquished by the implacable reactionary *realpolitik* of the Old.

[1] Milner: *England In Egypt*.
[2] Hobson: *Imperialism*, 123.

The economic effects of the war on Britain had been surprisingly small, and the war was followed by a boom—quickly to disappear. In many respects the war had had beneficial results, particularly on the chemical, scientific, and engineering industries. Before the war Britain had lagged badly behind her principal rivals in all three industries; by 1918 she could claim at least parity, and in many respects superiority. Britain had lost about a tenth of her overseas investments, which had amounted to some £4,000 million in 1914; she had also incurred a substantial external debt. This caused little concern, as the debt of £842 million to America was more than balanced by the £1,740 million owed to her by her allies. But £568 million of this was owed by Russia, and the other debtors were not in a condition to repay. It was some time before the British began to realise the full implications of this situation. In the immediate post-war euphoria it was assumed that Germany would substantially repay the Allies for their expenditure and that Britain's debtors would promptly meet their obligations. Neither assumption proved to be valid.

The psychological results of the war were to prove, in the long run, considerably more important than the physical, although the latter were serious enough. The British had lost some 744,000 men killed in the Army and Navy. This meant that one in ten men of the generation aged between twenty and forty-five during the war was dead. Most of them, it should be recalled, had been volunteers. In addition, 14,661 merchant seamen had been killed, and 1,117 civilians in German airship and aeroplane raids; the influenza epidemic of 1918–1919 killed 150,000 more, of whom more than 15,000 died in London alone. The British Empire mourned some 947,000 young men killed in action or dead of wounds; in addition, there were countless tens of thousands who had been physically or mentally scarred by the war. The available statistics can only afford us some idea of the physical results of the war. By 1921, in Britain, nearly 3,500,000 persons were receiving some kind of war pension or allowance;[1] some 160,000 wives had lost husbands in the war, and over 300,000 children had lost fathers.[2] The fact that struck commentators at the time, and

---

[1] *Report of the Departmental Committee of Inquiry into the Machinery of Administration of the Ministry of Pensions, p. 3.*

[2] The casualties of the other major belligerents were approximately as follows:
    Russia: 1·7 million dead, 4·9 million wounded.
    France: 1·3 million dead, 4·3 million wounded.
    Germany: 1·8 million dead, 4·2 million wounded.

which has become one of the most potent phrases of modern history, was 'the missing generation', particularly among the traditional ruling classes. But it was not simply a phrase. No nation of Britain's size can afford to lose three-quarters of a million young men dead and another million and a half wounded without grievous consequences. The great majority had been volunteers, and included men in the highly skilled professions. It has been suggested that of those who returned, there was a marked distaste for public life and for politicians. As Woodward wrote:

> The men who came back from the war have counted for less, perhaps, in the political life of their country than any generation during the last two or three centuries.

This contention was not wholly merited. Among the survivors of the so-called 'lost generation' were Anthony Eden, Clement Attlee, Walter Elliot, Duff Cooper, Harold Macmillan, Oswald Mosley, Walter Monckton, and the future Lord Halifax. But the men who dominated British politics in the inter-war period were those who had been born and brought up in Victorian Britain. This was not altogether surprising since the pattern of British politics is such that it is unusual for men under forty to rise to Cabinet rank. But there seemed to be—and was—a gulf in experience and attitude between the men who had served in the war and those whose experience was essentially pre-war.

This was seen less in specific policies than in general attitudes. The dominant—and understandable—feeling among the leading personalities in public life after the war was to return to the comfortable 'normality' of the pre-1914 situation. As R. H. Tawney has commented: '"Back to 1914" became a common cry.' They had no wish to build on the structures that had been so painfully created by the exigencies of the war, and which they consequently regarded as exceptional measures for exceptional circumstances. Thus, the new functional Ministries spawned by the war were thankfully and

---

Austria-Hungary: 1·2 million dead, 3·6 million wounded.
Over 60 million men were mobilised by the European belligerents, of whom 57·6 per cent were casualties, with more than 8 million killed and over 21 million wounded. These figures are very approximate, but are certainly not an under-estimation, and it cannot be emphasised enough that they are almost entirely related to males between the ages of 18 and 45, and they give little hint of the psychological and physical effects upon the survivors.

swiftly obliterated. Free Trade was revived as the national lode-star, and those politicians who had fought for the Tariff Reform cause for so long resumed their wearying struggle. All parties worked towards a return to the Gold Standard. Nothing, it seemed, had changed. The trouble was that everything had changed. But those who saw this, and had no desire whatever to go back to 1914, did not occupy the commanding political heights.

The structure of politics itself had changed drastically. The condition of the Liberal Party was very comparable to that of the Whig Party in the 1840s, described by Disraeli as 'absolutely forlorn . . . spoken of as a corpse, it was treated as a phantom', its remnants divided between Lloyd George and the defeated Asquith. But Lloyd George and the Conservatives—in 1914 apparently doomed to indefinite Opposition, and now in 1919 so firmly in control—had not been the only causes of the Liberal débâcle.

The most significant event in the downfall of the Liberals had been the emergence of the Labour Party, with its own leaders, candidates and programme, and now a separate, distinct, and individual force in British politics. In 1910 Labour voters had amounted to less than eight per cent of the votes cast; in 1918 it was 22·2 per cent. The Labour Party was in no sense whatever a revolutionary element, but its emergence aroused intense apprehension in the older parties. From this point the obsession of keeping Labour out of office became their dominant, if often unspoken, motivation.

The Redmondite Irish Nationalists had vanished almost as completely as the Austrian-Hungarian Empire. Of the eighty-strong phalanx that had swayed British politics since the late 1870s, only seven returned. The seventy-three elected Sinn Fein candidates contemptuously refused to take their seats in the British Parliament, and established their own, the Dail, in Dublin. The profound significance of this action was only gradually perceived.

An observer of the House of Commons at the beginning of 1919 could accordingly see at a glance the political effects of the war. The Conservatives, in opposition for so long, sat triumphantly on the Government benches, enclosing in their midst their Lloyd George Liberal captives. The followers of Asquith sat in a pitiful group, in an apparent condition of shock. The Irish had gone. Labour, with fifty-nine Members, was the majority opposition party.

*

The dominant personality in British political life was Lloyd George. Many of his contemporaries, and a number of subsequent commentators, have endeavoured to recapture his extraordinary personality, but without success. He comes down to us in vague terms, Keynes' 'half-human visitor to our age from the hag-ridden magic and enchanted woods of Celtic antiquity', 'rooted in nothing', 'void and without content', 'a vampire and a medium in one'. To Beaverbrook he was the Archetypical Pragmatist:

> To keep the seat of power, the place of patronage, he was prepared to stand out as the leader of Empire-minded men—or appear as the Liberal Apostle of Free Trade: as the Man of Peace in Europe—or as the Man of War against Turkey and France: as the hammer of the Russian Bolshevists—or their noble conciliator: as the Tribune of the British Working Class—or the champion of the Tory landlords against Labour: stern enemy of the Irish—or their tender friend spreading his covering wings about another Celtic race ground under the heel of the oppressor. He took up each position in turn during those tragic years of 1921 and 1922.[1]

That Lloyd George was an opportunist and, in political terms, an adventurer, may be freely accepted. So had been Disraeli; so was Churchill. In 1918 this was not only accepted but positively admired; he was 'the man who won the war', and 'the man who got things done'.

But although Lloyd George had successfully stormed the citadel of power, he had triumphed at heavy cost. He had split the Liberal Party. He was wholly dependent upon Conservative votes and Conservative goodwill for his survival. He headed a Coalition in which the Conservatives were dominant. His own shifts of policy reflected the strains and difficulties of the Government that he headed. He was to become the convenient scapegoat when the electorate turned against the Coalition.

To those who appreciate natural justice in human affairs, this is agreeable. Lloyd George's personal standards of political probity were not high; his standards of loyalty to friends and colleagues were even less exalted; he was more than willing to pay the price of Tory support; in political matters great and small he had few scruples and few standards. But no portrait of this remarkable individual can discount

[1] Beaverbrook: *The Decline and Fall of Lloyd George*, 10–11.

his extraordinary charm. He was always bubbling with life and vigour, and could be an enchanting companion. One sensed in his presence a glow of energy and spirit which few could resist, and he had full comprehension of the value of flattery in human affairs. Bonar Law was one of many improbable politicians who found 'the little man' irresistible, however much he might disapprove of certain aspects of his public and private life. The fact that Lloyd George had a mistress, to whom he was not invariably faithful, was well known in political circles, but—like Asquith's drinking—was never mentioned publicly, and remained unknown to the public until long after his death. But, in the mood of 1919, it is perhaps doubtful that even this knowledge would have fatally affected his political eminence.

Political power and prestige of the kind that Lloyd George enjoyed immediately after the 1918 General Election is very heady wine. He became careless and greedy, in matters financial particularly, and the atmosphere in 10 Downing Street was not edifying. Everything revolved around the Prime Minister's whims and prejudices, and the only road to favour was subservience. Lloyd George became intoxicated by his power, relished its trappings to the point where they dominated his horizons, and made him forget how shallow were the foundations of his occupancy of Downing Street. From past experience he should have known that the Conservative Party would only follow him while his national popularity remained, and would abandon him without remorse or compunction when it was evident that his usefulness to them was at an end. It was said of Lloyd George in 1918 that he could be Prime Minister for the rest of his life; conceivably, he might have been, had he continued to produce political success for his nominal followers and effective masters. But *hubris* was to be for Lloyd George, as for so many others, his fatal characteristic.

The collective personality of the Government was essentially that of its leader. Lloyd George was the first—and, to the time of writing, the last—'Presidential' Prime Minister. He treated Parliament with contempt, and rarely went there. He filled 10 Downing Street with cronies and sycophants. He could be—and often was—brutal to those colleagues who crossed him or who aroused his jealousy, and merciless when his own position seemed in jeopardy. He created the Lloyd George Fund, whose purpose was simply 'to promote any political purpose approved by the Rt. Hon. David Lloyd George', and for which a major source of revenue was the sale of honours and other favours. Until 1922 the income was shared fifty-fifty with the Conservatives; afterwards it all went to Lloyd George, and only he controlled it. This must have seemed a brilliant stroke, giving him a power of the purse that would ensure his domination of the Liberal Party. But Lloyd George grossly exaggerated the value of money in the new circumstances created by the arrival of a mass electorate, and the revelation of its existence and how it had been built up was to be the final blow to his declining reputation in 1922.

But for most of the Coalition Lloyd George's style and manner dominated it, and were to be his undoing. Churchill became increasingly disenchanted with his old companion-in-arms; Bonar Law was to become totally disillusioned; and the revulsion that Lloyd George's imperious and cynical conduct of affairs aroused in the junior members of his Government was to prove fatal to him in 1922 and to pursue him relentlessly for the rest of his career.

The second man in the Government—indeed, almost on a level with Lloyd George—was Bonar Law, formerly highly sceptical of Lloyd George but now a warm admirer. His hold on the Conservative Party was a strong one, but was in the real sense a reactionary one; Law did not lead, he listened and followed what his supporters said. He was plainly, and manifestly, the lynch-pin of the Government. His natural caution and melancholy had been emphasised by the loss of two of his sons in the war. Pessimistic, matter-of-fact, cautious, modest to the point of appearing nondescript, Law was in marked contrast to the other Coalition leaders—in Beaverbrook's phrase the glittering birds of paradise.

The Coalition leaders could count upon nearly 500 supporters in the House of Commons. They basked in the glow of military victory, as the dominant personalities in the most powerful nation in the world. It was a dazzling, brilliant, all-powerful alliance. Yet, within four years it was to disintegrate, collapse, and to perish unmourned. The story of this downfall is among the most remarkable in modern British political history.

It is not simply hindsight to detect in the Coalition from the outset certain important weaknesses. 'The war fought for democracy', one perceptive observer has written, 'had produced at the centre an atmosphere more like an oriental court at which favourites struggle unceasingly for position.'[1] Its leading members, with the notable

[1] Francis Williams: *A Pattern of Rulers*, 19.

exception of Bonar Law, were remarkably detached from their rank and file. Lloyd George was to become, so far as the House of Commons was concerned, virtually an absentee Prime Minister. He also developed a marked taste for personal international diplomacy, an obsession that increasingly divorced him not only from the House of Commons but also from the Government.

Churchill had only recently emerged from a period of signal political misfortune. The prodigy of 1900–15 had stumbled badly, and although he was back in office, much—if not all—of the early glitter had been severely tarnished. The grim shadow of the Gallipoli disaster hung over his reputation. The Conservatives disliked and distrusted him; the Asquithian Liberals considered him a renegade; organised Labour regarded him as one of their most implacable foes. Churchill was totally dependent upon Lloyd George for his political survival. In 1908, when Churchill had first entered the Cabinet, A. G. Gardiner had pondered the question of whether the mercurial young man had staying power. 'How will forty find him?' Gardiner asked, '—that fatal forty when the youth of roselight and romance has faded into the light of common day. . . .' By 1919 Churchill was forty-five, yet he retained many of the more alarming features of the *enfant terrible* that prompted Lloyd George to compare him with a chauffeur who drove steadily for months and then drove one over a precipice. Churchill had no political or personal following. As an anonymous commentator wrote in *The Times* in November 1920: 'His first party will still have no good said of him, his second believes him to be hankering after his first love, and latterly he has been advertising for a new Centre Party which is to combine the charms of the other two. But even if this third match came off and then turned out ill, Mr. Churchill would not be greatly embarrassed, for wherever he is there is the party.'

In the event, however, Churchill was indeed 'greatly embarrassed' when the match was broken off by the other party and he was left, totally alone and grievously exposed, in a political No Man's Land.

In 1919 Churchill could point to many conspicuous achievements; among them, however, was not that of inspiring trust or notable affection—particularly in the Conservative Party, where Bonar Law eyed him with conspicuous reservations.

Churchill's closest friend in the Government was F. E. Smith, now transformed into Lord Birkenhead and Lord Chancellor at the age of forty-five—a step described by *The Times* as 'carrying a joke too far'. Birkenhead was probably the most brilliant individual in public life, 'the cleverest man in the kingdom', as Beaverbrook described him. Sardonic, sharp-witted, and irreverent, he was the best of company when in the mood, adored by his family and close friends, and a superb speaker. But his public virtues were not as apparent as his deficiencies. After a spectacular start he had failed to reach the heights that had seemed open to him. Like Lloyd George, he had no real roots. His cynical, cavalier attitudes made more enemies than admirers. If, in Cabinet, he was a silent and respected member, whose eventual opinion carried great weight, and if he was deeply loved by those who knew him best, in public he gave a rasping, intolerant, bullying and unprincipled impression. Even in an age of hard-living politicians, Birkenhead's drinking and extravagance stood out conspicuously.

Austen Chamberlain was in many ways the most attractive of the Conservatives; certainly, in most respects, he was the most attractive of all the Chamberlains. But although he faithfully emulated his father's appearance and revered his memory, there was a vast gulf between Joseph and Austen. Indeed, acutely conscious of the ill-feeling that remained over his father's political action, Austen Chamberlain sought a reputation for honourable conduct that rendered him peculiarly vulnerable and ineffective. Controversy exists about the author of the famous phrase 'Austen always played the game and always lost it'—Birkenhead is the most likely author, although it has also been credited to Churchill—but it had substantial justice. And, in spite of much *gravitas* and earnestness, there was always something faintly preposterous, if also rather touching, about the frock-coated, top-hatted, monocled, Austen.

Curzon was, on the face of things, even more preposterous, but he was in fact one of the most complex and deeply interesting figures of modern politics. Although born in rich circumstances, his upbringing had been a hard and loveless one. He suffered from a lifelong weakness of the spine, which required wearing an uncomfortable steel brace. He was rarely free from pain, a fact that no doubt contributed substantially to the stiffness, formality and on occasion downright pomposity of his public manner. But perhaps there were other, deeper, causes for this. For all his qualities and achievements, he lacked constancy of purpose and self-confidence to a surprising degree.

He was always threatening resignation, always complaining of the treatment of his colleagues, yet always irresolute. As Churchill has tartly commented: 'He was too much concerned with what might be said about things, and too little with the things themselves.' There was truth in this jibe, but it did not contain the whole truth.

Curzon's record was impressive by any standards. His careers at Eton and Oxford had been outstanding, and he had entered the House of Commons in 1886 almost as of right. He had travelled widely and thought much; he had, above all, written much (one book on Persia ran to some 1,300 pages). Nor did he lack shrewdness; he devoted one section of an enormous book on the Far East to an unknown hamlet in Indo-China called Dien Bien Phu which had, as he pointed out at length, substantial strategic importance. He was in every respect a formidably equipped man. Yet it all added up to surprisingly little. The House of Commons found him a bore. He never rose above junior office, until, in 1898, he was appointed Viceroy of India. That searing experience has been related.[1] But, like Milner, he had risen again. In 1915, at the age of fifty-six, he had held senior office for the first time. From October 1919 he was Foreign Secretary, and one of the best equipped of all modern holders of that office. But, again, it added up to not very much in terms of real influence. Throughout his strange career Curzon eagerly coveted and sought after eminence. Few men have worked harder to achieve it, nor have recovered more completely from severe misfortunes and disappointments. But the curious fact is that at no time was he ever taken seriously as a politician of the first order. There was something in his manner, his seriousness, his celebrated meanness, and self-important grandeur that made him an object of ribaldry rather than respect.

Balfour, the other leading Conservative in the Coalition, was perhaps even more remote than Chamberlain, Birkenhead and Curzon from the political rank and file. His detachment from the political hurly-burly, which had always been marked, had become greatly accentuated by the passing years. Still bland, affable, charming, remote, and cold-blooded, Balfour moved on a different plane from the new men who gave the Coalition their Parliamentary power.

*

This Parliament has become known to history as being composed of

[1] See Volume I, 215–16.

'hard-faced men who look as though they had done well out of the war'; the phrase was that of the then unknown Stanley Baldwin, but it was echoed by others. Austen Chamberlain described them as 'a selfish, swollen lot'. Some historians have demonstrated that, statistically, this Parliament did not differ greatly from its predecessors. As usual, such statistics are irrelevant. There was clearly something about that overwhelming Coalition majority that observers found loathsome;[1] yet it was this body that was to turn against the Coalition with revulsion, and permanently to affect the course of British politics in the inter-war years.

For most of 1919 Lloyd George was in Paris, and the main burden of his activity was directed towards the settlement of the peace treaty in particular and international affairs in general. A substantial part of the Foreign Office was moved to Paris, and the processes of Cabinet Government were rendered infinitely more complicated by the frequent absences not merely of the Prime Minister but the Foreign Secretary, and often the Chancellor of the Exchequer as well. This was perhaps inevitable in the circumstances, but the results were unfortunate. Almost at once, the Government was plunged into a series of domestic problems from which it extricated itself with some difficulty and without enhanced reputation.

The first shock—and it was a very real and serious one—came over demobilisation. The mood of the Army had been manifested quickly after the Armistice by the refusal of troops, in camps at Dover and Folkestone, to embark for France and by the burning of Luton Town Hall. It was a difficult situation for the Government as peace had not been signed, but the mood of the Army was ugly. The principal cause was the decision to grant priority releases not only to men with jobs awaiting them in certain trades but also to men on leave who could produce written offers of employment. In effect, this meant that priority discharges were being given to men who had been in the Army

---

[1] This was the adjective employed to the author by the late Sir Edward Fellowes, Clerk of the House of Commons, who entered the service of the House in 1919, and retired in 1962. These people—particularly on the Conservative side—did not disappear at the end of this Parliament, as Duff Cooper, elected in 1924, has related. 'I soon discovered that the Die-Hards were not the stern, unbending Tories of my imagination, the descendants of those who had supported Pitt against Fox, Wellington against Grey, and Disraeli against Gladstone. They were mostly business men who had recently made fortunes, often by methods that did not invite close inspection.' (Duff Cooper: *Old Men Forget*, 141.)

for a short time, and militated against those who had been under arms for a longer period. The Government's plans were justifiable in the national interest, but hardly skilfully designed to placate a citizen army aching for release. Lloyd George blamed Milner; Robertson wondered if he could rely on any troops to quell the disturbances. The impasse was resolved by Churchill, who took over the War Office in January and swiftly ordered that demobilisation was to be firmly based on length of service. The disturbances subsided, although there were further isolated episodes in the summer.

Matters were not improved by the lavish generosity with which Parliament rewarded the commanders of the war. Peerages, honours, and substantial financial rewards showered upon the deserving and undeserving alike. The widow of General Maude received £25,000, a particular grant which received the attention of Philip Snowden in *Forward*. The resentment which these generous rewards to the senior officer class caused in the Army was profound, and fully merited, when they are compared with the plight of disabled ex-soldiers, war widows, and orphans. In itself, it was a small episode, but it was symptomatic of an attitude which had been acceptable before 1914 but which was now not. The refusal of the Glasgow Federation of Discharged Soldiers to admit ex-officers was an extreme reaction, but understandable.[1] At the outset, the hope of many veterans that the comradeship of the trenches would be carried into peace was compromised. Back to 1914, again.

This anger in the Army coincided with widespread industrial unrest, and the Government—and particularly Lloyd George—took fright. The miners, the railwaymen, and the transport workers revived the 'Triple Industrial Alliance' in February. The engineers were also in a belligerent mood, and in Glasgow a series of stoppages culminated in a general strike in the area which had violent scenes, caused the dispatch of tanks and troops, and lasted from January 27th until February 11th. Among those arrested were James Maxton and Emanuel Shinwell, of whom much more was to be heard. By February 1919 the startled and apprehensive Government found itself coping with striking soldiers, a formidable nationwide federation of trade unions capable of inflicting virtually a national strike, and rioting in

[1] It was characteristic of the mood of the Government that, on June 6th, the Minister of Labour, Sir Robert Horne, declared that the Glasgow Federation was 'now in touch with the Russian bolsheviks', and likely to form a Soviet.

Glasgow, Edinburgh and Belfast. But, except in Glasgow—where the Red Flag was flown from the flagstaff of the Town Hall, and the leaders of the rising were arrested and imprisoned—the Government acted cautiously and sensibly. Nevertheless, they were already reacting to situations and problems at home on a piecemeal basis, while their Prime Minister and senior Ministers were occupied at Versailles with the future map of Europe.

The measures taken by the Government were essentially ad hoc. Milner told Henry Wilson on February 5th that 'we are in chaos in England as regards these strikes, which under Lloyd George's régime are being dealt with by every sort of man and every sort of department, each acting on a different principle from the others'. The minimum wage level was maintained until September 1920, although it had been originally designed to expire six months after the Armistice. An out-of-work donation to ex-servicemen and unemployed civilian workers was extended beyond the original plan to confine it to firms working for the Ministry of Munitions. A Coal Commission, presided over by Mr. Justice Sankey, was set up to examine the grievances of the coalminers. Lloyd George also called—at the end of February—a National Industrial Conference, a characteristic dramatic and futile step, but one that at least served to lower the temperature for the time being. The fact that the Government consistently ignored the Conference's recommendations resulted in the eventual withdrawal of the trade union members, and marked another stage in the growing disillusionment of organised labour with the Coalition.

The Sankey Commission's final Report—issued in June—disclosed the gulf between the views of the miners and the owners. The Government had already approved a compromise wage increase; it now firmly rejected any idea of nationalisation of the mines, and in this seemed to be going back on its acceptance of the interim report in March in which Sankey had recommended representation of the workers in the running of the mines, and either nationalisation or some other system of unification 'by national purchase and/or joint control'. This was now reduced to acceptance of a one-man minority report by a member of the Sankey Commission, Sir Arthur Duckham, for amalgamation of collieries into district companies, with a minority of workers' representatives and a limit on profits. The miners indignantly rejected this solution, and the possibility of a nationwide coal strike now grew nearer.

Meanwhile, the railwaymen had been active. In the dispute between the Government and the railwaymen the principal difficulty was caused by the fact that the latter were convinced that after decontrol the owners would not increase wages. The Government's offer was a fair one; the minimum wage was to rise to forty shillings a week but—given the sharp rise in the cost of living since 1914—this was not a substantial improvement on the pre-war level of eighteen shillings. The failure seems to have been essentially one of communication, for which the somewhat rasping manner of the President of the Board of Trade, Sir Auckland Geddes, must bear considerable responsibility. The railway strike began on September 26th, and on October 5th the Government agreed to maintain the existing system for one more year.

These compromises and devices for putting off serious examination of the problems may have been unheroic, but they were successful in damping down the somewhat revolutionary tone that had been evident earlier in the year. The continuance of the wartime boom kept up wages and kept down unemployment, and the apparent success of responsible labour leadership succeeded even more effectively in diminishing the influence of the extremists. A special Trades Union Congress was summoned in December to consider the particular case of the miners, and it was resolved to undertake a publicity campaign in favour of nationalisation rather than to strike. In March 1920 the T.U.C. voted overwhelmingly against a proposal by the Miners' Federation for a general strike; the Government reciprocated by granting a wage increase to offset increases in the cost of living.

Nothing had been solved by these essentially political measures, and the Government was concurrently eagerly dismembering the government machinery that was essential to a controlled economy. But the Government had at least bought time in which tempers could cool, and had divided the unions. It remained to be seen what use it could make of the opportunity thus created.

*

No international treaty of modern times has come under such widespread criticism and abuse as the Treaty of Versailles, which was concluded on June 28th, 1919.[1]

Lloyd George's position—although perhaps not as difficult as that

[1] Lloyd George was persuaded that it would be appropriate to write to the King informing him of the fact, which he did with some reluctance; the letter was conveyed by air to the King by J. C. C. Davidson, Bonar Law's private secretary. (Davidson: *Memoirs of a Conservative*, 92.)

of Clemenceau—was difficult enough. The bulk of the Coalition M.P.s looked to him for severe reparations on Germany, and reacted with alarm to any suggestions of leniency. Northcliffe, now in sad decline, and embittered with Lloyd George for not including him on the British delegation, kept up a running fire of criticism in *The Times* and the *Daily Mail*. The eventual Treaty was considerably more lenient towards Germany than the bulk of the Coalition supporters had expected or wanted; yet, within a relatively short time, they were echoing the vehement criticisms of J. M. Keynes against its severity.

The proceedings of the Conference were a triumph for Lloyd George and a disaster for President Wilson. In fact, Lloyd George's attitudes were very close to those of Wilson, and he was an infinitely more accomplished negotiator than the American. Wilson's lack of experience and understanding of the details were painfully exposed, and matters were not improved by the attitudes and actions of Herbert Hoover, who sabotaged a reasonable proposal put forward by the British to maintain shipping controls and establish an international administration to supersede the blockade. Hoover vetoed the proposal out of hand and ordered that nothing should be done about feeding Germany until he arrived in Europe. Three months elapsed before the Supreme Economic Council was set up, with him in the dominant role. The new organisation was no improvement on that originally suggested, and three vital months had been wasted. Hoover's disagreeable personality did not assist matters. An agitation began in Britain against what was called 'the hunger blockade'.

Here, Lloyd George was in a very real difficulty. The Germans had been sinking the world's transport shipping up to the Armistice, and there was a severe shortage of ships. The American farming and business interests were putting strong pressure for the resumption of exports to Europe; the Germans pointed out the difficulties of paying for the food and insisted that its supply should be definitely assured by British or American credits before handing over their mercantile marine to the Allies; the French were all for maintaining the blockade to bring pressure upon the Germans. There was another factor. The only tangible asset in the Reichsbank was the gold reserve of some £120 million, and the French Government had its eye firmly fixed upon this valuable asset; the prospect of it disappearing to America to pay for food was not relished.

The deadlock was broken by Lloyd George, in a masterly display of negotiating skill, at the Supreme War Council on 8th March. The French eventually withdrew their main objections and the Germans were more forthcoming over the ships. By April the food supplies were entering Germany. Difficulties remained, but the deadlock had been broken.

Over the League of Nations Covenant Lloyd George was less successful. The British saw the League essentially as an instrument for international conciliation, and their proposals—which had been carefully prepared—were practical and realistic. Wilson, who ignored a studied hint by Lloyd George that heads of delegations should not sit on the League of Nations Committee, became its chairman. His interest was less in organisation than in establishing a code of international ethics. Furthermore, his own isolationism and that of his advisers led to serious omissions in the Covenant. Any matter which by international law was solely within the jurisdiction of a party to a dispute was excluded; French plans for a permanent international General Staff and commission to watch over armaments were rejected by Wilson as an interference with national sovereignty; Hoover's opposition to international economic controls had been based on the same attitude. The result was a compromise document that, on the whole, leaned more to the British interpretation than to Wilson's, but which contained several important ambiguities. The most crucial point concerned the guarantee by the participants of 'political independence and territorial integrity to great and small alike'. The British opposed any automatic guarantee, and it was decided that in cases of aggression the Executive Council would advise upon the matter. The French text, however, used the word *aviser*, or 'look to', which left them with the conviction that the League was pledged to guarantee the security of its members.

To say this is not to dismiss Wilson's vision. The concept of the League owed much to the contributions of Norman Angell, Lord Robert Cecil, and Smuts, but it was Wilson who was the only major international leader to grasp it and espouse it with genuine enthusiasm. The League had immense potentialities. Tragically, the British and French, upon whose support the League's future rested, were unexcited. 'Nobody wished any ill to the League', Duff Cooper later recorded of his then colleagues in the Foreign Office, 'but few believed it could do any good.'[1] Hankey—who was seriously considered

[1] Duff Cooper, op. cit., 157.

as Secretary-General—also reflected official disdain for this idealistic experiment. Wilson returned to America to wage an exhausting and heroic national campaign to secure the ratification of the Treaty and American endorsement of the League, in the course of which he suffered a paralytic stroke. For the remainder of his Presidency he was a broken man. The Senate did not ratify Versailles, and the United States remained aloof from the League, from Europe, and from foreign entanglements generally. 'The people are tired', Walter Lippmann wrote in *The New Republic*, 'tired of noise, tired of politics, tired of inconvenience, tired of greatness, and longing for a place where the world is quiet and where all trouble seems dead leaves, and spent waves riot in doubtful dreams of dreams.'

America's refusal to join the League was a major misfortune, but not a disaster. The United States was potentially a major world power, but only potentially. American power and influence were insignificant, and in either economic or military terms she was not to be compared with Britain or France. The disaster to the League lay not in American aloofness, but in British and French stupidity. Back to 1914.

The new boundaries in Europe provoked further strains between the British, French and Americans. The Wilsonian concept of 'self-determination' became somewhat difficult to define in the highly confused situation that followed the collapse of the German, Austro-Hungarian and Ottoman Empires. The delineation of the new Polish State and that of Czechoslovakia proved particularly difficult, and the French proposal for a separate Rhineland state was vehemently opposed by the British and Americans. Eventually agreement was reached by authorising the extension of Allied occupation of the Rhineland for fifteen years and its permanent demilitarisation.

It was over reparations, however, that the most severe difficulties arose. The British representatives on the Reparations Committee—the Australian Prime Minister W. M. Hughes, Lord Cunliffe, and Lord Sumner—put forward extraordinarily unrealistic estimates of Germany's ability and liability to pay. Lloyd George could not accept their figures—which at one point suggested that Germany could and should pay some £24,000 million in a generation. The Treasury believed that £3,000 million was a more realistic sum; the estimate of the then obscure J. M. Keynes was £5,000 million. Lloyd George persuaded the Council that the Treaty should merely state the principle of Germany's liability to pay and that the sum should be fixed after a detailed examination of her resources.

But while Wilson deserves better of history than he has received, the view that an innocent, peace-loving, sincere American President was taken for a ride by a guileful, cynical, selfish, narrow-minded clique of wily European politicians cannot stand up to any serious examination. What had been painfully exposed was Wilson's ignorance of Europe and of the realities of international diplomacy, and the sheer impracticability of many of his proposals. But there was a deeper reason. The Americans—and not least their President—were intoxicated by their arrival on the world stage. The actual contribution of the United States to the Allied victory had been important, but the Americans developed a grotesquely exaggerated estimation of its significance, and assumed that Wilson was negotiating from a position of great strength and could dictate terms. The realities of the situation were quite different, and Wilson was in fact in a relatively weak negotiating position against the British and French. In his message to the Senate, Wilson emphasised that the League was not 'a counsel of perfection [but] . . . a plain counsel of necessity', but he added that 'America may be said to have just reached her majority as a world power', which was simply not the case. And there was also truth in the statement of Senator William E. Borah, a vehement opponent of the League, 'that we are a part of the European turmoils and conflicts from the time we enter this League'.

The Treaty was approved virtually unanimously in Parliament. It was not long before new attitudes manifested themselves. MacDonald —still out of Parliament—was one of the principal opponents of the Treaty in the Labour Party. Later in the year the former Treasury official, John Maynard Keynes, published *The Economic Consequences of the Peace*, a brilliant and mischievous philippic in which the American President was mercilessly held up to ridicule and the European members of the War Council accused of imposing a Carthaginian peace upon Germany, which was vital to the future of Europe. Keynes became a national figure overnight.[1] His book had an enormous sale and was excessively venerated on all sides; its long-

[1] 'About 1922 the world suddenly got very full of arrogant and languid young people of uncertain sex engaged in the new Bloomsbury sport of expressing their bored yet intolerant confidence that art and brains ended with them and Maynard Keynes' (Douglas Jerrold: *Georgian Adventure*, 240).

term effects on British attitudes towards the Versailles Treaty and the League can hardly be exaggerated. His diatribe appeared *after* disillusionment had set in; it followed an existing trend rather than creating a new one. But it was a vitally important factor in the growth of what Etienne Mantoux subsequently called *meaculpisme* over the Treaty, which was to have baleful consequences in the 1930s. In Germany, the new Weimar Republic was saddled with the double stigma of having sued for peace and of having accepted an odious Treaty. The Treaty of Versailles created enduring grievances in both Germany and France, and fostered guilt and uncertainty in Britain. In Britain it suddenly became fashionable to deride, and be ashamed of, the Treaty of Versailles. France became the new menace to international peace and order, and Lloyd George her ally. Thus, by a remarkable shift of public attitude, Lloyd George's triumph swiftly turned into reproach and even obloquy. And, from other quarters, events were marching down relentlessly upon him and the Coalition Government which were further to diminish its stature and authority.

*

Throughout 1919, while Lloyd George was negotiating peace in Paris and his colleagues were coping with industrial unrest at home, the British Government was involved in a complex and embarrassing consequence of the war that brought it no credit and whose management provides us with an instructive illustration of the processes of the Coalition.

When the Soviet Government ended the war with Germany in December 1917, counter-revolutionary forces were raised by Generals Kornilov and Denikin, which were supported by the Allies. In the July of 1918 the British had landed forces at Archangel to protect substantial supplies already landed there. These actions were perfectly legitimate in the context of the war, but with its conclusion the position of the British in Russia at once became more equivocal.

The situation in Russia was, in any event, somewhat confused by November 1918. In the north, there was an Allied force of some 15,000 troops—of whom half were British—at Murmansk. In Siberia there were over 100,000 Czech troops, and some British, French, American and Japanese elements. In all, there were some 1,200 British troops in Siberia. The various governments in the area had been concentrated into a single Directorate at Omsk, whose War Minister was Admiral

A. V. Kolchak. In South Russia, General Denikin commanded a substantial army of over 30,000 men, which had received—and continued
to receive for some time—very heavy British assistance in material and
advisers.

Up to this stage there was no question of 'intervention' in Russia.
But in October 1918 some significant steps had been taken in this
direction. The British commander at Murmansk had been ordered to
take certain bases that clearly could only be of use against the Bolsheviks, and on October 18th the Cabinet in effect ignored Lloyd
George by deciding to retain the force at Murmansk, to recognise the
Omsk government, to maintain the force in Siberia, and also to
increase the scale of intervention by occupying the Baku-Batum
railway and stepping up supplies to Denikin. Three days later Kolchak
was declared head of the Omsk government. At this Cabinet Lloyd
George's opposition to any crusade against Bolshevism had been made
very plain; what had also become plain was that his views on this
matter were not shared by his colleagues. Smuts had been particularly
vigorous in his denunciation of Bolshevism, and the views of Milner
and Sir Henry Wilson were clear enough. Churchill was not at this
point a member of the Cabinet, but his views as Minister of Munitions
were of importance, and his alarm at 'the foul baboonery' of Bolshevism was very marked. Thus, although the Government had not
decided to intervene in Russia, it had decided not to reduce its
existing commitment of troops, and, by deciding to maintain Denikin,
had incurred a moral commitment of some importance.

On December 10th Lloyd George initiated another discussion in
the Cabinet on the issue of Russia, again making his personal views
very clear. The Foreign Office submitted a memorandum that stated
in effect that although there was substantial opposition in the country
to a major military intervention, any new governments set up under
British protection must be supported and maintained. Milner and
Wilson argued strongly against the withdrawal of the Murmansk
force, and Curzon said that the British were in honour bound to
remain until the anti-Bolshevik forces could properly organise themselves. Thus, the status quo was to be maintained. The troops stayed,
the blockade remained, and Denikin received his supplies of British
surplus war material. The Royal Navy policed the Baltic and the
Black Sea.

Early in January the division in the Cabinet became more marked.

On January 10th Churchill strongly opposed any suggestion of a withdrawal of men and support from the Omsk government. On the 16th, at a meeting of the Council of Ten in Paris, Lloyd George made a vigorous speech opposing Allied intervention in the Russian civil war, and suggesting the invitation of representatives of all sides to Paris. Wilson supported him, but the French and the Italians were not enthusiastic. On the 21st Wilson proposed that the representatives should meet after they had ended hostilities with representatives of the Great Powers on Princes' Island (Prinkipo) in the Sea of Marmara. The proposal was approved by the Council, and turned down by the White Governments of Siberia and North Russia, while the Red conditions for attendance were unacceptable. On February 12th, when the new Parliament met for the first time, the Prinkipo proposal came under strong criticism from the Conservative benches; in reply, Lloyd George put the case against intervention with vigour and skill.

In the Cabinet, however, his views were not prevailing. As soon as Churchill had gone to the War Office he had sent out a circular to station commanders enquiring if their men would accept service overseas, 'especially Russia'; the reply was to the effect that the men would muster for draft overseas except in Russia. It was accordingly necessary in future to have to raise volunteers for any forces in Russia. At Cabinet meetings on February 12th and 13th the gulf in attitudes between Churchill and Lloyd George became wider. Churchill wanted the Japanese to aid Kolchak, the British to declare war on the Bolsheviks and send volunteers to Russia, and accordingly 'crush' Bolshevism for ever. On February 14th he put his case personally to Wilson in Paris, who was hostile. On the following day Churchill put his plan to the Council of Ten, and Lloyd George—in London—hurriedly checked Churchill's activities.

Public debate on the situation was becoming more noticeable. The Labour leaders had never been enthusiastic about the Bolsheviks after the fall of Kerensky, but both they and the Asquithian Liberals now began to express concern about the British position. The Miners' Federation led the way; the Triple Alliance followed, and the T.U.C. followed this joint lead in opposition to the intervention. On March 3rd Churchill covered his flanks neatly by stating that 'in this theatre we have no special British interests of any sort to serve. . . . We are simply discharging a duty to the League of Nations . . . and endeavouring to prevent new areas of the world from degenerating into the welter of Bolshevik anarchy.' On the Conservative side, however, the Government was being urged not merely to maintain its position but actually to increase its assistance. This was in any event being done; volunteers and millions of pounds' worth of munitions were being sent to Denikin by Churchill. Already, the War Office was interpreting the decisions of the Cabinet in a vigorous spirit. On April 9th the Foreign Office joined in by issuing a horrifying list of alleged Red atrocities in a solemn Parliamentary Paper. Yet a week later, in the House of Commons, Lloyd George made one of his most powerful and effective speeches against intervention in the internal affairs of another country. On the previous day the General Staff had circulated its detailed plans for an offensive in North Russia!

It was now becoming clear even to observers outside the Cabinet that the Government was speaking with two voices. What was not sufficiently appreciated was the extent to which Churchill was operating not merely independently of the Cabinet but in some instances actually contrary to its decisions.[1] Nevertheless, enough was realised to make Churchill the particular object of the steadily mounting criticism in the Labour and Liberal parties of the enterprise. Nor was this unjustified. On June 14th Churchill and Henry Wilson secured Cabinet approval—both Lloyd George and Bonar Law being absent—for the offensive in the North on the grounds that it was essential for the preservation of the British force. Unfortunately for their plans, Kolchak at once suffered the first of a series of heavy defeats; the Cabinet reconsidered the offensive on June 27th, and assented to it when assured that it was vital for the preservation of the British force.

Up to this point the Government had been sustained by two hopes; the first was that a joint Allied policy would emerge from Paris, and the second was that the Russian situation would happily solve itself by the defeat of the Bolsheviks. By August 1919 it was evident that both these hopes had been dashed. Lloyd George, in May, urged the Supreme Council to aid Kolchak to make the Omsk regime the 'Government of all Russia'; any chances this overture had were

[1] Perhaps the best example of this occurred in May. On the 14th the Cabinet expressly rejected a proposal by Churchill to form additional units of the Slavo-British Legion. Churchill, after consulting Balfour, decided that it was a strictly War Office decision, and put the matter in hand. The Cabinet was informed of this *fait accompli* on June 11th.

dashed by Kolchak's military disasters.[1] Churchill put up a vigorous rearguard action, but the most that he could secure was the granting of a final batch of assistance to Denikin. By August 15th the Cabinet had decided to end all other intervention. But the War Office continued to assist Kolchak until October, and British troops were not withdrawn until the late autumn. The naval blockade continued until the winter, and on November 20th the Cabinet decided not to renew it in the spring. As late as September 25th, Churchill was still urging the Cabinet to approve 'war upon the Bolshevists with every means in our power . . . with a coherent plan on all fronts at once'. When, in the middle of October, it seemed that Denikin—whose forces were in the suburbs of Petrograd—might win, he issued a public letter that declared that 'There are now good reasons for believing that the tyranny of Bolshevism will be overthrown by the Russian nation'. It was, however, a false dawn. On November 8th Lloyd George, in a speech at the Guildhall, pronounced finally and definitely against intervention. On January 27th, 1920, the Cabinet was faced with a request for a new anti-Bolshevik combination: it decided that 'we have neither the men, the money, nor the credit, and public opinion is altogether opposed to such a course'.

Certainly the Labour opposition to the intervention had been vigorous. The party conference in June had passed condemnatory resolutions, and advocating 'the unreserved use of . . . political and industrial power' to change the policy of the Government. Those Labour leaders who opposed direct action were coldly received; the young Herbert Morrison described the intervention as 'a war against the organisation of the Trade Union movement itself, and as such should be resisted with the full political and industrial power of the whole Trade Union movement'. In September the T.U.C. had followed suit, and had set up the National 'Hands Off Russia' Committee. It has been argued[2] that this agitation had no effect on the Cabinet's decision, which had been taken before the activities of the Labour movement had developed. This is factually correct, but the nature of Labour opposition had been apparent long before the resolutions were carried, and it was an important element in strengthening the positions of Lloyd George and Austen Chamberlain in particular in the Cabinet. Bonar Law had acquiesced uneasily in

[1] Kolchak was captured and killed in January 1920.
[2] See S. R. Graubard: *British Labour and the Russian Revolution*, 82.

the intervention; his gradual shift against it was a decisive stage in the development of Cabinet re-assessment of the policy. Perhaps the clamour in the country had no bearing upon the decisions of the Cabinet, but it is difficult to accept this in its entirety, while rejecting the bold claims made at the time and subsequently by Labour leaders.

The entire episode did nothing to bring credit upon the Government. As Churchill had pointed out at the very beginning, it had a choice between full-scale intervention or withdrawal, and that any middle course would be the worst policy of all: '. . . he felt that if we did not decide upon a policy we should have a succession of disasters, followed by wholesale massacres and the extermination in one way or another of the whole of the people who had been supporting us. If we were unable to support the Russians effectively, it would be far better to take a decision now to quit and face the consequences.'[1] Nevertheless, given the prevailing political feeling at the time, the Government had some justification in continuing assistance so long as there was a fair chance of a White victory. If the gamble had come off, the policy would have had its own justification. It was not until the late summer of 1919 that majority opinion in the Cabinet definitely came round to Lloyd George's side and against Churchill.

By the policy of half-hearted intervention in Russia the Coalition had earned the hostility and contempt of Left and Right alike. Lloyd George was attacked by Labour for publicly opposing intervention and yet continuing with it, while he was under fire from the Conservatives for not seizing a chance of destroying Bolshevism once and for all. What the episode did reveal very clearly was that Lloyd George was no longer master in his own house, and that his personal influence, once so dominant, now stood for little when he was isolated in his own Cabinet. If the melancholy story of the British intervention in Russia brought no credit on the Government as a whole, it did even more harm to Lloyd George's already falling reputation, while Churchill became a particular target for Labour and Liberal vilification. The latter censure was rather more fair than the former, but it is not the least of the perils of personal government that all censure tends to concentrate upon its principal and self-styled exponent.

Thus, if 1919 was not a good year for the Coalition, it was an even

[1] War Cabinet Minutes, February 13th, 1919.

worse one for the Prime Minister, both in public esteem and in his control over his Cabinet.

*

As has already been noted, not the least of the crucial results of the 1918 election had been the virtual extinction of the old Irish National-ist Party and the triumph of Sinn Fein. The victorious seventy-three members refused to go to Westminster, and met at the Mansion House in Dublin as the Irish Parliament, Dail Eireann. On January 21st they issued a declaration of independence and ratified the establish-ment of the Irish Republic that had been publicly proclaimed outside the General Post Office in Dublin on Easter Monday, 1916. They then made an appeal for recognition by the participants in the Peace Conference at Versailles. To the British, loudly adhering to the principle of 'self-determination' for small nations, this was an acute embarrassment. It was to become something substantially more than an embarrassment. The Paris attempt came to nothing, but the Irish Race Convention in Philadelphia sent a committee of three to Paris and Ireland to report back, and produced a bitter indictment of British rule that was written into the Congressional Record. De Valera visited America in 1919 to further the Irish cause, and raised some five million dollars for the Irish National Loan, although he did not escape some embroilment in the labyrinthine viciousness of Irish-American politics.

Meanwhile, the British were confronted by the uncomfortable fact that the self-styled Irish Government was usurping many of the functions of the administration, including a Ministry of Defence. Funds were raised by Michael Collins, the Minister of Finance, and arms and ammunition were smuggled into Ireland from England; the famed Volunteers became the Army of the Republic, the Irish Republican Army (I.R.A.). It was not long before it began to operate. On the day that the Dail had declared independence, two armed policemen were killed at Solohead, County Tipperary, while attempt-ing to prevent the capture of a consignment of gelignite. They were the first victims of the events that were to be described with charac-teristic understatement as 'The Troubles'.

The first priority for the I.R.A. was to secure weapons, and all the initial attacks—principally directed against the Royal Irish Con-stabulary—were for this purpose. Small barracks were so consistently attacked that many had to be abandoned, and gradually the country-side fell into the control of the Nationalists, who became experts in the skilful use of the ambush. The I.R.A. technique was, in the words of Collins, 'an organized and bold guerrilla warfare', and set-piece battles on the lines of the Easter Rising, which Collins knew he could not win, were eschewed. It was not long before the R.I.C.'s morale began to drop sharply. Recruitment slumped, and resignations rose. This was the first victory for the new movement, and an important one. In 1919—which subsequently looked in retrospect a quiet year—there were eighteen murders and seventy-seven armed attacks, which included an attempt to ambush and assassinate the Viceroy, Lord French, on the outskirts of Dublin. The weapon of the boycott was revived, specifically against the R.I.C., and with considerable success.

The British Government decided to meet force with force. Sinn Fein was declared illegal in August 1919 and in September the Dail was also proclaimed. In March 1920 Sir Nevil Macready, Commissioner of the Metropolitan Police, was appointed Commander-in-Chief of the British forces in Ireland. As it was urgently necessary to increase the size of the R.I.C., recruits were sought in England, mainly among ex-soldiers. This was a creation of Churchill's, originally described as the 'Special Emergency Gendarmerie'. By the summer of 1920 they were arriving in Ireland, and were equipped with surplus khaki uniforms with the black belts and dark-green caps of the R.I.C. They were dubbed the 'Black and Tans', after a famous pack of hounds in County Limerick. In addition, another 1,000 men were recruited from among ex-officers in England, the Auxiliary Division of the R.I.C., the 'Auxis', who had a dark-blue uniform. The Black and Tans were paid ten shillings a day, and the Auxis a pound. Churchill subsequently claimed that they 'were selected from a great press of applicants on account of their intelligence, their characters, and their record in the war'. All other estimates have been considerably less favourable.

This decision to fight the I.R.A. was not surprising when the composition of the Coalition is considered. Bonar Law, Long and Birkenhead had been vigorous supporters of Ulster in the grim crisis of 1912–14; the Chief of the Imperial General Staff was Henry Wilson, who had always been a vehement supporter of Ulster and who had played an important part in the fatal decision to impose conscription in 1918; Churchill, who seriously misjudged the scale and nature of the situation, was certainly not a man to bow to rebellion; and Lloyd George himself was fully prepared to follow the course they charted.

The Irish rebellion developed slowly, and this fact reflected the divisions that still existed within the nationalist movement. Collins, who directed the I.R.A., was the only leading nationalist who was a member of the Irish Republican Brotherhood. His most open opponent in the movement was Cathal Brugha (hitherto known as Charles Burgess) who was a passionate fighter but lacked Collins' organising genius and subtlety—and, as events were to prove, his ability to compromise. De Valera endeavoured to mediate between them, without success. Arthur Griffith, the founder of Sinn Fein, to whom the example of Hungary's independence from Austria under the Dual Monarchy was always predominant sought freedom for Ireland through peaceful rather than violent means. He was Minister of Home Affairs in the Dail Government; De Valera was President (succeeding Brugha after his escape from Lincoln Jail in 1919), and Collins had become Minister of Defence.

Ireland raged throughout 1920 and most of 1921. The British forces in Ireland—military and police—numbered at least 40,000; the I.R.A. had about 15,000, but it has been claimed that there were never more than 5,000 men on active service at one time. Whatever their numbers, they sufficed. Losses have never been fully assessed, but one authority gives figures of 752 Irish killed and 866 wounded between January 1919 and July 1921, with the British losses put at 176 police and 54 soldiers killed, 251 police and 118 soldiers wounded. But the numbers were less relevant than the circumstances. On 'Bloody Sunday'— November 21st, 1920—fourteen British officers were hauled from their beds and shot by the I.R.A., in some cases in the presence of their families. That afternoon a party of Black and Tans opened fire into a football crowd in Dublin, killing twelve people and wounding sixty. Perhaps the burning of Cork by the Black and Tans in December 1920 was the most notorious single episode of all, while to Irishmen the death, after seventy-four days of hunger-fasting, of the Lord Mayor of Cork—Terence MacSwiney—in Brixton Jail was an example of English callousness. On October 9th, 1920, Lloyd George declared that 'we have murder by the throat'; other Ministers made frequent similar statements, Birkenhead promising that 'we shall use force and yet more force'; the situation only deteriorated further, and English opinion began to veer sharply against a Government that could neither make war nor achieve peace.

The fierce debates on the Irish situation brought into sudden and dramatic prominence a dashing, handsome, and highly articulate Coalitionist back-bencher. Oswald Mosley had been the youngest Member of the Commons when he had been elected for Harrow in 1918 at the age of twenty-two. His appearance was striking, he was clearly of a highly independent nature, he was rich, and he had swiftly developed into a most formidable debater. His genius at mob-oratory was as yet unknown. Shocked by the excesses of the Black and Tans, and contemptuous of the Government's blatant evasiveness on the issue of reprisals, he went for the Irish Secretary, Hamar Greenwood, Churchill, and the Prime Minister himself with a sharpness and skill that reminded older Members and observers of Lord Randolph in his prime, and others of the young Lloyd George. He crossed the Floor to assail Ministers to their faces, and was relentless in his probings and attacks. It was evident that the war generation had thrown up at least one politician of elemental fire and outstanding ability. It was also apparent to some shrewd observers that his personality did not lack elements of arrogance and impatience. It was not long before the Conservatives of Harrow became embarrassed, and then enraged, by the insulting independence of their Member. But, at the age of twenty-five, 'Tom' Mosley had definitely arrived. Married to a daughter of Lord Curzon, untroubled by money matters, fascinating to women and with an air of complete self-control and manifest ambition, he was suddenly seen as the most exciting prospect in British politics. The laurels were to wither quickly, but in spite of subsequent follies and worse, at least the Irish never forgot that he had been their fiery and dedicated champion against the evil obscenity of the Black and Tans. Nor should it be forgotten by others.

What efforts that were made towards peace had an air of fantasy. The Government of Ireland Act of 1920 had something for everybody; there would be two Parliaments in Ireland, one for Ulster and another for the rest of the country, while the Irish representation at Westminster was to be retained on a reduced basis; a Council of Ireland, drawn from the two Irish Parliaments, would preserve or restore Irish unity. It was a good example of Lloyd George's skill at apparently reconciling all sides; apart from the Ulstermen, it placated nobody. In the South, the Government lost control of the legal process and of the taxation system. The local authorities took their orders from the Dail Ministry of Local Government. The clashes between the I.R.A. and the Black and Tans increased in their intensity.

This was an Irish struggle which, for the first time since 1800, had no counterpart at Westminster. Churchill commented that 'the two supreme services which Ireland has rendered Britain are her accession to the Allied cause on the outbreak of the Great War, and her withdrawal from the House of Commons at its close'. The Labour and Liberal parties could not be, in numbers or political vigour, a proper substitute. The Act of 1920, for all its high-sounding utterances and imposing façade, was a victory for Ulster and a further postponement of the real issue. With Ireland in turmoil, and with the British Press becoming progressively more appalled at the situation, the moment for decision could hardly be postponed longer.

*

And all this was taking place in a darkening economic situation.

In 1919, when the industrial situation had seemed so menacing, the one gleam of solace had been provided by the booming conditions of British industry and commerce. Then this gleam was suddenly extinguished. As Tawney has commented: 'In April 1920 all was right with the world. In April 1921 all was wrong.'

The causes are not difficult to detect. Encouraged by the dizzy prospects of vast world trade, British manufacturers had invested heavily. These prospects, after the immediate post-war demand, almost vanished. Producers of food and raw materials suddenly found no markets. Exports of coal and cotton were cruelly hit, bringing poverty to those cities whose total livelihood depended on the prosperity of those industries. Government spending had been cut by nearly two-thirds (£2,696 million in 1917–18 to just over £1,000 million in 1920–1) while taxation had gone up. Prices fell, and unemployment rose, until by June 1921 it passed two million, or over ten per cent.

The Government, which had contributed to this disaster by the wanton dismantling of all the laboriously created machinery for economic control, now further added to the chaos. The official monetary policy was severe. In April 1920 the Bank Rate was raised to seven per cent to check inflation. It also checked investment and confidence. The Government, pursuing its policy of decontrol, also decided to relinquish its paternal supervision over the railways and the mines. The miners and the owners at once clashed; the owners offered 'new' agreements by which wages were cut and the old hated system of district rates was to be resumed. On April 1st a lockout began. The Triple Alliance did not show up to advantage, as the railwaymen and transport workers would not strike in sympathy. By the beginning of July the miners were beaten, and forced to accept the harsh terms of the owners. The national depression, and the farsightedness of J. H. Thomas and Ernest Bevin, had averted what would have been virtually a national strike, but the divisions and bitterness in the coal-fields was an important contributory factor to the further decline of Labour sympathy for the Government in general and Lloyd George in particular.

More and more, the phrase 'a land fit for heroes to live in' came to be seen as a mocking, cruel joke. At the Ministry of Health, Christopher Addison had attempted to meet the housing shortage by lavish grants to local authorities; he had no control over the market in land and labour, and no machinery to control the work. By 1921 the Government was paying over £900 for each house, and a Parliamentary and Press uproar developed against this extravagance. In March Addison was abruptly dropped from the Ministry and, a few months later, from the Government altogether. Addison joined the lengthening list of men who had been ruthlessly abandoned by Lloyd George when their usefulness expired, and he joined the equally lengthening list of those men who had a real personal grudge against the Prime Minister. The irony of it was that although Addison went, and his grandiose schemes with him, the principle that the State had a responsibility for housing the people had been initiated and accepted; furthermore, the fact that the scheme operated through the local authorities was another revolution of a kind. These principles, utterly novel in 1919 and unthinkable in 1914, have never subsequently been challenged. But Addison's 213,000 new houses did not look well beside a figure of over two million unemployed.

By chance rather than design, the unemployed were catered for. The 1911 National Insurance Act had been limited to the building, engineering, and shipbuilding industries, and covered some three million workers; in the war it was extended to munitions workers. When the out-of-work donation ended in 1920, it was evident that something must replace it. The new scheme covered some twelve million workers; it was designed solely to provide insurance, to be contributed to by workers and employers, against casual short-term unemployment. It was not intended to meet the situation that now, in the winter of 1920–1, fell upon the nation. The scheme was arbitrarily extended by virtual subsidies from the Treasury to meet the exceptional circumstances; the circumstances went on being exceptional.

The author of the 1911 Act had, without meaning to, provided the working classes with an important buttress against total disaster. Between 1919 and 1924 over £525 million was provided for unemployment relief. But the fact won him no gratitude; by 1921 Lloyd George's personal position had fallen spectacularly from the glories of 1918. He sought to redeem that position by triumphs abroad. With mounting disaffection at home, Ireland in a state of civil war, Russia now abandoned, and the nation in the midst of what the *Economist* described as 'one of the worst years of depression since the industrial revolution', the reactionary Conservative phalanx on the Government benches eyed the Prime Minister with decreasing admiration. In March 1921 Bonar Law resigned on grounds of ill-health, and was succeeded by Austen Chamberlain as leader of the Conservative Party. In the subsequent reshuffle the obscure Stanley Baldwin entered the Cabinet, at the age of fifty-four, as President of the Board of Trade. The former change was a portent that was not detected at the time. The latter was to be a vital contributory factor in the downfall of the Coalition and its leader. The Coalition had lost its lynch-pin.

CHAPTER FIVE

THE RETURN OF THE CONSERVATIVES, 1922–1923

B Y THE END of 1921 the Coalition had lost almost all of its original authority and prestige. As early as 1919 Harold Laski had written of Lloyd George that 'he seems determined to sacrifice upon the altar of his private ambition the whole spirit of our public life'. Edward Grey subsequently wrote that the Coalition moved him to 'indignation and despair such as I have never felt about any other British Government'. Arnold Bennett noted after a weekend at Cherkley with Chamberlain, Lloyd George, and Birkenhead: 'I never heard principles or the welfare of the country mentioned.' A subsequent commentator has written of this period:

> What strikes one most as one looks back upon that period is the general disarray of public life, the absence of firm principle in most of the moves and counter moves hatched at the country house gatherings and private dinner parties round which political activity on its highest levels revolved.[1]

The remoteness and *insouciance* of the Coalition leaders from this mounting disillusionment were remarkable. The many warnings that they received were ignored or dismissed. 'Who is going to lead you to victory if you smash the Coalition?' Birkenhead imperiously and contemptuously demanded of a discontented Conservative: 'Someone like Bonar or Baldwin?'[2] Fortified by all the panoplies and appurtenances of power, they wholly failed to notice the remorseless slipping away of their authority and political position. The old Liberal Party was politically dead; the new Labour Party was only gradually emerging; it was in the Conservative Party that the real opposition to the Coalition was slowly generating.

[1] Francis Williams, op. cit., 19.   [2] Winterton, op. cit., 115.

Lloyd George's strength still lay in his alleged wizardry in international affairs, but it had already been compromised by the criticisms of the Treaty of Versailles, and it was difficult to judge the Russian Intervention or the handling of the situation in Ireland as outstanding triumphs. Between the end of the war and the fall of the Coalition Lloyd George attended twenty-four major international conferences. To his increasingly irritated contemporaries, the value of these exercises seemed limited. The last was at Genoa in April 1922, and was intended to settle everything. In the event it settled nothing. The Americans, who were cast in the amiable role of generously writing off the war debts of the Allies, refused to attend. The French only came to repeat their claims for full reparations. The Germans and the Russians—fearful (and with cause) that they were to be played off against the other—came to a previous arrangement at Rapallo. Lloyd George's 'personal diplomacy', which had briefly dazzled his countrymen, was now a rather poor political joke.

Elsewhere, success had been mixed. In the Middle East the British had been obliged, as a result of French and American pressures, to withdraw from Persia; they also withdrew from Afghanistan. Iraq and Palestine became British mandates, and the clash between Arab commitments and the obligation to provide the new national home for the Jews in Palestine was already becoming evident. The British stayed in Egypt, but the old authority and control had gone.

In India new forces were stirring. The British declaration of 1917 that India would have 'responsible government . . . as an integral part of the British Empire' was given legislative enactment in the Government of India Act of 1919. It had established 'dyarchy' and emphasised again that the process of 'gradualness' was to be slow. At Amritsar, in April 1919, troops under the command of General Dyer opened fire on a crowd and killed 379 persons, including many women and children. The ugliest aspect of this deplorable incident was the support that Dyer received in Britain, and not least on the Conservative benches. Dismissed by the Government, he received a public subscription and warm tributes. This in itself demonstrated the new nervousness with which the British regarded the situation in India. The emergence of Gandhi and the outbreak of serious communal violence, met with armed force and the proscription of Congress, were unpleasant portents.

The main crises were, however, nearer home. By the early summer of 1921 the British were becoming sickened of the Irish nightmare. 'There is something wayward, *diabolical* in them (the Irish)', Morley wrote at the time.[1]

There were several factors involved in the sudden *volte-face* of the British Government, but the dominant one was the increasing revulsion in Britain at the war and the manner in which it was being conducted. There were those Ministers who still believed that the war could be won, but their numbers and influence were declining. The King was personally deeply troubled and consulted Smuts, who was visiting London in the summer of 1921. Smuts was a strong advocate of conciliation, and drafted a statement which he urged upon Lloyd George. The Prime Minister, who was confronted by the possibility of even more intense fighting, a divided Cabinet and a restless public, assented readily enough. When the King spoke in Belfast in June and appealed for unity it had an immediate response from the Irish leaders, and a truce was signed on July 8th. The King's initiative, as Mr. Taylor has said, 'was perhaps the greatest service performed by a British monarch in modern times'.[2]

The Irish Treaty of December 1921 was in many respects Lloyd George's greatest diplomatic and political triumph, but at the time the feeling was more that he was belatedly bringing to an end a tragedy for which he bore a substantial personal responsibility. And it was, like all of Lloyd George's interventions in the affairs of Ireland, too clever by half. The Irish delegates were bullied and tricked into submission. The retention of Ireland in the Empire was nominally achieved, but at the expense of the reality. Ulster was preserved—thanks to Bonar Law threatening to lead a Unionist revolt if she was interfered with—and the twenty-six counties were given a greater degree of autonomy than Parnell or Redmond ever claimed. The Conservatives had to swallow the Treaty, but without pleasure, and Carson delivered a cruel attack on Birkenhead in the Lords for his apostasy. In Ireland, de Valera denounced the work of the Irish plenipotentiaries. Their offence was that they had reached an agreement under threat of renewed war, without consulting their colleagues in Dublin, and had abandoned the dream of United Ireland.[3] The Dail approved the Treaty by sixty-four to fifty-seven after a debate of great bitterness and drama. The nationalist movement split into two

[1] J. H. Morgan: *John, Viscount Morley*, 55.   [2] Taylor, op. cit., 157.
[3] The best account of the negotiations is F. Pakenham: *Peace by Ordeal* (1935).

powerful groups, and real civil war began to flare all over Ireland, in which many Irish leaders—including Collins and Erskine Childers[1] —were to meet their deaths. The new Irish Free State was formally agreed to by the British Parliament on December 5th, 1922. The last British troops left twelve days later. The civil war lasted until April 1923. The wounds that it inflicted on Ireland were to be even more lasting and debilitating than those of the fight against the British.

The Conservatives could only see that, once again, they had been led up the path by Lloyd George, and then betrayed. If Ireland had been conciliated, possibly all might have been well. But the fighting that raged throughout Ireland, and episodes, of which the assassination in London of Sir Henry Wilson was the most significant, destroyed what chances the Coalition had of securing the fading trust of the Conservative ranks.

When a Government runs out of fortune, nothing goes right at all. The record of the Coalition was far from one of total failure. The Treaty of Versailles had many imperfections, but was a masterpiece of compromise with the emphasis on the liberal and progressive side. The placating of Labour in 1919 and 1920 may have been ad hoc, unplanned, and opportunist, but at least Labour *had* been placated. The intervention in Russia may have been a folly, but at least the British had withdrawn in time. The decision to fight Irish nationalism with the Black and Tans may have been an outrage to civilised opinion, but there had been a settlement that was, in the difficult circumstances, magnanimous and workable. The depression of 1921 may have afflicted the prople grievously, but the effects were infinitely less cruel than they would have been without the acceptance of the principle of government support for the needy. Lloyd George may not have built a land fit for heroes to live in, but 200,000 new houses had been built, and the State had taken a responsibility for accommodating the people. Nothing of major importance that had been

[1] Childers, the author of *The Riddle of the Sands*, who had accompanied the Irish delegation in the Treaty negotiations as its secretary, had resigned from his Clerkship in the House of Commons before the war and had involved himself in the Nationalist cause. It was he who, in his yacht *Asgard*, had brought the rifles to Howth in July 1914 (see Volume I, p. 277), which had been used in the Easter Rising. In the war he served in the British Army with distinction, before returning to Irish politics. Churchill subsequently denounced him as a 'mischief-making, murderous renegade', a grotesquely harsh depiction of a very talented and brave man. He wrote shortly before his execution at the hands of an Irish firing-squad that 'I die loving England, and praying that she may change completely and finally towards Ireland'.

gained in the war had been lost. The Montagu-Chelmsford Reforms in India may have been too little and too late, but they existed, and the Government had disavowed Dyer and all he stood for.

In political terms, however, all this added up to very little. Labour steadily gained seats in by-elections; Asquith had returned to Parliament, and new hope existed among the Asquithian Liberals; the Conservatives chafed at their erratic leadership. On the Left there was disillusionment with the social reforms produced by the Government; on the Right there was resentment at a series of compromises which smacked of weakness and vacillation, and, in the High Tory school, an increasing suspicion of the adventurer image of Lloyd George, Churchill, and Birkenhead. The blatant trafficking in honours came into the open in the summer of 1922; no one had heard of Maundy Gregory, but his handiwork was there to behold.[1] The 'Garden Suburb' Secretariat came under increasing criticism. By the August of 1922, when the House of Commons adjourned for the summer recess, the Government supporters and junior Ministers were in a condition of simmering revolt. Yet, so long as the ruling circle held firm, how could the leadership of the Coalition be changed?

Whichever way men looked in the summer of 1922, there was misfortune and disillusion. Unemployment had become the burning issue of the day, and was to remain so for the next twenty years. By December 1921 36·1 per cent of insured workers in shipbuilding were unemployed; in the iron and steel industries the figure was 36·7 per cent, and for engineering 27·2 per cent. These grim facts were reflected in the areas most severely afflicted: Northern Ireland (25 per cent), Scotland (21 per cent), the Midlands and the North-East (18 per cent each). In August 1922 Barrow-in-Furness had an unemployment rate of 49 per cent, and Hartlepool had 60 per cent. Demonstrations took place in almost all the major industrial cities. Unemployment pay—the 'dole'—saved the people from starvation, but not from anger and disillusionment.

The Government had reacted by deliberately adopting deflationary measures. A committee mainly of business leaders, headed by Sir Eric Geddes, was appointed to review Government Estimates and recommend economies. The committee published three reports in February 1922 that recommended economies totalling over £86 millions. The biggest cuts were to be in the armed services, but Education was to

[1] See Davidson: *Memoirs of a Conservative*, 280.

lose £18 millions, Health £2½ millions, and War Pensions £3·3 millions. What really symbolised the 'Geddes Axe' was the emphasis on the social services; teachers' and police salaries were to be reduced, and contributions to the tuberculosis, maternity and child welfare services were to be cut. Scheduled for abolition were the Ministry of Transport, the Ministry of Labour, and even the Labour Exchanges. It was a typical rich man's economy drive. The Government eventually accepted cuts of £64 millions, and reduced income tax to five shillings in the pound. The economy campaign subsided, but the mood of Labour was justifiably bitter.

Nor were others much mollified by the Government's attempts to satisfy all parties. The old duel between Free Trade and Protection had never died, and now flared up again. Protection was still a word from which politicians shrank, and the Safeguarding of Industries Act of 1921, which provided for duties of thirty-three and a half per cent on certain imports, was too feeble to protect British industry adequately, yet significant enough to alarm the Free Traders in the Liberal and Conservative sections of the Coalition. Such storms passed, and the Coalition struggled on, yet with its position impaired still further.

Nevertheless, there was no desire on the part of any of the party chiefs to end the Coalition. Faced with the alternatives of Asquith or Labour, the leaders drew together. In February 1920 the prospects of a formal new party had been seriously discussed, but had been opposed by the respective rank and files, and the notion of 'fusion' had been allowed to fade away. Early in 1922 the idea of a General Election was seriously canvassed, and then thwarted by the adamant opposition of Sir George Younger, the head of the Conservative organisation. In February, Lloyd George offered to make way for Austen Chamberlain, and Chamberlain refused on the grounds that Lloyd George's departure would be a disaster for the country and the Conservative Party. His decision was accepted, but Law—returning to the Commons in February—at once noted a change of feeling in the party towards the Coalition. On April 5th a Conservative, Joynson-Hicks, moved a motion of censure on the Coalition, which was defeated by 193 votes.

In these circumstances it needed a major political convulsion to change the Coalition without also bringing down the Conservative Party as well. This was the essential problem, and one which the

Coalition's critics within the Conservative ranks found insoluble until September.

At first, the crisis that suddenly flared up in the Middle East seemed ideally suited for Lloyd George. In spite of the opposition and lack of enthusiasm of many of his colleagues, Lloyd George had pursued a consistent pro-Greek policy in Asia Minor. The emergence at Ankara of a new Turkish national movement led by Mustapha Kemal, the most significant of the Turkish commanders at Gallipoli, prompted the French and the Italians to abandon their grants under the Treaty of Sèvres of 1920; the Russians also treated with Kemal. The Greeks, encouraged by Lloyd George, hung on. In the summer of 1922 they began to fall back in disorder under a series of massive and brilliantly conducted attacks by the Kemalists. By August they were in full rout, and the exultant Kemalists, having swept the Greeks into the sea at Smyrna—or those that could not be evacuated by the Royal Navy—swung northwards to the Dardanelles, where they were confronted by a small British force at Chanak. Frances Stevenson, Lloyd George's mistress and future second wife, noted in her diary on July 20th:

> D. very interested in the Greek advance against the Turks. He has had a great fight in the Cabinet to back the Greeks (not in the field but morally) and he and Balfour are the only pro-Greeks there. All the others have done their best to obstruct and the W.O. have behaved abominably. However, D. has got his way, but he is much afraid lest the Greek attack should be a failure and he should be proved to have been wrong. He says his political reputation depends a great deal on what happens in Asia Minor, though I don't think people care a hang what happens there. . . . He is perfectly convinced he is right over this, and is willing to stake everything on it.

Churchill, Birkenhead, and Chamberlain, hitherto highly unenthusiastic over Lloyd George's pro-Hellenic adventure, now saw in the Kemalist threat a potential disaster to British honour and prestige in the Middle East. Beaverbrook has described a sharp discussion on October 4th:

> The debate became bitter in tone. The accusation made against the Peace party was a charge of 'scuttle'—a word thrown like a brick-

bat. Birkenhead referred to our duty to Christian minorities and showed a lively interest in the British Nonconformist Conscience. Churchill talked of the might and honour and prestige of Britain which he said I, as a foreigner or invader, did not understand, and of how it would be ruined for ever if we did not immediately push a bayonet into the stomach of anyone in arms who contested it. He was always ready to fight England's foes. He was not departing from his honest and sincere convictions. Birkenhead was in a different position. Hard-headed, clear-sighted, free from any profound political faith, he was a team man, dazzled by preferment, and influenced by the mistaken belief that Lloyd George could get the votes.[1]

The Cabinet—without Baldwin, holidaying in Aix, and often without Curzon—rushed towards a major confrontation. On September 15th the Dominions were appealed to for assistance. By a crass error in timing, most of the Dominion Premiers read of the appeal in the newspapers before they officially received it. Not surprisingly, their reactions were generally bleak. The British woke up with amazement to discover themselves almost at war. Law published a letter on October 7th that opposed the actions of the Government if they were to be unilateral. This action came after the real drama, which occurred on September 29th, when General Harington was ordered to issue an ultimatum to the Turks, and did not do so. The Chanak Crisis fizzled out, but to many people it was decisive. Baldwin read of the Government's action in the newspapers, and came hastening home to express his dismay, and to join with Curzon in opposing the dispatch of the ultimatum. Bonar Law's denunciation was curt and scathing.

The revolt against Lloyd George now gathered momentum. The junior Ministers had already been irked by a characteristic hectoring lecture from Birkenhead, and it was clear that the annual Conservative conference in November was going to be a difficult occasion. The decision was made to hold the election before then. The Conservative organisation men—Younger, Sir Malcolm Fraser, Leslie Wilson—strongly opposed the decision, and Baldwin was the sole dissentient voice among the Conservative Cabinet Ministers. Curzon's doubts and anxieties were also increasing. After a deliberately

[1] Beaverbrook: *The Decline and Fall of Lloyd George*, 116.

belligerent speech by Lloyd George at Birmingham on October 13th, Curzon ostentatiously stayed away from a dinner party given by Churchill on the 15th, at which it was decided to call a party meeting at the Carlton Club on the following Thursday, October 19th.

It must be emphasised that the decision was made by the Conservative leaders. The purpose was, as Chamberlain put it, 'to tell them bluntly that they must either follow our advice or do without us, in which case they must find their own Chief, and form a Government *at once*. They would be in a d——d fix.' Just to ram the point home, the meeting was timed to take place just after the result of a by-election at Newport was due to be announced, at which it was confidently expected that an independent Conservative candidate would be at the foot of the poll.

This left only three days for the rebels. As Leo Amery has written:

> Unionists felt that they no longer had any policy of their own, but were being dragged along in the wake of an erratic Prime Minister whom they once again profoundly distrusted, by a little group of their own leaders who had lost, not only their principles, but their heads.[1]

Everything depended on Bonar Law. Beaverbrook, Baldwin, Amery and a young confidant, J. C. C. Davidson, urged him to go to the Carlton Club and speak against the Coalition. Law was tortured by doubts and misgivings, and up to the morning of the 19th his decision seemed in doubt.

Meanwhile, although unaware of the vigour and the strength of the forces against them, the Coalition leaders were not inactive. As Beaverbrook has recorded:

> Between Sunday the 15th and Thursday the 19th the struggle became less like a battle than a series of single duels. Every man's political soul was required of him. Promises and promotions and honours were sprinkled from Downing Street on the green benches with a hose. The orthodox Tories appealed to the age-long traditions of a Party now caught fast in the house of semi-Liberal bondage.[2]

Every stratagem was employed to buttress the still wavering Law. A memorial signed by eighty influential—and carefully chosen—

---

[1] Amery: *My Political Life*, II, 232–3.   [2] Beaverbrook, op. cit., 190.

back-benchers against the Coalition was submitted to him; Baldwin, Beaverbrook and Davidson kept up their urgings, aided by Younger, Wilson, and Lord Derby; on the other side, Salvidge reminded him of his 1918 promise 'never to let the little man go'. Law wavered miserably throughout the 18th. At one point he had written a letter addressed to the chairman of his constituency declaring his intention to resign his seat and retire from public life. Beaverbrook persuaded him not to send it. The *Daily Express* on the morning of the 19th announced that Bonar Law would go to the Carlton Club. As Members entered it, the news of the Newport by-election came in. The independent Conservative had won; the Coalition candidate was a bad third.

The actual meeting itself was full of drama. Chamberlain made a somewhat condescending speech in support of the Coalition, supported by Balfour. But the real sensation was Baldwin's contribution, which revealed, as his biographer has written, 'a new eloquence; direct, conversational, monosyllabic; rising and falling without strain or effort between the homeliest humour and the most moving appeal'.

I will not beat about the bush but will come right to the root of the whole difficulty, which is the position of the Prime Minister. The Prime Minister was described this morning, in the words of a distinguished aristocrat, as a live wire. He was described to me, and to others, in more stately language, by the Lord Chancellor, as a dynamic force, and I accept those words. He *is* a dynamic force and it is from that very fact that our troubles, in our opinion, arise. A dynamic force is a very terrible thing; it may crush you, but it is not necessarily right.

It is owing to that dynamic force, and that remarkable personality, that the Liberal Party to which he formerly belonged, has been smashed to pieces; and it is my firm conviction that in time, the same thing will happen to our party . . . until the old Conservative Party is smashed to pieces and lost in ruins.

The decisive speech, however, was Bonar Law's. Following his advice, the party resolved to fight the next election as an independent party by 185 votes to eighty-eight. That afternoon Lloyd George resigned as Prime Minister. The Conservative ex-Ministers issued a pained statement, stating that the victors of the Carlton Club meeting would have to live with the consequences of their unpatriotic actions without any assistance from them. The Coalition, to the amazed glee of the rebels, had fallen. The task of replacing it now pressed urgently upon them.

*

Having toppled the Coalition, the dissident Conservatives were now faced with the very real problem of forming a Government to replace it that would be representative of the Party and that stood a chance of winning an election. Law insisted that his election as Leader of the Conservative Party should precede his acceptance of the Premiership, and this took place at the Carlton Club on October 23rd. For the first time, prospective candidates were invited to attend the 'election'. Curzon moved, and Baldwin seconded, the motion, which was unanimously adopted. It was no more an election than Law's first one, eleven years before, but it was an important endorsement of his position and a clear warning to the dissident Conservatives.

With Austen Chamberlain, Birkenhead, Balfour, and Sir Robert Horne standing studiously aloof, it was not surprising that Law's Cabinet had a somewhat makeshift appearance. Baldwin became Chancellor of the Exchequer, Curzon—who had left the sinking Coalition ship at the eleventh hour—stayed at the Foreign Office, Derby returned to the War Office. Bonar Law tried to bring Reginald McKenna back to active politics at the Treasury, but without success. The Bonar Law Cabinet was largely composed of unknown political figures, of whom six were Peers; derided by Churchill as 'a government of the second eleven', it uneasily took up the offices lately held by more glittering and arresting personalities. Parliament was dissolved immediately, and the General Election was held on November 15th.

There was much truth in the subsequent comment of Philip Guedalla:

Mr. Bonar Law . . . became Prime Minister of England for the simple and satisfying reason that he was not Mr. Lloyd George. At an open competition in the somewhat negative exercise of not being Mr. Lloyd George that was held in November 1922, Mr. Law was found to be more indubitably not Mr. Lloyd George than any of the other competitors; and, in consequence, by the mysterious operation of the British Constitution, he reigned in his stead.

5   Ramsay Macdonald addressing the House of Commons, 1923.
By Sir John Lavery, R.A., R.S.A.

THE SOFT-WORD PUZZLE.

Mr. Baldwin. "CAN ANYBODY THINK OF ANOTHER WORD FOR 'SUBSIDY'?"

6 *Left to Right:* Austen Chamberlain, Baldwin, Birkenhead, Churchill,
Neville Chamberlain, Joynson-Hicks

7   Baldwin by Low in *The New Statesman and Nation*, November 1933

Sir Austen

LOW

8   Austen Chamberlain by Low in *The New Statesman*, March 1926

The downfall of the Coalition had been principally a reaction against 'Lloyd George-ism', and in his election programme Bonar Law emphasised the differences; he promised 'the minimum of interference at home and of disturbance abroad', severe economies, and the reduction of the personal power of the Prime Minister. 'We are asked to choose', Asquith's daughter, Lady Violet Bonham-Carter, commented in what was, in the main, a dull campaign, 'between one man suffering from Sleeping Sickness and another from St. Vitus's Dance.'

In fact, Lloyd George's campaign was notably quiet. His isolation —and that of his Liberal supporters—was painful. Their only hope was to placate Conservative vengeance, and Lloyd George did not even issue a manifesto. Bonar Law could not prevent local Conservative Associations from putting up candidates against his former colleagues in the Coalition, but he did nothing to encourage them. This attitude was approved by the Conservative managers, who hoped to attract Coalition Liberal support for those of their candidates who were contesting Asquithian Liberals.

These genial arrangements were disrupted by several local Conservative Associations, who felt deeply about the Coalition, and by Beaverbrook, who put up, and in some cases, financed, independent Conservative candidates against the National Liberals. This sharply changed the tone of the campaign, which became notably more vigorous and outspoken. Birkenhead and Churchill—prostrate after an emergency appendix operation but still vehement—were particularly sharp in their criticisms of the Bonar Law Government.

It was, in any event, a highly confused election. The Conservatives fielded 442 official candidates, and in the course of the campaign Bonar Law—to Beaverbrook's dismay—gave an undertaking that another General Election would be held before there was any major change in fiscal policy. This virtual negative to Protection was necessary to preserve party unity—not least at the top—and it was not unpopular. Free Trade remained the fiscal orthodoxy of the majority in all parties. The National (Lloyd George) Liberals put up 138 candidates, of whom 56 found themselves opposed by Beaverbrook-inspired unofficial Conservatives; the Asquithian Liberals had 339 candidates, and Labour 408. Never before, and never since, have so many candidates appeared in a British election, and rarely have the differences between them been so difficult to discern.

The result, however, confirmed the decision made at the Carlton Club. The Conservatives won 345 seats; Labour 142; 60 Asquithian Liberals were elected, and 57 National Liberals. Of the 56 National Liberals opposed by independent Conservatives, all but two had been defeated. F. E. Guest, indeed, lost his seat in East Dorset to the son of Hall Caine, the novelist, in spite of flaunting the pictures of Lloyd George *and* Bonar Law in his Committee Rooms. Churchill was overwhelmingly crushed at Dundee in a peculiarly harsh and bitter contest.

In terms of the votes cast, the figures showed what the Conservatives owed to the disunity of the other parties. They had won 5,383,896 votes; Labour 4,236,753; Lloyd George Liberals 1,678,088; and Asquithian Liberals 2,507,204. The practical effects of the Liberal split could be clearly and explicitly seen.

Labour's triumph—in terms of votes won rather than seats—was perhaps the most remarkable feature of all. The pacifists who had lost their seats in 1918—MacDonald, Philip Snowden and George Lansbury—were returned. The composition of the new Parliamentary Labour Party was also significant; the trade union domination of 1918–22 was ended. From having formed virtually the whole of the Parliamentary Labour Party, they now constituted little more than half. From Glasgow there came 21 exultant I.L.P.'ers, including Maxton and Shinwell, fortified by the belief that the victory of Socialism had already been won. There was also an infusion of educated middle- and upper-class men, of whom one was Major Clement Attlee.

When Parliament met, the Parliamentary Labour Party elected a new leader. The voting figures are given as 61–56 for Ramsay MacDonald against Clynes in the accounts of MacNeill Weir and Shinwell; Dalton states that MacDonald's majority was four; Snowden says that it was two. There is, at least, no doubt that MacDonald won, nor that the Clydesiders voted solidly for him.

Looking back, it seems that MacDonald was virtually the only sensible choice the P.L.P. could have made. But he had been out of Parliament for four years, and Clynes was an established, well-liked, orthodox trade union M.P. Furthermore, MacDonald had—quite justifiably—criticised the Parliamentary Party for its generally listless and feeble performance since 1918. The proposal, made in April 1920 at the instigation of Thomas, that MacDonald should advise the party on day-to-day matters had been defeated by twenty-two votes to eleven. The decision was understandable, and MacDonald's position would have been highly anomalous; but the rejection stung him, and his criticisms of the lack-lustre performance of the P.L.P. did not diminish.

Others—notably the Clydesiders—were also critical of the P.L.P. but for different reasons. As MacDonald put the matter in an article in the *Socialist Review* in 1919:

> I am constantly meeting people who do not appear to be able to understand that there is anything possible but one of two positions: either a wild, reckless, disorganised fight, unprepared by scouting, surveying the ground, studying maps, and an examination of the enemy's strength and weakness, or an abject living from day to day with your ears on the ground listening to 'the man in the street', mistaking commonplaces for wisdom, and the shifting position of disorganised majorities for progress.

In the difficult years of 1918–22 in the Labour movement, Mac-Donald's was consistently the voice of sanity and realism. When he contemplated the sufferings of the miners and their families he inveighed against:

> those who think that we have only to lay down tools to build the City of God in our midst. . . . Direct action may be forced upon us, as it was upon the miners, but to choose it as an ordinary weapon for redressing grievances and bringing Governments to their knees betokens insanity.

On several issues—notably on the British involvement in Russian affairs—MacDonald was as fierce as any Labour man, describing Churchill as 'the man of most evil influence in the Government'. On another occasion he wrote that 'If Mr. Churchill had been an unlimited monarch, he could not have spent the money and lies of the nation with more unstinted generosity'. (*Forward*, July 10th, 1920.)[1] Nevertheless, even on the issue of the Russian civil war it was

[1] This, it might be noted, was mild comment compared with some others on Churchill in Labour journals at this time. In one article in *Forward*, by William Stewart in the July 17th 1920 issue, entitled 'The Marlborough Rat', he was described as 'a madman or a blackguard'.

significant that MacDonald only recommended limited direct action. 'When Governments have to be checked by industrial action', he wrote, 'do not let us deceive ourselves, it is an act of revolution.' In his attitude to the Bolsheviks—first welcoming, then cautiously approving, and then fiercely critical—the combination of idealism and realism that characterised MacDonald can be clearly seen. 'How often have we to say it', he wrote on one occasion: 'Wars and revolutions settle nothing; they only begin settlements under the most adverse conditions.' As the works of the Bolsheviks became plainer to see, his contempt for their methods increased, at a time when it would have been easy to win favour and cheers by identifying Bolshevism with Socialism and by talking away Bolshevik actions as natural and understandable. The seizure of the Georgian Republic aroused his particular fury. In 1921 he published his book, *Socialism: Critical and Constructive*, which revealed his moderate position very clearly. In all, he published four books in the years 1919–21, edited the I.L.P. *Socialist Review* and contributed to many journals.

When he returned to Parliament in November 1922—having failed to win a by-election at Woolwich—it was at once plain that he would be a formidable rival to Clynes. To the Clydesiders in particular Clynes was antipathetic. His reluctance to break with the Coalition in 1918—of which he had been Food Controller—had been unconcealed; he had contributed to Horatio Bottomley's scurrilous and super-patriotic *John Bull*; and, on a memorable occasion, he had been howled down at a Labour meeting in Glasgow. Thus, although MacDonald was a moderate in the eyes of the new men, when compared to Clynes he was a substantial improvement. Above all, his record of courageous and unvarying hostility to the war now stood him in excellent stead. By any standard he was the best qualified man in the party to lead it, and—looking back—the only surprise about his election was the narrowness of his majority.

Labour was not the only party that needed to make changes. But the Liberal schism remained as deep as ever. 'For the moment the thing that gives me the most satisfaction is to gloat over the corpses which have been left on the battlefield', Asquith wrote: '—Winston, Hamar Greenwood, Freddie Guest, Montagu, Kellaway—all of them renegades.' These emotions, although understandable, were hardly likely to lead to party reconciliation. In the rank and file there was some feeling towards re-unification, but the leaders remained aloof.

Throughout the spring of 1923 the two Liberal groups sat on the Opposition benches in uneasy proximity, a divided and largely ineffectual force.

The short-lived Bonar Law Government had some achievements to its credit. In December, Law had to move the Bill that gave legislative force to the Irish Treaty of 1921, a task that he undertook with reluctance and distaste but discharged with skill. The Irish Question thus faded out of the sphere of British domestic politics, and was to remain dormant for nearly fifty years.

The two major crises that the Government faced were economic in their origin. In December 1922 Baldwin went to the United States to discuss the American Loan. Bonar Law considered that Britain should pay only the equivalent of what she received from her debtors, thus following the policy implicit in the Balfour Note sent to the debtor nations stating that the British recognised their obligations to the United States but also that 'our undoubted rights as a creditor nation cannot be left wholly in obeyance. . . . In no circumstances does Great Britain propose to ask more from her debtors than is necessary to pay her creditors—not more, but not less.' The response had been not merely negligible, but actively hostile.

The debt itself, furthermore, had been incurred in the form of goods (some of which had been sold at inflated prices), but its discharge by these means was prevented by American tariffs and by the insistence of the Foreign Debt Commission set up by Congress which wanted the money, with interest.

Baldwin returned with a settlement that committed the British to paying 3 per cent interest for ten years and $3\frac{1}{2}$ for 52 years; in practical terms, this amounted to paying £34 millions per annum for ten years and £40 millions thereafter. Baldwin considered that these terms, although stern, were reasonable. On his arrival at Southampton he held a highly injudicious press conference in which he announced the terms of the settlement and gave his opinion on them. Bonar Law was violently opposed to the settlement and carried his objections to the point of threatening resignation at a Cabinet meeting on January 30th. Derby's account informs us that:

With the exception of Lloyd-Graeme we were absolutely unanimous in saying that we ought to accept the terms, and it looked at the moment as if there would be a break-up of the Government there and then, but luckily somebody—I cannot remember who—suggested that we might adjourn and meet again the next day.[1]

The Times carried a letter, signed 'Colonial', which repeated the arguments put forward by Bonar Law in the Cabinet; some Ministers, noting the many similarities, suspected that Law may have inspired it. In fact, he had actually written it, an extraordinary action for a Prime Minister to take. But on the following day, faced by the unanimous opinion of the Cabinet, the Treasury, and the City of London, Law reluctantly withdrew his objections, and this storm passed.

With the French, however, no progress whatever was made. Poincaré's insistence upon immediate payment by Germany of her reparation commitments resulted in two unsuccessful meetings in December 1922 and January 1923 in London and Paris respectively. Law urged Poincaré 'to allow Germany a breathing space to restore her shattered credits before pressing her for payments she cannot at the moment make', but to no avail. After an unhappy and unfruitful meeting in January, the Prime Ministers parted with the cold regret 'that there should be irreconcilable differences on a subject so serious'. On January 11th the French started to occupy the Ruhr. The British, although hostile to the French policy, acquiesced in it. The Germans boycotted the French; the supplies of coal stopped, and German industry with it. By the end of the year there were ten millions unemployed in Germany, and the value of the mark had collapsed from 2,000 to the pound in January to 100,000 in May and to 5,000,000 in September. The banking system of Central Europe was in chaos. In September, after receiving assurances from a new German Government, the French withdrew. This was an ominous milestone on the downward march of Europe.

Meanwhile, the Government had achieved a major diplomatic success at Lausanne, where Curzon had been grappling single-handed with the aftermath of the Kemalist uprising. The Turks gained much, but Curzon secured the neutralisation of the Straits and the retention of the oil wells of Mosul. It was one of those rare conferences from which all the parties emerged reasonably satisfied.

Thus, by April 1923, the Government had weathered its immediate

[1] R. S. Churchill: *Derby*, 495. Philip Lloyd-Graeme, later Cunliffe-Lister, later Lord Swinton, was President of the Board of Trade.

storms, and the confidence of Ministers and back-benchers alike had risen. And it was at this point, when some stability seemed to have arrived at last, that the political situation was once again hurled into turmoil.

*

For some months Bonar Law had experienced difficulty in speaking, and his voice had actually failed during the 1922 election. This caused no great concern, and it was expected that a relaxing holiday would quickly restore him. He accordingly sailed to Genoa with his son Richard in the liner *Princess Juliana* on May 1st. They were met at Genoa on the 8th by Davidson, who was taken aback to see that Law's condition had not improved at all, and that he looked decidely worse. Law decided not to stay in Genoa, and to travel to Aix to spend some days with the Baldwins. Baldwin's cousin, Rudyard Kipling, was staying at Aix, and was shocked by Law's appearance. Beaverbrook was telegraphed to come out at once. Law went on to Paris, where Beaverbrook had arranged for Sir Thomas Horder to examine the Prime Minister. Even at this stage, although there was considerable concern, there was no serious anxiety.

Horder examined Law on the morning of April 17th at the Hotel Crillon, and diagnosed terminal cancer of the throat. Law was now under heavy sedation, and could hardly speak. For some weeks he had spoken yearningly of retirement, and Beaverbrook had argued strongly against entertaining such thoughts. Now Beaverbrook had to change course abruptly; but Law's condition was such that he was overwhelmed with relief at the prospect of his deliverance.

Law returned to London on Saturday, May 19th. Confronted by the precedent of March 1894,[1] Law let the King know that he would prefer not to be consulted about his successor, and on the morning of May 20th he laboriously wrote out his letter of resignation to the King.[2]

While he was writing it, Davidson was dictating a memorandum in another room. This document he had promised to Stamfordham 'as

[1] See Volume I, 142–3. The precedent was not, of course, exact, but it impressed Law.

[2] It was on this day that he told Thomas Jones that if his advice had been required, 'he would put Baldwin first'. (R. K. Middlemas (ed.): *Whitehall Diaries*, Volume I, p. 236.)

representing back-bench opinion'. It went to Aldershot together with Law's letter, and was conveyed by Law's son-in-law Sir Frederick Sykes and his secretary, Sir Ronald Waterhouse.

Both Davidson and Waterhouse were very keen that the succession should go to Baldwin, and Davidson's memorandum—which was unsigned—while carefully prepared to give an apparently balanced portrait, was in fact a cogent argument for Baldwin as against Curzon. According to Stamfordham, Waterhouse said that 'it practically expressed the views of Mr. Bonar Law'. Davidson has firmly denied that Waterhouse had any knowledge of its contents, and doubted that it had any real effect on the course of events. A lively dispute later developed as to whom Law did in fact prefer, and whether his views were deliberately misrepresented. Davidson and Waterhouse, supported by Amery and Jones, believed that on balance Law favoured Baldwin. Beaverbrook has argued vigorously in the other direction. None of these witnesses are, however, wholly reliable.[1] But the fact that Law, who was well enough to have conveyed advice, did not, was a powerful implicit voice against Curzon.

The King sought formal advice from Lord Salisbury and Balfour. Salisbury favoured Curzon, and Stamfordham records of his conversation with him:

Lord Salisbury then told me that he had seen Bonar Law this morning and in discussing the question of his successor he gave Salisbury the impression that in this very grave and complex situation he would on the whole be disinclined to pass over Curzon: but he added that he would rather not take the responsibility of any decision.

This was something less than a ringing endorsement of Curzon, and Balfour's advice was strongly against Curzon, basing his case firmly on the impossibility of the Prime Minister being in the Lords. No doubt Balfour found his task highly congenial. On his return he was asked 'And will dear George be chosen?', to which he retorted with evident satisfaction, 'No, dear George will not'. Although Balfour's argument against Curzon was constitutionally fallacious, it was persuasive. The King concurred in this opinion. On the afternoon of Tuesday, May 22nd, Baldwin was summoned to the Palace and invited to form an Administration. Meanwhile Curzon, out of telephone communication

---

[1] See Davidson, op. cit., 150–5, and Blake, op. cit., 520–5.

with London at Montacute, was summoned to London by Stamfordham. To Curzon, this summons could only have one meaning, and he travelled to London discoursing to his wife on his plans for the Premiership. He was greeted at the station by a large crowd of photographers. On his arrival at Carlton House Terrace an emissary from Austen Chamberlain—Oliver Locker-Lampson—arrived with a message that 'he and his friends earnestly hope for my appointment and that some of them, including Chamberlain himself, would willingly consent to serve under me, but could not do so under Baldwin'. Curzon replied that one of his first acts 'would be to end the breach in the Tory Party and ask him [Chamberlain] to rejoin the Government'.[1]

Then, Stamfordham called. He came, not with the expected invitation, but with the information that Baldwin was already at the Palace. Poor Curzon's dreams were shattered in an instant. And not only his. According to Davidson, the former Conservative Coalitionists were awaiting the news of Curzon's accession at Sir Philip Sassoon's Park Lane house. Beaverbrook was present, and eventually telephoned Downing Street. Davidson, already there, recorded the conversation:

I went into the Private Secretary's room, picked up the receiver, and heard the familiar voice of Beaverbrook. He said, 'David, you know that Curzon has been sent for', and I replied 'Yes, I know he has been'. He then said 'I am at Philip's house and the old gang have sent a message to Curzon to tell him that they will serve under him as Prime Minister', to which I replied, 'I am sorry Max, but it's too late: Baldwin has just come back from the Palace and is busy in the Cabinet Room making the new Government'. There was a roar like a lion and it sounded as though the telephone had been thrown across the room and crashed against the wall.[2]

Thus did the news come to Park Lane. Elsewhere, there was equal astonishment and, in many quarters, equal dismay. Beaverbrook claims that Bonar Law was astonished at Baldwin's selection, Davidson that 'Law was very pleased that the Prime Minister was to be in the House of Commons'.

The King's action was endorsed by a special meeting of Conservative M.P.s and Peers—candidates were not invited—on May 28th, in which Curzon proposed Baldwin's election as leader of the

[1] Mosley: *Curzon*, 271–2.   [2] Davidson, op. cit., 161.

party in a speech of superb malice. 'In a sense', he remarked, 'it may be said that the choice of Mr. Stanley Baldwin as Leader of the whole Conservative Party has been determined by the action of the King. But we all felt, and I am sure you will agree, that it was right that the choice of the Sovereign should be ratified and confirmed by the vote of the entire Party.' After a somewhat unenthusiastic recital of Baldwin's virtues, Curzon concluded that 'lastly (I breathe this almost *sotto voce*), Mr. Baldwin possesses the supreme and indispensable qualification of not being a peer'. Baldwin was duly 'elected'.

Curzon died in 1925, still to the majority a preposterous personality, but to some, for all his failings and foibles, a man of exceptional quality beset by exceptional misfortune. Curzon deserved the memorable tribute paid to him by Winston Churchill: 'The morning was golden, the noon-time silver, the afternoon bronze, and the evening lead. But each was polished until it shone after its own fashion.'

Curzon had only two years of life left to him, Law had even less. On October 20th his sufferings ended, and his ashes were buried in Westminster Abbey. 'It is not inappropriate', Asquith is alleged to have remarked caustically, 'that we have buried the Unknown Prime Minister beside the Unknown Soldier.'

Beaverbrook has given a moving account of the last meeting between Law and Lloyd George, at Beaverbrook's little house in Fulham, in September:

> Here were two men who had served in the highest office of state and each had come to an end. Bonar Law had come to the end of his life and the shadows of death were already gathering round him. Lloyd George had many years to live, but the shadows of decline were gathering round him. There were to be flashes of revived activity, moments of brilliance and an occasional false hope of further greatness still to be achieved. But these manifestations meant nothing. The path led inexorably downwards. The heights were behind and the valley was ever deepening before. Lloyd George was never again to hold any public office.[1]

*

By the time that Stanley Baldwin made his unexpected advance to the Premiership, the condition of European affairs already dem-

[1] Beaverbrook, op. cit., 233–5.

onstrated a sharp descent from the high hopes of November 1918. The first Assembly of the League of Nations at Geneva in November 1920 emphasised the divisions rather than the strengths of the new European and world order. It was a victors' assembly. None of the former enemy states were present—Austria and Bulgaria were admitted at the end of 1920, Hungary in 1922, Germany in 1926, and Turkey in 1932—and the United States of America and Russia were even more conspicuously noticeable absentees.

The effects of American withdrawal were immediate, and substantial. In the lengthy discussions at Versailles in which Wilson had persuaded Clemenceau to abandon the French demand for cession of the Rhineland, the Americans and the British had promised, in return for French withdrawal on this point, to give a guarantee to France against any future German attack. The action of the Senate in denying ratification of the Treaty until the Presidential elections of 1920 repudiated Wilson's pledge. The British Government decided that the new situation rendered their pledge inoperative. The French, to their dismay and chagrin, found that they had lost the joint guarantee that had been the prime advantage that they had secured from Versailles.

This episode blighted Anglo-French relations, never really to be restored. For the British, although less dramatically and obviously than the Americans, had demonstrated that their inclination was equally isolationist. The 'lessons' of the First World War were already being absorbed, and the pre-Entente policy of freedom from European entanglements was again in the ascendant. Such an attitude was strongly supported by the Dominions, whose influence on British policy was infinitely stronger than it had been before the war. As the events of September 1922 had served to emphasise, the Dominions were ill-disposed to become implicated in another European conflict unless Britain was specifically and manifestly imperilled.

The gulf in attitudes between Britain and France became steadily more evident. The French, deprived of their Versailles pledge, now attempted to secure protection from the League of Nations. The British saw the League as a conciliation body and an international forum, rather than as an organisation with executive functions and responsibilities. In short, the French wanted to give the League binding commitment upon its members to resist aggression; the British did not. In 1923 the French brought forward the Draft Treaty of

Mutual Assistance, which proposed that once the Council had declared that a member state was the object of aggression, all other members were obliged to come to its assistance. In 1924 they proposed the Geneva Protocol, which provided for the submission of disputes to the International Court of Justice or to the Council of the League; any refusal to do so would constitute an act of aggression. Both these proposals were defeated, principally as a result of British official and Dominion opposition.

The French were pursuing other lines in their search for the security that the war and the Peace Treaties had failed to provide. An elaborate series of defensive alliances was intended to avert a repetition of the 1914 situation, when British intervention had hinged on the neutrality of Belgium. Such treaties were negotiated and agreed with Belgium in 1920, Poland in 1921, and Czechoslovakia in 1924. These involvements led to others. Poland had an alliance with Romania, and Czechoslovakia had joined with Rumania and Yugoslavia in 'the Little Entente'; France joined, and, in 1927, forged additional military ties to cement the diplomatic alliances.

There were many flaws in the French strategy. The pursuance of security clashed with France's membership of the League, a fact that was emphasised in 1923 when she supported Poland in an attack on Lithuania and blocked League intervention. The new alliance, furthermore, increased the mistrust with which the British regarded French policies and their apprehension of European entanglements.

These divisions in the Anglo-French entente were aggravated and accentuated by the German question.

The central point of division was that of Reparations. By 1920 the British had come to the conclusion that to continue a policy of heavy reparations was probably impracticable and even undesirable. To a Cabinet in which Lloyd George and Churchill were members the spectre of Bolshevism was a very substantial one. The Rapallo Treaty, that had destroyed Genoa, alarmed the British in this direction, whereas it made the French even more determined to insist upon their rights under Versailles. This was the background to the elaborately staged action of January 1923, when the French occupied the Ruhr, which must be adjudged the most important single event of the 1920s to damage democratic forces in Germany and give encouragement to those of reaction.

A year earlier—indeed less than two weeks after Lloyd George had fallen at the Carlton Club Meeting—Mussolini had come to power in Italy.

Of all the 'victorious' nations, Italy had been a most conspicuous loser. The territorial gains at the head of the Adriatic were hardly adequate to compensate for the losses in the war; the war itself had not succeeded in endowing the Italians with a reputation for military competence; and it had plunged the national economy into appalling debts. Disillusion and bitterness stalked the land on the morrow of victory. The political parties were divided, venal, and incapable of providing stable government or competent administration. A series of coalition governments presided helplessly and feebly over a country increasingly riven with faction and disorder.

Three important elements viewed this situation with dismay and contempt. The wealthy landowners and industrialists wanted stability and security; the nationalists who had backed intervention in 1915 and who still believed in Italian greatness were bitterly hostile towards the pusillanimous Socialists and Liberals, a hostility that was based on the recognition of Yugoslav rights on the Dalmatian coast in 1920 and the evacuation of Albania in the same year; then, there were the ex-servicemen, abandoned and derided. These groups found their man in Benito Mussolini.

Mussolini had formed his first *Fascio di combattimento* in Milan in March 1919. For a time the movement seemed powerless, divided, and faintly absurd. Mussolini's authority was far from being accepted, and at times his position seemed precarious. But he was indispensable to the movement. For all his deficiencies as a leader, as a writer and an orator he towered over all his contemporaries. His subsequent career, and its dismal conclusion, must not blind the historian to Mussolini's very real abilities and popular appeal.

In 1920 and 1921 Italy was ravaged by industrial and agrarian disorder, which the Government was unable to meet. The Fascists posed as the champions of law and order, and the true patriots of Italy. In the elections of May 1921 the Fascists became bolder, and their tactics more open. They won only thirty-five seats, but the Fascist movement was now on the offensive; the declaration of a general strike in August 1922 gave the movement its great opportunity. The nation was yearning for stability, and when the Fascists embarked upon a policy of fighting socialism there was general approval. Emboldened, the Fascist leaders took command of the major cities of northern Italy. Negotiations with royalist, religious, and industrial representatives convinced Mussolini that the moment was ripe for a national *coup d'état*. With some trepidation, Mussolini ordered the Black Shirts to mobilise and march on Rome. The King —Victor Emmanuel III—refused to sign the declaration of martial law put forward by the government, and, urged by a Fascist mission led by Count Grandi, appointed Mussolini Prime Minister. The hero arrived in Rome by sleeping car from Milan on the morning of October 30th.

Other nations were quickly made aware of what the change meant. In August 1923 an Italian general and his staff were killed on the Greco-Albanian border. Mussolini issued an ultimatum to the Greek Government, and then bombarded and occupied the island of Corfu. Greece appealed to the League of Nations. The Western Powers referred the matter to arbitration; Corfu was returned to Greece in return for the payment of substantial damages to Italy. Mussolini had gained a cheap triumph. What was more significant was the refusal of the European Powers to apply the principles of the League. The Corfu Incident, small in itself, was of profound significance for those who wished to emulate Mussolini's achievement.

The Weimar Republic in Germany was buffeted most brutally from its birth. It was born in the shadow of defeat, humiliation, and internal anarchy. For the first four years of its existence it was involved in constant crisis, internal and external.

The first attempt to overturn the Republic came in March 1920, in the so-called Kapp *Putsch*. This episode exposed the equivocal position of the Army, as the Defence Minister—Noske—could not persuade the commanders to envisage troops firing on troops. The Kapp 'government' was brought down by the Socialists and the trade unions, and the Republic was saved. But the ugly demonstration of where power really lay in Germany poisoned the air; the army, allegedly aloof from the political foray, bided its time and awaited the leader who would restore their former supremacy. On the Left, opposition to the army was increased after a rising in the Ruhr, in March 1920, was put down with severity. This episode, coming so swiftly after the Kapp *putsch*, also demonstrated the fact that the Republic needed the army.

But the problem of reparations, in an economy severely hit by the war, was the dominant and perpetual crisis. In strict logic, the case for reparations—particularly to France and Belgium—was justified. But the brutality of the French attitude occasioned the crisis. The occupation of the Ruhr in January 1923 sent inflation, which had been serious since 1919, spiralling catastrophically. The life savings of respectable, thrifty people became of absolutely no value. The reserves of the trade unions were obliterated. Violence swept across Germany. Walter Rathenau, the foreign minister and author of Germany's economic war planning, was assassinated in June. Other leaders of the Republic were in mortal danger. On November 9th Adolf Hitler and General Ludendorff led the Munich *putsch* which, easily crushed, destroyed the until then potentially serious situation in Bavaria. 'Hitler was arrested and imprisoned', the British Ambassador wrote in his memoirs—published in 1932—'and thereafter disappeared into oblivion'.

But the ailments of the Republic were on the mend. In August 1923 Gustav Stresemann became Chancellor of a coalition. His first action was to end the policy of passive resistance to the French occupation of the Ruhr, which ended in September. Draconian measures, worked out by Schacht and Luther, were introduced to restore the economic situation. Britain and the United States responded to appeals for assistance, and, with reluctant French agreement, the Dawes Plan revalued the rate of reparations. Foreign loans—principally from the United States—were arranged to invigorate the German economy and German industry. It was an essential step, and one that restored Germany with dramatic suddenness in the 1920s. The protests of the extreme Right were impassioned, but as Germany recovered her economic position and her diplomatic respectability, these shrill accusations of betrayal faded into apparent insignificance. But the bitterness against Versailles could not be obliterated, and awaited darker days to be exploited again.

*

It was at this hour that Stanley Baldwin came to the Premiership.

A more complex personality has seldom held the supreme political position in the State. It is still difficult to focus accurately on him. He comes down to us in many vignettes, sniffing at books, muttering restlessly to no-one in particular in the House, parading as the simple country gentleman, the romantic Celt, the modest scholar, or the Man of Reliability, the personification of Trust. That he was also at root an honest and sincere man is also incontestable. What is not clear is when he was being devious and when he was honest. It was also a matter of bafflement to his contemporaries, and in this lay perhaps his greatest strength. He portrayed himself as a practical, common-sense Englishman; as a commentator in *The Times* remarked in 1930, he 'cultivates the character of an amateur in politics to a point which is maddening to ardent politicians'. He had been selected as Bonar Law's Parliamentary Private Secretary because, in the words of Lord Edmund Talbot, he was 'discreet enough to be safe and stupid enough not to intrigue'. If his Ministerial career had not been outstandingly successful, he had cultivated the House of Commons assiduously, and with quiet skill. As has been written of him, 'the House of Commons was his village. He had an ear like an old man sitting in the sun outside a village inn.' Harold Macmillan has written of him that he:

> had a unique hold on all sections of his party and the House as a whole. He was rarely attacked with any vigour, and if the House was excited or unruly he would usually and without difficulty reduce the temperature. His fairness in debate, the width and generosity of his approach to life, the charm of his manner, and even the skilful way in which he could avoid a difficult argument or awkward situation by a few minutes of reminiscence or philosophising; all these qualities made him a supreme Parliamentarian.[1]

The decline of the Coalition had brought to the surface emotions and attitudes hitherto unappreciated. As Thomas Jones wrote of Baldwin, 'he felt things deeply, and his conscience was more active than his intellect'. His reaction to the Coalition had been perhaps the most decisive element in its downfall. 'Beaverbrook and I fought for the soul of Bonar Law', Baldwin once commented on that episode. 'Beaverbrook wanted to make him a great man after his fashion. I showed him there were better things to be'. The Coalition Conservatives had been astounded at his apostasy, and much of their subsequent bitterness was directed against him personally. They found it impossible to take him seriously as a major political figure, and had yet to learn that he was, like Gladstone, 'terrible on the rebound'—or, as *The Times* commentator of 1930 put it, 'his spiritual home is always the last ditch'.

[1] Harold Macmillan: *Winds of Change*, 313.

Not the least of his most valuable political attributes was the fact that he was a most likeable man. As Leo Amery has written of him, 'Baldwin was a personality, with a breadth of outlook, a tolerance and a warm humanity which commanded the admiration, as well as the affection, of those who chafed under the weaknesses of his leadership'.[1]

The contrast between this agreeable, tolerant, broad-minded man of business and the personalities of the Coalition was marked indeed, and did him no harm at all. The real exhaustion of the war was now becoming apparent. Like a victim grievously wounded yet alive and exhilarated by his survival who subsequently plunges into deep shock and depression, Britain by 1922 was at last feeling the full psychological and physical consequences of the war. The indications were apparent on all sides, and had been manifested by the general approval of the fall of Lloyd George and by the almost alarming conservatism of the Labour Party. The revulsion against suppressing Ireland was, as Austen Chamberlain (among others) noted, deeply significant. The reaction to Chanak was no less revealing. The British had had enough of fighting, of adventurous living, of sacrifice. Unemployment hung like a pall over the land, particularly in the north. The spectre of grievous industrial disputes haunted all men of sensitivity, glancing nervously at the situation on the Continent. As Europe struggled and seethed in the grim aftermath of the war, the British drew in upon themselves.

Baldwin enjoyed particular support on the Left and in the more liberal sections of the Conservative Party. Attlee has written of him that 'he always seemed more at home with our people, particularly the older trade union people, than with his own lot'. Macmillan has written:

The young and progressive wing of his party had a special regard for him. His speeches, particularly on industrial problems, struck just the note which we thought appropriate and illuminating. The fact that the Right Wing and especially the so-called 'industrials' had little love for him, confirmed our feelings.

Baldwin had already given a demonstration of that quality, in a speech in February 1923:

Four words of one syllable each are words which contain salvation

[1] Amery, op. cit., 398.

for this country and for the whole world. They are 'Faith', 'Hope', 'Love', and 'Work'. No Government in this country today which has not faith in the people, hope in the future, love for its fellow men, and which will not work and work and work, will ever bring this country through into better days and better times. . . .

The historian must often ponder on why it is that, so often, a single speech or a single phrase in a speech, establishes or destroys a political character. It is something that is inexplicable for those who were not there. It is a matter of the combination, the magical combination, of orator, theme, words, audience, and occasion. That phrase struck the House of Commons like a bullet. It was widely reported, a fact which in itself demonstrates how wide and deep was the appeal of Baldwin's message.

But his real strength lay in the fact best expressed by John Buchan in his biography of Montrose:

There is a moderation which is in itself a fire, where enthusiasm burns as fiercely for the whole truth as it commonly does for half-truths, where moderation becomes not a policy but an act of religion. . . . The moderate man can never become a barren dogmatist.

Baldwin was a deeply sensitive man. Lloyd George once remarked of him that 'Baldwin is one of us, he is a Celt at heart and that is why many of you find him difficult to understand'. And his son has written that 'Before an important speech the colour would leave his face, the sweat would sometimes roll off his brow, and he has confessed time and time again that he felt he might be sick'.

Baldwin's successes over the next ten years so astonished men who regarded themselves as superior to him in capacity and experience that they tended to endow him with qualities that he did not in fact possess. Lloyd George described him as 'the most formidable antagonist whom I ever encountered'. Churchill has described him as 'the greatest party manager the Conservatives ever had'. Beaverbrook, so often worsted by Baldwin, left a posthumous portrait of a man of almost diabolical cunning.

All this came later. At the time, it seemed impossible that this amiable nonentity would be anything more than a *locum tenens*. But Baldwin had many shocks in store for his critics, his party, and his country.

He made no really serious overture to the Coalition Conservatives to return to the fold. One historian[1] has written that he 'badly muffed the opportunity to bring about a reconciliation', but Baldwin's timing was much better than this implies. It was Baldwin's view that the time had not yet come for a reconciliation, an impression increased after a bleak interview with Austen Chamberlain. Of greater importance was the fact that in the party as a whole, and particularly in the Cabinet, there was no great urge towards reconciliation. The actions of Birkenhead and Horne in particular since the fall of the Coalition were resented, and those who had been subjected to the collective and individual arrogance of the Coalition Conservatives had no desire to repeat the experience. Furthermore, if they returned they would have to be given senior offices, a factor which was no doubt on the minds of those who held those offices. There was not only no real desire for reconciliation, but no real need. The only change of real note that Baldwin made was to appoint Austen's half-brother, Neville, to the Treasury, after yet another attempt to woo McKenna back to politics had failed. Neville Chamberlain had entered Parliament in 1918 after a successful period as Mayor of Birmingham and a very unsuccessful one as Director of National Service in the Lloyd George Government, which left an enduring impression on both men. He was nearly fifty when he entered national politics.

It was in fact Neville Chamberlain who was responsible for the only measure of note produced by the first Baldwin Government, the Housing Act of 1923, which gave a subsidy of £6 a year for twenty years for each house built within certain dimensions by local authorities or private enterprise. These were houses built only for sale, and the Act benefited the lower middle classes. This fact, when combined with the wretchedly small size of the houses to be subsidised, the restriction to houses for sale, and the emphasis on private enterprise, caused bitter hostility from Labour. Neville Chamberlain's somewhat grim version of State paternalism, well laced with characteristic superciliousness at the stupidity of his critics and a certain moral sanctimoniousness, enraged the Opposition, and made him a special target even from this early stage of his official career.

Nevertheless, the significance of what Neville Chamberlain had done was considerable. A Conservative Government had perpetuated rent restriction; it had accepted the principle of the Addison scheme

[1] C. L. Mowat: *Britain Between the Wars*, 164.

that the State had a responsibility for housing; and it had accepted the importance of the local authorities in any housing programme. At the time these facts were obscured by the outcry that the limitations of the scheme aroused.

The economic situation showed no sign of improving. By October the national average of unemployment was 11·7 per cent. Talk of protective tariffs was heard again, and was a dominant topic at the Imperial Economic Conference held in London in October. Nevertheless, the nation was wholly unprepared for the statement of Baldwin on October 25th at the annual party conference at Plymouth, to the effect that Protection was essential. The actual words are worth recording:

> Mr. Bonar Law's pledge given a year ago, was that there should be no fundamental change in the fiscal arrangements of the country. That pledge binds me, and in this Parliament there will be no fundamental change, and I take those words strictly. I am not a man to play with a pledge. . . . This unemployment problem. is the most crucial problem of our country . . . I can fight it. I am willing to fight it. I cannot fight it without weapons. . . . I have come to the conclusion myself that the only way of fighting this subject is by protecting the home market (*loud and continued cheering*). I am not a clever man. I know nothing of political tactics, but I will say this: Having come to that conclusion myself, I felt that the only honest and right thing as the leader of a democratic party was to tell them, at the first opportunity I had, what I thought, and submit it to their judgement.

Baldwin had decided to raise the Protection issue while on holiday in Aix in August after, in the words of G. M. Young, 'meditating deeply on his own discomforts as Prime Minister and the precarious condition of his party'. But there is no evidence that he envisaged an election on the issue, nor that he proposed to fulfil Bonar Law's pledge, at this stage. This only matured in September, after consultations with his colleagues, but Baldwin's Plymouth speech envisaged a full autumn session and made no reference to an election. But the fact of the speech—and the manner in which it had been received—aroused apprehensions that Lloyd George might seize the issue and the initiative. The Protectionists were eager for an election, and were confident that with Liberal divisions and the fear of Labour the party would win easily. Baldwin had forced the issue, but he did not, as was subsequently charged, stampede his colleagues into an election. The decision was reached on November 12th.[1]

At the time, and for many years afterwards, it was commonly said that Baldwin had been guilty of an act of political lunacy. The Conservatives had a comfortable majority. Protection could be brought in, if need be, by the back door by the process of 'safeguarding' more industries on an ad hoc basis. It was only some time later that the shrewdness of Baldwin's move was seen. Perhaps he has been credited with more skill and subtlety than he deserved, and his precise motivation remains somewhat obscure. Nonetheless, the effect of his action was to bring Austen Chamberlain, Birkenhead and their supporters scuttling back from any tentative alliance with Lloyd George. It removed any possibility of Lloyd George himself raising the banner of Protection. By securing the agreement of the Cabinet to the election he took the issue away from the party to the country.

The gamble did not come off electorally when the election was held in December. Free Trade still had powerful allies. The total Conservative vote dropped only slightly, and that of the Labour Party rose only fractionally. The Liberals, hurled into an uncomfortable embrace by the old unifying cry of Free Trade, improved their position slightly. But the Conservatives lost badly in terms of seats. Although they were still the largest party in the Commons, with 258 seats (as opposed to 346 in 1922), they were in a minority in the Commons and the country to a Liberal-Labour coalition. Labour had won 191 seats, and the Liberals 158. As 1923 came to a close, the nation suddenly realised that it was confronted by the real possibility of a Labour Government taking office with Liberal support. There was a wave of violent criticism against Baldwin for having exposed the nation so wantonly to this peril, and wild schemes were devised for a Conservative-Liberal Coalition against Labour with, possibly, Balfour as Prime Minister—the 'impossibility' of a Peer being Prime Minister evidently now forgotten.

The sudden emergence of the hideous spectre of a Labour Government convulsed London. The City trembled. The ample proportions of the Carlton Club could scarce contain the prophets of doom and sulphurous mutineers. Brutal intrigue flourished at every groaning table, and savage mutiny was discussed nakedly over the port wine.

[1] See Keith Middlemas and John Barnes: *Baldwin*, 239.

Defeated Conservative candidates hastened back to London, aflame with resentment that their services had been so incontinently denied to the State at this critical juncture. Heads were seen to wag mournfully in the most influential circles. Visions of the Red Flag floating insolently over the Palace of Westminster loomed before the outraged eyes of The Elect (but, alas, unelected). The Empire was doomed! Trade would fall! Britain was finished! And Baldwin must go!

There are, indeed, few spectacles more heart-rending than the Conservative Party on the morrow of defeat, seeing the country going to the dogs, and helpless to avert the catastrophe. But seldom has this assumed such tragical proportions as it did in December 1923. The fate of civilisation fluttered in the balance, and it was infinitely galling for the Conservatives to behold the calm indifference with which the British people proceeded upon their daily tasks. If only they knew what was in store for them! Bolshevism! Misery! Devastation! The mockery of the world! And the fools don't give a damn! In such moods of sedition, fury, and contempt did the Conservatives angrily adjourn to celebrate a gloomy, but not frugal, Christmas. There are occasions when the historian's emotions of pity and distress overwhelm him, and thus he must avert the gaze of his reader from this melancholy episode in the annals of this historic political confederation.

After a good Christmas, the mood of the party was more benign. After all, things were not as bad as all that. If Mr. MacDonald and his Muscovite collaborators assumed office, they would do so under the lowering gaze and majority votes of the Conservatives and Liberals. The latter, after all, were not all *that* bad, and could be relied upon to demonstrate some lingering traces of patriotism. There would be a brief interlude, which would prove once and for all that Labour was unfit to govern, and then The People would recover their senses.

Baldwin was under heavy pressure to resign, but stood calmly apart from this absurd clamour. On January 21st the Liberals marched to their doom. The Government was defeated in the House of Commons on a motion of no confidence moved by Clynes and supported by Asquith. On the following day Baldwin resigned and Ramsay MacDonald kissed hands as the first Labour Prime Minister, inspiring the King to sombre reflections on what 'dear Grandmama' would have thought.

CHAPTER SIX

THE TRIALS OF LABOUR AND THE DIFFICULTIES OF BALDWIN, 1924–1929

IF THE GENERAL ELECTION of December 1923 was, both in its origins and its result, one of the more perplexing episodes of modern British politics, its consequences were to be of weighty significance. The principal casualty was the Liberal Party, so hurriedly flung together in such embarrassing circumstances, and so dismally unsatisfied by the sensation and the results of its loveless consummation. This melancholy reunion has been well described by Asquith:

At 7 o'clock Sat. evening the rites of Liberal Reunion were celebrated at an enthusiastic meeting in the Town Hall [at Paisley]. Ll. G. arrived with his Megan, and I was accompanied by Margot and Violet. I have rarely felt less exhilaration than when we got to the platform amid wild plaudits and a flash-light film was taken, 'featuring' me and Ll. G. separated only by the chairman—an excellent local Doctor. I spoke for about quarter of an hour, and Ll. G. then plunged into a characteristic speech—ragged and boisterous, but with quite a good assortment of telling points. He was more than friendly and forthcoming, and the meeting was full of demonstrative fraternity. When it was over, Ll. G. and Megan, and their bodyguard of secretaries and detectives, were swept off by their host, Lord Maclay, to some baronial retreat, and we supped here in peace.[1]

The old flame of Free Trade had prompted this reconciliation. For Asquith the issue was so fundamental that the prospect of a Protectionist Conservative Government was anathema. His attitude was supported by Lloyd George at a party meeting on December 18th.

[1] Jenkins, op. cit., 499.

From that moment it was certain that the Baldwin Government would fall.

But there were many Liberals—including Churchill, who had lost again, this time at Leicester as a Liberal Free Trader—to whom Asquith's decision was the moment of final rupture from the Liberal Party, and who regarded the prospect of a Labour Government with horror. Asquith commented sardonically:

> You would be amused if you saw the contents of my daily post-bag; appeals, threats, prayers from all parts, and from all sorts and conditions of men, women, and lunatics, to step in and save the country from the horrors of Socialism and Confiscation . . . The City is suffering from an acute attack of nerves at the prospect of a Labour Government.

By putting in the Labour Government, Asquith had done the Liberal Party irreparable damage. No doubt, the Liberals' false position would have been exposed sooner or later, and the necessity for choice could not have been postponed indefinitely. But, as Asquith and Lloyd George had each repeatedly emphasised, a wide chasm separated Liberalism from Socialism. Certainly, a wide gulf separated most Liberals from the Labour Party. Churchill was not the only Liberal who viewed Asquith's decisions with dismay, and who concluded that British politics were moving towards a choice of two parties and two philosophies, in which the ancient Liberal creeds were increasingly irrelevant. There was to be no real co-operation between Labour and Liberals throughout 1924. The Labour M.P.s tended to regard the Liberals with scorn; the feeling was reciprocated, Asquith describing the new Government (in private) as 'a beggarly array'.

It is also arguable that the election had been unfortunate for the Labour Party. The Red Dawn had broken unexpectedly soon. The National Executive boldly declared on December 12th that 'should the necessity for forming a Labour Government arise, the Parliamentary party should at once accept full responsibility for the government of the country without compromising itself with any form of coalition'. But behind these brave words there was much unease and uncertainty. At a meeting of the Labour leaders on December 11th at the Webbs' house it was accepted that Labour could not refuse office, but MacDonald's reluctance was manifest and understandable. They agreed that their approach should be a moderate one. This reflected MacDonald's ambition to 'gain the confidence of the country'; it also recognised the reality of the minority position of a Labour Government; but, most important of all, it demonstrated that Labour had little positive to offer in legislation or policies. Labour came into office with a multitude of attitudes and beliefs but with few positive proposals and little agreement on the few that there were.

Apart from its psychological unpreparedness, Labour had a marked shortage of men who could claim to have any apparent qualifications for public office. MacDonald appreciated this very clearly, and the barrenness of the field was apparent when the new Government was announced. Lord Parmoor—a former Liberal M.P. and brother-in-law of Beatrice Webb—became Lord President of the Council; Haldane became Lord Chancellor, for the second time in his interesting career; Lord Chelmsford became First Lord of the Admiralty, a surprising elevation for a former Viceroy of India with allegedly Conservative inclinations. The Labour Left was almost totally ignored, the most conspicuous absentees being E. D. Morel and George Lansbury. The only Clydesider in the Government was John Wheatley, who turned out to be its only major success. The principal posts went to Snowden (Treasury), Arthur Henderson (Home Office), and J. H. Thomas (Colonial Office). This Ministry could not be described as revolutionary in personality or in policy. The spectacle of Ramsay MacDonald in Court Dress with silver-buckled shoes and sword, and Jimmy Thomas in full fig brought solace to those apprehensive of the coming Bolshevik Revolution and aroused unease in those who had anticipated more radical attitudes. The new Ministers seemed enchanted at their positions, and quickly brought to their tasks that solemnity of mien and pomposity of manner that are deemed appropriate for those who nobly bear on their shoulders the destinies of a great nation and a mighty Empire. As Clynes (Lord Privy Seal) subsequently wrote:

> As we stood waiting for His Majesty, amid the gold and crimson of the Palace, I could not help marvelling at the strange turn of Fortune's wheel, which had brought MacDonald the starveling clerk, Thomas the engine-driver, Henderson the foundry labourer, and Clynes the mill-hand, to this pinnacle.

But the Conservative Right Wing was still aghast at the prospects. 'The enthronement in office of a Socialist Government', Churchill thundered wildly from his wilderness, 'will be a serious national misfortune such as has usually befallen great states only on the morrow of defeat in war. It will delay the return of prosperity, it will open a period of increasing political confusion and disturbance, it will place both the Liberal and Labour parties in a thoroughly false position. . . . Strife and tumults, deepening and darkening, will be the only consequence of minority Socialist rule'.

*

In these difficult circumstances, Labour did surprisingly well and laid the foundations for its own future. There were two really substantial achievements in social reform. John Wheatley—whose early death was to be a tragedy for the Labour Party—took Chamberlain's housing policy and entirely re-cast it. He increase . the subsidy from £6 a year for twenty years to £9 a year for forty years, with the option open to local authorities to add a further £4 10s. for forty years if the controlled rent was insufficient to meet the cost; he put the main burden and responsibility firmly on the local authorities, and insisted that the houses must be built to rent. He secured an expansion of the building industry by promising that the scheme would operate for at least fifteen years. The Wheatley Act was a real revolution, and it was noticeable that its main principles were unchallenged. Its principal deficiency lay in the fact that it did not tackle the problem of slum-clearance; the building of new houses was, of course, vital, but did not meet the problems of overcrowding and wretched conditions in the worst areas. And, once again, the unemployed and the really poor did not immediately benefit.

Only in the field of education did Labour have a policy, largely the work of the historian R. H. Tawney. The Minister, Charles Trevelyan, restored much of the work of H. A. L. Fisher between 1918 and 1921 that had been scrapped or shelved by the Geddes economies, particularly in secondary education; but he initiated studies that resulted in the system whereby the compulsory minimum school-leaving age was to be raised to fifteen[1] and a separation was created by examination between primary and secondary education at the age of eleven, thus creating two categories of talent. Subsequently, this latter arrangement came under heavy and justified criticism in the 1960s and was

[1] The Fisher Act of 1918 had established it at fourteen and had abolished all previous exemptions.

abandoned. At the time it was regarded as a remarkable step forward, and as completing the transformation of British state education that had had its first tentative advances in the Forster Act of 1870 and in the Balfour Act of 1902.

In foreign affairs, to which MacDonald devoted almost all his attention and energies, some real progress was made. Labour in this respect at least was lucky. The Franco-German dispute had passed its peak, and the Dawes Plan was the first realistic assessment of reparations that had a chance. It was to MacDonald's credit that the British Government seized upon it, and urged France and Germany to accept it. The British reaped some tangible benefit from their role of honest broker; the share of reparations from Germany, together with some payments from France, enabled the British to meet the obligations to the United States incurred by Baldwin.

MacDonald also set the tone for the improvement in international relations which Austen Chamberlain was to develop subsequently. He personally attended the League of Nations, and actively supported the Geneva Protocol: the Government fell before it was ratified, and the Conservatives were hostile to it. But the role of international conciliator was one to which MacDonald took naturally, and one which he accomplished well. He was never, as some of his admirers (and many of his critics) have averred, a devout believer in the League of Nations as an effective replacement for the international bilateral system. But he did believe that in a forum such as the League the rules of international politics could be reorganised to avert a repetition of the disastrous pre-1914 system. In this, as in so many other matters, the difference between MacDonald's outlook and that of the Conservative leaders was one of degree; but that degree was important. The Geneva Protocol would not have stopped Hitler or Mussolini or Japan; it imposed no obligations not already inherent in the Covenant. But the principle of the reference of all disputes to arbitration was an important one, and might possibly have borne fruit if it had been wholeheartedly pursued and backed by successive Governments.

All this was viewed with suspicion by the Liberals and alarm by the Conservatives, who viewed another aspect of the Labour foreign policy with open hostility. Anglo-Russian relations since the end of the war had veered between the bad and the critical. Continued anti-British propaganda from Russia, studied insults, and hectoring communications, had not disposed any British Government to view the

Soviet Government with anything but reluctant acceptance of the unpleasantness of its existence. There was some substance in Churchill's concluding words in *The Aftermath* that 'Russia, self-outcast, sharpens her bayonets in her Arctic night, and mechanically proclaims through half-starved lips her philosophy of hatred and death'.

Suspicion of international Bolshevism ran very deep in British political circles, and touched even level-headed men like Baldwin. The Conservative-dominated Press never omitted to emphasise the barbarous intentions of the Soviets, and the blood-curdling utterances of Zinoviev—the bellicose president of the Communist International —did not help to warm Anglo-Russian relations.

In this unpromising situation the Labour Government acted with what could be regarded as courage or foolhardiness. On February 1st the Soviet Government was officially recognised, and was invited to a conference in London to settle outstanding differences. This gesture was bleakly rewarded. The conference began in mid-April, and dragged on inconclusively throughout the summer. It was resumed in August, and broke down on the evening of August 5th; under heavy Labour back-bench pressure the Government reconvened the conference, and agreement was reached on the following evening. Two treaties—covering commercial relations and pre-Revolution obligations—were signed on the 8th; the British Government also agreed to recommend to Parliament the granting of a loan to the Soviet Union. The treaties and the loan were immediately vehemently attacked both by the Conservatives and the Liberals, Lloyd George being among the most vigorous of the critics. Largely as a result of Russian intransigence, the position of the Government had been fatally compromised by the embarrassing *volte-face* of August 5th–6th.

If these Bolshevik flirtations aroused the wrath of the Opposition, Labour supporters had been profoundly disappointed by the failure of Labour to effect a miraculous cure in the economic situation. The claim that 'only Labour can speak to Labour' had had an unexpectedly early repudiation.

Snowden's views on national economic policy showed little advancement, if any, on those of Mr. Gladstone. In his 1924 Budget expenditure was cut and taxes reduced; even the McKenna Duties were abolished. This was, of course, the reason why the Liberals had backed Labour—to preserve Free Trade. But in Snowden they had discovered an advocate more ardent and bigoted even than themselves. The McKenna Duties had, after all, been introduced when Asquith was Prime Minister and maintained by Lloyd George. Now, even that fig-leaf of Protection was removed.

This did nothing to alleviate the condition of the unemployed or the part-employed. Eventually, and with manifest reluctance, Snowden announced a scheme of public works costing £28 millions, a modest enough nod in the direction of Keynes, the only foremost economist now advocating such policies. Labour did not merely accept the *status quo*; in many respects it demonstrated an alarming conservatism on economic matters, combined with a reluctant acquiescence in the system among the rank and file.

In industrial disputes the Government did not fare much better. Faced with strikes of dockers and London tramwaymen, the Government threatened to use the Emergency Powers Act. The unions were astounded, and their leader—Ernest Bevin—called the strikes off. An angry division opened between the T.U.C. and the Government.

By the late summer of 1924 the Liberals were becoming increasingly impatient with their leaders for continuing their support of the Government. Lloyd George's opposition to the Anglo-Russian Treaties forced Asquith's hand, and it was evident that the Government would be defeated on this issue when Parliament reassembled in the autumn. But before then, the Government sealed its own doom. A prosecution was initiated against the Communist J. R. Campbell for publishing a 'Don't Shoot' appeal to soldiers in *The Workers' Weekly*. Urged by back-benchers, and with MacDonald's approval, the case was dropped by the politically inexperienced Attorney-General, Sir Patrick Hastings. At once the Conservatives alleged improper interference in the course of justice, and received substantial Liberal support. A Vote of Censure was tabled at the end of September. Asquith proposed a characteristic compromise, whereby the matter would be considered by a Select Committee. This was rejected by the Government, which was defeated by 364 to 191. Parliament was dissolved.

Behind the Campbell case there lay the same prejudices and apprehensions that had greeted the Russian Treaties. Were there, in fact, mysterious and sinister forces at work behind the apparently moderate façade of the Labour Government? Such fears were sedulously fostered by the Conservatives, and appeared to have had some justification when, shortly before polling day, a letter from Zinoviev giving instructions to the British Communists was made public by the Foreign Office. The matter was handled clumsily by MacDonald, with the result that the Conservatives were able to allege that the Prime Minister was incompetent as well as being implicated in the great Bolshevist Conspiracy.

In fact, as we now know, and many suspected at the time, the Zinoviev Letter was a forgery. The Conservative Central Office had been partly responsible for its publication. Although it is doubtful if it had much effect on the eventual result, it did give a very neat clincher to the Conservative allegations concerning the Peace Treaties and the Campbell Case. It seemed to give strong emphasis to the dire and alarming warnings of Churchill that Labour was indeed 'driven forward by obscure, sinister, and in part extraneous forces'. It was a squalid episode.

But the Zinoviev Letter was a misfortune for Labour for another reason, as it provided it with a magnificent excuse for failure and defeat. The inadequacies that had been exposed in the Government in its brief existence could be ignored and forgotten by the movement. All could be blamed on misrepresentation by the Opposition, the hostility of the capitalist Press, and the unscrupulous use made of the 'Red Scare'. Thus, when Labour returned to office in 1929, it proceeded to repeat its more grievous errors of 1924 with fervent exactitude.

But the election was far from being a disaster for Labour. It lost sixty-four seats and gained twenty-four, and was still ten seats better off (151) than in 1922; largely as a result of running more candidates, it put up its national vote by a million. The real losers were, again, the Liberals. They lost a hundred seats, and among the fallen was Asquith, whose long career thus came to a sad close. He went to the Lords as Earl of Oxford and Asquith; he did not find the new atmosphere congenial: 'It is an impossible audience; as Lowe said fifty years ago, it is like "speaking by torchlight to corpses in a charnel-house",' he glumly recorded. In his last years he wrote a certain amount, without much distinction, and presided benignly over his brilliant and loud-speaking family, a genial and much-loved patriarchal figure. His last years were clouded by persistent financial difficulties, which were only partly alleviated by the commercial success of the irrepressible Margot's memoirs and articles. He died in 1928 and, in spite of several studies and two full-length biographies, remains an enigma.

But Asquith did not relinquish the Liberal leadership until 1926, and in the meanwhile the forty surviving Liberals in the Commons had only Lloyd George to lead and guide them there, a prospect that not all found heartening.

The Conservatives returned triumphantly with 419 Members. There was now no criticism to be heard of Baldwin. The nation settled down to five placid years of solid Conservative rule. Her first little Labour fling was over.

*

Understandably, Protection had been notably absent from the Conservative programme in the 1924 General Election. It would have to wait for 'clear evidence that on this matter public opinion is disposed to reconsider its judgement'. This, although it did not satisfy the more ardent Protectionists, went far to close the divisions in the Conservative ranks, removed the only common ground of unity in the Liberal leadership, and focused the issue on whether or not Labour was 'fit to govern'. To emphasise the remarkable contrast with 1923, Baldwin, in an unhappy hour for his Administration, offered the Chancellorship of the Exchequer to Churchill, now returned as 'Constitutionalist' Member for Epping, and ardent exponent of anti-socialism.[1]

The other rebels returned to the Conservative fold. Horne was offered, but refused, the Ministry of Labour, and never held public office again. But Birkenhead became Secretary of State for India; Austen Chamberlain went to the Foreign Office; Balfour, in 1925, succeeded Curzon as Lord President on the latter's death. One by one the great pre-war and wartime political figures were disappearing. Bonar Law and Curzon were dead; Asquith was in retirement, Carson was a spent force, McKenna was out of politics, and, although it was not certain at the time, Lloyd George's star was definitely in the descendant. Milner died in 1925, Asquith in 1928, Rosebery—long

[1] Churchill had contested the Abbey Division of Westminster as an 'Independent and Anti-Socialist' candidate in March with strong but unofficial Conservative support, and had lost to the official Conservative candidate by only forty-three votes. In May he had spoken at a meeting organised by Sir Archibald Salvidge—now the dominating figure in Liverpool—and addressed a gathering of Scottish Unionists in Edinburgh presided over by Arthur Balfour. Although nominally a 'Constitutionalist' at Epping, his candidature was warmly supported by the local Conservative Association, and a year later he renewed his membership of the Carlton Club.

forgotten—in 1929, Balfour in 1930, and Birkenhead in 1931. Each had been out of office and responsibility for some time before their deaths, although Balfour had been by far the most durable.

Curzon has received more biographies and biographical studies than his colleagues and contemporaries could have expected. There is always something irresistibly attractive about early success and eventual near-triumph, but this cannot wholly explain Curzon's great subsequent fascination for biographers and historians. Behind his excessively deliberately impressive façade, Curzon was a passionate and sensitive man. He had a real scholar's approach, and was genuinely learned and a man of taste and discernment. He bore disappointment with public fortitude, and although he was mocked for his idiosyncrasies and airs, his capacities as a negotiator were formidable. As Churchill and others who had cause to resent him have emphasised, he was a difficult man to dislike for very long. His financial meanness was proverbial—and is well-attested—and he was inordinately vain. But he was also very generous with time, kindness, and attention to young people whom he wished to help, and many of the best stories about him either originated with him or were told by him cheerfully against himself. He had wit, style, intelligence, and a profound devotion to public duty. The more one examines his life and career, the less is one surprised by the interest and admiration which he subsequently aroused.

Curzon's decline and death made Baldwin's task much easier. The Conservative Party was at last formally reunited. And British politics could, after nearly a decade of violent fluctuations of fortunes, alliances, and allegiances, resume a coherent pattern. The Liberal Party had been the most spectacular casualty of this decade. In July 1914 it stood, 260-strong in the House of Commons, fortified in the country by a substantial and effective organisation. Now, it had forty Members of the House of Commons, and its once-formidable organisation was reduced to isolated and embittered fragments. Driven out of the cities by Labour, and out of the counties by the Conservatives, it found succour only in the Celtic fringes. The Labour Party, despite its first somewhat hapless experience of office, viewed the future with a new confidence and spirit.

We may conclude this account of the events of October 1922–November 1924 with some comments made by Churchill in a newspaper article on October 5th, 1924:

9   Philip Snowden by Low in the *Graphic*, 1927

10　Lloyd George by Low in *The New Statesman*, March 1926

11 'The Recruiting Parade' by Low, 1924. Lords Rothermere (*left*) and Beaverbrook (*right*) hold the banner of Anti-Socialism over Mr Churchill's motley army, which includes Birkenhead (in busby) and Baldwin

12   Strube in the *Daily Express*

Max, Lord Beaverbrook.

13   Beaverbrook by Low in *The New Statesman*, March 1926

When the Coalition Government was destroyed at the Carlton Club only two years ago, it was perfectly clear to many of us that a period of political chaos would ensue. To the best of my ability, I warned the public of what was in store. But nobody would listen. Everyone was delighted to get back to party politics. Dear to the hearts of all the small politicians were the party flags, the party platforms, the party catchwords. How gleefully they clapped their hands and sang aloud for joy that the good old pre-war days of faction had returned!

They have had their wish. We have had two years of insensate faction.

*

The Baldwin Government of 1924–9 operated in the context of continuing decline and hardship in the old industries—particularly in the North of England—and mounting prosperity elsewhere. The historian viewing the 1920s is struck by the sharpness of the contrasts —the misery in the mining towns, for example, and the glittering revival of London Society, the utterly different worlds of Aneurin Bevan and Michael Arlen, of James Maxton and Lady Cunard, George Orwell and Dornford Yates. Unemployment never fell below one million, yet by 1927 there were nearly two million motor vehicles, and the era of the private car, mass-produced and relatively cheap, had arrived. Income tax was low, and was to be made even lower by the Baldwin Government; virtually all the wartime restrictions had gone; Europe at long last reposed in apparent tranquillity and peace. With the United States of America locked in its isolation, and passing through a period of confusion, introspection, wealth and hedonism under the distant supervision of a succession of nondescript and often corrupt leaders, and Stalin's Soviet Union occupied with its ferocious internal difficulties, the position of Britain and her Empire appeared stronger than ever. The Labour Government's controversial Russian Treaties were curtly abrogated; the Geneva Protocol dropped. The phenomena of Gandhi in India and Adolf Hitler in Germany seemed to have passed. The British viewed the policies of Mussolini in Italy with benignity. Europe, demonstrating its extraordinary resilience and strength, was recovering rapidly physically, politically, and economically. There was a freshness in the atmosphere, a resurgence of hope and of confidence, symbolised by the Treaty of Locarno, signed in London on December 1st, 1925, and regarded as Austen Chamberlain's greatest achievement.

Locarno was a non-aggression pact between France, Germany, and Belgium, guaranteed by Britain and Italy. It also ended military staff talks between Britain and France. It was a perfect example of politicians successfully stopping the last war, but at the time it was widely applauded, and not least because it seemed to remove Britain definitely from any close commitments in Europe, and particularly in Eastern Europe. To all outward signs, 'normalcy' had indeed been achieved. It was 'back to 1914' accomplished, and a 1914 with distinct improvements. There was no sense of the shortage of time, and certainly none that this was a transient gleam of sunlight in the darkness of the twentieth century.

But it was not sunlight for all. One per cent of the population of Britain still owned some two-thirds of the national wealth. Three-quarters of the people earned less than £100 a year. Rural and urban poverty remained stark and grim. Imports were higher than before the war, and exports never recovered their previous position. British agriculture endured another prolonged slump, until by 1931 only 5·67 per cent of the employed population worked on the land and land values had plummeted. The European economic recovery was not matched by the British. And, over all, hung the concentration of depression and unemployment among the pre-war industrial giants, coal and cotton, shipping and steel.

For many years it was fashionable to depict the General Strike of May 1926 as a catalytic event. Before it, it was asserted, Labour and employers were set on a collision course. The strike, this version runs, 'purged the poison' in industrial relations, which from then onwards were harmonious, reasonable, and sympathetic. 'Our old country can well be proud of itself', King George wrote when it was all over, 'as during the last nine days there has been a strike in which 4 million men have been affected; not a shot has been fired and no one killed; it shows what a wonderful people we are.' Foreign observers were astonished and impressed by what had *not* happened. And the strike entered a familiar realm—that of historical mythology. But in fact it was a clear reflection of a very serious social and economic situation.

The dominant feature of that situation was the persistent unemployment level of over one million. This experience was unique and unprecedented. There had been cyclical unemployment before the war, but nothing in memory comparable to what the Cambridge economist Pigou called 'the intractable million'. This unemployment tended to be explained by the dislocation of the international trading monetary systems caused by the war. By this reasoning, the only hope lay in the restoration of this system which involved currency stabilisation (by means of return to the Gold Standard) and the reduction of wartime tariffs. Free Trade remained the economic doctrine in firm possession of the field, and, as the General Election of December 1923 seemed to demonstrate, the belief of the people. Of the main political parties, only a minority of the Conservative Party was wedded to Protection. Labour, the Liberals, and a substantial element in the Conservative Party, were vehement advocates of Free Trade. Philip Snowden was a dedicated Free Trader; so was Churchill. These two men were at the Treasury from January 1925 until November 1931.

The politics of 1925–31 were to be the politics of unemployment, which dominated all other issues, but which defied the endeavours of the politicians, and notably those of the pre-1914 era. Early in his career, in 1902, Winston Churchill and his friends had entertained Joseph Chamberlain, then at the zenith of his fame, to dinner. As the young men present had just combined to embarrass the Government of which they were supporters and Chamberlain one of its principal members, the evening had begun uneasily. But the mood warmed, and at the end Chamberlain had repaid his hospitality by telling his hosts that 'Tariffs are the politics of the future'.[1] But in 1924 no politician of the first rank had grasped that unemployment was now the politics of the future, and that the kind of unemployment that now afflicted millions of people and darkened the lives of millions more was not susceptible to the machinery and attitudes of the past. A few younger men grasped this fact, but they were outcast and ignored voices. There was, accordingly, an air of marked and real irrelevancy about the speeches and actions of Government and Opposition alike during these vital years. They took the wealth of the nation for granted; they understood that there would be ebbs and flows in the process of economic expansion; they endeavoured to mitigate the unfortunate consequences of recessions; but their eyes were usually on more traditional and exciting concerns. It was not wholly without significance that the fiercest schism in the Conservative Party in the period was over Churchill's attempt to reduce the cruiser-building programme, nor that the finest debates in the House of Commons were

[1] Churchill: *My Early Life*, 385.

over the revised Book of Common Prayer. The political centre was drifting away from the true concerns of the people.

Normal unemployment, based on pre-war experience, was about four per cent. It was considered that the problem centred on the remaining six per cent—the 600,000 persons who formed the 'new unemployed'. Concentration of unemployment was in the north and in the Celtic fringe, where the ailing industrial giants of pre-war years were situated. Coal and cotton together accounted for about sixty per cent of the 'abnormal' unemployment. Together they employed 1,500,000 workers, and were the largest industries in the country. The textile and coal industries had formed fifty-five per cent of the total value of British exports in 1913; in 1913, cotton alone provided a quarter of this total value of exports, but exports fell by nearly half between 1912 and 1929. In 1913 Britain had exported 73 million tons of coal; by 1921 this had shrunk to 25 million, and although there was a recovery, the average figure in the 1920s was 50 millions. Accordingly, coal production fell by some 30 million tons a year comparing 1913 with 1929. The principal causes were the increase of coal exports by Germany in the 1920s, the loss of the Baltic markets to Poland, and the elimination of the valuable trade with Russia. The movement to oil, gas, and electricity at home was an additional, but not a crucial factor.

Cotton had been killed by competition. Britain's best market had been India; here, domestic production trebled between 1913 and 1929. By 1929 Japan—not a competitor at all in 1913—had captured nearly twenty per cent of the world market. Thus, in both coal and cotton the British were severely undercut in prices and at least equalled in quality.

The iron and steel industries were heavily dependent on the ship-building industry. Shipbuilding contracted sharply after the war. There was an immediate post-war shipping boom that had abruptly stopped before the end of 1921. The decline in exports aggravated what would have been in any case a serious situation. The war had resulted in a dramatic boom in iron and steel, the installation of new equipment, and the building of new factories. Much of this now stood idle. The production capacity of British steel was some 12 million tons; only twice in the 1920s did actual production exceed 9 million tons.

The solutions to these chronic problems were sought along two separate but not unconnected lines.

Free Trade was an integral and essential part of the gold standard system. But a return to the gold standard was regarded as essential for other reasons. The pre-war rate was seen as a crucial token of London's financial leadership, and it was believed that its restoration would re-establish its former primacy. In this attitude there was some realism. In the disordered condition of Europe in the early 1920s *some* established economic leadership was required, and Britain was considerably better equipped to undertake this than any other single nation. Prestige and confidence are crucial to success in international banking. There was accordingly much to be said for the arguments that were brought forward by the City and the Treasury and that were accepted by all Governments.

Furthermore, the messianic quality of Free Trade must never be under-estimated. The belief that Free Trade encouraged international co-operation and good feeling was deeply imbedded. The return to general Free Trade had much political content in it. A series of international conferences agreed that the elimination of trade barriers was highly desirable, if not actually essential, for international harmony. But, of all the international trading nations, Britain was the only one that kept it in effect. Throughout the 1920s, as a result of the assistance given to the few safeguarded industries, there was a tariff level of some five per cent for foreign imports, which was negligible. At the same time, the tariff barriers abroad to British exports were steadily, if stealthily, rising. But at the same time as the restoration of the pre-war trading and monetary system was thus being eagerly sought, there was a general refusal to accept the permanence of the decline of the staple export industries. The cause of their decline, it was argued, was the high cost of their products. But the solution was sought not in better equipment and marketing but in the reduction of wages, and what was, after 1927, described as 'rationalisation' to reduce production costs. The former became an article of faith, shared even by Baldwin, who said (July 30th, 1925) that 'All the workers of this country have got to take reductions in wages in order to help put industry on its feet'. The effects of this attitude were to precipitate the confrontation between the coal-owners and the miners that reached its culmination in May 1926.

It is to over-simplify the matter to state that Free Trade as practised in Britain in the 1920s implied *no* government control of the economy. What was important was *how* it attempted to do so.

The function of the Treasury was principally to regulate government expenditure. Monetary policy was the field of the Bank of
England. Industrial policy was the responsibility of the Board of
Trade and the Ministry of Labour, which were subordinate to the
Treasury. 'Balancing the Budget' was a hallowed principle. In this, as
in other fields, the Government was expected to give the nation a
lead. Every Chancellor was expected to provide for a surplus and to
achieve it by taxation and reductions in government expenditure. As
it was generally agreed that taxation—particularly direct taxation—
was too high at even five shillings in the pound—and which Churchill
reduced to four shillings—this meant that the real 'balancing' was to
be achieved by the latter. It was also regarded as essential that the
Budget contained interest payments on the national debt, for moral
rather than for practical purposes. Thus, every Budget in the 1920s
contained a provision for about £60 millions which went on the 'debit'
side automatically, and had to be met from the static 'credit' side.

With these attitudes and this machinery, and having turned its back
upon Protection, and with a dramatic but thinly informed Free Trade
Chancellor of the Exchequer, the Baldwin Government had little to
offer towards the restoration of the old exporting industries. It is fair
to add that Labour had little to offer, either. If Churchill was an
hereditary Free Trader, Snowden was a fanatical one.

Baldwin's personal obsession was with industrial peace, haunted
by the potentialities of employer–employee antagonism. 'There is only
one thing which I feel is worth giving one's strength to', he said on
January 1st, 1925, 'and that is the binding together of all classes of our
people in an effort to make life in this country better in every sense of
the word. That is the main end and object of my life in politics.' In a
party in which there were strong elements on the front and back
benches burning for a confrontation with the unions, Baldwin's voice
was one of sanity and compassion. On March 6th, 1925 he destroyed
a back-bench Bill to abolish the political levy, the Labour Party's
principal source of income, with a speech in his own distinctive style,
rambling, sincere, modest, and yet compelling. He ended with the
words 'Give peace in our time, O Lord', and the Bill was dead. But
it was only a temporary victory.

Neville Chamberlain proved a progressive and reasonably imag-
inative social reformer at the Ministry of Health. The implications of
Birkenhead's reactionary views on India were not yet fully evident.

Only Joynson-Hicks, at the Home Office, was an obviously unfortunate appointment. It was, in Churchill's words, 'a sedate, capable, government'. It gave financial incentives to exporters; it relieved industry of three-quarters of local rating assessments; it financed public works on a modest scale; it restored the McKenna Duties ; it provided unemployment relief for an indefinite period by abandoning the insurance principle; it introduced contributory old-age pensions; it put into practice—on Churchill's urgings—the principle that the Defence estimates should be based on the assumption that no war with a major power would break out within ten years; it established, in the British Broadcasting Corporation and in the Central Electricity Board, the machinery for national corporations that was later to be used as precedents by their opponents; it lowered the voting age for women from thirty to twenty-one, and gave them the same residence qualification as for men. But it could not, and did not, resolve the fundamental problems.

The first serious blunders occurred in Churchill's first Budget in 1925, when he imposed new taxes on artificial silk at a time when the textile industry was seriously turning to the development and production of man-made fibres, and when he announced the return of Britain to the Gold Standard at the pre-war parity of $4.86. It was the last decision that was the major error. Churchill had not taken it lightly, but he was seriously out of his depth in this field. 'We are often told,' he said in introducing the Gold Standard Bill, 'that the gold standard will shackle us to the United States . . . I will tell you what it will shackle us to. It will shackle us to reality. For good or ill, it will shackle us to reality.' At the time, the decision was enthusiastically applauded, particularly as a further indication that 'normalcy' was returning. But Keynes spelt out in a series of articles in the *Evening Standard*—subsequently published as *The Economic Consequences of Mr. Churchill*—some of the implications:

> The whole object is to link *rigidly* the City and Wall Street . . . The movement of gold or of short credits either way between London and New York, which is only a ripple for them, will be an Atlantic roller for us.

The principal consequences may be swiftly categorised:
The primacy of the Bank of England over monetary policy was restored. The Bank saw its relationship with the Government as that

of 'the ordinary duties of banker to client', and the supremacy of the Treasury over the Bank, which had seemed to be established in 1917 when Bonar Law had secured the resignation of Lord Cunliffe, was lost. This might not have been so serious were it not for the fact that the Bank of England was inadequately equipped to meet its responsibilities.

The fact that the pound was over-valued in relation to other currencies reduced the value of British exports.

The consequent necessity to build up reserves to support the new value of the pound removed sums that could—and should—have been used to assist industry.

The British economy was henceforth linked to a world-system which the British did not dominate. The conditions of 1925 had no relevance to those of 1914. A large proportion of British assets had been sold to pay for the war, and exports could no longer produce the surplus necessary to finance and buttress her position.

Above all, the decision was symbolic of the fact that neither the Government nor its principal advisers had grasped the enormity of the new problems facing the British economy and British industry. It was a step backwards into a dream-world in which Britannia ruled the waves and the pound sterling commanded awe and respect throughout the world. The reasons *why* the pound sterling had commanded this respect were inadequately appreciated.

It is relevant to look at what was written in warning and in retrospect by Hubert Henderson, perhaps the wisest of contemporary economists, and certainly among the most percipient. On April 4th he wrote warningly:

> We make bold to say that a return to gold this year cannot be achieved without terrible risk of renewed trade depression and serious aggravation of unemployment.

And, on May 9th:

> In short, it was Mr. Churchill's duty, if he decided to take the plunge back to gold, to insist that expensive social measures must be ruled out meantime. Nor is that all. Relief to the income-tax payer should no less have been ruled out. The sacrifices of the return to gold fall entirely upon business and do not touch the salaried man. Mr. Churchill should accordingly have used his

Budget surplus . . . exclusively to help industry through the transition . . .

We are driven to the conclusion that Mr. Churchill's great but peculiar abilities are not well suited to the realms of finance. . . . It is with regret that we are disposed to write him down as one of the worst Chancellors of the Exchequer of modern times.

Perhaps most important of all was the point made by Keynes:

He [Churchill] was just asking for trouble. For he was committing himself to force down money-wages and all money values, without any idea how it was done . . . [the result] must be war, until those who are economically weakest are beaten to the ground.

*

The resultant confrontation, long developing, was immediate.

Churchill's Budget had not only been massively irrelevant to the general economic problem, it had actually been harmful to industry, and particularly to the textile and coal industries. For the latter, 1925 was the worst year on record and the return to $4.86 substantially increased the cost of British exported coal. With the recovery of the Ruhr coalfields, this additional burden—estimated by some as an increase in cost of two and a half per cent, by others as high as ten per cent—was catastrophic. The owners proposed to meet it by the classic methods of revoking the existing wage and working condition agreements, reducing wages, and increasing the working day. But the miners had had enough, and were backed strongly by the General Council of the T.U.C. in their 'resistance to the degradation of the standard of life of their members'. There was strong workers' solidarity with the miners, and by July the situation had become critical. Baldwin's proposal for a subsidy to the industry was strongly opposed by the bulk of his colleagues, but, confronted by the real possibility of a General Strike, the Government agreed to an interim subsidy for a period during which a Royal Commission would examine the industry. This had Churchill's support, albeit with reluctance at any surrender to the Unions—a reluctance not diminished by the statement of the miners' leader, A. J. Cook, that 'we have already beaten not only the employers but the strongest government in modern times'. Herbert Samuel was made chairman, and nine months' peace had been purchased. The satisfaction of the unions at the Government's apparent climb-down stirred angry mutterings on the Conservative benches and in the Cabinet, which were not appeased by the prosecution in October of twelve members of the Communist Party.[1] Certainly in the Cabinet the view was beginning to prevail that a confrontation with the T.U.C. was inevitable, and that it should come soon, on ground of the Government's own choosing. On the unions' side, the approach was less clear. The Government perfected its plans for a national emergency; the unions did nothing in particular.

It was clear to observers—and also to Baldwin—that there was a considerable gulf in attitudes between the Prime Minister and a substantial element in the Conservative Party towards the crisis. Duff Cooper and Harold Macmillan were not the only progressive younger Conservatives who sat for industrial constituencies—Oldham and Stockton-on-Tees respectively—and who were shocked not only by the condition of their constituents but by the indifference of a considerable number of their colleagues towards these conditions. Baldwin's 'hard-faced men' and what the progressives called 'the industrials' were active, influential, and vocal in the party, and constituted one of Baldwin's principal difficulties. They despised his moderation, and were fearful of the menace of Socialism which Baldwin rightly regarded with relaxed indifference. Thus, as Baldwin greatly increased his reputation with the Opposition, his authority within his own party was constantly imperilled. It was to this audience that Joynson-Hicks, Churchill, Birkenhead, and even Neville Chamberlain, with his rasping contempt for the Labour Party, constantly played. Baldwin believed strongly that vital constitutional principles were involved in the threat of a General Strike, but his own instincts for conciliation were affected by the need to retain his party's support. The clash between these instincts and the political reality explain his actions in 1926 and 1927.

The Samuel Commission reported on March 11th, 1926. Parts of its proposals were positive, but the key recommendation was for the immediate reduction of wages. The owners were unimpressed by the positive proposals, the miners were incensed at the endorsement of the owners' principal demand. Cook urged 'not a penny off the pay, not

---

[1] All were convicted under the Incitement to Mutiny Act, 1797, and given moderate prison sentences, a fortunately very rare example in modern times of a purely political trial in Britain.

a minute on the day', and was obdurate to all proposals that did not meet this central criterion. Birkenhead's celebrated remark that he thought the miners' leaders the most stupid men he had ever met until he met the owners seems ill-merited. Negotiations continued throughout April, with little movement on either side. The agreement expired at the end of the month, and on May 1st the owners resorted to another classic tactic, the lock-out.

On the same day a special union conference placed authority in the general council of the T.U.C. and approved the proposal for a General Strike on May 3rd. The Government and the T.U.C. stumbled into confrontation. There were two days of confused negotiations and discussions, eventually broken off by the Government late on May 2nd when the Cabinet learned that the machine-men of the *Daily Mail* —acting entirely independently—had refused to print the Monday edition unless a fiery leading article by the editor, Thomas Marlowe, was amended. There is still considerable doubt whether this provocation was or was not deliberate. Certainly Marlowe hastened to inform the Cabinet. There is no doubt that it was welcomed by a majority of the Cabinet as a *casus belli*. Their plans—carefully matured by the permanent under-secretary of the Home Office, Sir John Anderson, and J. C. C. Davidson—were ready, and a State of Emergency had already been proclaimed. Baldwin, although deeply depressed, really had no choice but to break off negotiations. In the previous August, in defending the interim subsidy, he had given a strong warning to any who intended to have 'a deliberate and avowed policy to force a stoppage of this kind on the country', and his authority could hardly have survived another apparent climb-down. He was, like the T.U.C., caught irrevocably by events. The T.U.C., also trapped in a false position and unsure of its course, had to press on. The General Strike began at midnight on May 3rd.

Both sides surprised themselves and each other. The strike was virtually total, an unpleasant shock for the Government; the Government's emergency plans, and the flood of eager volunteers to work them, were a considerable surprise to the unions. Baldwin was calm and moderate, as were most of the union leaders. Churchill was given the relatively harmless job of editing a government newspaper, the *British Gazette*, which he did with characteristic élan. It was an inflammatory, one-sided, and provocative propaganda broadsheet, which aroused a considerable degree of resentment, and not least in its insistent demands for 'unconditional surrender'. The counter-attack took the form of the *British Worker*, which never attained the *Gazette*'s circulation nor could match its frenzied style.

More serious was Churchill's attempt to commandeer the B.B.C., which its managing director, John Reith, successfully repelled with the support of Davidson and Baldwin. But a price had to be paid. The B.B.C., behind an impressive façade of impartiality, was in fact strongly supportive of the Government, and its influence was far greater than that of the *British Gazette*. Its most notorious action was to refuse permission to the Archbishop of Canterbury to broadcast an appeal for a settlement drawn up by leaders of the Church and the Nonconformists on May 7th; it was eventually broadcast, in amended form, on May 11th. But it was also, like Baldwin and unlike Churchill, in favour of a negotiated settlement. On May 12th the T.U.C. gladly accepted a compromise formula proposed by Samuel and called off the strike. By this stage the mood had grown ugly, and there was general agreement by contemporary observers that it was as well that the strike ended when it did. Certainly, Churchill did not emerge with an enhanced reputation. 'Throughout the 1930s', as George Isaacs has written, 'suspicion of Churchill was one factor in preventing any attempt by the trade unions to make a closer alliance with him in opposition to the foreign policy of the Baldwin and Chamberlain governments.' A reading of the issues of the *British Gazette* gives part of the answer.

The announcement of the end of the strike had shocked the majority of the strikers, exhilarated by their solidarity, and they determined to fight on. When some employers tried to capitalise on the Government's victory, the strike was in effect resumed voluntarily until Baldwin categorically denounced the owners' tactics. But the memories of this attempt by some employers to cut wages and impose humiliating conditions for accepting men back were to prove very enduring.

The abandoned miners maintained their stand, and the owners were relentless. Baldwin and Churchill—who followed his characteristic principle of 'in victory, magnanimity'—could not persuade the latter otherwise, and eventually the miners had to capitulate unconditionally. As Amery has written, they 'struggled back to the pits on the owners' terms, including longer hours, a beaten and resentful army'. But they had not fought entirely in vain. The crude tactic of the general strike was never to be repeated, and its failure gave strength to those union leaders, notably Ernest Bevin and Walter Citrine, who had always believed in compromise, and it seriously damaged the wilder union leaders. But the solidarity of the workers had made a deep impression upon many sensible employers. With Government support, Sir Alfred Mond, the head of Imperial Chemicals, initiated employer–union discussions which achieved little of immediate practical value, but which were highly significant of the new mood.

Unhappily, this did not include the politicians. The die-hard Conservatives were determined to capitalise on their success, and carried Baldwin reluctantly with them. The Trade Disputes and Trade Union Act of 1927 deliberately set the clock back twenty years, although not quite to the Taff Vale Judgement.[1] Sympathetic strikes, or any strike designed to coerce the Government, were made illegal, and union members who wished to pay the political levy now had to 'contract in' rather than 'contract out', thereby jeopardising a substantial part of the income of the Labour Party. It was a mean and useless act of vengeance that only temporarily affected the Labour Party income and created a lasting and justifiable resentment. Given the overwhelming feeling in his party and in the Cabinet, Baldwin had little choice but to acquiesce. It won him no further friends in the Conservative ranks, but it was a remarkable tribute to the estimate that his opponents had formed of him that the respect and trust he had created in the Labour Party were not seriously affected.

It was a persistent criticism of Baldwin at the time—and subsequently—that he did not 'lead' his Government, that he waited upon events, was vacillating, and was usually unsure of his course. These strictures had justice in them, but in retrospect they enhance, rather than diminish, his character and intelligence. His principal mistakes had been to bring back Birkenhead, Churchill, and Joynson-Hicks, and particularly to the posts he offered them, but he had had little choice if he was to re-unite the Conservative Party after the schism of 1922–3. He held together his Cabinet effectively for five years, and during that period did much to reduce the venom in industrial relations that had built up so ominously since the war. Baldwin did not have the answer to unemployment, but at least he understood what it meant. Although not a political innocent, and quite capable of swift, severe, and effective action in the lower levels

[1] See Volume I, pp. 212 and 231.

of public life, he had a humanity and basic moral standards that were far higher than those of Lloyd George or many men then active in politics. He was a refreshing personality, and it is probably more to Baldwin than to any other British politician that the nation owed the fact that it faced the terrible crisis of 1939–40 united. But for this imperishable achievement he was to receive little gratitude, particularly in the Conservative Party.

*

Regarded in retrospect, the years 1924–9 represented a lull in the international anarchy that had been rampant since 1914 and which was to be resumed in the 1930s, and through which we have been living ever since. The Treaty of Locarno was described by Austen Chamberlain as 'the real dividing line between the years of war and the years of peace', and such it appeared to be. In 1926 Germany joined the League, and in the same year the Preparatory Commission of the League on Disarmament was established. The international renunciation of war by the signatories of the Kellogg Pact in 1928 seemed another important step forward. The problem of reparations seemed to have been definitely settled by the Young Plan in May 1930. The Allied troops left the Rhineland. In Russia Zinoviev and his associates were removed in 1927–8, and the strident propagandist interference of the Third International was replaced by belated attention to the lamentable circumstances of the internal affairs of the Soviet Union; the presence of a Soviet representative on the Disarmament Commission from 1927 was seen as a hopeful portent.

In reality, nothing much had changed, despite a greatly improved atmosphere. But, after the inter-European relations of 1906–25, anything would have seemed an improvement. Europe remained the dominant centre of the world, on which all attention was fixed and whose actions directly affected virtually every part of the world. International affairs were still conducted wholly on a national or at best a regional basis. The pre-1914 system of local alliances had not disappeared. The smaller new nations were still subservient to the big ones. The tendency towards autocratic government throughout the world was sharply apparent, and was seen particularly in Russia, Italy, Spain, Portugal and Greece. The triumph of democracy, so freely forecast at the end of the war, had failed to materialise.

This was not how the British saw the situation at the time. The condition of Europe was enormously better in 1929 than it had been even five years before. An incident here and there might rattle the tiles, but such breezes quickly faded away. The calm warmth of peace, prosperity, and optimism glowed throughout Europe. The scars of the war had healed. The nightmare was over.

Yet, for those who wished to see them, there were some ominous signs. Mussolini, addressing a large audience at Florence, on May 17th, 1930, struck what was to become the dominant theme of the 1930s:

> Words are a very fine thing; but rifles, machine-guns, warships, aeroplanes and cannon are still finer things. They are finer, Black-shirts, because right unaccompanied by might is an empty word. . . . Fascist Italy, powerfully armed, will offer two simple alternatives: a precious friendship or an adamantine hostility.

And, in an article in the *Saturday Evening Post* in February 1930, Churchill pointed to the necessity to form a 'United States of Europe', and wrote:

> The Treaty of Versailles represents the apotheosis of nationalism. . . . The empire of the Habsburgs has vanished. That immense, un-wieldy, uneasy but nevertheless coherent entity has been Balkan-ized. Poland has escaped from her eighteenth century dungeon, bristling with her wrongs and dazzled by the light. The whole zone of Middle Europe, from the Baltic to the Aegean, is split into small states vaunting their independence, glorying in their new-found liberty, acutely self-conscious and exalting their particularisms. They must wall themselves in. They must have armies. They must have foundries and factories to equip them. They must have national industries to make themselves self-contained and self-supporting. They must revive old half-forgotten national languages just to show how different they are from the fellows across the frontier. No more discipline of great empires: each for himself and a curse for the rest. What a time of jubilee!

It was perhaps not without significance that 1929 saw the publication in Britain of several outstanding anti-war books, of which the most popular were Robert Graves's *Good-Bye To All That*, Edmund Blunden's *Undertones of War*, and Siegfried Sassoon's *Memoirs*. R. C. Sherriff's play *Journey's End* was also firmly in the spirit of revulsion against the Great War that was now so apparent.

One other development of the 1920s must be recorded. At the Imperial Conference of 1926 a report of a committee presided over by Balfour was accepted. For the first time an attempt was made to define the relationship of the members of the Empire. Britain and the Dominions, the vital sentences ran, were 'autonomous Communities within the British Empire, equal in status . . . united by a common allegiance to the Crown, and freely associated as members of the British Commonwealth of Nations'. This definition was formally ratified in the Statute of Westminster in 1931. The formula was in reality merely a statement of the existing situation and the relationship between the 'old' Dominions. Virtually no consideration was given to the implications for the future; significantly, the Report stated (paragraph III) that:

It will be noted that in the previous paragraphs we have made no mention of India. Our reason for limiting their scope to Great Britain and the Dominions is that the position of India in the Empire is already defined by the Government of India Act, 1919 . . .

This bland assumption was to be swiftly challenged.

*

By 1928 it was apparent that the Baldwin Government was losing ground. It had had its achievements, but it seemed dull, uninspired, and was clearly unable to solve the intractable problem of unemployment. As John Boyd Orr wrote in 1927:

A ruling class living on dividends, masses of the people on the dole, and a Government trying to maintain an uneasy status quo, is a picture which fills thinking people with despair.

It was particularly in economic and industrial matters that the Government's performance was regarded, with good cause, as pedestrian and incomprehending. Churchill's last three Budgets were characterised by ingenious but unsatisfying expedients to provide a technical surplus; it was only too clear that there was a complete absence of strategic and serious economic thinking at the level that the Liberals were now advocating, which John Strachey and Sir Oswald Mosley were proselytising, and which some Conservative back-benchers—notably Robert Boothby, Harold Macmillan and Oliver Stanley—were urging. Churchill robustly dismissed Keynes's proposals as 'camouflaged inflation', entranced the Commons with his brilliant speeches, and proceeded on his temporising way.

Keynes declared that his principal objective was 'the transition from economic anarchy to a regime which deliberately aims at controlling and directing economic forces in the interests of social justice and social stability', and the adamant rejection of such attitudes disturbed many Conservatives. As Amery subsequently wrote:

> The combination of deflation and free imports which he [Churchill] stubbornly maintained bore its immediate fruit in wage reductions, long-drawn industrial conflict and continuous heavy unemployment; its long-term results in the conviction of the working classes that Socialism alone could provide a remedy for unemployment.

But could Labour provide this remedy? This was certainly the impression that it confidently gave. But closer inspection revealed that Labour thinking on the subject had not advanced at all since 1924, and that the differences between Labour and Conservative attitudes and policies were minimal.

For years Labour speakers had convinced themselves, and their audiences, that sufficient national wealth was available for assisting the unemployed, but by the middle of the 1920s they concluded that it was not. Snowden had a horror of inflation, and wrote in 1920 that 'Government borrowing in this country has reached a point which threatens national bankruptcy'. In 1924 he had pursued a rigid Treasury policy. In 1925 Labour abandoned the proposal of raising funds for unemployment assistance from direct taxation. In 1927 Snowden was warning that 'the microbe of inflation is always in the atmosphere', and he was undoubtedly, and unhappily, correct when he wrote in 1929 that 'there is a good deal more orthodoxy in Labour's financial policy than its critics appear to appreciate'. Echoing Snowden was William Graham, who in many respects was even more 'orthodox' than Snowden, and who was declaring in 1929 that 'Labour has no desire to increase expenditure, but to decrease it'. These were not merely election-year soothing noises. As events were to demonstrate, Snowden and Graham meant what they said.

The one really constructive Labour programme was put forward by Oswald Mosley, John Strachey, and Allen Young in 1925 in *Revolution By Reason*, which emphasised that:

At present Socialist thought appears to concentrate almost exclusively upon this transfer of present purchasing power by taxation, and neglects the necessity for creating additional demand to evoke our unused capacity which is at present not commanded either by the rich or the poor.

They recommended the nationalisation of the banks, planning by an Economic Council, subsidies to industry, and bulk purchasing of raw materials. Mosley also was prepared to abandon the Gold Standard and let the pound sterling fall to its true value. Such proposals were regarded with distaste and incomprehension by the party hierarchy, and Labour took office in 1929 still firmly committed to the vaguely defined attitudes of 1924.

The only other serious thinking on the subject came from the Liberals.

In 1925 the Liberal Industrial Enquiry had been initiated, in which politicians and economists collaborated at length and in detail, and in which the prominent intellects were those of Keynes, Hubert Henderson, Philip Kerr and Seebohm Rowntree. The first fruit was the first 'Yellow Book', published in February 1928, entitled *Britain's Industrial Future*, which advocated government planning and substantial investment in industry. It was the parent of the 'Orange Book' *We Can Conquer Unemployment*, issued in March 1929. Its central features were an emergency programme of public works—principally in roads and housing—and long-term planning. It caused a sensation, and may be regarded as the most brilliant and far-seeing programme put forward by any political party in Britain in this century.

It was at once subjected to vehement counter-attack and distortion by both main parties. On this at least they were united. The Government issued a reply which described the Liberal proposals as irresponsible and impracticable, and which would require a dictatorship to operate. Keynes retorted with justification that 'Mr. Baldwin had invented the formidable argument . . . that you must not do anything because it will mean that you will not be able to do anything else'.

The Conservatives, after deriding the Liberal programme as being unsound and impracticable, then dwelt heavily upon their own record since 1924. The De-Rating of Industry Act had relieved industry of some £27 million, which could be used for investment. There had been a record of steady development in the public services which would be continued, though a Conservative Government would not follow 'hasty and ill-considered schemes which could only lead to wasteful and unfruitful expenditure'. The 1925 Pensions Act had been of substantial benefit; 930,000 houses had been built since 1925; infant mortality had been reduced from 75 to 65 per 1,000 births, and much more besides. It was a familiar Conservative refrain—'Safety First', 'You never had it so good', 'Don't let Labour ruin it'.

Labour produced a reply of sorts to the Liberal programme, written by G. D. H. Cole, which was singularly unimpressive, and contained not a single original thought or proposal. The Liberals' scheme was assailed for its 'irresponsibility', and vague references were made to Labour's 'more diversified plans'. What were they? In MacDonald's account at the Albert Hall on April 29th, 1929, they consisted of the following:

> Roads will be built as a system, bridges broken and reconstructed, railways reconditioned, drainage carried on, afforestation advanced, coasts protected, houses built, emigration dealt with, colonial economic expansion planned and carried out.

Thus the Conservatives went to the country in May 1929 with considerable confidence on the cry of 'Safety First'. The strategy misfired for several reasons, of which the principal one was that the fears of Labour, which had been whipped up so successfully in 1924, had virtually disappeared. The Liberals were much more formidable than they had been five years before. And the Conservatives, running on their record, had little positive to offer. The aftermath of the General Strike—particularly the Trade Disputes Act and the breaking-off of diplomatic relations with the Soviet Union on the flimsiest of pretexts in 1927—had hurt it in the traditional Tory working-class electorate, and undid much of the good done by Baldwin's common sense and reason. A party political broadcast by Churchill set the tone:

> We have to march forward steadily and steadfastly, along the highway. It may be dusty, it may be stony, it may be dull; it is certainly uphill all the way, but to leave it is only to flounder in the quagmires of delusion and have the coat torn off your back by the brambles of waste.

The election contained two innovations—broadcasts by the party leaders, of which Baldwin was the most impressive and Lloyd George the least—and the use by the Conservatives of mobile cinemas, which were particularly effective in remote rural areas.

The results were inconclusive for Labour and Conservatives, but a bitter disappointment to the Liberals. In this, the distrust of Lloyd George may have been the major factor; the strength of the Labour and Conservative organisations was certainly another; but perhaps the most important element was the fact that the Liberal programme was too revolutionary in the context of 1929. Nevertheless, the Liberal performance was not unimpressive. They put up 512 candidates and secured 5·31 million votes. It was in terms of seats won that the acute disappointment lay. Labour, with 8·4 million votes, won 287 seats; the Conservatives, with 8·6 million, won 261; the Liberals, with their 5·31 million, won only 59. The election had at least been a decisive vote of no confidence in the Baldwin Government. 13·7 million votes cannot be lightly disregarded. But it had been wholly indecisive about the alternative.

Another remarkable—and historic—statistic about this election should be emphasised. The total registered electorate was now nearly 29 million, an increase of 7½ million since 1918—and those figures had then included Southern Ireland. Even more remarkable was the fact that the number of women electors (15,196,000) exceeded that of male voters by some 1½ million. It may be recalled that the total electorate, including Southern Ireland, had been 7,267,000 in the 1906 General Election. This comprised some 27 per cent of adults over 21, and only 58 per cent of male adults. The 1918 electorate had been 78 per cent of all adults. By 1929 virtually the entire adult population was entitled to the vote. What Churchill lamented as 'the age of mass effects' had arrived.

Baldwin did not meet Parliament as he had in 1924, and promptly resigned. MacDonald formed his second Administration.

MacDonald's leadership had come under serious criticism after the 1924 defeat, and there had been talk of replacing him by Henderson, which Henderson himself had effectively quenched. But the uneasiness remained, and was not assuaged by the revelation that MacDonald had accepted the gift of a Daimler car from a Scottish biscuit manufacturer (who had received a baronetcy) while he had been Prime Minister, nor by his fierce counter-attacks to criticisms levelled against him by the I.L.P. Those who viewed him closely increasingly doubted his commitment to socialism, and were alarmed by his enjoyment of

London society. 'Ramsay MacDonald,' Beatrice Webb sharply noted, 'is a magnificent substitute for a leader. He has the ideal appearance. . . . But he is shoddy in character and intellect.' But there was no serious move to challenge his leadership in the Parliamentary Labour Party, and although many of his colleagues—notably Snowden—had their views on his capabilities, they judged that any attempt to change the leadership would be doomed to failure. But this did not mean that they accepted the high estimates of his leadership that were widely held in the Labour movement.

The *Annual Register* for 1929 comments:

The fall of the Baldwin Ministry, while hailed with exultation by the progressive parties, was not deeply regretted by the bulk of its own supporters, who found much to criticise in its leading personages. Mr. Baldwin had been more amiable than forcible, and had shown himself too much inclined to wait on events instead of trying to direct them. Mr. Churchill had proved himself the most able debater in the party, if not in the House, but as a financier his success had been questionable; he had not fulfilled his promises of reducing expenditure, and he left to his successor a formidable task in the financing of the de-rating scheme.

Thus, not greatly mourned, Mr. Baldwin's Ministers gathered their political belongings and reluctantly moved from the balmy warmth of office into the cool shades of Opposition. 'We all parted very happily' Amery wrote in his diary, 'voting ourselves the best government there has ever been, and full of genuine affection for S.B.'

CHAPTER SEVEN

THE TURNING-POINT, 1929–1931

THE MORROW OF defeat in 1929 found the Conservative Party in an ugly and fractious mood. As in 1923, the bulk of the criticism fell upon Baldwin and his closest associates, particularly J. C. C. Davidson, the party chairman, and the author of 'Safety First'. The party was, as Austen Chamberlain noted, 'divided, disgruntled, and confused', and in an article in the *Saturday Review* in November, Harold Macmillan wrote:

> The Conservative Party has no clear policy on immediate problems; it has no clear goal towards which it feels itself to be striving. It has too many 'open questions' and too many closed minds.

Beaverbrook had been politically quiescent for some time. He had been absorbed by his rapidly expanding and highly successful newspaper empire, and had been downcast by variations in his own health and by the deaths of his mother and wife. Now he made a dramatic return with the 'crusade' of Empire Free Trade, which was in fact Tariff Reform and Imperial Preference jumbled up and clothed in a new guise. It was not a coherent programme, and perhaps it was simply because of this that it had such success. It became fashionable in the top Conservative circles to depict Beaverbrook as an evil, unscrupulous, calculating megalomaniac of limitless ambition. He certainly had many faults, but these were hardly to be numbered among them. Beaverbrook had beliefs, and he loved crusades. Above all, his greatest joy lay in stirring things up, a characteristic that deeply shocked respectable public men—particularly when they were on the receiving end of Beaverbrook's disfavour or mockery. He was a marvellous raconteur and mimic; he was also a superb journalist and public speaker and, when in the mood, wonderful fun. His political judgement veered from the wrong to the execrable, and his devotion

to his friends and relentless hostility to his foes belied the label of
'calculating'. He was warm, opinionated, often intolerable, always
brash, yet to the end possessed of a magnetism and vitality that made
all others seem bleak and dreary. Empire Free Trade was much more
of an imposture than Tory Democracy had been, but when Beaverbrook hurled himself into a crusade things were likely to happen.

In July 1929 the first happening occurred. At a by-election at
Twickenham, the Conservative candidate announced his conversion
to the new creed; he was disowned by the Central Office, but several
Conservative M.P.s announced their intention of speaking for him
and did so. The Conservatives lost the seat; each faction ascribed the
loss to the action, or inaction, of the other. This was an interesting
beginning.

At least two ex-Ministers, Amery and Neville Chamberlain, were
dedicated Protectionists, and several back-benchers—particularly the
right-wingers who had grumbled against Baldwin since 1923—were
sympathetic to Beaverbrook's crusade. Baldwin, who could scent
trouble more quickly than most politicians, sought a *modus vivendi*, but
by the end of the year no real progress had been made. The Rothermere and Beaverbrook newspapers were in full cry, and their cause
gave a good excuse for critics of Baldwin to group themselves behind
it. The 'crusade' became a party—the United Empire Party. At a
public dinner early in 1930 Rothermere proposed Beaverbrook as the
new leader of the party, to which Beaverbrook replied by describing
Rothermere as 'the greatest trustee of public opinion that we have
ever seen in the history of journalism', and declaring that he would
serve loyally under Baldwin 'subject of course to his adoption of the
policy in which I so earnestly believe'. He went on to announce that
Empire Free Trade candidates would be put up wherever necessary.

This challenge could not be lightly dismissed. Serious attempts were
made to provide a formula that would placate Beaverbrook and not
alarm the Free Traders in the party hierarchy. At one stage, at the
beginning of March 1930, it seemed as though an arrangement had
been reached. Beaverbrook seemed to be soothed, and Rothermere
was angered by Beaverbrook's apparent betrayal. To the dismay of
the Conservative leaders this rift proved to be brief. Early in April
Beaverbrook charged that the Conservative leaders had broken their
side of the bargain by nominating a candidate at a by-election at
Nottingham who was opposed to Empire Free Trade. Beaverbrook

virtually demanded that the candidate be disowned; Davidson refused. A few days later, basing his case on a Conservative party policy circular, Beaverbrook declared open war again against the leadership. He refused to appear on the same platform as Baldwin. At another by-election, at East Fulham, a Conservative with Beaverbrook–Rothermere support won a Labour seat, which was hailed by the *Mail* and *Express* as evidence of the strength of the cause of Empire Free Trade. By now, the United Empire Party had a membership of 170,000.

The Conservative Party was becoming extremely nervous at these uncomfortable developments. An immediate scapegoat was Davidson, who resigned in June under fire, and was replaced by Neville Chamberlain.[1] But the assaults on Baldwin, far from abating, drew new encouragement. As one commentator noted:

> The Conservative revolt against Mr. Baldwin's leadership is gaining strength, and preparations are being considered for definite open actions. The resignation of Mr. Davidson from the Chairmanship of the party organization has stimulated the movement . . . it is hailed by the anti-Baldwin faction as a success in the campaign against Mr. Baldwin himself.

Baldwin was twice compelled in the summer and autumn to summon party meetings to pass motions of confidence in himself (in October he won by 462 to 116)—a sure sign of declining authority. By the end of the year it seemed certain that his tenure of the leadership could not be prolonged much further.

But the disruptive activities of the Press barons, and the considerable success of Empire Free Trade, did not constitute the only strains within the Conservative Party.

As has been related, the steps towards Indian self-determination had been cautious. The Morley–Minto and Montagu–Chelmsford Reforms had improved Indian representation without affecting the reality of British supremacy. The fact that Britain was in India, and would remain there indefinitely, was subject to little active dispute in British politics, and particularly in the Conservative Party. Seeley's statement of 1883 that withdrawal 'would be the most inexcusable of

---

[1] Davidson's achievements had been many, but perhaps the most durable was the establishment of the Conservative Research Department, subsequently often— and wrongly—credited to Neville Chamberlain.

all conceivable crimes and might possibly cause the most stupendous of all conceivable calamities' represented the established view. Radical criticism of Empire had been assuaged by the gradual—and very gradual—movement towards self-government. Reform and the widening of Indian responsibilities was one thing; abandonment was quite another. As Morley had declared:

> There is a school of thought who say that we might wisely walk out of India and that the Indians could manage their own affairs better than we can. Anybody who pictures to himself the anarchy, the bloody chaos that would follow from any such deplorable step might shrink from that sinister decision.

The first step in the revival of Indian nationalism had been taken in reaction to Curzon's partition of Bengal in 1905. Nevertheless, India had been relatively quiescent until the end of the Great War. The Amritsar massacre in 1919, the anti-Turkish policies of the Lloyd George Government, and the general ferment of ideas aroused by the war all played their part. But there had been cause enough for disaffection in the past. The factor that added a crucial new dimension to the situation was the personality of Mohandas Gandhi. In this frail, determined, saintly but politically highly acute man all the streams of Indian protest merged and met. 'An Englishman', he wrote, 'never respects you till you stand up to him. Then he begins to like you. He is afraid of nothing physical; but he is very mortally afraid of his own conscience if ever you appeal to it, and show him to be in the wrong.'

Gandhi's first campaign of non-violence had begun in August 1920, and developed into civil disobedience a year later. Ugly flames began to glow. Communal and race riots had totalled sixteen between 1900 and 1922; between 1923 and 1926 they rose to seventy-two.

On the British side, the key figure in the 1920s was Birkenhead. He accepted the principle of 'gradualness' only in the sense that 'rendered the final attainment so remote as to be incalculable'.[1] In a speech made in 1925 he said that 'I am not able, in any foreseeable future, to discern a moment when we may safely, either to ourselves or to India, abandon our trust'. In private he was even more explicit: 'To me it is frankly inconceivable', he wrote to the then Viceroy, Reading, in December 1924, 'that India will ever be fit for Dominion self-government.' Birkenhead knew nothing about India. His faculties were now

[1] Gopal: *The Viceroyalty of Lord Irwin*, 3.

in decline, and the defects of his personality were now becoming distressingly apparent.[1] He had not long to live, but in his relentless quest for money he was to sadly compromise his once glittering reputation, signing his name to books he had never read, and dictating bored and inaccurate reminiscences to a secretary after dinner. When he had his first serious haemorrhage he said to his brother, 'I'm done for, Fred'. In reality, he had been 'done for' many years before. After 1922, all was melancholy anticlimax. He died just before the vulture descended. He was bankrupt, and with nothing to leave save gleaming memories and the haunting sense of undefinable and irrevocable loss.

Birkenhead's two most important actions as Secretary for India were the establishment of the Simon Commission in 1926, required by the 1919 Act to review its workings and appointed by Birkenhead to forestall a possible Labour-nominated body and which was boycotted by the Indian political leaders, and the appointment of the Hon. Edward Wood (who was created Lord Irwin) as Viceroy. The majority of the Simon Commissioners—who included Clement Attlee —were as adamantly opposed to the idea of Dominion Status for India as was Birkenhead; for, as he wrote to Irwin, it meant 'the right to decide their own destinies'. This was, of course, the point.

To Birkenhead's surprise and dismay, Irwin proved to be a shrewd, sympathetic, and sensitive Viceroy. He pursued a humane, enlightened and realistic policy. The Independence for India League was founded in 1928, and plans were prepared for further campaigns of civil disobedience. Gandhi's dramatic Salt March to Dandi (March 1930) focused Indian and world attention on the movement. The demand for Dominion Status was being rapidly overtaken by the campaign for complete independence.

It was Irwin's outstanding quality that although he realised that law and order must be preserved, he recognised the eventual need to negotiate. When the Conservatives fell in June 1929 he had no difficulty in persuading Wedgwood Benn, the new Secretary of State, to call a conference attended by representatives from Britain, the Indian States, and British India. A public correspondence was carefully prepared, in which Simon would propose a conference and MacDonald would state the view of the Government that the granting of Dominion Status was inherent in the 1917 Declaration of the Montagu–Chelms-

---

[1] One episode was the provision to him of £10,000 out of Party funds as compensation for loss of earnings (Davidson, op. cit., 276–7).

ford proposals. But the Simon Commission objected to being involved in a correspondence about Dominion Status, and the two announcements—the conference and the interpretation of the 1917 Declaration —were published in the *Gazette of India* on October 31st. The so-called 'Irwin Declaration' came as a thunderbolt to the Conservative Party.

Birkenhead and Reading assailed the Declaration at once, vehemently supported by Churchill. Baldwin first approved it, and then, when he realised that the Simon Commission had not been involved and that the bulk of his party was opposed to it, back-pedalled. This was hardly impressive, but as the months passed it became increasingly clear that Baldwin's sympathies lay more with Irwin and the Labour Government than with their opponents in the Conservative Party. The Conservative reactions to the Irwin Declaration confirmed many in India in their suspicions of British good faith, and the good effects of the Declaration were quickly lost. The Congress Party turned once again to civil disobedience.

The lead was quickly taken by the fading Birkenhead, and by Churchill. After Birkenhead's final decline and death in 1931, Churchill was the dominant figure in the Tory rebellion. Churchill vigorously denounced the granting of Dominion Status, and urged that 'it is necessary without delay to marshal the sober and resolute forces of the British Empire and thus preserve the life and welfare of all the people of Hindustan'. This had been an ominous warning shot, but worse was to follow. The Government, with Baldwin's support, called the first Round Table Conference in 1930, which was boycotted by Congress. By the end of 1930 Churchill was the leading spokesman of the newly formed India Defence League, and his speeches were becoming increasingly frenetic. 'Gandhi-ism', he declared (December 12th, 1930), 'and all it stands for will, sooner or later, have to be grappled with and finally crushed.' He demanded that Congress be broken up and its leaders deported. On February 12th he alleged that 'every service that has been handed over to Indian administration has been a failure'. On February 23rd:

It is alarming and also nauseating to see Mr. Gandhi, a seditious Middle Temple lawyer, now posing as a fakir of a type well known in the East, striding half-naked up the steps of the Viceregal Palace, while he is still organizing and conducting a defiant campaign of civil disobedience, to parley on equal terms with the representative of the King-Emperor.

When, in January 1931, MacDonald called for further consultations with the Indian leaders, and the Congress leaders were released unconditionally from jail, Churchill came into open division with Baldwin on January 26th in the Commons. He violently attacked the Round Table Conference; in one of his best speeches, Baldwin made it plain that he supported the Government. Churchill resigned from the 'Parliamentary Business Committee' and left the front benches. He was not to return to them for eight years. On March 12th he and Baldwin clashed again, and again Baldwin more than held his ground in the debate, quoting from Churchill's celebrated speech on General Dyer a decade before, with devastating effect. Wedgwood Benn, the Secretary of State for India, followed Baldwin with the words 'After the historic speech to which we have just listened there is really, from the point of view of the Indian situation, nothing to add to this debate'. This was not Churchill's opinion.

India was the issue, but it was not the only factor in Churchill's departure. He himself has described his position:

> My idea was that the Conservative Opposition should strongly confront the Labour Government on all great Imperial and national issues, should identify itself with the majesty of Britain as under Lord Beaconsfield and Lord Salisbury, and should not hesitate to face controversy, even though that might not immediately evoke a response from the nation.[1]

He had made his dissatisfaction with Baldwin's unheroic attitudes evident immediately after the 1929 election, and following the Irwin Declaration in October he had written an article in the *Daily Mail* in which he described the granting of Dominion Status as 'a crime'. He became the leading spirit of the India Defence League, and drew a black picture of an India dominated by 'Brahmins who mouth and patter the principles of Western Liberalism and pose as philosophic and democratic politicians', in which 'the British will be no more to them than any other European nation, when the white people will be in India only upon sufferance, when debts and obligations of all kinds will be repudiated, and when an army of white janissaries,

[1] Churchill: *The Gathering Storm*, 32–3.

officered if necessary from Germany, will be hired to secure the armed ascendancy of the Hindu'. The dismissal by the Labour Government of the High Commissioner in Egypt, Lord Lloyd, had also incensed Churchill. 'The British lion', he informed a large audience in Liverpool, 'so fierce and valiant in bygone days, so dauntless and unconquerable through all the agony of Armageddon, can now be chased by rabbits from the fields and forests of his former glory. It is not that our strength is seriously impaired. We are suffering from a disease of the will. We are the victims of a nervous collapse'.

Not the least of the consequences of the Churchill–Baldwin dispute over India—which Duff Cooper described as 'the most unfortunate event that occurred between the two wars'—was that it alienated Churchill from the younger and liberal-minded Conservatives. For his principal supporters he was thrown back upon those elements in the Party whose knowledge of the subject was as limited as his, and who were impelled forward not only by reactionary ignorance about India but by their loathing of what they regarded as Baldwin's 'neo-Socialism'. It was bad company to keep, and most of it swiftly deserted Churchill after the India dispute was eventually resolved. But an even greater tragedy was that, by the extreme violence of his speeches, Churchill debased the coin of alarmism, with the result that when, from 1933 onwards, he was warning his fellow-countrymen of the real perils from Germany, they remembered his dire prognostications of doom if India received even a mild version of Dominion Status. They also remembered much else about this flamboyant, melodramatic, disturbing politician. Thus it was that he became, in Beaverbrook's words, 'a busted flush', a haunted, and sometimes desperate, impotent observer of the events of the next eight years.

But his campaign seriously embarrassed successive Governments in their attempts to find an agreed settlement. This campaign lasted from 1931 until 1935. In 1933 there was a well-planned attempt to destroy the Government's policy at three levels in the Conservative Party machinery. In February, an attempt to get the National Union to disavow the policy was only defeated by 189 to 316. In October, at the Annual Conference, the Government won by 737 to 344. In October 1934 it survived by only 17. Churchill led the attack with unmatched brilliance; it was melancholy that such oratory should have been so devoted. In February 1935, in a national broadcast, he declared that 'two million bread-winners in this country would be tramping the streets and queuing up at the Labour Exchanges', and warned that one-third of the population of Britain 'would have to go down, out, or under, if we ceased to be a great Empire'.

Thus, from 1929 to 1935, the Conservative leadership was exposed to constant harassment from the Right in its attempts to achieve a settlement in India. Indian nationalist opinion was outraged by descriptions of Gandhi as 'a half-naked fakir', and by the repeated statement that Indians were not in a condition even to have Dominion Status. And the Government itself, by being forced to make some concession to its critics, provided a form of Dominion Status that was infinitely less generous than that accorded to the 'white' Empire. All this gave an immense impetus to the total Indian Independence movement.

This lay in the future at the beginning of 1931. The language of the disputes within the party had got notably sharper throughout 1930. At the party meeting on June 24th, Baldwin had described the Press Lords as 'an insolent plutocracy', and read out a letter from Rothermere demanding consultation as to offices in a future Conservative Government. Beaverbrook retorted with spirit by calling on Conservatives to send their party subscriptions to the Empire Crusade, and wrote that 'Baldwin's successive attempts to find a policy remind me of the chorus of a third-rate review. His evasions reappear in different scenes and in new dresses, and every time they dance with renewed and despairing vigour. But it is the same old jig'. The manner in which his newspapers handled the news was well demonstrated when a banner headline declared an 'Australian Resolution for Empire Free Trade'. It transpired to be a resolution passed by the Kyabram Urban District Council in favour of E.F.T., 'provided there was no interference with the tariffs set up to protect Australian industries'. A not insignificant qualification!

Neville Chamberlain was writing as early as July 1930 that 'I have come to the conclusion that if S.B. would go the whole party would heave a sigh of relief. Everywhere I hear that there is no confidence in his leadership or belief in his determination to carry any policy through.'

These movements against Baldwin were unhappily more symptomatic of internal confusions exacerbated by frustration at loss of office than evidence of serious re-thinking in the Conservative Party about the philosophies and future of Conservatism. In any event, Baldwin's critics did not combine. The cause of the Protectionists was not helped by the fact that Beaverbrook's crusade was so obsessed with the Imperial aspect, and was linked to Rothermere's avowed aim to supplant Baldwin as leader. Churchill did not warm greatly to Empire Free Trade, which he regarded as a somewhat unreal cause; the raising of the banner of Britain's Imperial greatness by Churchill did not, however, greatly attract Beaverbrook. Nonetheless, although the forces against him were divided, it was evident that Baldwin's position was precarious at the beginning of 1931.

*

The short-lived Labour Government of 1929–31 was not, as its detractors claimed, standing evidence of Churchill's often repeated charge that Labour was unfit to govern. Its principal failure lay in only one field, that of unemployment, but it was the deep misfortune of that Government and of the party that it was the one field in which Labour had claimed special qualifications—with flimsy evidence. It was also the one that really mattered.

A perverse political godparent seems to have attended the birth of the Labour movement. She gave to it a fine cause for which to fight; she tended it carefully in its fledgling years, enabling it to grow and prosper under the benevolent and condescending guardianship of the Liberal Party; she permitted it to have sufficient independence in which to gain experience, yet without the opportunity to court disaster; she so arranged matters that, when the child was gaining in strength and confidence, those of its Liberal guardian faltered and failed, enabling it to seize its inheritance. But this political godparent failed to bestow the one priceless gift on the child when it emerged from youth; she denied it fortune when in office. There are indeed times when one feels warm sympathy with the bitter complaints of the Labour movement that on no occasion has it ever come into office in calm, or even reasonably calm, times. The political godparent of the Conservative Party denied that federation much, but she ensured that it had generous amounts of good luck in the matter of the taking and leaving of office. In 1929, as in 1945 and even 1964, the Conservatives were removed from the scene a fraction before the political tempests began to rage, leaving Labour to turn haggard and dismayed into the unexpected storm.

Ramsay MacDonald was sixty-two in 1929, and was in reality older than his years. He had been in at the birth of the party, and had borne almost alone the righteous opposition to the Great War. His origins had been humble, yet there had always been about him, in manner, speech and talents, a certain aristocratic aloofness which many found attractive, and many others impressive. He was absolutely convinced of the constitutional road to social reform, contemptuous and even fearful of any suggestions for direct action or outside interference in the proper processes. Yet he was never a House of Commons man; as he once remarked on the Treasury Bench to Herbert Morrison, 'I hate this place'. He was the nominee of the I.L.P. members in 1922, and yet a vast gulf of attitude separated him from them. In 1923 he declared that 'public doles, Poplarism,[1] strikes for increased wages, limitation of output, not only are not Socialism, but may mislead the spirit and policy of the Socialist movement'. What, then, was MacDonald's road to Socialism? Indeed, what *was* his Socialism?

Whenever one approaches this central problem, the man and his message seem to take on a vague, empty, mystical, entity. MacNeill Weir wrote that it was

> that far-off Never-Never-Land born of vague aspirations and described by him in picturesque generalities. It is a Turner landscape of beautiful colours and glorious indefiniteness. He saw it, not with a telescope, but with a kaleidoscope.

This was perhaps a true, although hardly kind, estimate. Mac-Donald was certainly a romantic. He was also a shy and remote man. After the death of his wife in 1911 he wrote:

> I feel the mind of the solitary stag growing upon me. My fireside is desolate. I have no close friends in the world to share either the satisfaction of success or the disturbance of defeat. So I get driven in upon myself more and more, and I certainly do not improve.

It is at once apparent on reading MacDonald's articles and letters that here is a man of exceptional intelligence and sensitivity. The shadow of his illegitimacy[2] certainly assisted this latter aspect, and his enjoyment of the company of the great and the rich was probably

---

[1] In 1921 the Poplar Borough Council refused to pay its share of the expenses of the London County Council in protest against inequities of local rates in rich and poor boroughs, and the word 'Poplarism' was used to describe local authorities' defiance of the Government.

[2] Something that he shared with Ernest Bevin.

more the result of very human gratification at acceptance and security rather than of simple vanity or snobbery. But such traits in a Labour leader were bound to be misinterpreted—and were. Furthermore, his intellectual intolerance of others—and particularly his colleagues— may have been often justified, but was not calculated to make relationships any easier. He was jealous of possible political rivals, and as he aged he at times seemed obsessively concerned to demonstrate his own omniscience. A magnificent public speaker—Beatrice Webb probably did not exaggerate when she called him 'the greatest artist of British politics'—his diffuseness, impatience with detail, and vague but sincere Utopianism served better on a public platform than in dry debate in the Commons or technical discussions in Cabinet. And, even by 1929, his intellect was fading. This was at least partly the consequence of sheer exhaustion and strain. In 1924 he had doubled the offices of Prime Minister and Foreign Secretary, and the pressures of this double burden had played an important part in the maladroit handling of the Campbell Case and the Zinoviev Letter. He was bad at delegating responsibility, was not an efficient administrator, forever conscious of the precariousness of his position and both suspicious and contemptuous of most of his colleagues. And he did not lack vanity.

But in 1929 MacDonald was not able to be his own Foreign Secretary. Arthur Henderson had insisted upon this office, and MacDonald had conceded his claim with reluctance and ill grace. Henderson was sixty-five, and since 1903 he and MacDonald had worked closely together, although often in disagreement. Henderson was warm-hearted, approachable, and gregarious. The Labour Party was the sum total of his life, and his Socialism was confined to what has been appropriately described as 'a vague gradualism'. As the same commentator has written:

. . . his speech-making was mediocre, he wrote nothing. He was dull, practical, teetotal and deeply religious, with all the sterling qualities and limitations of his type. Above all, he was utterly devoted to the Labour movement, which he came to regard as an end in itself. He was, as his biographer has written, 'the incarnation of the Party as a Party'.[1]

Henderson was at least likeable, and was liked. MacDonald was respected. But Philip Snowden was perhaps even more remote than

[1] R. Skidelsky: *Politicians and the Slump*, 68.

his leader. He was working-class self-help Yorkshire, crippled, proud, independent, and bitter. He regarded MacDonald and Henderson with almost equal contempt and dislike. His wife, Ethel, was not an endearing personality, and was deeply disliked in the Labour movement. By this stage, Snowden had no time for the I.L.P. and perhaps even less for the trade union leaders. His political phraseology fully merited the adjective 'vitriolic'. It is possible to say harsh words and yet still be liked, but Snowden's virulent invective had an unforgivable quality about it. He meant every word. But there was no question that Snowden should not be Chancellor of the Exchequer again. Like MacDonald and Henderson, he was one of the party's veterans, in a confederation already excessively awed by the principle of seniority. Like them, he believed in gradualism. Unlike almost anyone else in the party, he actually wanted to be Chancellor. His vigour in debate, and authority of manner when discussing financial and economic matters, made the place his for the asking. As Boothby has written:

> To every outworn shibboleth of nineteenth century economics he clung with fanatic tenacity. Economy, Free Trade, Gold—these were the keynotes of his political philosophy; and deflation the path he trod with almost ghoulish enthusiasm.

This was a bad appointment, if inevitable, but another was much more disastrous. With justifiable unease, MacDonald appointed the garrulous, and indolent J. H. Thomas to be Lord Privy Seal with special responsibilities for unemployment, assisted by a three-man committee consisting of George Lansbury (Ministry of Works), Thomas Johnston (Under-Secretary for Scotland) and Sir Oswald Mosley (Chancellor of the Duchy of Lancaster).

Mosley's imperious march from Coalitionist gadfly to Socialist intellectual had been viewed with scepticism and distaste by many in the Labour movement. When one appreciates Mosley's wealth, glamour, manner, and the publicity his every action almost effortlessly acquired, these emotions are understandable. But the combination with John Strachey, which had produced *Revolution By Reason*, brought to the Government the only serious intellectual force that it possessed. He was also its only serious revolutionary. In the words of Harold Nicolson: 'The exuberant dynamism of the Chancellor of the Duchy was ill-attuned to the cheerful lethargy of the Lord Privy Seal.' But there was a good deal more to the situation than that. Mosley was still in a tearing hurry. Fame, and the discovery that he was by far the best public orator in the country, reminding many of the not-forgotten brief glories of Victor Grayson, had encouraged neither the slender elements of modesty in his character nor his patience for slower minds. Humourless and implacably self-confident, he firmly believed that he had the answers to all the ills that plagued the nation. Furthermore, he entertained few apprehensions of his capacities to lead it. Here were the ingredients of a famous disaster, and a major national misfortune.

It would be difficult to conceive a more ill-assorted quartet, but the appointment of Thomas ensured that nothing very revolutionary was likely to emerge. As Mr. Skidelsky comments with justice of him:

> Totally devoid of constructive ideas, intimate with the City and big business, the boon companion of half the House of Commons, the jingoistic upholder of imperial and national unity, his appointment gladdened the conservatives and dismayed the radicals.[1]

These were the diverse and fallible human instruments with which the new Government would endeavour to cure the chronic disease of mass unemployment. It was highly improbable that any positive agreed proposals would emanate from the Thomas group, but the presence of Snowden at the Treasury ensured that any which did slip through would be met with freezing hostility and the certainty of rejection.

*

Although Henderson was Foreign Secretary in title, foreign affairs remained the obsession of the Prime Minister. He warmly supported Irwin's policies in India, pressed forward eagerly with international disarmament, and had his reward in the London Naval Conference of March 1930, in which Britain, America and Japan agreed to ratios which were certainly not to the advantage of the British. Henderson, for his part, worked successively for the resumption of full diplomatic relations with the Soviet Union; the final withdrawal of Allied troops from the Rhineland; the acceptance of the principle of compulsory arbitration in international disputes; and a sharp reversal of policy in Egypt, starting with the removal of Lord Lloyd as High Commissioner and culminating in negotiations towards an Anglo-Egyptian Treaty.

[1] Skidelsky, op. cit., 70.

These initiatives, in the context of 1929–30, can be fairly regarded as enlightened, progressive, and sensible. In this field at least, Labour had gone far to prove that it was responsible and fully fitted for government.

But in October 1929, with the sudden and dramatic collapse of the American stock market, there came the first of a series of events that was to shatter the illusory tranquillity of the second half of the 1920s. The impact upon Britain, it requires emphasis, was not so grievous as it was elsewhere in Europe, but it was bad enough. British exports fell in value from £839 million in 1929 to £666 million in 1930, and then to £461 million in 1931. By July 1930 unemployment had gone over two million, and by December had risen to over 2½ million.

In this darkening situation, Ministers looked helplessly about them In February 1930 Mosley produced a dramatic programme of increased pensions and allowances, protection of home industries by tariffs, import restrictions, bulk purchase agreements; a far more extensive use of public money to finance development; and the rationalisation of industry under central control. These were in fact the same proposals as he had enunciated in 1925, with a certain watering-down of some of the more extreme proposals.

The 'Mosley Memorandum' was submitted to the Cabinet in February; it was definitely rejected in May. Mosley resigned—to be succeeded by the more docile Clement Attlee—and took his case to the Parliamentary Party, where he was defeated by 202 votes to twenty-nine. He then put it before the annual party conference in October, and was only narrowly defeated. In December he published his manifesto, and was supported by seventeen M.P.s, who included Strachey and Aneurin Bevan, a young miner who had recently been elected for Ebbw Vale. In February 1931 Mosley announced the formation of the New Party to put his policies into effect. He was expelled from the Labour Party, supported only by Strachey. Thus did the Government lose perhaps the most able man in its ranks, and turned away from the only policies that had any real hope of success in the deteriorating situation. Thereafter, Mosley's career took him into channels that were to lose him the support of Strachey and of most of his other adherents, and to lead him to the bathos of the British Union of Fascists, and to the immortal denunciation of A. P. Herbert —'A curse on both your blouses!'

All the Government could do, and all that it did do, was to increase the unemployment benefits to the unemployed and abandon the principle of contributory relief. For this they were assailed by the Opposition for their extravagance and from the Labour back benches for their niggardliness. The Government retreated into a cloud of impressive-sounding Commissions and Committees. A Committee of Enquiry into Finance and Industry under Lord Macmillan was appointed in November 1929; in 1930 an Economic Advisory Council under MacDonald's chairmanship was set up. Later in 1930 a Liberal-Labour committee was established, followed by a Royal Commission. Most serious of all, Snowden virtually abdicated the Government's responsibility when he agreed to the appointment of a Committee on National Expenditure chaired by Sir George May in February 1931. Until the Committee reported the Government could only mark time. Meanwhile, what Churchill called 'the economic blizzard' grew even more fierce. The collapse of the Credit Anstalt in May caused further drainage of gold from London. Unemployment approached the figure of three million.

*

One solace for Labour throughout this turbulent period had been the acute divisions within the Conservative ranks, culminating in Churchill's resignation from the front bench over India at the end of January 1931 and a crucial by-election at St. George's Westminster in March. This was, as the *Annual Register* remarked, 'a campaign of unusual scurrility, instigated not by Communists or Socialists, but by titled Conservatives'. Hostility to Baldwin's leadership had become so acute that Baldwin had seriously considered resignation, but had been persuaded to stand and fight. Baldwin in a corner was a very formidable quantity. At St. George's the Beaverbrook–Rothermere factions propelled forward a candidate of little capacity but imposing support. At one point Baldwin brooded over the possibility of fighting the by-election himself, but thought better of it. Duff Cooper, who had lost his Oldham seat in the 1929 election, was nominated as the official Conservative candidate.

Baldwin now exercised again his genius for a diversionary attack. The 'Press Lords' were an easy target, of whom Baldwin had made good use in the past, but now came the opportunity for a knock-down blow. On March 18th he spoke on behalf of Duff Cooper, and turned on the 'Press Lords':

They are engines of propaganda for the constantly changing policies, desires, personal wishes, personal likes and dislikes, of two men. What are their methods? Their methods are direct falsehood, misrepresentation, half-truths, the alteration of the speaker's meaning by publishing a sentence apart from the context, such as you see in these leaflets handed out inside the doors of this hall; suppression and editorial criticism of speeches which are not reported in the paper. These are methods hated alike by the public and by the whole of the rest of the Press. . . . What the proprietorship of these papers is aiming at is power, and power without responsibility—*the prerogative of the harlot throughout the ages.*

It was this final phrase—proposed by Baldwin's cousin, Rudyard Kipling—which electrified the audiences and a wider public. 'I saw the blasé reporters, scribbling self-consciously, jump out of their skins to a man', Duff Cooper's wife later recorded, with vividness rather than total factual accuracy. Duff Cooper rode to an easy victory, Beaverbrook swiftly came to terms with Baldwin, and the latter's critics in the Conservative Party relapsed either into sullen silence or hastened to proclaim their fealty. Neville Chamberlain, whose hand had been reaching eagerly for the succession, had to maintain his patience. Never again, except in the difficult summer of 1936, was Baldwin's leadership in any serious jeopardy.

*

The Conservatives resolved their internal difficulties only just in time. By the early summer of 1931 the Labour Government was in serious trouble. Unemployment continued to rise with inexorable force, the value of British exports fell, Ministers became distraught and helpless, awaiting the solemn judgement of the May Committee. The party was confused and demoralised. By the time the May Committee reported at the end of July, withdrawals from London were running at nearly £2·5 million a day, and unemployment was over three million.

The Report of the May Committee was released after Parliament had risen for the summer recess. Its salient conclusions were that there would be a deficit of £120 millions by April 1932; that new taxation, to raise £24 millions, was required; and that immediate economies, totalling £96 millions, were needed, of which £66½ millions were to be achieved by the reduction of unemployment relief, including a twenty per cent reduction in benefit payments. By this time the situation was almost out of control; a run on sterling had already begun, and the May Report caused a panic among foreigners with short-term British investments.

The Bank of England obtained credits at the beginning of August, but by the 11th the drain was resumed; MacDonald returned hurriedly from Lossiemouth to be told by the bankers that the crisis was one of confidence in the Government, which the Government alone could restore. A balanced Budget and a determined drive for economies—in unemployment benefit in particular—was required. They also proposed meetings between the Government and Opposition leaders, to which MacDonald agreed. The first meeting took place on August 13th, when MacDonald and Snowden met Baldwin and Chamberlain, with Samuel and Donald Maclean representing the Liberals in the absence of Lloyd George, who was recuperating from an operation.

A Cabinet Economy Committee drew up a tentative list of economies totalling £78½ millions; after long sessions, the Cabinet agreed to £56¼ millions on August 19th. But at a meeting with the Opposition leaders on the next day (August 20th) the impression was given that the £78 millions had been agreed. On the same afternoon there was a confused meeting with the General Council and the National Executive, at which it had become clear that the T.U.C. would not accept any reductions in unemployment benefit.

On the afternoon of the 21st, after a day of Cabinets, Snowden and MacDonald reported to the Opposition leaders the true figure of £56 millions; they retorted that these were wholly inadequate. The Opposition was now dominating the Government. On the following morning the Cabinet was summoned again to be told by MacDonald and Snowden that further economies were required. A major split among Ministers now appeared, but there was agreement to submit to the Opposition a new set of proposed economies of £68½ millions, including £12¼ million saved by a ten per cent cut in unemployment allowances.

The Government was now tottering towards collapse, without leadership, hopelessly confused, sorely divided, and subjected to the fierce blasts of conflicting pressures. MacDonald, Snowden, and J. H. Thomas now clutched towards other possibilities of rescue. A cool head and a refusal to be stampeded might have saved the situation, but these were not provided. The waves of the prevailing panic in London swept into the Cabinet Room, and Ministers swayed helplessly in its harsh billows.

It is not possible to decide exactly when the idea had been implanted in MacDonald's mind of extricating himself simultaneously from his acute dilemma and his quarrelling colleagues by seizing the possibility of heading a National Administration. Perhaps the basic psychological need had been there throughout, and he had been sending signals to the Conservatives since 1929. The circumstances of August 1931 were sufficient to tempt him profoundly.

Others were thinking on similar lines, if from different perspectives.

The momentum towards coalition was greatly assisted by the fact that Lloyd George was convalescent; and, although consulted by Samuel and Maclean, was effectively removed from the real negotiations. The Press—and notably *The Times*—was by now pushing the Government hard. But of far greater significance was the mounting concern of the King, who returned from Balmoral and saw MacDonald on the morning of August 23rd. MacDonald told him of the gravity of the position in the Cabinet, and the King decided to consult Samuel and Baldwin. In the normal course of events Baldwin, who was strongly opposed to the idea of coalition, would have been the first to be summoned, but he could not be found immediately (he was discussing the crisis with the editor of *The Times* at the latter's house, and later lunched with Sir Samuel Hoare at the Travellers' Club). Accordingly, as a result of Baldwin not having told the Davidsons— with whom he was staying—of his plans, Samuel, who did favour coalition, was the first to see the King.

Possibly this did not make much difference. The King was now firmly in favour of the principle of coalition, and his dominant and overriding concern was—properly—with national unity at an hour of crisis. Samuel strongly fortified these attitudes. His advice was that if the Government could not agree on the necessary economies, it should be replaced by a National Government, preferably led by MacDonald himself. This suggestion fell upon very receptive ears. Thus, when the King saw Baldwin in the afternoon, the main question put to him was *not* his general advice on the crisis but whether he and his colleagues would serve in such a Government. Put in such terms—virtually an appeal to Baldwin's patriotism—there could only be one answer. The King 'was greatly pleased with Mr. Baldwin's readiness to meet the crisis which had arisen, and to sink Party interest for the sake of the Country'. Baldwin was not, however, enthusiastic or optimistic about the prospects. It remained very much the King's solution, which —for different reasons—also attracted Samuel and Neville Chamberlain.

That evening the crisis reached its culmination when the Cabinet received the reply to its enquiry to the American bankers J. P. Morgan and Company, about the prospects of a loan; it was to the effect that this could only be considered if the bankers were convinced that the Government was sufficiently in earnest. The Government was now firmly in the hands of its opponents. MacDonald appealed to the Cabinet to agree to the larger sum of £78 millions; eleven Ministers were prepared to do so, but ten were not. Accordingly, MacDonald asked all Ministers to place their resignations in his hands, to which they consented. The distracted and perplexed Cabinet adjourned in circumstances of considerable confusion, under the impression that it would be replaced on the following day by a Conservative–Liberal Coalition. But the King urged MacDonald to reconsider the matter, and told him that 'he was the only man to lead the country through this crisis'. The King also agreed to MacDonald's request for a meeting of the party leaders on the next morning. Later that evening Baldwin, Samuel, and Chamberlain entered 10 Downing Street by a back entrance; in the discussion Chamberlain and Samuel urged Mac-Donald to remain Prime Minister, as head of a Coalition Government. Baldwin said nothing.

Thus was the situation on the night of August 23rd–24th. The Government had in effect resigned, but MacDonald, at the personal appeal of the King, had agreed to reconsider his own position. Samuel was enthusiastic for coalition, but Baldwin was not. His judgement was that the best, as well as the most obvious, course was for the Government to resign, for him to form a Conservative Government with suitable guarantees for immediate legislation, and then to dissolve.

But the meeting at Buckingham Palace on the morning of the 24th was dominated by the King, who opened by saying that he trusted that there was 'no question of the Prime Minister's resignation: the leaders of the three Parties must get together and come to some arrangement. His Majesty hoped that the Prime Minister, with the colleagues who remained faithful to him, would help in the formation of a National Government, which the King was sure would be supported by the Conservatives and the Liberals. The King assured the Prime Minister that, remaining at his post, his position and reputation would be much more enhanced than if he surrendered the Government of the country at such a crisis.'[1] After this, there was very little to say, and this momentous meeting took little over thirty minutes. The agreement was that the new Government 'will not be a Coalition in the ordinary sense of the term, but co-operation of individuals' and that its task would be purely to resolve the economic crisis. Thus was born the National Government.

Baldwin and Samuel left to inform their colleagues, and MacDonald to break the astounding news to the Cabinet. Ministers were too stunned to protest. Perhaps most did not grasp the enormity of what had happened. 'We uttered polite things, but accepted silently the accomplished fact', Sidney Webb recorded. 'Lord Sankey proposed a vote of thanks to MacDonald which was passed unanimously and, without further leave-taking, his colleagues left the room.'[2]

In a very literal sense, this was the King's Government. If he had not pressed the idea on MacDonald and had not asked him to reconsider his resignation, and had not conducted his meetings on the 23rd and 24th with the determination to have a National Government, it is very unlikely that it would have been created. If Lloyd George had not been prostrated, it is doubtful whether the King would have been as enthusiastic, and Baldwin would have shied violently from the prospect. If MacDonald's vanity had not been so vulnerable to the urgings of the King, Chamberlain and Samuel . . . But these speculations must remain of academic amusement. For good or ill, the Second Labour Government had gone, and much else besides. Baldwin's instinctive suspicion of coalitions was to be fully justified, and MacDonald's proven inability and weakness in stress were to become even more marked. But in the apprehension and drama of the hour the unhappy long-term consequences of the King's leadership were impossible to discern.

[1] Harold Nicolson: *King George V*, 465–6.   [2] Skidelsky, op. cit., 383.

CHAPTER EIGHT

NEW DANGERS AND TRIBULATIONS, 1931–1935

THE 'ECONOMIC BLIZZARD' of 1929–31 was the turning-point not only for Britain. It marked the doom of the Weimar Republic, and gave Hitler the chance that had seemed so forlorn when his Munich *putsch* had been so ignominiously scattered. It plunged the United States into a terrible depression, from which it was slow to emerge. It rocked, and sometimes fatally disturbed, governments and financial institutions across Europe. The growing confidence of the 1920s was dispersed and destroyed. Anarchy, confusion, and dismay renewed their briefly interrupted dominance.

It was not surprising that in the vital years 1931–5 the majority of British politicians were obsessed by primarily domestic problems, of which the economic situation was the most central. The principal exception was India, and the passage of the Government of India Act, eventually achieved in June 1935, evoked prodigious debate in Parliament—covering some four thousand pages of *Hansard*—and very considerable and heated controversy outside it. For all its imperfections, in its recognition of Indian rights it did indeed constitute 'a monument to the sincerity of declared British intentions'.[1] The adoption of a general ten per cent tariff in 1932 and the Ottawa Conference of the same year marked a significant change from the temporising economic policies of the 1920s without representing a shift of sufficient substance to meet the remaining problem of concentrated industrial unemployment. Neville Chamberlain's Unemployment Act of 1934 abolished the hated 'means test' that had been introduced in 1931, and established an Unemployment Assistance Board intended to provide a more fair and consistent system. But it was still based on the

---

[1] *Oxford History of Modern India*, 370.

insurance principle, and did not receive the warm approval from Labour that it merited.

The British were oppressed by their own concerns. There was an increasingly evident isolationist mood. 'Right or Left, everybody was for a quiet life', as the Permanent Under-Secretary at the Foreign Office, Sir Robert Vansittart, subsequently wrote. To arouse apprehension and a sense of awareness of what was happening in Europe was, as Boothby has written, 'like boxing a stone wall'. Nor was this particularly surprising. The British were engaged in the process, which was not fully achieved by 1939, of pulling themselves out of another major economic crisis. Although they experienced no hardship on the scale of the American Depression, it was a grim period for many. The intractable million of unemployed remained intractable, and there was consequently little interest in foreign affairs. To most, what happened in Germany was of insignificant interest, no more relevant to the lives of the multitude than upheavals in Egypt or difficulties in India—indeed, probably less relevant. It was only very slowly that the realisation dawned that the emergence of Hitler did indeed have a direct and personal relevance, and by then it was too late.

Throughout the 1930s—and, indeed, until 1945—Britain was ruled by essentially Conservative Governments. The National Government formed on August 24th, 1931, consisted of MacDonald, Baldwin, Neville Chamberlain, Sir Samuel Hoare, Cunliffe-Lister, Samuel, Snowden, Lord Sankey, Thomas and Lord Reading. By his actions over India, Churchill had excluded himself; Austen Chamberlain— who was chagrined by the offer of the Admiralty—was evidently ageing; a more surprising omission was that of Amery who, after a lifetime of battling for the cause of Protection, was left out of the Government that at last accepted it. The Liberals did not fight hard for their former faith; under the formula of 'agreement to differ' initiated by Lord Hailsham, they opposed Chamberlain's Import Duties Bill, with little effect or even enthusiasm, and in 1932 resigned (with Snowden) when they considered the results of Ottawa—which were largely nugatory, and admirably described as 'a repudiation of Free Trade principles in theory, though not in practice'[1]—the final apostasy. Lloyd George denounced Ottawa vigorously: 'the mutilated statues of Peel, Cobden, and Bright have been finally relegated to the scrap-heap to be melted down to provide material for the bronze

[1] Taylor, op. cit., 334.

figures of Chamberlain (père et fils) on a pedestal showing in bas-relief the great anti-food taxers MacDonald, Snowden, Runciman, and Samuel as pouting supporters; at the base Baldwin gazing triumphantly at a prostrate Beaverbrook with his Empire Free Trade banner in the dust'. This did not aid the cause of Liberal reunion. In reality, the Liberals were broken, even more so than Labour.

The economic crisis that had created the National Government was not miraculously averted; indeed, after Snowden[1] brought in an emergency Budget on September 10th that substantially carried out the recommendations of the May Committee and cut unemployment benefits and the salaries of Government-paid persons by an average of ten per cent, the crisis actually got worse. The main cause was a disturbance in the Fleet at Invergordon which was described as a mutiny and involved ten thousand men; this necessitated a hasty revision of the Government's plans, but not before Britain had been unceremoniously forced off the gold standard. The heavens did not fall.

Snowden's Budget had been vehemently opposed by the embittered Labour Party, and the Conservatives now pressed for an election. Neville Chamberlain is generally credited for evolving the formula in which the National Government appealed to the country for 'a doctor's mandate' whereby the three parties would fight independently but together under this ingenious banner, and not oppose each other. It was, in practical terms, a ganging up on Labour. Thus, the Conservatives campaigned for a modest Protectionist policy, the National Liberals heroically stood by Free Trade, and National Labour pledged that the tariff issue would be impartially examined after the election. Baldwin, with even greater vagueness, said that the Government 'must be free to consider any and every expedient which may help to establish the balance of trade'.

The election was, of course, a direct vote of no confidence in Labour and left the Lloyd George Liberals in limbo. It was, as Mowat has commented, 'the coupon election all over again, though, let it be granted, without the coupons'.[2] It was not the most elegant of campaigns, and the Labour Party was justified in feeling sore about the alarmist character of the National programme, and not least by Snowden's charge that their modest proposals were 'Bolshevism run

---

[1] Snowden went to the House of Lords in November as Lord Privy Seal, and was replaced as Chancellor of the Exchequer by Neville Chamberlain.

[2] Mowat, op. cit., 409.

mad'. But the tide was running harshly against them. In a mood of uncharacteristic panic, impregnable Labour citadels collapsed, and a considerable number of young Conservatives fighting forlorn ventures found themselves in the House of Commons. In the Northumberland mining constituency of Morpeth a Labour majority of more than 16,000 in 1929 produced in 1931 a comfortable Conservative majority; in Gateshead, Ernest Bevin, fighting his first election, experienced a Labour majority of 16,700 becoming a Conservative one of 12,938. Many former Liberals clearly voted Conservative; evidently a considerable number of Labour voters did not bother to vote at all; probably many who did switched their allegiance. The results were devastating—not only for Labour but for Lloyd George, and for Mosley, whose New Party fought twenty-four seats without success, Mosley himself losing his seat. The New Party did even worse in total votes (36,377 in 24 constituencies as opposed to 70,844 in 26) than the Communists.[1]

Labour, deserted and reviled by its former leaders, had gone down to catastrophic defeat, only a stunned fragment of fifty-two crawling back to the House of Commons. Of the former front bench, only Lansbury—who became leader—Attlee and Stafford Cripps survived. Lloyd George's party was reduced to a family quartet. Suddenly, there was no Parliamentary Opposition, and, although Labour was to win back a hundred seats in 1935 and make a modest revival, it was to remain a minority party with no real prospect of office until the events of 1940 brought its leaders into a very different Coalition than that which reigned in 1931.

*

Throughout the 1930s, Britain made a considerable economic recovery. In 1932 Chamberlain introduced his modest tariff of ten per cent, and cut Bank Rate to two per cent. Although there was still a tendency for governments to shy violently away from anything that savoured of 'planning', Government interventions were far more substantial—if unsystematic—than they had been in the 1920s. Keynes was still regarded as heretical, and unemployment was only slightly reduced. (It was 1·2 million in 1929, 2·7 million in 1931, 2·5 million in 1933, and 1·4 million by 1937.) The general level of British exports remained depressingly low. But the overall picture was one of substantial improvement, particularly in the consumer and service

[1] R. Skidelsky: *Oswald Mosley*, 279.

industries, and in the south there was a really remarkable transformation in the 'white collar' professions and industries. The 1930s were, in fact, the golden years of the British middle class.

But although this Parliament was not initially dominated by issues of foreign affairs or rearmament, these gradually consumed its increasing attention, acting as a darkening back-drop to the concerns of Members of Parliament with the economic depression, unemployment, and the apparently interminable India debates, in which Hoare conducted the Government of India Bill through its complex and extended stages with considerable skill and moderation, thus marking him out for future promotion. His young Under-Secretary, R. A. Butler, was clearly a rising man, as were Duff Cooper, W. S. Morrison, Walter Elliot, and a notably flamboyant and publicity-conscious Minister, Leslie Hore-Belisha, Minister of Transport from 1934 to 1937, and immortalised by the flashing 'Belisha Beacons' for pedestrian crossings introduced under his regime. Each was spoken of as a future Prime Minister. But the star of Anthony Eden was rising much faster —perhaps too fast for his own good. Little notice was taken of Harold Macmillan, who, rebellious and intense, aroused irritation in the party hierarchy and made little immediate impact.

Of the senior Ministers, only Neville Chamberlain enhanced his reputation, his massive competence and self-assurance evoking respect but little affection, particularly in the Labour Party. Simon's arrogant legalisms were equally resented. MacDonald, contemptuously dismissed by Churchill as 'The Boneless Wonder', was in marked and pathetic decline. Cunliffe-Lister, although outstandingly able, was too acerbic for most tastes. Jimmy Thomas blundered along harmlessly enough at the Colonial Office, delighting the King with his racy conversation and enjoying his celebrity as a favourite of the House of Commons.

But what of Baldwin? Although only a year younger than Mac-Donald, and sixty-four in 1931, he was clearly still highly alert and physically very fit. But, as has been emphasised, he was a very sensitive man, and the events of 1929–31 had hurt him deeply. He had been much closer to quitting in January 1931 than most contemporaries —and several historians—have realised. He was still estranged from a substantial element in the Conservative Party, which, with Churchill's vigorous encouragement, was incessantly barking at his heels over India throughout the Parliament. He was held in politics partly through sheer habit, partly because he had not abandoned his vision of the Conservatives as a truly national party, partly because he felt that the task of national reconciliation which he had begun had not been completed, and, perhaps principally, through a profound sense of national duty at a time of serious crisis. But these were not the only factors. His reluctance to see Neville Chamberlain take his place, which was entirely natural after recent events, and his strong desire to defeat Churchill and the die-hards over India, also played their part.

But although Baldwin was, as Bonar Law in the Lloyd George Coalition, its lynch-pin, he was not the Prime Minister, and he was excessively meticulous in recognising and emphasising this fact. It would have been far better if MacDonald had been quietly shunted into retirement in 1932 or 1933 and Baldwin had taken his place, but Baldwin's loyalty stood against such a desirable action. Such attitudes might have been appropriate in quiet times, but by 1933 it was evident that the international situation was deteriorating rapidly, and that the brief Age of Locarno had ended. These were not circumstances in which MacDonald would have shone at any time of his career, and were certainly ill-fitted for its melancholy twilight.

Since the war, successive British Governments had followed policies of non-commitment—particularly in Europe—wary association with the League, and the pursuit of the goal of disarmament. What was lacking was any realistic assessment of the perils facing the European system and any sense of the shortage of time available. These failings were apparent in politicians of all parties. But in their defence it must be emphasised that nothing comparable to the advent of Hitler had been seen in Europe before, and, even now, it is a phenomenon that still astonishes and awes. The old concept of the Balance of Power in Europe had been tacitly abandoned, and had been replaced by what Lord Strang has called 'an almost Cobdenite non-interventionism'. It is difficult to improve upon Strang's estimate:

> In the inter-war years . . . no clear policy was framed. The new problems of a changed and changing world tended to be interpreted in terms of old conceptions. Our position in the world had altered for the worse and we did not seem to recognise this in our actions. We continued too long to believe the horrors of the war of 1914–18 would have convinced all civilised powers that they must not have another war. We behaved as though we could play an effective part

in international affairs as a kind of mediator or umpire without providing ourselves with the necessary arms and without entering into firm commitments, whereas the truth was that, for lack of international solidarity in face of the common menace, we were in mortal peril.[1]

Hitler came to power early in 1933 at a time when France was weakening and her political structure was crumbling, and the British were preoccupied with other concerns. Their reactions to Hitler were confused. In October 1932, when the pattern of future events was becoming more clear, Baldwin warned the annual Conservative conference of the deteriorating situation in Europe and that 'we are coming to the parting of the ways in Europe'. Two months after Hitler's assumption of power Sir Horace Rumbold, the British Ambassador in Berlin, reported that his regime had brought to the surface 'the worst traits in German character, i.e. a mean spirit of revenge, a tendency to brutality, and a noisy and irresponsible jingoism'. Anthony Eden reported to Baldwin after a meeting with Hitler in February 1934 that 'he has simplicity of manner and a sense of humour', and gave it as his opinion that 'I find it very hard to believe that the man himself wants war. My impression is much more that this country has plenty to do internally and to be thus preoccupied for five years to come.' The only British politicians who took Hitler seriously from the outset were Baldwin, Churchill, and Austen Chamberlain, the last saying in the Commons on April 13th, 1933:

> What is this new spirit of German nationalism? The worst of all-Prussian Imperialism, with an added savagery, a racial pride, an exclusiveness which cannot allow to any fellow-subject not of 'pure Nordic birth' equality of rights and citizenship within the nation to which he belongs. Are you going to discuss revision with a nation like that?

But this was exactly what most people were very willing to do. The alleged iniquities of Versailles had been sedulously cultivated by German propagandists since the setting up of the 'War Guilt Section' in the German Foreign Ministry in the 1920s. The success of these methods may be seen from a statement of Lord Lothian in 1939:

> I do not think it possible to understand British policy without

[1] Lord Strang: *Home and Abroad*, 154.

realising the fact that a great many people felt that the internal persecution in Germany was in great part the result of the denial to Germany of the rights which every other sovereign nation claims.

Arthur Henderson, in *War and Peace* (1934), wrote that the injustices of Versailles must be redressed, and that Labour would not fight to defend them; he added that sanctions would be sufficient to curb Hitler, and that there was no need to rearm.

The gradual revelation of what Nazism really was did not invariably carry with it the assumption that it denoted aggressiveness *outside* Germany. *The Times* claimed (July 10th, 1934) that the violent and aggressive speeches of the German leaders were only for home consumption. Indeed, there was a respectable body of opinion that constantly reiterated that internal revolutions were always ugly affairs, and that responsibility came with power. We find even Churchill writing in October 1937:

> Although no subsequent political action can condone deeds or remove the guilt of blood, history is replete with examples of men who have risen to power by employing stern, grim, wicked and even frightful methods, but who, nevertheless, when their life is revealed as a whole, have been regarded as great figures whose lives have enriched the story of mankind. So it may be with Hitler.

And, again, in September 1937:

> One may dislike Hitler's system and yet admire his patriotic achievement. If our country were defeated, I hope we should find a champion as indomitable to restore our courage and lead us back to our place among the nations.

The argument that a strong Germany was a powerful 'bulwark against Communism' was one that was emphasised repeatedly by the Nazis, and it was one that gained particular approval in the British business and conservative communities. The reports of pogroms against the Jews tended to be discounted by people cynical of propaganda; there were some who actually applauded the Nazi attitudes. Lord Londonderry—admittedly a notable example—wrote to Ribbentrop in 1936:

As I told you, I have no great affection for the Jews. It is possible to trace their participation in most of those International disturbances which have created so much havoc in different countries.

The Anglo-German Fellowship contained many leading people from these backgrounds who firmly believed in the truth of this argument. As Michael Astor has commented:

In the nineteen-thirties the majority of Conservatives thought that Fascism was, in some ill-defined way, more or less all right. And the majority of Socialists thought that Communism was more than more or less all right. And in these judgements they were both all wrong.[1]

Thus, even those who accepted the essential evil of Nazi Germany and distrusted its presence in Europe, did not accept that conflict was in any sense unavoidable. Indeed, it was this group—substantially in the majority in the Cabinet—that was particularly susceptible to the argument that a policy of controlled and judicious concessions would damp the fires of German chauvinism and make it a tolerable neighbour. Lothian was not unrepresentative when he said in 1933:

Like most Liberals, I loathe the Nazi regime, but I am sure that the first condition to reform it is that we should be willing to do justice to Germany. The second is that Liberal nations should be willing to stand together to resist any unjust pretension which she herself may later put forward.

The tragedy of Europe was that the latter condition became increasingly obscured. The development of Lothian's argument may well be seen in a leading article in *The Times* written by Geoffrey Dawson in 1936:

The truth is that British public opinion is probably far ahead of the Government in its conviction that a clear understanding with Germany will have consequences more profound and more conducive to a stable peace than any other single object of our foreign policy. There is little sympathy here with the view, which has sometimes seemed to prevail on the Continent, that the proper way

[1] Michael Astor: *Tribal Feeling*, 143

to treat Germany is to ring her about with vigilant allied states, sometimes masquerading as the League of Nations, like trained elephants round a tiger in the jungle, to prevent her expansion in any direction beyond the limits imposed twenty years ago.

Behind all British attitudes there lay the haunting terror of another war. The argument of Sir Edward Grey that the 1906–14 arms race had somehow 'caused' the Great War was particularly emphasised in radical circles; it accordingly became logical to argue that a refusal to rearm oneself would in itself reduce the chance of war. The prevalent attitudes were well described by Churchill in a newspaper article in 1932, before Hitler came to power:

> There is such a horror of war in the great nations who passed through Armageddon that any declaration or public speech against armaments, although it consisted only of platitudes and unrealities, has always been applauded; and any speech or assertion that set forth the blunt truth has been incontinently relegated to the category of 'war-monger'. . . . The cause of disarmament will not be obtained by Mush, Slush, and Gush. It will be advanced steadily by the harassing expense of fleets and armies, and by the growth of confidence in a long peace.

All commentators agreed that the next war would be unspeakably worse than the last. 'Who in Europe', Baldwin asked, 'does not know that one more war in the West and the civilisation of the ages will fall with as great a shock as that of Rome?' Churchill also painted the picture in colours so appalling that the effect, far from stimulating his audiences to a comprehension of the perils of evasion of the issue, confirmed them in their fears.

If diagnosis of the new threat to Europe was confused, cure was even more controversial. MacDonald was fading rapidly. 'The thought that this vain old man, whose mind was only just turning over, was Prime Minister of a still great country, was rather depressing', as one sardonic observer has written.[1] Simon had little of value to contribute, and was markedly hostile to the idea of rearmament. He presided, furthermore, over a very divided Foreign Office. The retirement of Rumbold from Berlin and the appointment of Sir Eric Drummond, the former Secretary-General of the League of Nations,

---

[1] Kenneth Clark: *Another Part of the Wood*, 185.

to Rome were to prove major errors. Of Rumbold's successor, Sir Eric Phipps, Baldwin complained that his reports 'had too much wit and not enough warning; they did not alarm the Cabinet enough'. Drummond's association with the League was not the swiftest road to Mussolini's confidence. With a pacific, aloof, and limited Foreign Secretary, a vehemently divided Foreign Office, and confusing reports from the principal capitals, the Cabinet was not well served.

In the Labour Party the dominant phrase was 'collective security', a perfectly respectable and sensible theoretical philosophy but one that tended to wither into generalities when closely approached. Until 1935 at any rate, the one thing on which Labour agreed was the futility of rearmament. Richard Crossman has commented on the attitude of the *New Statesman*:

> Week by week throughout the 1930s we predicted the imminent collapse of Western capitalism and denounced in despairing terms successive betrayals of Western democracy . . . At home we attacked appeasement as a base surrender to Hitler and simultaneously opposed rearmament and predicted the total destruction of London by Hitler's air force if war broke out. I doubt whether any other periodical in modern history has preached such a despairing, self-immolating gospel with such gusto as we did in the 1930s.[1]

The essential conflict in Labour attitudes can be best seen in a resolution passed at the annual conference in October 1936, which was strongly condemnatory of the dictatorships, urged that 'the armed strength of the countries loyal to the League of Nations need be conditioned by the armed strength of the potential aggressor', but 'declines to accept responsibility for a purely competitive armament policy'.

If 'collective security' meant anything, it meant rearmament and the League of Nations. Yet here British politicians were in a quandary. The concept of the League as a centre of conciliation was a practicable one in the atmosphere and conditions of the 1920s, yet, as had been demonstrated in the Corfu Incident and was shown again by Japan in Manchuria in 1931, the League could be flouted at will. If, on the other hand, one interpreted 'collective security' in the sense of a series of national treaties, one was brought back to the sombre 'lesson' of 1914 that such entanglements deprived Britain of freedom

[1] *New Statesman*, May 3rd, 1968.

of manoeuvre, encouraged German chauvinism, heightened tensions, and led to war.

Britain's natural ally was France, even if few British Ministers recognised this fact. As a result of Locarno, there was no military co-operation. And France was herself entering a period of severe domestic difficulties that made a consistent policy almost impossible and sapped the initiative of French politicians, to whom it became an accepted fact that no war could be launched on Germany without British assistance. French foreign policy—particularly towards Germany—was increasingly dominated by concern about what the British felt. In the meanwhile, unperceived in London, the French military superiority over Germany was being remorselessly eroded.

There were few enough other potential allies. Fear of Russia had faded, but deep suspicions remained. On a practical basis, what could Russia do in the event of a western European war? Her army was to be grievously weakened by the purges of 1936–8. Her fleet and air force were derisory. The Left in Britain always favoured rapprochement with Russia on ideological grounds, but few suggested Russia's incorporation into any kind of western European military alliance beyond her current obligations. There was no movement in British foreign policy in the 1930s to make any serious overtures to Russia, and it is difficult to see how any practicable arrangements could have been made. The prevalent view was that put forward by H. A. L. Fisher in his *History of Europe*, published in 1936: 'The Hitler revolution is a sufficient guarantee that Russian Communism will not spread westward. The solid German bourgeois hold the central fortress of Europe'. 'A Communist Germany', Lloyd George said (September 27th, 1933) 'would be infinitely more formidable than a Communist Russia'.

The United States of America hardly counted at all in these considerations. Preoccupied by her own severe domestic problems, still aloof from the League, concerned by the rise of Japan, her remoteness from the grim drama that was unfolding in Europe was complete. The occasional international forays by President Franklin D. Roosevelt were regarded with impatience by the British, and it must be conceded that a considerable emptiness of purpose lay behind the European activities of the United States. In retrospect, the unwillingness of the British to try to draw the United States out of isolation is almost as strange as their apprehensions of American naval strength in the

1920s had been. But all the evidence demonstrates that any such attempts would have been futile.

Thus, everything depended upon the British.

As this menacing situation slowly unfolded, a critical difference of attitude became evident in Britain among the ranks of those who increasingly chafed against policies of inaction.

In this respect, it is instructive to return to Churchill, whose voice was the most challenging and insistent throughout this period. Churchill was not particularly concerned about Fascism *per se*. It would be tolerable only, he wrote, 'if the sole alternative was Bolshevism'. He expressed warm admiration for Mussolini, of whom he was writing in October 1937:

> It would be a dangerous folly for the British people to underrate the enduring position in world-history which Mussolini will hold; or the amazing qualities of courage, comprehension, self-control and perseverence which he exemplifies.

On every issue of flagrant aggression in the 1930s apart from those inflicted by Germany, Churchill's reactions were muted. He said in February 1933 of Japan's invasion of China:

> I do not think the League of Nations would be well advised to have a quarrel with Japan . . . I hope we shall try in England to understand a little the position of Japan, an ancient state, with the highest sense of national honour and patriotism and with a teeming population and a remarkable energy. On the one side they see the dark menace of Soviet Russia. On the other, the chaos of China, four or five provinces of which are now being tortured under Communist rule.

In the Abyssinia crisis of 1935 his position was highly equivocal. He said that 'no one can keep up the pretence that Abyssinia is a fit, worthy and equal member of a League of civilised nations', and warned that Britain must not become 'a sort of bell-wether or fugleman to lead opinion in Europe against Italy's Abyssinian designs . . . We are not strong enough to be the lawgiver and the spokesman of the world'. On the issues raised by the Spanish Civil War he was more emphatic —at least until the spring of 1938. A strong supporter of non-intervention, he also made it quite clear that he preferred a Fascist Spain to a Communist one.

Throughout, from the end of 1933 onwards, Churchill had his eye fixed upon the revived menace of German militarism. He considered that, compared to this threat, all other dangers were minor. But although this determination of priorities was to prove absolutely correct, it contained a very serious political and moral deficiency. For, if Italian aggression in Abyssinia or Japanese aggression in Manchuria were somehow morally and politically defensible as acts of national policy in which the League of Nations had no *locus standi*, what about the remilitarisation of the Rhineland? And if Fascist governments in Italy, Japan and Spain were perfectly tolerable, why not tolerate that of Germany? By taking these stands, Churchill cut himself off from a very real element in Britain that was increasingly nauseated by Fascist excesses everywhere; his lack of sympathy and understanding for the young men who went to fight in Spain was significant of the gulf of attitudes between himself and them. Abyssinia brought the Labour movement out of its feckless slumber; Spain aroused the young. Churchill's limitation to *German* ambitions failed to take advantage of a very sizeable group of British opinion. Thus, when he belatedly attempted to stir the still substantial League of Nations Union constituency in Britain in the 'Arms and the Covenant' crusade, his own position was severely compromised.

'Appeasement' has become one of the most dangerous and misleading of all modern political phrases. Briand had used the word to differentiate his policies from those of Poincaré; everybody subscribed to Anthony Eden's statement in 1936 that 'the appeasement of Europe' was the prime objective of British policy. This was, of course, the classic policy of England if, by appeasement, one meant the preservation of peace. But there was a substantial difference of emphasis between the foreign policy, and the circumstances, of 1933–7 and those of 1937–9. Indeed, it can be well argued that there was no foreign policy in 1937–9 apart from the avoidance of war at virtually any price.

British foreign policy between 1933 and 1937 was unquestionably lacking in distinction or purpose. Simon's tenure of the Foreign Office (1933–5) was hapless, and Hoare's brief occupancy in 1935 was a fiasco. 'Everyone seemed to be over-excited', he subsequently complained. 'There appeared to be no generally accepted body of opinion on the main issues. Diametrically opposed views were pressed upon me, and sometimes with the intolerance of an *odium theologicum*.'[1] Eden

---

[1] Templewood: *Nine Troubled Years*, 137.

(1935-8) was far from being the vigilant foe of the dictators that he has been subsequently portrayed as. The central features of British policy in these years were to reach accommodations with Germany on specific issues—as demonstrated in the Anglo-German Treaty of 1935—to avoid conflicts arising in Europe—as in the Rhineland crisis of March 1936—and to attempt to retain the co-operation of Italy— as in the so-called British, French, and Italian 'Stresa Front' of 1935. The latter policy collapsed over Abyssinia in the storm that followed the revelation of the Hoare–Laval Pact,[1] and the Stresa Front was accordingly a dead letter almost from the outset. Nevertheless, the thinking behind the Hoare–Laval Pact was very enduring, and lasted until May 1940. There were many serious fallacies in this approach, but a case could be made out to the effect that here was a valid policy of cynical realism. But it was not conducted in that spirit on the British side up to 1937, and after that it became part of Chamberlain's approach of all-round conciliation. By then, as the Italians rightly estimated, the British had little to offer as a potential ally, and little to be fearful of as an opponent.

The fundamental fallacy that ran through British policy and attitudes—and not only Governmental—was the assumption that Britain's unilateral efforts would be sufficient. Any attempt to 'encircle' Germany would have met strong opposition from all sides, and yet if this was regarded as unacceptable and unrealistic, what was the alternative?

As the reactions to the German reoccupation of the Rhineland in March 1936 were to emphasise, the concept of a preventive war was even less acceptable. The comment of the *Spectator* (March 27th) was representative: 'The reoccupation of German territory by German troops is no cause for war.' The coup was denounced by the *New Statesman* and the *Manchester Guardian*, consistent opponents of re-armament, and vehemently opposed to all war. But all the latter could suggest was that Britain and France should insist on the with-drawal of the troops under the threat of 'international ostracism'. If war was unthinkable between civilised nations, and was the most stupendous of all conceivable evils, what remained except a series of bilateral deals? And, in the context of relative British and German military strength, how could this result in anything save a series of capitulations? By March 1938, when the first major act of German

[1] See pp. 286-9.

aggression occurred, the British had moved into a situation in which the options had been reduced to one between concessions and war.

So far as an effective British foreign policy was concerned, the issue of armaments was much more crucial *before* 1938 than it was then. 'The practical choice', Simon wrote in January 1935, 'is between a Germany which continues to rearm without any regulation or agreement, and a Germany which, through getting a recognition of its rights and some modification of the peace treaties, enters into the comity of nations, and contributes, in this and other ways, to the European stability.' It was significant that in the summer of 1935 the Cabinet authorised the Service Ministries to make their defence preparations 'with a view to achieving a reasonable state of preparedness by 1939'. Preparedness for what? It was all too reminiscent of the War Council's resolution on the Dardanelles in January 1915. But at least it recognised the significance of time. The 1934 assessment had envisaged 1942 as the likely period of crisis, now the odds were dimly seen to be shortening. But the major crisis was to occur a year earlier. In 1938 the military imbalance between Britain and Germany was still considerable, but was closing. But by then the conviction of British inferiority was dominant in Chamberlain's mind. Thus, the paramount object in 1938 was to maintain peace, even if Czechoslovakia had to be sacrificed for this purpose. It was in the period 1934–7 that British weakness was so fatal for the peace of Europe.

*

In the writing of recent history it is very necessary for the participants to get in first. First impressions tend to be dominant; if they are formidably deployed no amount of subsequent revisionism can match the effect created by the original version. Churchill's opening volume of his Second World War memoirs, *The Gathering Storm*, has perhaps had a greater impression on post-war attitudes—and not least in the United States—than any other single work. Although its impact upon historians is diminishing, it is still considered a reliable primary source for examining the 1930s.

Churchill's thesis is a very simple one. The Second World War was 'the Unnecessary War'. As he writes:

It was a simple policy to keep Germany disarmed and the victors adequately armed for thirty years. But this modest requirement the might, civilisation, learning, knowledge, science, of the victors were unable to supply.

But, in reality, it was not nearly as simple as that. This policy required several crucial elements—not the least of which was to deny to Germany one of the rights of a sovereign state while at the same time building her up as one. The policy also required a situation whereby, in order to enforce German inequality, the European Powers would be prepared to revert to military action. By 1933 this situation did not exist. In one of his earliest speeches on the subject, in August 1933, Churchill warned that 'there is grave reason to believe that Germany is arming herself, or seeking to arm herself contrary to the solemn treaties *extracted from her in her hour of defeat*' (my italics). It was the latter comment that contained the difficulty.

It was with very profound reluctance that the British turned away from the chimera of total disarmament. None of the former Great Powers had given so much practical demonstration of their good faith. By 1933 the R.A.F. was numerically sixth in the world; the Navy had a smaller complement of men than at any time for forty years, and the Fleet was substantially ageing; the condition of the Army was the worst of all. Nine cavalry regiments, sixty-one batteries and twenty-one infantry battalions had been scrapped in the Regular Army; the Territorials were 40,000 below strength; mechanisation had virtually stopped; equipment was obsolete and in small supply; the Ordnance Factories were virtually phased out. Total Defence expenditure in 1926–7 had been £116 millions; in 1932–3 it was down to just over £100 million. The Disarmament Conference limped along until 1934. At the celebrated by-election in East Fulham in 1933 an anti-war Labour candidate rode to triumphant victory. No election is ever won or lost on a single issue, and there were other factors involved in East Fulham. But it was the successful candidate's principal theme, and the impact it made upon other politicians was understandable. In 1934 the Peace Pledge Union was created, followed by a Peace Ballot organised by the League of Nations Union— whose most interesting (but rather unnoticed) feature was the statement by some 6¾ million people that they favoured military sanctions by the League in the face of aggression. But sanctions by the League of Nations was not the same as unilateral rearmament. In the 1935 election, accordingly, Baldwin had to maintain a precarious balance; in the context of 1932-4 this balance was even more delicate.

There was, of course, a genuine and highly vocal pacifist anti-war element in the rearmament debate after 1933. In the Labour Party George Lansbury and Stafford Cripps were its most vehement exponents, Cripps actually declaring in November 1936 that he 'did not believe it would be a bad thing for the British working class if Germany defeated us. It would be a disaster to the profit-makers and capitalists, but not necessarily for the working class.' If these were extreme views, they were very close in content to those of moderate men like Attlee and the Liberal leader Sir Archibald Sinclair. In the debate on the 1935 Air Estimates the Labour spokesman attacked 'the squandering of so much money on the enlargement of the Air Service. . . . We are sick to death of all this mad talk about rearming.' In the 1935 General Election Herbert Morrison described Neville Chamberlain and Churchill as 'fire-eaters and militarists. . . . Chamberlain would spend money on the means of death, but not on the means of life.' In the 1935 election one Labour pamphlet declared that:

> The Unionist Party wants war. Your husbands and sons will be cannon-fodder. More poison gas will mean dearer food. Register your distrust of the war-mongers by voting Labour.

In the debate on the Defence White Paper in 1935, Attlee said that 'We reject the use of force as an instrument of policy. We stand for the reduction of armaments and pooled security . . . Our policy is not one of seeking security through rearmament but through disarmament.' The impossibility of reconciling the desire to 'fight' Fascism without rearming made all Labour Party contributions to the debate in the 1930s singularly unhelpful. There were, however, some voices of realism, and the most brutal was that of Ernest Bevin who, at the party conference on October 8th, 1935, destroyed Lansbury's leadership.[1]

In the Government, the reluctant acceptance in 1933-4 of the necessity to begin a modest rearmament to repair the ravages of years of neglect and low expenditure clashed with the optimism of a European settlement. As Lord Halifax (the former Lord Irwin) commented in December 1935:

[1] See p. 278.

Are we in fact to judge the question so serious that everything has to give way to the military reconditioning of our Defence Forces? Such a conclusion, in fact, appears to me to rest on premises not only of the inevitability but of a certain degree of certainty as to the early imminence of war, which I am not prepared to accept.

In this, Halifax represented a very substantial view—and not only in the Conservative Party. War remained the supreme, the total, horror. As Churchill himself said, 'Another Great War would cost us our wealth, our freedom, and our culture, and cast what we have so slowly gathered of human enlightenment, tolerance, and dignity to different packs of ravening wolves . . . It would be like the last—only worse.'

Thus, the British rearmed in a spirit of depression, believing almost to the end that the weapons would never be used.

The governmental organisation for rearmament was itself cumbersome and complicated. Sir Maurice Hankey had established himself into a position of immense influence in Whitehall, greater than that of any other single official and more substantial than that of most Ministers. He was hostile to all proposals for reorganisation, and his negative attitudes almost invariably carried the day. Hoare's portrait of the situation is confirmed by subsequent knowledge:

> The complicated machinery that Hankey had most efficiently developed had become so intricate that it was often difficult to obtain a quick or clear decision upon specific questions. Rearmament had ceased to be the sole concern of the Service Departments and almost every Minister, Service and Civil, had come to take an interest in it. The result was the creation of innumerable committees for dealing with every kind of defence question, and an inevitable tendency to defer decisions until most of them had been consulted.[1]

This might not have been serious were it not for the fact that the Prime Minister was incompetent and vacillating, the Foreign Secretary was blandly untroubled by the European situation and instinctively hostile to rearmament, the Chancellor of the Exchequer was obsessed by the economic problems and profoundly reluctant to allocate expenditure for rearmament, and the Service Ministers—two of whom, Hailsham and Londonderry, were in the Lords—were

[1] Templewood, op. cit., 330.

politically weak and technically limited. Of the entire Cabinet, only two men grasped the realities and the new necessities—Baldwin and Cunliffe-Lister. But Cunliffe-Lister was Colonial Secretary, and Baldwin, checked by his unfortunate loyalty to MacDonald, could not at that stage move too far ahead of his colleagues and his party—at least not too obviously. But he at least sent up some public warning signals, and made evident the reality of his concern. In private his alarm was much greater, and it was principally because of his efforts that the rearmament programme was begun, and the Ten Year Rule abandoned.

It is not the case that MacDonald was the determined believer in disarmament, with Baldwin a reluctant follower. Up to 1933 Baldwin believed strongly in it, and particularly in the elimination of what he regarded as the barbarism of aerial bombing—a factor that made the Air Minister, Londonderry, and his chief bombing zealot, Trenchard, highly uncongenial to him. On this matter he tried very hard in 1932 to get an agreement at Geneva, and in his celebrated speech of November 10th he meant every word:

> I think it is well also for the man in the street to realise that there is no power on earth that can protect him from being bombed. Whatever people may tell him, the bomber will always get through. The only defence is in offence, which means that you have to kill more women and children more quickly than the enemy if you want to save yourselves.

This often-derided statement was, in the context of 1932, absolutely true. But by 1933 Baldwin realised that the moment for genuine all-round disarmament had probably passed; by the beginning of 1934 he was absolutely convinced that it had. But his preoccupation was always to be on aerial defence. For this he was prepared to cut official corners and give to those engaged in this task virtually everything they wanted that he could supply. 'A country which shows itself unwilling to make what necessary preparations are recognisable for its own defence will never have force—moral or material—in this world', he said in 1935. Again, emphasis must be placed on the word *defence*. It was the key to Baldwin's thinking and activity on rearmament questions, a key that almost all observers and historians have missed. By 1933, and even more by 1934, Baldwin had developed what can be best described as 'the Armada complex'. The Defence of the Realm—particularly from the air—was his personal, and almost total, obsession.

Baldwin was not—and nor did he pretend to be—an expert on foreign affairs. As Prime Minister in the twenties he had worked on the old principle of letting each Minister run his own shop without interference unless a particular crisis or problem arose, much as Asquith had done, and Lloyd George had not. If the Ministers were well chosen and able, this arrangement had much to be said for it. But as number two to MacDonald, and with Simon at the Foreign Office for purely domestic political reasons, it had very little to be said for it. But Baldwin, although no expert, saw the reality of the danger looming in Europe and the need to take some action to counteract it. But he concentrated on one particular aspect, the negative one of air defence, and could not and did not see the matter in the wider perspective that it desperately needed. And, by 1935, he was tired, and assailed by other problems.

Baldwin's other great concern was to carry public opinion with him. The many speeches, some elliptical and confusing ('the bomber will always get through', 'When you think of defence of England you no longer think of the chalk cliffs of Dover; you think of the Rhine'), that he gave on the subject did not provide the clarion call that Churchill and some others sought, but they went far further than any others made by Ministers. He was convinced that the British could not be, and would not be, stampeded into increased expenditure on armaments unless the necessity was very evident. Perhaps he read too much in the East Fulham by-election, but all the evidence we possess emphasises that Baldwin's general diagnosis of the public mood was correct. He therefore concentrated upon building the foundations not only of rearmament itself but of a cautious change in public awareness of the seriousness of the European situation. In this, Hitler was his best ally, but in this period Hitler was demonstrating that the portrait of him as a mere ranting paranoid gutter politician of considerable brutality left out a great deal. At home, ruthlessness and rearmament, the consolidation of his own position, the support of the Services, and the dramatic revival of nationalism, brilliantly stage-managed by Goebbels; abroad, the combination of menacing threats to the weak, and bland overtures to the strong. He played on fears and hopes, weaknesses and optimism, with intuitive genius. Hitler and Baldwin were the two best politicians in Europe, and every violent action or gesture by Hitler enabled Baldwin to carry his own policies further forward; but at this stage Hitler, too, had to act warily.

Furthermore, despite Baldwin's real affection and regard for the Labour Party—a regard greatly increased by the gallant manner in which the diminutive Parliamentary Party kept going in the 1931–5 Parliament, and to which he paid a noble and merited tribute in 1935 —he was convinced that it was in no condition to take office again in the immediate future. He was particularly alarmed about its attitude towards rearmament. With Lansbury and Cripps—with Attlee not far behind them—denouncing all armaments, even defensive, and deriding warnings about present or future dangers, this apprehension was not surprising. Baldwin also had considerable respect for the recuperative powers of the Labour Party. He understood, as did no other Conservative politician of the inter-war period, the strength of the foundations of the party, and he noted its ever increasing membership and voting power. He regarded the 1931 election, rightly, as a freak, and it was not only East Fulham that impressed him; all indications were of the revived spirits and increased public support for the Labour Party.

These apprehensions were fully confirmed by the by-election results, which were devastating for the Government from the autumn of 1933 until the summer of 1934. East Fulham was the first shattering blow in October 1933, when the Labour candidate John Wilmot campaigned on a shrill pacifist platform and was warmly supported by Lansbury, who pledged that he would disband the Army and disarm the Royal Air Force, close every recruiting station, and 'abolish the whole dreadful equipment of war'. The swing to Labour was 26·5 per cent. In November the pattern was repeated at Kilmarnock (24·8 per cent), Shipton (25·2 per cent), Rusholme and Rutland (18·6 per cent in each case) and Market Harborough (23·6 per cent). In February 1934 Cambridge was held, but with a large anti-Government swing, and in April the Government held Basingstoke with a greatly reduced majority, and lost Hammersmith North and West Ham. In March, Labour gained control of the London County Council for the first time ever, and in the autumn of 1934 the movement against the Government was even greater than at East Fulham. The disarmament issue was obviously not the only factor, but the disturbing element for Baldwin was that these by-elections, held in very different constituencies in very different regions, demonstrated the same ominous pattern of Labour recovery. The fact that when Admiral Sir Roger Keyes hung on to Portsmouth against an 8·8 per cent swing this was regarded as a signal triumph gives some indication of the seriousness of the situation. A Labour Government, with Lansbury as Prime Minister, was, on the basis of these indications, a very real possibility.

Baldwin's operations were, therefore, on several levels. Within the Government he pushed his very reluctant colleagues, and supported by only a relatively few senior officials, of whom Vansittart was the most notable and outspoken, in the direction of rearmament, particularly in the air. In public, without being alarmist he gave his warnings—on occasions in terms more dire than his experts believed were merited by the facts. But he also heavily stressed the specifically defensive nature of rearmament. It was a calculatedly gradual and cautious exercise, intended to get the results without inflaming the Labour Party or opening irreparable divisions in his own Government. And, in the main, he succeeded.

It was generally accepted—and in this Baldwin and Churchill were in full agreement—that the threat to Britain came from the air. This was the dominant obsession of the 1930s. In October 1933 the Cabinet had set up a Defence Requirements Committee under Hankey, to examine 'the worst deficiencies' in the Armed Services; it reported in February 1934, and stated that Germany was 'the ultimate potential enemy'. The fact that Germany was rearming—and rearming fast— was well known; indeed, there was little attempt made to conceal it. But it was the rebuilding of the Luftwaffe that caused the British the greatest alarm. This was partly the result of recognition of the fact that the German Army was not a direct menace to the British, but it was principally based upon a very widespread fear of an aerial pre-emptive strike of devastating proportions. At that stage the German Navy seemed to pose no serious threat to the British, and exponents of naval expansion usually spoke in terms of the dangers presented by the Japanese and Italian navies. Once again, the submarine danger was discounted.

Thus, the debate on rearmament was from the beginning essentially about *air* rearmament, with the result that both the older Services— and particularly the Army—fared badly in the distribution of what funds were made available. The lamentable condition of the Army, and particularly in its equipment, when war did break out was commentary enough on this order of priorities. But it also reflected the general refusal to consider the possibility of it being involved once again in a major land war. The British remained convinced that they were, in Churchill's phrase, 'sea-animals rather than land-animals', and of all the Services the Navy had suffered least from the rigorous economies of the 1920s. But the Great War had demonstrated the superlative quality of the British soldier, however ill-commanded, and very serious deficiencies in the Navy. The latter were not adequately met; the former was forgotten. Duff Cooper, one of a string of un-distinguished Secretaries of State for War, subsequently complained that he had spent most of his time at the War Office—during which he wrote a lengthy and flattering biography of Haig—writing papers about the role of the Army, and that it was a relief to move to the Admiralty where no doubts about the role of the Navy existed.[1] His even less distinguished successor, Hore-Belisha, wrote to Neville Chamberlain in 1937 that 'My view after the fullest survey, including a visit to France, is that our Army should be organised to defend this country and the Empire, [and] that to organise it with a military pre-possession in favour of a Continental commitment is wrong'. When he introduced the Army Estimates for 1936–7 Duff Cooper apolo-gised to those cavalry units that were to be mechanised, remarking sympathetically that 'It is like asking a great musical performer to throw away his violin and devote himself in future to a gramophone'. The 1920s and early 1930s had been a miserable period for the Army; now, when rearmament at last began, it remained at the bottom of the list in terms of material, finance, and political leadership. No serious thought was given to what its role in a future conflict was to be. Again, the essentially defensive nature of the Government's military thinking, and the blind reliance on the French—a view in which Churchill, crying 'Thank God for the French Army', fully concurred —dominated. And so, the Army continued to languish. Its subsequent feelings about politicians were understandable and merited.

In taking these views, Ministers demonstrated the basic insularity of British attitudes, and their complete failure to comprehend the wider picture, which was a threat to the whole of Europe and to that balance of power to which they dutifully gave lip-service. It was France, and Central Europe, that were in mortal peril, not Britain. And it was the Wehrmacht, with its air arm and massive mechanisa-tion, that held the reality of political-military power in Europe. But

[1] Duff Cooper, op. cit., 207.

while the British Government was not particularly concerned about the Wehrmacht or the German Navy, although it should have been, it became progressively excessively frightened by the emergence of the Luftwaffe. No one—including Churchill—appreciated the basic fact that the Luftwaffe was essentially the air arm of the German Army, and that it was this combination that posed such a threat to Europe. In 1937 the Cabinet was informed that it must expect an immediate German air attack of sixty days in the event of a war, with probable casualties of 600,000 dead and 1,200,000 injured (the actual civilian casualties in the whole of the Second World War were 295,000, of whom 60,000 were killed). Churchill, in 1934, described London as 'the greatest target in the world, a kind of tremendous fat cow', and dwelt upon the hideous effects of air attack. In March 1934 he warned that Germany would be strong enough in the air within a year or eighteen months to threaten 'the heart of the Empire'. Baldwin gave an assurance that such an eventuality would not be permitted to arise. A year later, again in response to Churchill, he acknowledged that Germany had indeed achieved 'parity' in the air—as will be seen, incorrectly—and that a greatly enhanced programme would have to be introduced. It is very difficult indeed to escape the conclusion that Churchill's campaign was extremely helpful to Baldwin, so far as *air* rearmament was concerned.[1]

It is important on these matters to separate the true facts from those that people believed at the time. In July 1934 the Luftwaffe possessed

[1] Although Churchill urged rearmament for all Services, he devoted himself principally to the Air Force. Indeed, some of his evaluations of future military and naval conflicts read very curiously indeed in the light of later—and even current—experience. He himself later admitted that he had not fully appreciated the revolution in mechanised warfare which had been propagated by Captain Basil Liddell Hart, to whom the Germans had listened with great respect and profit. He was sceptical of the value of the tank. He discounted the effectiveness of aerial attacks on modern warships and greatly exaggerated the advances in anti-submarine techniques. He was convinced that a future land war would be essentially static, and that 'One thing is certain about the next war, namely, that the armies will use their spades more often than they use their bayonets' (April 24th, 1938). 'The idea that enormous masses of mechanical vehicles and tanks will be able to overrun [modern] fortifications will probably turn out to be a disappointment.' But Churchill assumed that the major land powers in Europe likely to be opposed to Germany—France, Czechoslovakia, and Poland—would act together and were reasonably well equipped. He assumed also the paramount need for such an alliance, with the British playing their part on the sea and in the air. For all his errors, Churchill had a vision of the kind of alliance that was essential to meet the German threat. In this he was virtually alone.

some 400 military aircraft, and some 250 that were readily convertible to military uses; it had, in addition, some 1,450 civil and training aircraft of various types. The threatening factor was that Germany had an aircraft industry that was capable of producing at least 100 aircraft a month; by December 1934 the Luftwaffe consisted of 1,888 aircraft, of which 584 were operational military aircraft. These figures were bound to cause concern, but gave no reason for panic.

The issue was bedevilled by the fact that the Foreign Office—and Churchill—possessed much more alarming figures of German expansion. Vansittart was by now absolutely obsessed by the German threat, and particularly by the fear of 'a knock-down blow from the air' at the outset of a war, and his alarming memoranda descended upon Ministers like a cataract. The Air Ministry indignantly defended its estimates of German air strength, and the struggle gradually took the strange form of the Air Ministry producing arguments *against* the dramatic expansion of the Air Force for which Vansittart and Churchill were clamouring.

In point of fact, the Air Ministry figures were accurate, and the Foreign Office estimates of German aerial rearmament between 1933 and 1938 were greatly exaggerated. In 1934 Baldwin took a figure roughly between the two extremes, and was right. But when, in March 1935, Hitler made a false claim to Simon and Eden of air 'parity', it seemed that he had been wrong.

It has become almost an article of faith in Britain—and elsewhere —that, had it not been for Churchill's loud and insistent voice in the wilderness, the National Government would not have rearmed at all, and that the Battle of Britain would have been lost. As Churchill himself once wrote in a very different context, these broad effects are capable of refinement. In particular, the obloquy he and others heaped on Baldwin is now clearly seen to be grossly unfair.

It is impossible, of course, to gauge the effect on Ministers of Churchill's speeches on this issue. Probably Baldwin welcomed them. His celebrated 'confession' of May 22nd, 1935, that he had been 'completely wrong' the previous November in his estimate of future German air expansion was certainly not unhelpful to his own cause. But Churchill was a solitary and discredited figure with no following worth taking seriously. When he forced Baldwin into making apparently very damaging admissions of government inadequacy in aerial rearmament, he aroused many Conservatives who might despise

Churchill personally but who were alarmed by his message. Baldwin arranged for Churchill to receive confidential information through his friend Desmond Morton; he also, as will be recorded, brought him in as a member of the Air Defence Research Committee. The Statement on Defence published in March 1935 was by far the clearest statement of the Government's concern and marked the vital step away from deficiency programmes to real rearmament. But these were not in response to Churchill's speeches; they were the result of Baldwin's own activities. When Baldwin became Prime Minister in June 1935 and was master of his own house again, he at once removed Londonderry and appointed Cunliffe-Lister—who went to the Lords as Lord Swinton—as Secretary of State for Air, with his full support and encouragement to undertake a revolutionary programme of expansion and innovation. 'It could not have been achieved without Baldwin's support', Swinton has recorded: 'we knew it and were grateful.' 'It is by no means clear', Churchill's latest biographer has conceded, 'that Churchill was able to assist significantly in the technical development of air defence.'[1] Other estimates are even less enthusiastic.

It is necessary to emphasise that the really vital decisions were taken between 1933 and 1935 within the Government circle. It may also be noted that Churchill's 'ten-year rule' had been abandoned in 1932, and that the run-down of the armament industries in the 1920s meant that the process of rearmament was likely to take a long time. In these circumstances Baldwin's initiation of a study of British industrial potentiality by Lord Weir, Sir James Lithgow, and Sir Arthur Balfour, which produced the scheme for 'shadow' factories, which could be swiftly moved to the production of military equipment, was to be of central importance. Under the chairmanship of Sir Henry Tizard, a committee for the scientific survey of air defence was set up at the end of 1934, and swiftly produced a most remarkable discovery, developed by Robert Watson-Watt—Radio Direction Finding. It then moved towards the next vital step, that of incorporating this new technique into the operational tactics of the R.A.F. By itself, radar was a valuable technical assistance; incorporated operationally, it could give the R.A.F. an outstanding defensive capability.

[1] H. Pelling: *Winston Churchill*, 371. See also R. Rhodes James: *Churchill: A Study in Failure 1900–1939*, Chapter Six.

Meanwhile, the Air Defence Research Committee—the policy overlord of the Tizard Committee—was moving towards the courageous decisions to order the Spitfire and Hurricane off the drawing-board and to set up the 'shadow' factories to produce them. These decisions owed everything to Cunliffe-Lister and Baldwin.

Exactly what *was* achieved requires emphasis. In 1934 the R.A.F. had based in Britain 564 aircraft, which were wooden biplanes with fixed undercarriages. By 1939 this had increased to 1,476 aircraft, of the most modern type. The personnel was increased from 30,000 regulars and 11,000 reservists in 1934 to 118,000 regulars and 68,000 reservists in 1939. In 1934 there were 52 airfields in the United Kingdom available for war needs; by 1939 there were 138, and in that year the expenditure on 'works' was more than three times the cost of the entire R.A.F. in 1934. Indeed, if Kingsley Wood in 1938 had not abandoned one of the 'shadow' factories at West Bromwich, the total of Spitfires available would have risen by some 1,000 by 1940. Swinton's 'Scheme F', approved by the Cabinet in February 1936, provided for the construction of eight thousand aircraft in three years; in April 1938 'Scheme L' provided for twelve thousand in two years. The creation of the R.A.F. Volunteer Reserve was in many respects equally significant. The British had started late, but their quality in aircraft and pilots was exceptional. The former owed little to successive Governments, and everything to private enterprise, funding, and initiative, as did the invention of the jet propulsion engine by Frank Whittle. Swinton deserves all praise for his actions, but the true heroes were the British air pioneers, and particularly the designers and engineers.

In immediate political terms, the price paid for this quality was substantial. In terms of numbers, the R.A.F. was not impressive in 1938. Calculations were based on the necessity for providing for 1939; thus, in the crucial year of 1938, the R.A.F. had only 93 of the new fighters in operation, all of which were Hurricanes, and which experienced difficulties in firing their guns above 15,000 feet. Certain aircraft—notably the turret-firing Boulton Paul Defiant, which Churchill greatly favoured—turned out to be quite useless, and the twin-engined bombers Wellington and Blenheim were highly vulnerable, although excellent aircraft in many respects. The Hampden was a more prescient design for the needs of war. The Hurricane and Spitfire, moreover, were under-gunned, and the latter never achieved its full performance until equipped with three-bladed propellers in 1940—a development urged for some time by the de Havilland Company. By 1938—and even by 1939—the R.A.F. was not an impressive deterrent force. The Germans did not know of its unique R.D.F. defensive operational capacity. Bomber Command had less than 100 obsolete long-range bombers. Meanwhile the Luftwaffe had a fully efficient first-line strength of 3,609 aircraft, supplemented by 552 modern transports; personnel numbers had risen from 20,000 in 1935 to over half a million by 1939. If the Government—on Vansittart's urgings—had expanded the R.A.F. dramatically, it would have been a quantitative expansion, with obsolete aircraft.

The public debate on the situation was becoming very confused. The MacDonald–Baldwin Government had taken a definite decision to rearm in 1934, and the White Paper of March 1935 seemed to mark a very decisive moment. But the unhappiness of the Government was manifest, and in discussion of the ratio of strength in the air the term 'parity' introduced a highly complicated element into the controversy. Was parity meant in numerical or qualitative terms? What, indeed, *was* 'front-line strength'?

Matters were not made easier by Baldwin's decision to appoint Churchill to the Air Defence Research Committee in the summer of 1935. Churchill insisted on maintaining his freedom of action in Parliament and on the admission of his friend Professor Lindemann to the Tizard Committee.

Lindemann had been Professor of Experimental Philosophy at Oxford since 1919. He had had a brilliant beginning as a physicist, and the Clarendon Laboratory stands as his monument—a poor joke in 1919, and under his aegis developed into the most advanced low temperature physics laboratory in the world. He fought for the status of science with absolute and concentrated ardour. But by the 1930s Lindemann no longer moved among the foremost figures of his profession, by whom he was generally regarded with aversion. Lindemann was not an attractive man. He was a snob; he could be savagely vindictive; he had a very high estimate of his own intellectual calibre and a low one of other people's. Sir Roy Harrod has written of him:

His experience of men was very limited. One might gain the impression, and he himself perhaps believed, that he knew everyone who was everyone. But his acquaintance really only extended to a thin top crust—prominent people in politics, diplomacy and London Society. . . . He was quite out of touch with the course of contemporary thought, and this considerably cramped his style.

He had sedulously cultivated Churchill since the 1920s. Each man was fascinated by the other. As Lindemann was a total abstainer, a non-smoker, a philistine in art and literature and a fastidious vegetarian the connection of interest between himself and Churchill may seem difficult to diagnose. Churchill has written that 'Lindemann could decipher the signals of the experts on the far horizons and explain to me in lucid homely terms what the issues were'. One commentator has surmised that:

Through Churchill, Lindemann could vicariously enjoy the pleasures of life; through Lindemann, Churchill could vicariously engage in mathematical calculations and scientific investigations.

There is no need to examine the controversial question of whether Lindemann was or was not Churchill's evil genius. What is undeniable is the fact that he was a divisive and almost disastrous influence on the Tizard Committee. He and Tizard had been colleagues and close friends in the past; swiftly there developed a deep and bitter enmity between them that poisoned relations and hindered the work of the Air Defence Research Committee to the point that Swinton—in order to keep the Committee together—had to disband it in 1936 and recreate it without Lindemann. But Lindemann had his revenge later.

Regarded now, many of Lindemann's arguments and theories verge on the farcical. The most ludicrous of all was a proposal for research on aerial mines, which has been rightly described as 'a completely blind alley for research on which valuable time and money were wasted'. Another proposal for a 'cloud of substance in the path of an aeroplane to produce detonation' seems to belong more appropriately to bad scientific fiction than to a serious understanding of scientific and technological matters. Lindemann put forward his ideas with intense vigour, and reacted harshly to criticism; Churchill urged them on the A.D.R.C. with comparable energy. Much time was lost in the pursuit of these fantasies. Swinton became exasperated. 'The differences of opinion on the Tizard Committee', it has been written, 'could have had a serious effect on the rapid growth of radar.'

There was another disadvantage to these arrangements. Churchill, as a member of the A.D.R.C. was privy to what was going on; he was also to some extent an associate in the decisions taken. This did not prevent him from attacking the Government incessantly in public for its dilatoriness. On this matter Swinton has written:

> Winston certainly believed in my expansion plans. . . . At the same time he was determined to use anything he could find to attack the Government. So he used every evidence, good or bad, relevant or irrelevant, he could find about German air strength to attack the Government. The meaningless phrase of Baldwin's about 'parity' played into his hands. And the last thing he bothered about was consistency. He knew I should go on with the plans we both believed in; and at the same time he could go for the Government.
>
> He was, I am sure, genuinely horrified when the result of attacks on the Government, to which he had contributed so much, resulted in Neville sacking me.

In this debate, it is very easy to make out a good case for each side. The Baldwin Government was in effect introducing rearmament by stealth, and making long-term plans for air defence that were far-seeing, courageous, and absolutely right. Churchill did not believe in rearmament by stealth, particularly in the air. He wanted a bold, well-publicised, defiant programme that would provide Britain with her defence needs and warn Germany of the perils of incurring Britain's enmity. Ministers could point to the progressive expansion of expenditure on armaments after 1934; £102·7 millions in 1932–3 to £198 millions in 1937–8. Churchill could point to the fact that this was not nearly enough *relative* to Germany, and this was the vital point.

But what was rearmament *for*? Hardly anyone—perhaps not even Churchill—accepted the inevitability of war. Was it to strengthen British diplomacy in a new appalling jungle world? Was it merely for national defence? Was it to check German and Italian ambitions? Baldwin's view—which he never set out clearly in public—was that the defence programme should have as its main objective that of deterrence. When Churchill made the same point in a meeting with Baldwin in November 1936 Baldwin interrupted him to say 'I am with you on that' . . . 'I am with you there wholeheartedly'.[1] Although the development of Bomber Command was a notable exception, the

[1] See R. Rhodes James, op. cit., 294.

priority of Ministers was, and remained, strictly defensive. Chamberlain reluctantly supported the need for a rearmament programme, but watched jealously over its cost. As he wrote in February 1936, 'If we were to follow Winston's advice and sacrifice our commerce to the manufacture of arms, we should inflict a certain injury on our trade from which it would take generations to recover, we should destroy the confidence which now happily exists, and we should cripple the revenue'. Principally as a result of his insistence, the 1936 White Paper on Defence pledged to rearm 'without impeding the course of normal trade'. For the MacDonald–Baldwin Governments, rearmament was a grim necessity, undertaken without zest and, with the exception of the Air Ministry, carried on without urgency.

We are accordingly presented with a very curious situation. By 1936, it is evident Ministers were at last deeply disturbed at the imbalance—which they exaggerated—between the British and German air forces. They were quite unconcerned at the other military imbalances. They were oppressed by the horrors of a future war. They accepted the fact that Germany was already approaching the capability of waging a substantial war. Yet they did not see rearmament as the answer. Nor was it the answer; but, having accepted that it was necessary, they did not see its place in the determination of policy towards the Dictators. There was a crucial absence of interest and urgency in the Cabinet on the subject—with the exceptions of Baldwin and Swinton, whose attention was concentrated on the R.A.F. Accepting military weakness as a fact, their colleagues gradually moved to accepting the solution to the European problem by other means. From this there came the conviction, almost the obsession, that Hitler could and must be negotiated with, and that the problems of Europe were fully capable of a peaceful solution. The 'deterrent' argument faded, even before Baldwin's retirement. By 1937 there was a tacit assumption in the Cabinet that Germany possessed overwhelming military superiority. We find Chamberlain writing in January 1938:

> Until our armaments are completed, we must adjust our foreign policy to our circumstances, and even bear with patience and good humour actions which we should like to treat in very different fashion.

None of this is to deny the existence of an imbalance by 1937. But what is so striking is the failure to enter into military conversations with the French, to examine the true nature of the German military threat—which was on the land—or to take the kind of measures that a Government which feels its national existence imperilled would be expected to take. Ministers became paralysed by the spectacle of German military renaissance, and accepted its preponderance. Thus by the time that Chamberlain succeeded Baldwin in May 1937, there was a general acceptance of the argument that diplomatic settlement provided the only hope of escape from disaster. Their general attitude was enshrined in the words of Castlereagh:

This country cannot and will not act upon abstract and speculative principles of precaution.

By the end of 1937 even Churchill was hesitant. In an article written in October he declared that:

Three or four years ago I was myself a loud alarmist . . . In spite of the risks which wait on prophecy, I declare my belief that a major war is not imminent, and I still believe that there is a good chance of no major war taking place in our time. . . . Well was it written: 'Agree with thine adversary quickly whilst thou art in the way with him.'

This was indeed the policy of the new Prime Minister. But much was to occur between the summer of 1935 and Neville Chamberlain's accession to the Premiership in May 1937.

CHAPTER NINE

THE LAST BALDWIN GOVERNMENT, 1935–1937

B Y THE early summer of 1935 the fluctuating fortunes of the National Government began to show clear signs of marked improvement. Although the chronic problems of the most afflicted industrial areas remained, the Government could claim that it had taken some positive action to alleviate their most severe difficulties. It was true that here the realities of unemployment, part-employment, and wretched conditions of work for those who could obtain employment were still overwhelming features of the daily lives of the people, but elsewhere in the country prosperity was rising. After the trauma and fears of 1930–2, national confidence had returned. In Parliament, the divisive and protracted India dispute was approaching its conclusion. The Labour and Liberal leadership was feeble and tentative. Both parties were weighed down by public memories of the 1929–31 débâcle, particularly in the middle classes. The Roehm purge, and Hitler's claims, had led to the general acceptance of the principle of cautious rearmament. The Anglo-German Naval Treaty of June 1935, which limited the German Navy to thirty-five per cent of the British, and submarines to forty-five per cent, was criticised, and not vehemently, only by a small group of Conservatives. To the majority, it appeared to be a notable coup for the Government; the fact that it was a unilateral revision of Versailles, undertaken without any consultation with France, and accordingly a severe blow to the concept of the 'Stresa Front', was not widely appreciated. Thus, after the strains of the previous two years, the Government seemed to be moving into a calmer and more hopeful period. In by-elections, the Labour resurgence fell away. It was Jubilee year. Conservative morale began to mount.

In June came the long expected reshuffle when MacDonald at last stepped down as Prime Minister and was replaced by Baldwin. MacDonald's career had dwindled into a pathetic twilight, in which his always somewhat diffuse speaking style had drifted into meaningless vapidity. To the younger politicians it was difficult to recognise in this often rambling and vain old man the architect of the Labour Party, the courageous and reviled opponent of the war, and the first national leader that the Labour movement had produced. He deserves much better of history than the derisive mockery which has followed him beyond his death in 1937. But it had been a profound national misfortune that he had held the Premiership so long after it was clearly evident that he was no longer capable of holding any serious public office.

Baldwin's belated resumption of power gave him the opportunity of making several overdue changes. The pompous and legalistic Simon was moved from the Foreign to the Home Office, and was replaced by Hoare. This was only a marginal improvement. Hoare was a prim and not wholly lovable personality, witheringly immortalised by Birkenhead as 'the last of a long line of maiden aunts', but he was very ambitious and undoubtedly able, and had a heightened reputation as a result of his patient handling of the Government of India Act. No one realised the price that had been paid in mental and physical exhaustion during this struggle. Anthony Eden became Minister Without Portfolio for League of Nations Affairs, also in the Cabinet. Eden, high-strung and eager to advance, was unhappy about this dual arrangement, and with good cause, but Baldwin persuaded him to accept. Although Eden seemed too young and inexperienced to take the Foreign Secretaryship, Baldwin had developed a high estimate of him. He was certainly by far the most exciting, attractive, and impressive of the new generation of Conservatives that had emerged from the war, with a good intellect, an excellent record, and considerable personal charm, and who was dedicated to his work. It was difficult to discern at that stage of his meteoric career that behind this most impressive façade there was a brave, sensitive, honourable, but nervous and irresolute personality.

Halifax, whom Baldwin had long admired and liked greatly, became Secretary of State for War, and two young Conservatives of high promise, Oliver Stanley (Education) and Walter Elliot (Agriculture), entered the Cabinet. The National Labour presence was rather disproportionately represented by Ramsay and Malcolm

MacDonald and the perennial Jimmy Thomas, with Lord de la Warr as a senior Minister. The most significant appointment was that of Cunliffe-Lister to the Air Ministry. His energy and ability as chairman of the Air Defence Research Committee had impressed Baldwin, who was also resolved to get rid of the imperious Lord Londonderry. The latter took his removal to the leadership of the Lords badly, and took his dismissal from the Government in November even more ill. Londonderry has received rather more praise for his tenure of the Air Ministry—notably from Churchill—than he really merited, but there were other factors in his downfall. He and his wife ran what was virtually the last *grande tenue* establishment in London, and the fact that their great wealth was based substantially upon coal revenues did not heighten his stature in Baldwin's eyes. The Londonderrys' sedulous courting of MacDonald also distressed Baldwin, who had a genuine affection and respect for his colleague and disliked seeing him basking foolishly amidst the glories of Londonderry House. But there were considerations of policy as well. Londonderry was a 'bomber', and in October 1934 had made a boastful speech on the subject which had been a source of considerable public embarrassment to the Government and of great personal annoyance to Baldwin. Londonderry was furthermore, a member of London Society that was markedly friendly to the German government and notoriously hostile to Jews.

Cunliffe-Lister was by far the best of Baldwin's new appointments, but it was a deep misfortune—as he himself subsequently realised— that in November he accepted a peerage and went to the House of Lords as the Earl of Swinton. This removed from the Commons not only one of the most able Ministers in the Cabinet but the architect of the renaissance of the Royal Air Force and the most emphatic exponent of effective rearmament. Cunliffe-Lister's abrasiveness and lack of respect for exalted reputations had prevented him from developing a real following in the party, but the respect he had gathered might have made him a strong challenger to Neville Chamberlain for the succession. As he remarked in his old age, 'I still kick myself. I was a damned fool.'

Londonderry's removal in November enabled Baldwin to transfer Halifax to the office of Lord Privy Seal and to bring in another promising young Conservative, Duff Cooper. Again, this promise was not to be fulfilled. In the Government, but outside the Cabinet, were other coming young men favoured by Baldwin—W. S. Morrison,

Thomas Dugdale, James Stuart, R. A. Butler, and Leslie Hore-Belisha. For some time Baldwin had been deeply concerned at the lack of young men of ability and sense of public service in the Conservative ranks that he was looking for in the party, and he was understandably worried about the advanced average age of the Cabinet. But his promotions look odd in the light of later experience. Of his personal favourites only Eden and Butler proved to be of top calibre, and he overlooked equally promising men, most notably the rebellious Harold Macmillan and the rapidly developing Victor Cazalet. Nonetheless, it was a bold infusion of new blood, and emphasised the fact that the Labour Party had nothing comparable in talent, in Parliament or out of it, in this generation at this level.

Baldwin himself was ageing, if not as noticeably as MacDonald, and the virtually twenty years of high office and thirteen of the party leadership had taken their toll. He commanded unequalled respect and affection, and he was, like the old Gladstone, still capable of rising from time to time to great events and important occasions. But the capacity to cover all aspects of Government without becoming too immersed, of surveying the operations of an Administration with a keen eye for the most critical, had been eroded. He cared deeply about rearmament—'a country which shows itself unwilling to make what necessary preparations are recognisable for its own defence will never have force—moral or material—in this world'—and had done more than any other senior Minister to put the Government on this unpopular but necessary course. But he did not see the whole picture. He was tired, under strain, and he recognised the fact. Chamberlain was to be the dominating influence in his last Government. But he felt that he should remain to take the Government through a General Election that could not be long postponed; he was concerned about Neville Chamberlain's likely approach to rearmament as Prime Minister; and he had deep forebodings about the monarchy. King George had never fully recovered from a major illness in 1929, and the Jubilee in the summer of 1935, although a personal triumph, had been a further strain on a weakened physique. The personality of his heir, and his fitness for the tasks before him, were matters of concern. Baldwin, accordingly, stayed on. His final Premiership was to be dismally undistinguished, and, indeed, marked by only one major public achievement and a series of public humiliations. But at least

Swinton was given his head at the Air Ministry, and that was to prove a major element in the salvation of the nation in 1940.

No places were found for Amery, Churchill, or Lloyd George. The former was becoming regarded, cruelly, but not wholly without cause, as an over-serious long-winded bore, and he had no following. But he had also proved himself an able and courageous Minister, and his continuing exclusion—in which Neville Chamberlain played some part—was a major misfortune. Churchill was deeply chagrined by his ostracism, but it would have been a most remarkable act of charity to have given office to a man whose dominant occupation over the previous four years had been to denounce the Government on almost all possible occasions, and often in the most violent terms. In these circumstances the fact that Baldwin was 'very hostile' to the idea of Churchill's return was wholly understandable.[1] Chamberlain was also strongly opposed to the reinstatement of what he called 'this brilliant, erratic, creature', and the opinions of the evident heir-apparent had to be taken into serious account. The only really surprising aspect was that Churchill, both before and after the 1935 election, thought that he had a serious chance of inclusion.[2] Subsequently he was more philosophical. 'There was much mocking in the Press about my exclusion. But now one can see how lucky I was. Over me beat the invisible wings. And I had agreeable consolations. I set out with my paintbox for more genial climes without waiting for the meeting of Parliament.'[3] The possibility of a Lloyd George–Baldwin coalition—although discussed—was never realistic.

The new Government was swiftly presented with an ominous challenge to the assumptions of the 'Stresa Front', when Italian designs upon Abyssinia moved from threats to active preparations for invasion.

The Cabinet received very conflicting advice. The Minister in Addis Ababa, Sir Sidney Barton, cabled that 'I can think of only one course likely to prevent perpetration of what may be widely regarded as an

---

[1] Thomas Jones: *A Diary with Letters*, 145.

[2] In January he had spoken on behalf of his son, Randolph, who had put himself forward as Independent Conservative candidate in a by-election at Wavertree (Liverpool). This was not inspired by the older Churchill, as was generally believed at the time, but Randolph Churchill got over ten thousand votes and Labour captured the seat. This episode, coming so soon before the change of Government, was in itself sufficient cause for Churchill to be passed over by Baldwin. But it was only one element.   [3] Churchill, op. cit., 141.

international crime, and that would be for England and France to tell Italy that she cannot have Ethiopia'. But the counsel of Sir Eric Drummond, formerly the first Secretary-General of the League, and now Ambassador in Rome, was dismissive of the League and of any conciliation procedures and favoured pressure on the Emperor Haile Selassie to make concessions to the Italians. His attitude reflected the firm views of Simon and Vansittart to exploit Mussolini as a counter-weight to Hitler, and the urgings of Barton were ignored. There was little enthusiasm among Ministers for making this a major issue, let alone a *casus belli*, and certainly none at all among the Chiefs of Staff. Their annual review of the condition of Imperial Defence was a very sombre document. 'By the signing of the Treaty of Locarno', they observed, 'the United Kingdom undertook definite commitments and to that extent made our participation in a European war more likely without in any way reducing our responsibilities in the Far East.' Confronted with a rearming Germany and a powerful and menacing Japan, the prospect of making an additional enemy was not alluring.

The bulk of the Conservative Party shared Churchill's view that it was 'a very small matter' and that 'no one can keep up the pretence that Abyssinia is a fit, worthy, and equal member of a League of civilised nations'. But the possibility of an Italian invasion aroused surprising passions outside Westminster, and was a major element in the downfall of George Lansbury, who was savaged and humiliated by Ernest Bevin at the annual Labour conference in October. The full extent of public feeling was not fully evident until December, but even in June and July Ministers realised—particularly with an election looming within twelve months—that they had to walk warily. While they sought in private a formula that would extricate themselves from this unpleasant embarrassment, in public Hoare was dispatched to Geneva to pledge on September 12th the full commitment of the British Government to the Covenant of the League, and, in particular, to 'steady and collective resistance to all acts of unprovoked aggression'. Eden was not the only Cabinet Minister to be startled by the vigour of a speech that, in the words of Lester Pearson of Canada, 'moved us to cheers and almost to tears'. Hoare had trapped the Government in its own self-made snare. Its policy was now reduced to big words, the League, and the private resolution not to put these grave matters to the test.

The Labour Party was passing through deeply emotional heart-searchings about its attitude towards national and collective security, which was now sharply exacerbated by the mounting crisis over Abyssinia. Lansbury, an avowed and dedicated pacifist, was greatly loved, and his offer to resign if his extreme views were an embarrassment to the party had been rejected at the 1934 party conference. By October 1935 this embarrassment had become very real with the majority of the party and the T.U.C. strongly supporting the League. The key issue was sanctions, which Lansbury passionately opposed, but there were other factors which had made his leadership a source of irritation to many in the party. With an election looming, Lansbury's age and lengthy emotional speeches jarred on many of his colleagues, but none dared challenge his overwhelming popularity. His speech to the 1935 conference opposed sanctions and won a tremendous ovation. But in a speech of notable brutality Ernest Bevin stamped upon the possibility, which Lansbury had clearly hinted at, that he might remain as leader despite the division of view between himself and the bulk of the party, in one passage: 'You are placing the Executive and the Movement in an absolutely wrong position to be taking your conscience round from body to body asking to be told what you ought to do with it.' Some who were present claim that Bevin used the words 'trailing your conscience', others 'hawking your conscience', but the exact words were not the point. The resolution against which Lansbury had spoken so vehemently was passed by more than two million votes, and his speech in reply to Bevin was listened to with impatience and had no effect. Lansbury resigned, and the Parliamentary Party, after asking him to reconsider his decision, elected Attlee for the remainder of the session. It was assumed that this would be a very temporary measure. This assumption was to prove wrong.

Thus, the trade union and Labour movements had committed themselves to the principle of firm action through the League against Italy. Their reasoning may have been confused, but the meaning was clear. A surge of emotion seemed to be sweeping the country, and to this Ministers could not be indifferent.

In June Hoare had warned the Cabinet that there was every prospect of it being placed in 'a most inconvenient dilemma' over Abyssinia, and had informed his colleagues that 'Either we should have to make a futile protest, which would irritate Mussolini and perhaps drive him out of the League into the arms of Germany, or we should make no protest at all and give the appearance of pusillanimity'. The same basic point was made more bluntly by the head of the Civil Service, Sir Warren Fisher: 'If Italy persists in her present policy', he wrote to Baldwin, 'is England really prepared not merely to threaten, but also to use force, and is she in a position to do so?' The answer to both questions was clearly negative. Thus, by September, the British were exactly in the dilemma that Hoare had warned about in June, and he was very substantially responsible for making the situation even worse by his dramatic Geneva speech. Electoral factors undoubtedly played a considerable part in this chaos. As Ministers read it, the Peace Ballot—published in June—demonstrated strong support not only for non-military League action against an aggressor but also for military. It was certainly Hoare's judgement that 'there would be a wave of public opinion against the Government if it repudiated its obligations under Article 16 [of the Covenant]. . . . It was abundantly clear that the only safe line for His Majesty's Government was to try out the regular League of Nations procedure'.[1] By this stage the Chiefs of Staff had laid out to the Cabinet the full military and diplomatic implications of years of neglect of the armed forces. The French, still embittered by the Anglo-German Naval Treaty, remained only very guardedly co-operative. When the French Foreign Minister, Laval, put the question of full British adherence to the Covenant to Eden with characteristic bluntness on September 2nd, he got a lame answer.[2] On September 9th and 10th Hoare met with Laval, and reached agreement that they would take no action at Geneva that would lead to war.

Why, then, did Hoare proceed to Geneva and deliver his dramatic call to arms? Chamberlain's account of a dinner with Hoare and Baldwin on September 5th relates that it was he who urged a firm line which 'might force Italy to a halt, which in turn might make Hitler waver',[3] and that Hoare and Baldwin agreed. But Hoare went further than this in public. He later wrote that he was personally determined to make 'a revivalist appeal to the Assembly. At best it might start a new chapter of League recovery, at worst it might deter Mussolini by a display of League fervour. If there was any element of bluff in it, it

[1] Quoted in Correlli Barnett: *The Collapse of British Power*, 361.
[2] Lord Avon: *Facing the Dictators*, 258.
[3] Keith Feiling: *Neville Chamberlain*, 268.

was a moment when bluff was not only legitimate, but inescapable.'[1] A cynic might observe that it was the only option left. But there was another consideration, to which Hoare referred in his speech: 'The recent response of public opinion [in Britain] shows how completely the nation supports the Government in the full acceptance of the obligations of League membership.'

Hoare had gone considerably further than the discussions in the Cabinet had warranted, and it is not clear whether Baldwin saw the final text of his speech. But although Hoare returned to a hero's welcome the reactions of other Ministers were understandably less glowing. At a long Cabinet on September 24th these mounting apprehensions surfaced, but Ministers had to conclude that 'the serious consequences of receding from the previous attitude [of support for the League] were emphasised from the point of view of domestic policy no less than from that of foreign policy. It was pointed out that any weakness or vacillation would bring serious consequences'. Baldwin was not the only Minister who remarked upon the equal perils of maintaining the present course. But now they had no choice.

Throughout this dismal proceeding Baldwin had not given any serious lead to his colleagues, and the error of having two Cabinet Ministers from the Foreign Office was being revealed. Baldwin's position and attitudes are extremely difficult to describe, let alone analyse, during these critical weeks. The evidence is confused and fragmentary, but the very absence of clear evidence in his own papers or in the Cabinet archives leads to the conclusion that Baldwin was himself very confused, baffled, and profoundly concerned. He did not let the crisis slip turbulently past him while he observed it serenely from a sage shore, as many have implied. He watched the terrible maelstrom with bewilderment and fear, but with his mind concentrated upon other matters. He left far too much to his subordinates, whom he had just appointed, and he had committed himself too deeply to the League in the appointment of the ardent Eden and the newly converted and unstable Hoare. And, then, there was the startlingly belligerent Neville Chamberlain, whose influence as the heir-apparent was rising sharply, and who had informed the Cabinet on May 27th that 'the Italians had behaved so badly that it would be impossible morally, and indeed, almost indecent to come to terms with them'. Hoare had taken his lead from Chamberlain.

[1] Templewood, op. cit., 166.

Thus, with a Cabinet whose senior members were so confident, yet himself knowing of the dismal inadequacies of the force behind these fine challenges, his attention concentrated on other priorities, Baldwin struggled along and hoped for the best. His Government had drifted into a position from which only a dramatic and humiliating climb-down by the Italians could possibly save them. And the possibility of this deliverance was rapidly disappearing.

Meanwhile, Baldwin was receiving conflicting advice about the best time for the General Election that must come before the autumn of 1936. The view of the Conservative Central Office was that the main issue of the election would be unemployment, and particularly the conditions in the depressed areas; it was also obvious that Labour would continue to exploit the armaments issue. Neville Chamberlain, somewhat surprisingly in view of his fiscal opposition to rearmament, urged that the Government should fight on rearmament and foreign policy, but his arguments were based less on national than on party political calculations. Baldwin disagreed strongly with these cal-culations. He wanted his mandate for rearmament, and was equally prepared to exploit the public feeling over Abyssinia, but he did not want another single-issue election on the 1923 pattern, and in any event he was convinced that rearmament was not an issue on which an election could be won. He therefore proposed to fight it over the broad front of the Government's achievements and the deficiencies of Labour. He held his counsel about the timing until the European situation seemed clearer. At the party conference at the beginning of October he had, in the account of Thomas Jones, 'a great ovation. Denounced the isolationists, reconciled the Party to the League by supporting rearmament, and reconciled the pacifists to rearmament by supporting the Covenant. Spoke strongly in favour of Trade Unions. All with an eye to the election, on the date of which he was inscrutable.'[1]

But on October 3rd the Italians actually invaded Abyssinia. The League branded Italy as an aggressor, and the question of economic sanctions was urgently considered. The dominant factors in the British approach were their refusal to act alone—and certainly not without full French support—their apprehensions of the situation in the Mediterranean if war broke out with Italy, and, above all, the desire of Ministers and the Foreign Office not to antagonise Mussolini

[1] Jones, op. cit., 155.

fatally. Sanctions were accordingly imposed, but with the notable exception of oil. It was something more than a slap on the wrist, and something less than a harsh blow. Ministers groped towards a convenient escape from their predicament, while making strong pronouncements about support for the League. Greater attention should have been given to Baldwin's warning in his October 3rd speech that 'His Majesty's Government have not, and have never had, any intention of taking isolated action in this dispute'. On this point Baldwin was emphatic, but he left the actual details to Hoare and Eden. It is a serious charge against Baldwin—and a just one—that he did not devote as much attention to what was going on in the Foreign Office at this time as he should have. As Vansittart, the chief author of the looming disaster, subsequently wrote:

> It is wrong to suppose that he [Baldwin] had no care for foreign affairs; he had some, but not enough: he could not find time to masticate the mass of Foreign Office papers. Seeing the limitations of time and himself he preferred to leave details to experts without authority.[1]

This is a severe judgement, and one not merited as a general one on Baldwin's involvement in foreign affairs throughout his career; but it was certainly justified in the context of the Abyssinian crisis.

It is not clear what were the decisive factors that prompted Baldwin to decide on an autumn election. He wanted his 'mandate' for rearmament, and his concern at the deficiencies revealed by the latest report of the Defence Requirements Committee was genuine. With the international situation so ominous, the prospect of taking the Government into the last months of a dying Parliament was not an alluring one. There was also the incalculable factor of Baldwin's sensitivity to public opinion. He sensed, rather than knew, that the Labour resurgence was receding, and that the Liberals offered no real threat. In the period when polling on the Gallup pattern was unknown (its first tentative appearance in Britain was in 1938) politicians had to rely upon visits to their constituencies, by-election results, the advice of the party officials, the economic indicators of confidence or recession, and the newspapers. When they had done all this, the judging of this vast new electorate was basically one of guesswork. In 1923 and 1929 Baldwin had guessed wrong; this time he was right. Parliament

---

[1] Vansittart: *The Mist Procession*, 352.

was dissolved, and the election held on November 14th. Meanwhile, the labyrinthine discussions in Geneva and Paris continued on their uneasy course.

Mr. Taylor has summarised the subsequent campaign:

> It was a confused election. Essentially both Labour and the National parties, apart from a few extremists on either side, were saying the same thing: all sanctions short of war. Labour implied that the government were not operating sanctions seriously: Conservatives alleged that Labour, if in power, would topple over into war. Both sides were in a muddle themselves and therefore muddled their charges against each other.[1]

But this was not the whole story. The election was not fought over Abyssinia or rearmament in isolation from other issues, of which economic ones were the most significant, but they figured so prominently in the debates between the major politicians that it is unwise to accept that, as Mr. Taylor claims, 'the electors showed little interest in these questions'. The Labour accusations of Conservative 'warmongering' did not diminish after the removal of Lansbury, and were intense throughout the campaign. The Labour Manifesto declared that 'This Government is a danger to the peace of the world, to the security of this country. . . . Whilst paying lip service to the League, it is planning a vast and expensive rearmament programme which will only stimulate similar programmes elsewhere . . . the best defence is not huge competitive national armaments, but the organisation of collective security against any aggressor and the agreed reduction of national armaments elsewhere.' One particularly vitriolic accuser was Herbert Morrison, a bitter and ambitious former Minister of Transport who had built up a formidable and ruthless organisation in the London County Council (and also a very formidable enemy in Bevin) and who was consumed by the conviction that if he had not lost his seat in 1931 it would have been he, and not Attlee, reigning in Lansbury's place. Perhaps he was right, but it was a lucky escape for the Labour Party and for the nation.[2] But in the 1935 election Morrison's was the dominant Labour voice, and he was relentless on

[1] Taylor, op. cit., 383.

[2] After the election, when he was in Parliament again, he and Arthur Greenwood stood against Attlee. In the first ballot the votes were: Attlee 58, Morrison 44, Greenwood 32. Greenwood withdrew, and on the second ballot Attlee defeated Morrison by 88 votes to 44.

the charge of armaments, with Attlee, a trenchant speaker on occasion, but no demagogue, limping behind.

Baldwin's responses subsequently earned Churchill's withering contempt—and not only his. At the time Churchill confined himself to Epping, equivocated on Abyssinia, was strong on rearmament, and pledged his warm support for his leader. 'Things are in such a state that it is a blessing to have at the head of affairs a man whom people will rally round', he wrote enthusiastically to Baldwin on October 7th. '. . . I will abide with you in this election, and do what little I can to help in the most serviceable way.'

Baldwin in fact handled the matter of rearmament not only with considerable political skill but also with rather more honesty than later evaluations—principally Churchill's—afford him credit. He reiterated the point that rearmament was necessary for defence, but defence alone. He pledged that 'there will be no great armaments', and in further response to the drum-beat of Labour attacks—'What they really want is big armaments in order to play the old game of power politics', Attlee was charging—issued a statement just before voting that made this point again:

> The Government will undertake a programme planned only, so far as all the defensive services are concerned, to provide adequately for our country's safety. The sole desire of Ministers is to secure that the country and the Empire are again placed in a position to safeguard their interests in case of any eventuality. Beyond that point it is not intended to go.

The allegation has persisted that Baldwin tricked the electorate over rearmament in 1935, and, in Churchill's devastating accusation, that 'having gained all that there was in sight upon a programme of sanctions and rearmament, he became very anxious to comfort the professional peace-loving elements in the nation, and allay any fears in their breasts which his talk about naval requirements might have caused. . . . Thus the votes both of those who sought to see the nation prepare itself against the dangers of the future, and of those who believed that peace could be preserved by praising its virtues, were gained.'[1] This was harsh, and not justified. Churchill's case would be strengthened if the evidence supported his own claim that

---

[1] Churchill, op. cit., 180.

'I fought my contest in the Epping Division upon the need for re-armament and upon a severe and *bona fide* policy of sanctions'. In fact, he ran it on classic anti-Socialist lines, warmly supporting the economic and social programmes of the Government, warning about the German peril but praising Baldwin, whom he described as 'a statesman who has gathered to himself a greater fund of confidence and goodwill than any man I recollect in my long public career'. Believing, as he did, that it would be 'a terrible deed to smash up Italy', references to sanctions—*bona fide* or otherwise—were not at all prominent in his campaign. It is in no sense to denigrate Churchill's prolonged and courageous campaign for rearmament in the 1930s to emphasise that all aspects of his subsequent version, and particularly the violent assault on Baldwin, should not be accepted. Churchill himself was a tough, and not always wholly scrupulous, professional politician. In his memoirs, although Baldwin receives more than his deserved share of criticism, there is one passage of genuine admiration: 'He had a genius for waiting upon events and an imperturbability under adverse criticism. He was singularly adroit in letting events work for him, and capable of seizing the right moment when it came . . . I should have found it easier to work with Baldwin, as I knew him, than with Chamberlain.'[1]

Baldwin received what he later described as his mandate for the continuation of his policies. It was, in a very real sense, a personal triumph. Baldwin had the capacity to inspire trust and respect that no British politician of the century has possessed. Normally a hum-drum commonsense speaker, with an instinctive understanding of his audiences, he had the capacity to move unexpectedly into heights of oratory that constantly astounded his colleagues and critics. As a radio speaker he was particularly impressive. In contrast, Attlee was waspish and sounded mean, like an embittered tax inspector; Morri-son was cockney and vicious; Cripps was learned and politically wild; Churchill seemed to belong to another age, almost as absurd as MacDonald; Lloyd George was a gone goose, courted only by those with flickering memories and vague expectations.

The real and valid charge against Baldwin in 1935 is not that he deceived the nation on rearmament, but that his Abyssinian policy was a fraud. The Opposition was deeply split on the issue, and in these circumstances the apparently balanced and judicious approach of the

[1] Churchill, op. cit., 221–2.

Government had an appearance of statesmanship and responsibility. It was this façade that was probably decisive in the Conservative victory, and laid the foundations for the subsequent tumult within and outside the party.

But it had not been a landslide. The Conservative vote was 11·8 million, that of Labour 8·3 million—a margin that emphasises how justified had been Baldwin's apprehensions of the Labour revival in 1933 and 1934. But in terms of seats the majority was much greater —432 to 154. The Liberals dropped again, and both MacDonalds were defeated, the elder by Emanuel Shinwell at Seaham in a particularly unpleasant contest. Both quickly returned to the Commons for other constituencies. Churchill departed with his family and paint-box to Spain. Ministers turned again to the embarrassments of Abyssinia.

*

By this stage, these had become acute. The strategy of the Government —if such a patched-up inchoate process can be adorned with such a description—was to create sufficient European moral, political, and economic pressure to make Mussolini draw back from his adventure and then offer him the hand of warm friendship and closer alliance in the Stresa Front. This overlooked the fact of French disillusionment over the Anglo-German Naval Treaty. Also, unknown to Ministers, there was a serious security leak in the British Embassy in Rome, and Mussolini had other sources in London that gave him the true picture of the flickering British resolve. He pressed forward to 'avenge Adowa', and the wretched poverty-stricken people of Abyssinia found themselves facing modern weapons and an exultant, cruel, and inept invader. Partly through their courage, but principally through Italian incompetence, logistical difficulties, and the sheer size of the country, the Italian onslaught was something less than a *blitzkrieg*. But in Britain, disgust at the Italian excesses rose sharply.

Hoare and Vansittart—principally the latter—devised an escape-route. With French aid, Mussolini would be offered most of Abyssinia, but not all of it; Selassie would retain his title and a fragment of land. This tactic had a considerable element of practical sense in it, but it took no account whatever of the passions building up in Britain. It also conveniently ignored the warm approval given to Hoare's September speech, and the fact that an election had just been fought and won on strong support of the League. It therefore included all factors save that of public opinion and practical politics, and presents us with a perfect example of political insensitivity by a leading official born and brought up in an age when everything was settled in the Westminster Square Mile. But the weak Hoare eagerly went along with it, and so did a not totally comprehending Baldwin.

The proposal that Hoare and Vansittart took to Paris on December 7th to present to Laval, was that Abyssinia would be partitioned, with Italy receiving the principal—and most valuable—areas, while the Emperor Selassie would retain his former limited kingdom with a corridor to the sea. The war would end, the Stresa Front would be triumphantly re-created, sanctions dropped, and the regrettable interlude successfully terminated. Laval enthusiastically endorsed it, and made proposals (which were accepted) even more favourable to Italy. The plan ignored the fact that Mussolini was under no serious pressure to end his campaign—and on this the British and French greatly exaggerated reports of discontent and difficulty in Italy—and that political and public opinions in Britain and France, and particularly the former, were wholly unprepared for such an abrupt *volte-face*.

The Hoare–Laval Pact was deliberately leaked in Paris—it is still not clear by whom—and in London Ministers and Members of Parliament were subjected to a storm of protest which Duff Cooper subsequently described as the most violent and intense he experienced in his political career. *The Times* blasted the proposals with a leader headed 'A Corridor For Camels', and Conservative back-benchers reported an unparalleled outburst from their constituents.

But the real revolt came from the new Conservative M.P.s, who had taken the election pledge that 'the League of Nations will remain the keystone of British foreign policy' seriously, and were outraged by the rapidity with which their election speeches had been made to look, at the very best, absurd. The Foreign Affairs Committee, chaired by Austen Chamberlain, was the centre of the revolt, and when fifty-nine Government supporters signed a motion critical of the Pact Ministers belatedly realised the full dimensions of the storm. The League of Nations Union, then at the height of its membership and influence, was in itself a force not lightly to be mocked, and made its fury known. As the events of June 1936 over the ending of sanctions were to demonstrate, the League by itself could not have changed the policy. The revolt was within the Conservative Party, and particularly by the new M.P.s. This was what brought Hoare down.[1] When the Chief Whip told Baldwin that 'our men won't stand for it' Hoare's doom was sealed.

Austen Chamberlain became the spokesman of this angry dissident group, and with the Conservative Party, the Press, and the Opposition in uproar, it became evident that Hoare, contentfully resting in Switzerland and believing that he had pulled off a major diplomatic coup, must be sacrificed. In such situations Baldwin could act swiftly. Hoare, his nose encased in plaster after a heavy fall while skating, was summoned back to be given his quietus. Forlorn, undignified, incredulous, and overwhelmed, he tearfully pleaded his case, but unavailingly. Hoare had cause for his unhappiness at the brutality of his treatment, although his colleagues also had merited grounds for complaint of his conduct of affairs. They considered that he had over-committed them on September 12th, and they had certainly not expected him to come to firm undertakings with Laval at this stage, nor to issue a communiqué after his talks with Laval that announced the creation of a formula 'which might serve as a basis for a friendly settlement of the Italo-Ethiopian dispute', which had precipitated the initial intense international speculation before the full details were leaked in Paris. Hoare noted that the Cabinet had agreed on December 10th that the terms were 'the best, from the Abyssinian point of view, that could be obtained from Italy' and 'the lowest terms which the French Government and the Secretary of State for Foreign Affairs thought that Italy might agree to'. On grounds of collective responsibility, all Ministers were implicated. But then the unexpected storm hit them, the party went into open rebellion, and the mob had to have a victim.

Baldwin, in one of the worst speeches of his career, tried to explain matters away in the House of Commons without success. A party revolt of real magnitude was only narrowly averted. Hoare was replaced by Eden, and the Hoare–Laval Pact was emphatically dead. So, too, was the League of Nations. All that remained was the inevitable Italian victory, the exile of Selassie who had become, improbably, an inter-

[1] For a recent study of the crisis see D. Waley: *British Public Opinion and the Abyssinian War, 1935–6*. The crisis also occasioned one of the King's more memorable utterances when he remarked (in private), 'No more coals to Newcastle, no more Hoares to Paris'.

national hero, and, in June 1936, the abandonment of sanctions, mocked into their grave by Neville Chamberlain as 'the height of midsummer madness'.

For the Government, this had been a very ugly shock. At no time in the life of the National Government, not even at the height of the storms over India, had there been a party revolt of such intensity and gravity. No one could recall an occasion when a newly elected Government had been plunged so swiftly into a crisis of survival. Luckily, Churchill had been studiously absent and had made no comment whatever, and Austen Chamberlain was hardly an intimidating leader of a *putsch*. But Ministers went on their Christmas holidays profoundly shaken and very perplexed, and none more than Baldwin. The overwhelming majority of a month earlier suddenly looked much less secure.

As has been emphasised before in this narrative, every Parliament has its particular and peculiar characteristics. This one was to prove exceptionally volatile and unpredictable throughout the ten years of its life, and was to provide Ministers with frequent and salutary surprises. It was to humiliate, and then to revere, and finally to excoriate, Baldwin; it was to give Neville Chamberlain the very rare tribute of a standing ovation and then to destroy him; it was to howl Churchill down, then to ignore him, and later to give him support of a kind that neither Gladstone nor Lloyd George had ever experienced —but on its own terms. It was to prove itself a restless, disturbed, emotional, apprehensive, and bloody-minded Parliament, at no time to be taken for granted. It was, both in its leading personalities and in its collective character, the most brilliant and passionate Parliament of the century. A strong and glorious lustre shines upon all who served in it.

As Ministers dispersed for Christmas, some vague inklings of these remarkable and disturbing characteristics had been forcibly borne upon them.   *

When Parliament returned, it was to mourn the passing of the Sovereign. King George V had succeeded to the throne in 1910 in the midst of a major constitutional crisis, for which he was ill-equipped by experience or temperament, and from which he had emerged with a healthy and abiding suspicion of most politicians. Throughout the war his influence had been on the side of the soldiers, and his relationship with Lloyd George had never been close. The King was a sensible, formidable, man, not an intellectual but possessed of considerable intelligence; deeply conservative, yet he never permitted his personal prejudices—which were very strong—to interfere with his conception of his public duty. His crucial intervention in the Irish war in 1921 has already been noted, as has his selection of Baldwin over Curzon in 1923. His treatment of the Labour Ministers was always scrupulously correct, and his personal friendship with Jimmy Thomas was warm and genuine. His part in the creation of the National Government in 1931 was based upon deep concern for the national interest.

The inevitable remoteness of the monarchy had been remarkably diminished by his annual Christmas radio broadcasts. Together with Franklin Roosevelt and Baldwin he had instinctively understood the fundamental technique of this new medium, and mastered it effortlessly. His calm, gentle, conversational, guttural, friendly and sincere homilies had a considerable impact, and the intense enthusiasm with which he had been greeted at his Jubilee in the summer of 1935 had startled most observers and had astonished the King himself. He regarded himself as the Father of his people, and to a remarkable degree was thus regarded by them.

He spent the Christmas of 1935, as always, at Sandringham, but it was evident to those close to him that he was seriously unwell. His condition deteriorated suddenly. On the evening of January 20th it was announced by his doctors that 'the King's life is moving peacefully to its close', and he died during the night. In the January bleakness his body was borne to Sandringham station after lying in state in the small Sandringham church guarded by his tenants and estate workers, and thence to an ice-cold Westminster Hall. 'The coffin remains there', Harold Nicolson, just elected as National Labour M.P. for West Leicester, wrote, 'just a wreath of flowers and the crown, its diamonds winking in the candle-light.' For several days a huge silent procession filed past the catafalque, soldiers with bowed heads standing at the corners. It was an unforgettable, awesome, intensely moving, spectacle. On one occasion the place of the soldiers was taken by the King's four sons.[1] Then the King was taken to Windsor. The public grief and gloom were genuine, and widespread.

[1] King Edward VIII, the Duke of York, the Duke of Gloucester, and the Duke of Kent.

In that same bleak January King Edward VIII was proclaimed with due ceremony. Remote from his parents, he was in public a charming and accomplished performer, but also known to those who had observed him closely to be moody, shallow, and self-indulgent. Although far from being a misogynist, he had not married, and had a marked prediction for what was derided as 'Café Society'. But it was his association with a married American woman, Mrs. Ernest Simpson, which gave those in the know the principal source of alarm, and not least because the relationship was deliberately flaunted. The people knew nothing of this, it was a London story. The new King inherited the vast respect for the monarchy that his father had increased in his reign, and the admiration that he had established in his own right as a fresh, vital, and glamorous personality. His admirers believed that he would provide excitement, and would inject new life into the monarchy. But others, including the Prime Minister, looked on with apprehension, hoped that their fears were groundless, but were still assailed with many forebodings. They could not have calculated how the brief reign of King Edward was to have such a major effect upon the course of British politics in 1936.

*

Ministers had little respite after the Hoare–Laval catastrophe. The pressure for a Minister of Defence from Conservative back benchers became so insistent that some response had to be made to it, in itself an indication of the Government's new nervousness about its supporters. With the notable exception of Swinton, few Ministers were enthusiastic, most were strongly opposed, and the strong influence of Hankey was cast in the balance against the proposal. The fact that Churchill, now returned but studiously restrained, was known to be thirsting for the position did not improve its chances, particularly as far as Neville Chamberlain was concerned. The result was a classic and lamentable Whitehall compromise, whereby a 'Minister for the Co-ordination of Defence' was created, with no powers and little staff. Furthermore, the new Minister was the Attorney-General, Sir Thomas Inskip, whose surprise at the appointment was widely shared. But the choice had been deliberate, and Neville Chamberlain had been the key voice in Inskip's selection; as he approvingly noted, Inskip 'would excite no enthusiasm but he would involve us in no fresh perplexities'. It was one of Baldwin's worst appointments. Inskip was to prove a thoroughly bad Minister, secretive, nervous, difficult to work with or for, and with none of the drive and energy that the post required. If he had possessed these qualities, of course, he would not have been selected. It was not without significance that Churchill's speeches subsequently began to strike a nastier note after this final (as it appeared) blow to his career. 'He thought, no doubt,' he later wrote of Baldwin, 'that he had dealt me a politically fatal stroke, and I felt he might well be right.' In reality, the stroke had been delivered by Chamberlain.

The announcement was made on March 12th, five days after Hitler had marched German troops into the demilitarised Rhineland in flagrant violation of Versailles and Locarno, swiftly following this coup by proposals for settling outstanding issues, the first example of a technique of swift actions followed by soothing words that was to become grimly familiar. But this was the first time, and everyone was caught off balance. The French looked frantically towards London, but the Government willingly accepted the advice of Eden that the French should be strongly discouraged from taking any military action—not that they intended any—and that renewed attempts should be made to reach 'as far-reaching and enduring a settlement as possible while Herr Hitler is still in the mood to do so'. Harold Nicolson noted that 'The feeling in the House is terribly "pro-German", which means afraid of war'.[1] The *Spectator*'s dismissal of the event as 'a small thing in itself' was excessive, but there was remarkably little disposition to criticise the Germans for, in Lothian's memorable phrase, walking into their own back-garden, and considerable impatience at alleged French belligerence. Even Churchill, who knew that the proposed appointment of the Minister of Defence (as he thought it would be) was at hand, was cautious. There was widespread agreement with the statement of Eden that Hitler's offer of negotiations was evidence of Germany's 'unchangeable longing for a real pacification of Europe', and that 'it is the appeasement of Europe as a whole that we have constantly before us'. There was no wave of public opinion faintly comparable to the revulsion against the Hoare–Laval Pact; indeed, all the evidence was that the British were largely indifferent to the event, and certainly strongly opposed to any steps that contained the possibility of war. As the French leaders well knew, the same attitudes prevailed in their country. The Russians

[1] Nicolson: *Diaries and Letters, 1930–1939*, 254.

The Right Honourable J. H. Thomas, P. C., M. P.

14   J. H. Thomas by Low in *The New Statesman*, July 1926

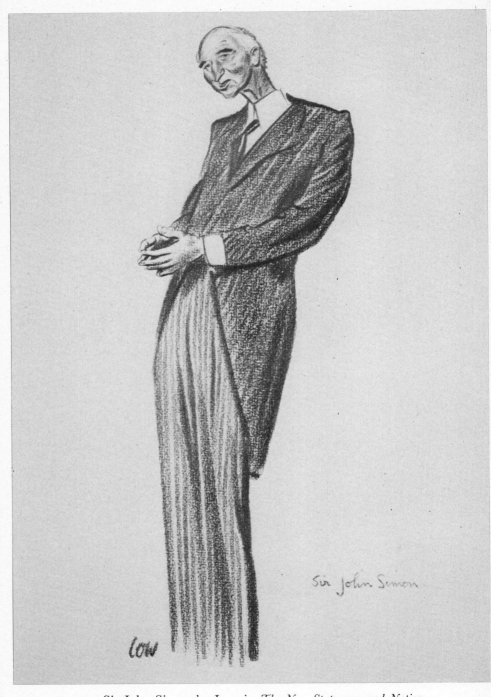

Sir John Simon

low

15   Sir John Simon by Low in *The New Statesman and Nation*,
December 1933

STILL HOPE

16   Illingworth in *Punch*, 21st September 1938

17   In Low's bitter commentary on Munich, Neville Chamberlain and
Halifax play with the innocent little lambs (led by Sir John Simon)
while Beaverbrook rejoices on the right

18   Winston Churchill by Low in *The New Statesman*, May 1926

proposed League sanctions against Germany, which killed what little hope there might have been of any serious reaction from the League. Hitler's soothing assurances turned out to have no real content, and no serious negotiations took place. He had won his first major victory at no cost. But the stirrings of unease in Europe that had begun in 1933 were now given substantial impetus. Austen Chamberlain's fame was now far eclipsed, and he had become a forlorn and even faintly comical figure, but when he warned the House of Commons that Austria would be next, and that 'if Austria perishes, Czechoslovakia becomes indefensible', Members were now beginning to listen.

The Government endured a wretched summer. The collapse of Abyssinian resistance, the flight of Haile Selassie, his hopeless and moving appeal to the League, the ignominious abandonment of sanctions, and his exile in England, were eloquent commentaries enough on the policy pursued by the Government. But when Neville Chamberlain denounced sanctions in June, and the League of Nations Union rose in its wrath, this time the Conservatives did not rise with it. The incident was instructive in another sense. It was the first serious public intervention in foreign affairs made by Chamberlain, was made without reference to his colleagues, and could be read as a humiliation for the young Foreign Secretary. As Swinton subsequently wrote, 'a man beaten once in politics at this level can be beaten again. Chamberlain knew from that moment that he had the measure of Eden.'[1] The Government's supporters accepted the inevitability of the facts, but the episode made them restless. In the House of Commons Arthur Greenwood denounced 'this trembling, vacillating, cowardly government, which is leading people backward instead of forward', and Lloyd George depicted Ministers as being in full retreat, 'running away, brandishing their swords—still leading!' The speeches and articles of Churchill had now real bite in them again. He accused MacDonald and Baldwin of excelling 'in the art of minimising political issues, of frustrating large schemes of change, of depressing the national temperature, and reducing Parliament to a humdrum level. . . . If the supreme need of John Bull after the war and its aftermath was a rest-cure, no two nurses were better fitted to keep silence around a darkened room and protect the patient from anything in the nature of mental stress or strong emotion.'

[1] Swinton: *Sixty Years of Power*, 166.

Then, the Spanish Civil War erupted. At first it seemed a simple military coup by the Spanish Army, but the supporters of the left-wing Government resisted fiercely. Italy and Germany sent military aid to General Franco's rebels, and the Soviet Union assisted the Government. The 'simple military coup' had flared into a terrible civil war, conducted with great brutality on both sides, and now expanded as a major international issue. But it was something more than this. The ideological struggle of Socialism against Fascism excited a considerable number of British people, notably the young, and with a strong element of the intellectuals. Others, who were uninterested in the ideology, saw the war as another part of the collective Fascist menace to Europe. On the other side were those who strongly supported Franco, were fearful of the possibility of the 'Reds' winning, and saw in the war the dread form of international Communism penetrating Western Europe. It became a deeply divisive issue, on which each group held to its opinions with fierce passions.

But it did not seriously divide the Conservative Party. The Government—with the strong support of Churchill, for some time a devout Franco supporter—decided to keep out; so did the French. A Non-Intervention Committee was established in London, and found its endeavours literally thankless. Labour, which originally supported non-intervention, switched into strong opposition when it was obvious that the Germans and Italians were intervening massively and in contemptuous indifference to the wails of the farcical and impotent Non-Intervention Committee. The League did absolutely nothing. Its new Secretary-General, the malevolent and obsessed Frenchman, Avenol, was a dedicated anti-Communist, and the atmosphere in Geneva itself was poisonously pro-Fascist. Interest in the League had dropped sharply in Britain after the Abyssinian débâcle, and although it continued its normal proceedings in its monstrous new edifice rising beside Lake Leman, it did so in an atmosphere of disillusionment and declining morale. It neither sought, nor was it offered, any role in the Spanish crisis.

But although the war was much more divisive on the Left than on the Right in Britain, the Government's compromises did not appear heroic even at the beginning, and increasingly looked distinctly like intervention on the Franco side when the scale of German and Italian intervention became evident. As Labour concern, anger, and contempt grew, Ministers found it increasingly difficult and embarrassing to hold to their chosen line. They did so, but were evidently highly uncomfortable as they battled the rising tumult of scorn.

There were several indications that Baldwin himself was becoming severely rattled by the storms through which his Government was passing. He over-reacted to Press rumours of a Churchill-led plot against his leadership and startled the House by the observation that it was 'the time of year when midges come out of dirty ditches', a comment both crude and absurd. But he had good cause for his alarm and confusion. The Government seemed incapable of getting anything right. First Hoare–Laval, then the Rhineland, then the Inskip appointment, then in May it was discovered that Jimmy Thomas had leaked to friends in the City the fact that income tax was going to rise by 3d and had to leave public life in a hurry, then the sanctions storm, and now Spain. Meanwhile, Churchill was maintaining his hostile salvoes from the back benches and in the columns of the *Evening Standard*, Austen Chamberlain was becoming a regular spokesman of doom,[1] and there were several other areas of turbulence behind the Prime Minister. It was not surprising that Baldwin was very close to a nervous breakdown. But his mounting army of critics did not fully appreciate the true cause of his weariness, strain, and preoccupation. Throughout this crucial summer the Prime Minister's principal concerns and attentions were concentrated upon what became known as 'the King's Matter'.

*

The relationship between the King (then still the Prince of Wales) and Mrs. Ernest Simpson had been well known in London Society for over a year. Mrs. Simpson was an American lady of much grace, intelligence, and charm, who had been married once before, and was whispered to have 'a past'. The Prince of Wales was clearly infatuated with her, and several of his friends considered her influence upon him a good one, but none had any idea that he contemplated marriage. When he became King his reliance upon her became, if anything, even greater. While the British Press maintained a discreet silence over the affair, those of Europe and the United States blazoned it. The

[1] He died in March the following year, and was the subject of a memorable tribute in the Commons by Lloyd George. 'The younger members felt that they had been carried back through Lloyd George to Gladstone away to the battles of the Reform Bill and the administration of the Duke of Wellington' (Nicolson, op. cit., 296).

King himself did little to conceal his feelings, and a cruise in the Mediterranean on the yacht *Nahlin* in the summer with Mrs. Simpson in prominent attendance further alarmed Ministers. On October 27th Mrs. Simpson obtained a *decree nisi* from her husband, and the loyal Press merely reported the fact without comment. This action was the direct result of an appeal by the King to Beaverbrook, who persuaded his colleagues in the newspaper industry to handle the divorce with the minimum of publicity. Beaverbrook had no knowledge that the King intended to marry Mrs. Simpson, and in fact received assurances from her solicitor, Mr. Theodore Goddard, to that effect. 'Even if I had known that he did propose marriage', Beaverbrook later wrote, 'I would still have done what I did. But the fact remains that I did not know, although I was having conversations with the King almost every day.'[1] The nation as a whole had no inkling of the situation, but in London it was the main topic of gossip and speculation. 'King and Mrs. Simpson only source of conversation', Victor Cazalet, M.P. for Chippenham, noted at the beginning of November. 'Everyone has ideas, nearly everyone is miserable about it . . . Some think he will have to abdicate, others think he will marry her, still again some think he may do it morganatically.' On November 19th Cazalet was present at a dinner given for the King and sat next to Mrs. Simpson:

Every minute he [the King] gazes at her and a happiness and radiance fills his countenance such as makes you have a lump in your throat. She believes that if she left he would deteriorate and drink. I think she's right; she is the one real friend he has ever had. She does have a wonderful influence over him, but she knows how stubborn he is, and how difficult to influence.[2]

Not all estimates were as favourable, particularly in the Royal Family itself. Baldwin approached the problem with embarrassment and caution. There is no evidence at all to support the view held by some that he was intent on removing the King from his throne. Indeed, it is clear that he was groping for a solution which would avert what he and many others genuinely regarded as a disaster. For all his faults and weaknesses, King Edward was a highly attractive man, and it was believed that he had great potentialities. But Baldwin believed—and probably rightly—that the possibility of Mrs. Simpson

---

[1] Beaverbrook: *The Abdication of King Edward VIII*, 33.
[2] R. Rhodes James: *Victor Cazalet*, 186.

as Queen of England was wholly unacceptable to the British people. It can be argued with some merit that Baldwin and the Cabinet were assuming an attitude which they never tested, and that the King was being judged by a wholly unrepresentative segment of the nation on standards which belonged more suitably to Victorian times than those of 1936. But it is significant that Labour supported Baldwin completely, and there are other indications that the British belief in the Royal Family as a standard-bearer of moral rectitude was very strong.[1]

Baldwin's caution and embarrassment were in part responsible for the misunderstandings which arose between himself and the King, but the latter was less than frank with the Prime Minister about his intentions. He also concealed his determination to marry Mrs. Simpson from his solicitor, Beaverbrook, and close adviser Walter Monckton. As Monckton recorded:

> I thought throughout, long before as well as after there was talk of marriage, that if and when the stark choice faced them between their love and his obligations as King-Emperor, they would in the end each make the sacrifice, devastating though it would be.[2]

Indeed, it was not until November 17th that the King informed Baldwin of this fact. Up to this point Baldwin had fought against the fact, but with waning optimism, that the King was serious, but it was now evident that he was utterly resolved. Baldwin, and many others, were torn by conflicting emotions. It was obvious that the King was deeply in love, and his determination to marry his mistress was honourable. But monarchs had had lovers before and had not married them, a point which Baldwin—who was not a puritan—gently put to the King. But the King was adamant.

The position was impossible. The Royal Family, the Cabinet, the Liberal and Labour leaders and Dominion leaders would not have Mrs. Simpson, either as a 'real' Queen or a morganatic one. On November 25th Baldwin told Attlee and Sinclair of the situation, and asked their attitude if the King persisted in rejecting the advice of his Ministers and they resigned. Attlee and Sinclair said that in that event they would refuse any invitation to form an alternative Administration. Churchill was also present at this crucial meeting, and

---

[1] See, for example, Hugh Dalton: *Call Back Yesterday*, 114.
[2] F. Donaldson, *Edward VIII*, 207.

Baldwin's biographers state that he said that 'though his attitude was a little different, he would certainly support the Government'. The attitude of other Ministers—notably Neville Chamberlain—was much less sympathetic than that of Baldwin to the King, and there was a strong feeling that Baldwin was not pressing the matter urgently enough. It was to Baldwin's credit that he refused to issue the virtual ultimatum which had been originally drafted by Sir Warren Fisher and Sir Horace Wilson, and toughened up further by Chamberlain. Baldwin's caution and care were more appropriate to the situation, both in human and in political terms. For these qualities he was to be harshly treated by the ex-King in his embittered exile, but historians have endorsed Baldwin rather than his accusers.

But the crisis could not be averted indefinitely, and the Press was becoming justifiably restive and unhappy at remaining silent on one of the most sensational and important stories in modern journalistic history while the American and European newspapers devoted great resources of time and space to the story.

Until December 3rd, the British public was wholly unaware of the crisis. The catalytic event was the statement by the Bishop of Bradford, Bishop Blunt, on December 1st that he wished the King were more aware of his duties as head of the Anglican Church. The innocent Bishop was referring to the King's lax attendance at church, but when the *Yorkshire Post* seized the statement, the London Press decided to break its long and wholly voluntary silence. To the dismay and surprise of the King and Mrs. Simpson, the general tone was one of hostility and censure. The King was not used to public criticism, and had clearly reckoned—even if subconsciously—on the power of his enormous popularity.

A swift turmoil followed. A proposal for a morganatic marriage—originally aired in discussion with the King by Esmond Harmsworth—briefly flared into prominence in the discussions, and then was curtly and definitively quenched by the Cabinet and by the uniformly hostile reaction of the Dominion leaders. Attlee wholly concurred that the suggestion was unacceptable. By the time that Baldwin informed the King of the unanimous rejection of this alternative, the matter had at last become public knowledge. Mrs. Simpson left London for the South of France, and was persuaded to urge the King publicly to abandon her and thereby to retain his throne. He refused. Beaverbrook and Churchill became strong advocates for delay, but it was apparent to Beaverbrook that the King had made up his mind. As he put it bluntly to Churchill, 'our cock won't fight'. Churchill, however, plunged on vehemently to the dismay of his friends. On December 5th he issued an emotional appeal for 'time and patience', and by implication accused the Government of acting unconstitutionally. 'They have no right whatever to put pressure upon [the King] to accept their advice by soliciting beforehand assurances from the Leader of the Opposition that he will not form an alternative administration in the event of their resignation, and thus confronting the King with an ultimatum . . . if an abdication were to be hastily extorted, the outrage so committed would cast its shadow forward across many chapters of the History of the British Empire.'

Churchill's actions were motivated principally by his reverence for the monarchy and personal friendship for the King. He was shocked by the King's evident fatigue and the effects of the prolonged emotional pressures to which he had been subjected. But his bitterness against the Government came through in his statement, and aroused intense resentment, and not less in the Labour and Liberal leaders who knew that Churchill had been present at the November 25th meeting. His intervention was not only clumsy, but it was based on wrong information—his statement said that it was quite possible that the King's marriage 'may conceivably, for various reasons, never be accomplished at all'—and it was also much too late. Churchill later realised that Baldwin 'undoubtedly perceived and expressed the profound will of the nation'. This may have been going too far, as the nation was never consulted, but it certainly was the profound will of Parliament. 'I do not find people angry with Mrs. Simpson', Harold Nicolson recorded on December 3rd, 'but I do find a deep and enraged fury against the King himself. In eight months he has destroyed the great structure of popularity which he had raised.'[1] This popularity was undeniable. When in the mood—and, as he had grown older, this was an increasingly important qualification—he had a magnetism and persona which a wide variety of individuals found irresistible. He was genuinely kind and interested in individuals, and his evident melancholy was very attractive. David Kirkwood, who regarded himself as a fervent republican, was among many who succumbed completely to his interest in and sympathy for the problems of his constituents. But, quite unconsciously, he had built up expectations far beyond his

[1] Nicolson, op. cit., 282.

capacity—or, indeed, any man's—to fulfil. Thus the revelations of early December had a far greater effect upon his millions of admirers than they would have in the case of most monarchs. He had, in short, become excessively idealised. It was not his fault, but when it was evident that he fell far below these high estimations the reaction was disproportionately severe.

In any event, the die was cast on December 5th. The King, through Walter Monckton, informed Baldwin of his intention to abdicate. Mrs. Simpson's offer to withdraw was made on December 7th, but it was superfluous, although sincere.

London was torn between 'the King's Friends', known as 'the Cavaliers', and 'the Roundheads'. This was rather overdramatic. There could only be one outcome, given the incompatibility of the position of the King and that of his constitutional advisers. When Churchill rose on December 11th in the House of Commons to renew his plea for patience and delay he was shouted down, and angrily stalked out of the Chamber. Winterton has described this episode as 'one of the angriest manifestations I have ever heard directed against any man in the House of Commons',[1] and Amery recorded that Churchill 'was completely staggered by the unanimous hostility of the House'. His last duty to the King was to assist him in preparing his farewell wireless message to the nation. On December 10th he abdicated, and was succeeded by his shy and retiring brother, the Duke of York, who became King George VI, and whose first act was to create his brother the Duke of Windsor. After his farewell broadcast, the Duke drove down to Portsmouth and embarked in H.M.S. *Fury* for France. King Edward VIII's brief reign was over.

The Abdication Crisis, although dramatic and intense, left few visible scars. The monarchy was strengthened rather than weakened by Edward's departure. His successor was a tense and nervous man, with none of the bonhomie of his father or brother, inexperienced and unprepared. But he was clearly a good and sincere man, devotedly and happily married to a woman of exceptional charm and intelligence. His nervousness manifested itself in a stutter which was a source of intense worry to himself but which became as distinctive and as familiar as Churchill's lisp. His sense of duty was profound, and he gradually established a position of trust with the British people equal to—and perhaps even greater than—that of his father.

[1] Op. cit., 223.

But the Abdication Crisis had had other serious long-term consequences, which historians have tended to underrate. For one thing, 'the King's Matter' had occupied a wholly disproportionate amount of the time and energies of the Prime Minister and his colleagues for many crucial months. It was almost certainly a major contributory factor in Baldwin's near-breakdown in the summer, and it dominated everything else in his mind. His plea to Anthony Eden 'not to trouble me too much with foreign affairs just now' was the result of this central preoccupation. The crisis had probably delayed Baldwin's retirement for perhaps a year, and had dramatically restored his position. Churchill's, on the other hand, had been well-nigh destroyed.

Baldwin's speech to the House of Commons on December 10th was a Parliamentary masterpiece, and it completely restored the position he had appeared to have lost through the year. The speech itself appears somewhat confused, and it was certainly not a carefully prepared oration, but at the time these characteristics deeply impressed that most critical of public audiences. 'It was Sophoclean and almost unbearable', Harold Nicolson wrote, '. . . We file out broken in body and soul, conscious that we have heard the best speech that we shall ever hear in our lives. There was no question of applause. It was the silence of Gettysburg. . . . No man has ever dominated the House as he dominated it tonight, and he knows it.'[1]

To his enemies this was yet another example of Baldwin's superb Parliamentary guile, his unique capacity to enter into an informal blundering conversation with the House of Commons which could almost hypnotise the assembly and win it over completely to his cause. But it is very doubtful whether, on this occasion, Baldwin had deliberately calculated the effect. He was a very tired man, under a very heavy strain. But, whether deliberately conceived or not, this speech and his conduct during the crisis destroyed the last rebellion against him which he had faced since he had unexpectedly become Prime Minister in 1923. Fate was to deal with him harshly in his last years, which he bore with uncomplaining fortitude. He was to be subjected to virulent abuse from his embittered and frightened countrymen, not discouraged by those whom he had politically worsted. He remains a strange, not precisely delineated, personality. But, at the close of the disastrous year of 1936, his control of the House of Commons was, once again, total.

[1] Nicolson, op. cit., 286.

These events had profound implications on the wider political situation. Churchill had been endeavouring to create a national movement that would give his personal campaign for rearmament and an aggressive approach towards the Dictators a much greater constituency than he had previously achieved. One attempt had been the 'Focus' group, which held its first meeting in June 1935, and which included Violet Bonham-Carter, Gilbert Murray, Kingsley Martin—the editor of the *New Statesman*—but which achieved very little. Nonetheless, it formed the basis for the 'Arms and the Covenant' movement which made real progress in 1936, and whose first meeting was due to be held at the Albert Hall on December 3rd.

On November 12th Churchill had had one of his greatest personal triumphs in the House of Commons. The House had reconvened after the summer recess in an ugly mood. The Opposition was deeply stirred by developments in Spain and the Conservatives were still distraught by almost a year of Ministerial ineptitude and vacillation. On the debate on the Address Churchill delivered perhaps the most brilliant of his philippics on the condition of British air deficiencies, which included this unforgettable passage:

> The Government simply cannot make up their minds, or they cannot get the Prime Minister to make up his mind. So they go on in strange paradox, decided only to be undecided, resolved to be irresolute, adamant for drift, solid for fluidity, all-powerful to be impotent. So we go on preparing more months and years—precious, perhaps vital, to the greatness of Britain—for the locusts to eat.

Baldwin's reply was one of the most disastrous in his career, and has shadowed it ever since. He took the House into his confidence, and said that he would speak with 'appalling frankness'. He spoke of the situation that he confronted in 1933:

> Supposing I had gone to the country, and said that Germany was rearming and that we must rearm, does anybody think that this pacifist democracy would have rallied to that cry at that moment? I cannot think of anything that would have made the loss of the election from my point of view more certain.

As a statement of historical fact it was incontrovertible, but the House of Commons was genuinely shocked. Churchill's subsequent distortion of this passage, and his deliberate claim that it referred to the 1935 election,[1] should not delude the historian to underestimate the impact of that speech on the House of Commons. 'His voice and thought limp as if he were a tired walker on a long road', Harold Nicolson noted. 'The House realises that the dear old man has come to the end of his vitality.'[2]

But from these depths the Abdication Crisis had rescued Baldwin; it had also hurled Churchill down. As Harold Macmillan has written: 'It was not possible to restore the situation.' The Arms and the Covenant movement struggled on with little effect, and Churchill's already waning public prestige had received so devastating a blow that, as he himself subsequently wrote, 'it was the almost universal view that my political life was at last ended'.

---

[1] The literature on this speech is somewhat disproportionate, but the glee with which Churchill and G. M. Young jumped on it and misquoted it has resulted in a powerful counter-attack, notably by R. Bassett in *The Cambridge Journal*, November 1948, and by Barnes and Middlemas, op. cit., 970–3.

[2] Nicolson, op. cit., p. 178.

CHAPTER TEN

TOWARDS THE ABYSS, 1937–1939

STANLEY BALDWIN RETIRED in a warm glow of popular esteem immediately after the Coronation of King George VI in May 1937, and became Earl Baldwin of Bewdley. 'No man', Nicolson wrote, 'has ever left in such a blaze of affection.' There was no challenge or question as to who his successor should be. Neville Chamberlain, the most successful Minister in the 1924–9 Government, had been second to Baldwin since 1929, and, as has been related, had nearly succeeded him early in 1931. Since 1931 he had been the architect of Britain's modest economic recovery, and as Chancellor had dominated both the National and the last Baldwin Governments— albeit at a discreet public distance. He worked hard, was a dedicated public servant, and was a first-rate Departmental Minister with a mind of his own and an incisive manner that although it did not attract over-much affection aroused considerable respect. His succession to Baldwin was a formality. Churchill proposed his election as leader of the Conservative Party and it was unanimously approved.

Neville Chamberlain is one of the most difficult of modern British politicians to portray with accuracy and justice. Only Baldwin was subsequently more denigrated and reviled, but with the distance of time a more objective portrait must be attempted.

Chamberlain had been brought up in the heavy shadow of his father, and his early life had been one of relative failure. After a disastrous attempt to make Joseph Chamberlain another fortune by growing sisal in the Bahamas, he had immersed himself in Birmingham business and politics with only modest success. In 1917 he had been briefly Minister for National Service, and had been summarily dismissed for alleged incompetence by Lloyd George, thus establishing a mutual and unrelenting antipathy. When he entered Parliament in 1918 he was in his fiftieth year, having achieved little of note in his life. Even the fact that he had been Mayor of Birmingham was regarded more as the result of his name than of his capacities.

But from this point his rise had been swift. He worked hard, and his experience had made him a practical social reformer. But although in private charming, sensitive, kind, and warm, his public façade was bleak. 'Neville's manner freezes people', as Austen Chamberlain wrote. '. . . Everybody respects him, but he makes no friends.' 'In manner he is glacial rather than genial', Arthur Salter wrote in 1939. 'He has neither the spontaneous ease of intercourse of some of his colleagues, nor the *fausse bonhomie* of others. It is unfortunate, and of some importance, that his expression often tends to something like a sneer, and his manner to something like a snub, even when there is nothing in either his intentions or his feelings to correspond . . . His instinctive attitude to a critic, even one who intends to be helpful and constructive, is to bear down, not to consolidate or to compromise. An opponent must be opposed; and a supporter who shows signs of independence must be disciplined.'[1]

It must be admitted that Chamberlain's disdain for the bulk of his political contemporaries was not wholly unmerited, nor his contempt for the vapid temporisings which are the stock-in-trade of most politicians, and which were particularly evident in the inter-war Parliaments. But it was his most conspicuous political defect that he could not and did not conceal these emotions. Furthermore, he appeared to have a sadistic pleasure in exposing ignorance, laziness, and shallow thinking. Although a limited man, he towered over most of his colleagues, and not least in his application. His shyness was a major element in his failure to make those casual friendships which are so essential to popularity in the House of Commons. It was his place of business, never his home. His only recorded visit to the Smoking Room was artificial, embarrassing, and not successful. Like Stafford Cripps, he was contemptuous of what he perceived to be the idleness and lack of dedication to the public service of the great majority of his fellow politicians. Admittedly, he was too quick to pass hostile judgement. But, if he was intolerant—as he was—it can be argued that he had much to be intolerant about.

Chamberlain was, as Lord Strang has written, 'a man of cool, calm mind, strong will and decisive purpose, wholly devoted to the public cause and with a firm confidence in his own judgement'. The last was

[1] Arthur Salter: *Security, Can We Retrieve It?*, 284–5.

both the key to his success and to his eventual failure. 'Unhappily', he once wrote, 'it is part of my nature that I cannot contemplate any problem without trying to find a solution to it.' But his solutions were created from a narrow base of knowledge of human nature.

Initially, Chamberlain did not entertain any illusions about Nazi Germany, as a long letter he wrote to the Secretary of the United States Treasury, Henry Morgenthau, in March 1937 demonstrates.[1] But the passage by the United States Congress of the Neutrality Act and the pacifist tone of the Commonwealth Prime Ministers' Conference in the summer of 1937 were important—indeed, crucial—influences. Equally influential were the attitudes and despatches of the British Ambassador in Berlin, Sir Nevile Henderson, a persistent, skilful, and lamentable advocate of settlement with Germany. Gradually, Chamberlain moved in the direction of a rapprochement with Germany, and from there it was but a short step to an almost obsessional search for peace, which characterised the policy of 1938 and culminated in Munich.

As the months passed, Chamberlain's personal control grew. At the beginning of 1938 Vansittart was shunted into honorific impotence at the Foreign Office; Eden was in effect dismissed shortly afterwards, and Swinton was removed. Halifax, although nominally Foreign Secretary, played a minor role in 1938, but his attitudes were close to those of the Prime Minister. Even closer were those of Sir Horace Wilson, his former Chief Industrial Adviser.

This was entirely deliberate. Chamberlain's first objective was to get the Cabinet that he wanted and the advisers whose judgements coincided with his own assessments. Chamberlain did not share Baldwin's relaxed and somewhat old-fashioned view of the role of the Prime Minister. Certainly, he did not welcome strong personalities or divergent views in his immediate or official circle. This feature of his personality could be put down to extreme self-confidence, to authoritarianism, or to a fundamental insecurity. Whatever the real motivation—which was probably a combination of these three factors—the result was that men of independence and high calibre were either ignored or got rid of. Churchill made hopeful overtures, which were rejected out of hand. Amery was left to languish in his political wilderness. Eden, Vansittart, Swinton and Ormsby-Gore were fired, and replaced by docile nonentities. 'To a somewhat exceptional extent',

[1] See James: *Churchill*, 359.

Salter wrote of Chamberlain, 'he regards unquestioning loyalty, obedience, pliability, as giving better claims to his favours than signs of personal initiative or judgement. . . . He prefers the even running of his craft to the vigour of the individual oar.' By March 1938 Chamberlain had established a congenial, subservient, and mediocre Government which he personally dominated, usually ignored, and, as some thought, bullied. If he had none of Austen's public charm, he had certainly inherited that element in his father's personality that frightened men. The Labour Party hated him; he had succeeded in building up a small group of dissident young Conservatives who were shocked at Eden's removal; but his mastery of the House of Commons and the Cabinet was complete. His weapons were immense application, mastery of his subject, and a freezing belligerence which his opponents found profoundly intimidating.

Some of his contemporaries, seeking for the clue to his character, have noted his intellectual vanity and implacable self-assurance. Others have remarked upon his conviction that no problems were beyond resolution by analysis and consequent clear policy, with the result that, once his mind had clamped down upon a matter and the policy determined, there could be and would be no turning back. These critics felt that life, and particularly political life, is a much more complex business than this, and also that Chamberlain consistently omitted the personal elements in his calculations. In short, he jumped to conclusions too quickly, was secretive and solitary, was unsparing in his dedication to his chosen solution and contemptuous of its critics, had little understanding of human nature, and pursued policies that were both superficial and dangerously rigid.

There was certainly much truth in these criticisms. The most merited of all was Chamberlain's distaste for criticism and his solitariness. Very few people had any clear understanding at the time of what his policies were. The Cabinet was usually bypassed and then told what had been done. Only a very limited group of officials had his ear. It was only many years later, with the availability of his papers and those of his colleagues, that it was possible to discern the movement of his thought. At the time, the majority were perplexed onlookers of events of massive importance to them yet in whose outcome they were denied any role. Subsequently, we have a clear picture in 1937 of a man puzzled and alarmed by the foreign situation, by the slow pace of British rearmament, by the timorous attitudes of the Commonwealth

Prime Ministers at their conference in the summer of 1937,[1] by the evident realities of German strength and French pusillanimity, and, above all, by the deep fear of Britain being sucked into another European war virtually by mistake or for reasons not central to British interests. 'I do not see', he wrote in November 1937, 'why we shouldn't say to Germany "give us satisfactory assurances that you won't use force to deal with the Austrians and Czechoslovakians, and we will give you similar assurances that we won't use force to prevent the changes you want, if you can get them by peaceful means".'

By the beginning of 1938, however, one is presented with a man who has reached his conclusions. This was not, as has so often been alleged, a policy of surrender, nor was it simply a desperate search for peace at any price. It was at root a matter of priorities. The integrity of France and the Low Countries was one; German ambitions to the East were not. This, at any rate, was how it began. Increasingly, however, the policy of 'appeasement' acquired in 1938 a self-righteous and even sanctimonious character which repelled its few critics at the time and subsequent commentators. But it was a gradual development. There was no public declaration of doctrine or policy; it was only as events unfolded, and government reactions seen, that the development of Chamberlain's attitudes could be discerned. Thus, throughout 1938, the House of Commons, the Cabinet, and the British people, all anxious for peace yet bewildered and dismayed, jogged nervously along the mysterious course that the imperious Prime Minister had vaguely charted in 1937 but to which he became irrevocably committed.

With the exception of Spain, 1937 had been a relatively quiescent year in European affairs, and even Churchill's independent trumpet was giving a more uncertain note. British rearmament, particularly in the air, proceeded, but hardly with coherence or fervour. What was more serious was the general Ministerial acceptance of German superiority, and their grossly exaggerated fear of the German air potential. They were also puzzled and concerned by the fact that the very large increases in the Air Estimates since 1934 did not appear to be giving them the large air force that they had expected. The real price for their neglect of the aircraft industry was now having to be

[1] See D. C. Watt: 'The Commonwealth and the Munich Crisis' in *Personalities and Policies*, 159–74.

met. The decision to go for the next generation of fighters and bombers had been courageous and right, but the facilities simply had not existed for this leap forward and had to be created. This inevitably caused delays that seemed inexplicable to Ministers, and was one of the factors in Swinton's unmerited downfall. The fact remained that although by the beginning of 1938 the British were not in a good position *vis-à-vis* the Germans they were in nothing like as bad a position as Ministers and their advisers believed. To remedy the situation there would have had to be a complete reversal of the distant attitude towards France, the acceptance of French guarantees to Czechoslovakia, a sharp and dramatic increase in rearmament, the introduction of military conscription, the purchase of war material from abroad—particularly the United States—and the concentration of British and Dominion forces closer to the area of crisis. None of these were done, or even seriously contemplated, by the Prime Minister. He freely negotiated from a position of weakness that could, even at this late hour, have been strengthened.

The British Government was, accordingly, severely and excessively frightened of Germany. Eden had written after the reoccupation of the Rhineland that 'The myth is now exploded that Herr Hitler only repudiates treaties imposed on Germany by force. We must be prepared for him to repudiate any treaty even if freely negotiated (a) when it becomes inconvenient, and (b) when Germany is sufficiently strong and the circumstances are otherwise favourable for doing so.' Baldwin warned the Dominion Prime Ministers in 1937 that 'the only argument which appeals to the dictators is that of force'. But the Government continued to view the situation as Britain *versus* Germany, and at no point seriously considered the strategical potentialities of an effective European alliance. Indeed, under Chamberlain, such a combination was anathema. Thus, the chimera of maintaining freedom of action and of playing a major European role without entering into any European commitments danced enticingly before the new Prime Minister.

Accordingly, Chamberlain was dominated by conflicting illusions. The first was his Victorian assumption that Britain, as the dominant world power, could deal directly and independently with the German leaders on a realistic and indeed *realpolitik* level. The second was that Germany was militarily so powerful and Britain so relatively weak that everything possible must be done to avert a war crisis. The third, which became increasingly central in his mind, was that reasonable men could always find reasonable solutions to problems, once the latter were identified. Alliances against Germany would be provocative; Halifax was able to inform the Cabinet, without protest, after the German occupation of Austria in March 1938 that 'nothing was more likely to aggravate the difficulties of the present situation than any suggestions that our ultimate objective was to unite France, Italy and ourselves against Germany'. Thus Ministers, while privately sharing Churchill's celebrated sentiment of 'Thank God for the French Army', kept the French carefully at a distance, and flirted vaguely with the Italians. 'If only we could get on terms with the Germans, I would not care a rap for Musso', Chamberlain wrote in his diary. The dream of an all-encompassing deal with the Germans increasingly obsessed the Prime Minister.

Viewing this situation in calm retrospect, with all the facts at his disposal, the historian can easily be contemptuous and condemnatory of the Chamberlain Government. But the situation that confronted them at the time must be clearly appreciated.

All of its members had passed, either personally or very closely, through the agony of the Great War. Those who had not fought in it had experienced the bitter loss of close relatives and friends. They had seen the subsequent turmoil in Europe, and the advent of a vast and malignant Communist state in Russia. Their own nation was barely recovering from the consequences of that war. They had hoped for, and had worked for unavailingly, a comprehensive disarmament programme. They had been compelled to rearm in the face of the German military renaissance. But they could not believe that another and more terrible catastrophe could not be averted. They could not believe that reason could not prevail. Few had any illusions about the character of Nazi Germany, but they could not accept that a deal could not be made with its leaders. But it was to be a *British* deal. No more fatal *ententes*!

This was certainly the progression of Chamberlain's logic, coupled as it was with his lack of serious interest in any Eastward ambitions that Germany might have. He shared the opinion of Eden, set out to the Imperial Conference in 1937, that any declaration of British willingness to regard an attack on Austria or Czechoslovakia as a *casus belli* with Germany 'would be going far beyond our obligations under the Covenant and far beyond where the people of this country were prepared to go'.[1] The same point was made by Halifax in his discussions with Hitler in November 1937 when he told the German leader that on matters such as Danzig, Austria, and Czechoslovakia 'we were not necessarily concerned to stand up for the *status quo* as today, but we were concerned to avoid such treatment of them as would be likely to cause trouble'. While this was not precisely an open invitation, it was perilously near one. Chamberlain made the same point in his discussions with the new French Foreign Minister, Delbos, at the end of November 1937. This looked like cold-blooded *realpolitik*. What British interests were involved in the independence of Austria or Czechoslovakia? Was either worth a war? Why should not they be sacrificed, and used as British bargaining offers in the achievement of an Anglo-German settlement? It was certainly a cold-blooded approach, but it was certainly not *realpolitik*.

With this narrowing of British concerns there went an earnest search for concrete British proposals—which included the possibility of the return of the annexed German colonies—to put before the Germans as part of the overall settlement which was developing into an obsession with the Prime Minister and his senior colleagues— among whom Eden must be included. Eden's abrupt removal from office early in 1938 owed less to fundamental differences on foreign policy than personal factors. There was at least one element of principle in their rift, their very differing judgements of how to handle Mussolini. But Chamberlain had been eyeing Eden very carefully and closely since 1935, and had been unimpressed. Perhaps he had detected the irresolution beneath the confident façade, and the intense emotionalism and ambition of this glittering but unsure young man. His confidence in his judgement could not have been reduced by Eden's feeble and deferential resignation speech. Chamberlain felt that he had little to fear from that quarter, and events were to prove him right.

Eden's successor, Halifax, was a man of several complexities. Brought up in a strange home, heir to his title only through the deaths of his brothers, deformed at birth with a withered arm, a Fellow of All Souls and a highly successful Viceroy of India, he skilfully erected an impassable wall between himself, his contemporaries, and historians. He was shrewd, yet also naïve. He was calculating, yet also sensitive and emotional. His shyness and apparent aloofness perplexed and

[1] Cabinet Papers. Quoted in Barnett, op. cit., 465.

antagonised many, but his kindness and sincerity won him a multitude of friends and admirers. He was at times sentimental and innocent, at others cold and realistic. He had common sense, yet also a capacity for wishful thinking. His strong dedication to the Church often tore at his innate Yorkshire pragmatism and sense of cynical reality. A devout man of principle, yet he was one whom one would compare in some respects to Balfour, of whom Churchill wrote that, had he been alive at the time of the Renaissance, he would not have needed to read the works of Machiavelli. Thus he was, through 1938, an eager and docile follower of Chamberlain's strategy and yet was the first to wake up to its implications and consequences. The more one examines this perplexing man the less is one surprised that he was to be, in May 1940, the first choice of the King and the Conservative Party to be Prime Minister, nor that the Labour Party was willing to serve under him. There were depths in that austere personality that historians have consistently failed to recognise, yet which contemporaries understood.

Unhappily, Halifax was barely given a walking-on part in the events of 1938. His meeting with Hitler and his colleagues in November 1937 had persuaded him that a deal could indeed be made with the German leaders, loathsome though they were. But while Halifax was impressed by Hitler's expressed contempt for the British 'fairy-land of strange, respectable, illusions' Chamberlain was more struck by the fact that Halifax's visit had created 'an atmosphere in which it is possible to discuss with Germany the practical questions involved in a European settlement'. This decision now developed into his dominant preoccupation. Throughout 1938 Halifax—and the Foreign Office— were little more than observers of the drama. This role was also given to the Cabinet, the House of Commons, and the British public. Chamberlain took in 1938 an even more arbitrary and personalised 'Presidential' role than even Lloyd George had established at the height of his power, and his awed and undistinguished colleagues followed dutifully and in ignorance.

Halifax's own attitude in 1938 was substantially based upon his profound personal admiration and affection for Neville Chamberlain. In Chamberlain there was a most marked, and remarkable, contrast between the public and private persona that was without parallel in modern British politics before the advent of Edward Heath. Chamberlain, who in public was so sharp, sneering, and unappealing, was in

private beloved and revered by his family and close friends. As Halifax
has himself written:

> It was not universally known with how many sides of life Cham-
> berlain moved on terms of close and intimate relationship. Few men
> had a more real enjoyment of all things of beauty and art, whether
> in the world of nature or of men, which make life colourful and rich,
> and few had his knowledge and deep appreciation of all that is
> greatest in music. No one was a truer lover of the countryside.

These words have sometimes been quoted mockingly, but they
partly open the door to why Chamberlain received the love and
veneration that he did. His gentleness and kindness moved people
who had had experience of other types of politicians. He was, in
private, shy and modest, and he was a devoted husband and father.
Those who penetrated the public façade—including Churchill[1]—were
surprised and impressed by the real man. His total control over his
Government was not merely that of being Prime Minister. He had
surrounded himself with some men who loved him and others who
feared him. Those who did neither had been cut down. Neville
Chamberlain was a decent, kind, sensitive, vain, authoritarian and
ruthless man. By March 1938 he was in complete command, and
marched forward without fear or doubt into the eager arms of his
enemies. They, too, believed that a deal could be made. But it was to
be on their terms.

*

The first shock to Conservative confidence in Chamberlain was the
forced resignation of Eden and his Parliamentary Under-Secretary,
Lord Cranborne, on February 20th; twenty-five Government back-
benchers abstained in protest in the subsequent debate. Eden's speech
of explanation left most Members wondering what the dispute had
really been about, and Eden himself was scrupulously—some felt
excessively—loyal to the Government. But it was a nasty jolt. In
reality, the causes of his departure had been personal rather than on
policy. Chamberlain's increasing absorption with foreign affairs, his
growing self-assurance, and his impatience with Eden and the Foreign
Office were the main causes. Chamberlain's discouraging reply in
January to a vague suggestion by Roosevelt for a world conference

[1] Churchill, op. cit., 494-5.

was made without consultation with the Foreign Secretary, and had been another episode in a lengthening list of incidents in which Eden had been virtually ignored. The final dispute was over the precise wording of a formula to give Mussolini *de jure* recognition of his Abyssinian empire in return for the withdrawal of Italian intervention in Spain. But the event not only provoked the first Conservative revolt against Chamberlain, but began the movement that was to deflect his course in 1939 and bring him down in 1940.

Then, on March 13th, Hitler annexed Austria. 'Europe', Churchill told the House of Commons, 'is confronted with a programme of aggression, nicely calculated and timed, unfolding stage by stage, and there is only one choice open, not only to us, but to other countries who are unfortunately concerned—either to submit, like Austria, or else to take effective measures while time remains to ward off the danger and, if it cannot be warded off, to cope with it.' Hitler's strategy was in fact not as carefully planned as Churchill and others assumed, and the *Anschluss* was a hurriedly launched affair, but apprehension began to mount sharply.

Chamberlain did not see matters thus gloomily, nor did Halifax. Both had become convinced by the 'encirclement' theory, whereby alliances would drive the Germans into some mad-dog act to escape. 'The more closely we associate ourselves with France', Halifax informed his colleagues, 'the more we produce on German minds the impression that we are plotting to encircle Germany and the more difficult will it be to make any real settlement with Germany.' Chamberlain said that 'the seizure of the whole of Czechoslovakia would not be in accordance with Herr Hitler's policy, which was to include all Germans in the Reich but not to include other nationalities'. Halifax 'distinguished in his own mind between Germany's racial efforts, which no one could question, and a lust for conquest on a Napoleonic scale which he himself did not credit'.[1] The Cabinet Foreign Policy Committee, to which these words were addressed, accepted their argument. Any resolution that there might have been was effectively dampened by a grim assessment of the British military situation by the Chiefs of Staff. But, again, it was an assessment only of the *British* position, and took no account whatever of the Czechoslovakian forces, the French Army, nor the German deficiencies which had become evident in the invasion of Austria. British military weak-

[1] Barnett, op. cit., 474.

ness was not the major factor—if, indeed, a factor at all—in Chamberlain's mind, although later it was to be used as an excuse for the policies of 1938. But it did have its impact upon other Ministers.[1]

As Austen Chamberlain, Churchill, and others had warned, this *coup de main* placed Czechoslovakia, with its three million Germans, immediately in a highly vulnerable position. Hitler's strident denunciations of the treatment of the German minority made the point clear. 'The overriding consideration with Chamberlain and his colleagues', Hoare, now back in office at the Admiralty, has recorded, 'was that the very complicated problem of Czechoslovakia ought not to lead to a world war and must at almost any price be settled by peaceful means.'[2] Chamberlain's strategy was to take the initiative and to place the maximum pressure upon the Czechs to come to terms with their German problem on German terms and thereby to deny Hitler the excuse to attack their country on that issue and draw in their French allies. Meanwhile, some bold words were used publicly about honouring obligations which perplexed the House of Commons, made the position of Chamberlain's small band of Conservative critics difficult, but did not deceive Hitler. As Strang later wrote: 'The ambivalence of our policy of trying to deter the Germans from armed action by pointing out the probability of British intervention, and to discourage the Czechs from fighting by hinting at its improbability, was not long concealed.' British politicians and the Press did not expect an immediate crisis, and tended to take at face value the resolution of the Government. The French, although they suspected that Hitler's menacing threats against Czechoslovakia were militarily unrealistic, went along—if uneasily—with the British strategy. The Sudeten German Nazi leader, Konrad Henlein, made a highly successful visit to Britain, even impressing Churchill. The discussions about the situation became increasingly confused. Hitler divined that the moment was approaching for another opportunistic coup.

The crisis came in September. In a daring stroke, looking to London and Paris, President Benes appeared to concede all the Sudeten German demands, knowing that even this would be inadequate for Henlein and Hitler. He also discovered that it was

---

[1] Even Duff Cooper, the most Francophile and anti-German member of the Cabinet, told Harold Nicolson in May that 'the Germans are so beastly powerful'. (Nicolson, op. cit., 344.)

[2] Templewood, op. cit., 344.

inadequate for London and Paris. On September 13th there were manufactured disturbances in German regions against the Government which were easily controlled, but on the 15th an alarmed but determined Chamberlain flew to Berchtesgaden with Sir Horace Wilson and Strang to see Hitler and to try to achieve his all-European settlement. There was no question in Chamberlain's mind of consultation with the Cabinet, of a concentrated policy with the French, and none whatever of any consultation with the Czechoslovak leaders. This was to be a straightforward Anglo-German negotiation—and one, furthermore, in which neither the British Cabinet nor the Foreign Office were involved. The two men discussed the matter alone. Chamberlain's proposal was that, in return for the preservation of the rest of the country, the Sudeten German areas would be separated from the rest of Czechoslovakia if they so desired. Lord Runciman, who had been dispatched on a special mission in August to 'mediate' between Henlein and Benes, had initially concluded that the claims of the Germans could be met within the framework of the Czechoslovak state; in his final report he switched hurriedly to the cause of 'self-determination'.

But Chamberlain returned to find his colleagues troubled and to learn of ominous rumblings in the Conservative Party. *The Times* had published an infamous leading article which remarked that 'the general character of the terms submitted to the Czechoslovak Government could not, in the nature of things, be expected to make a strong *prima facie* appeal to them'. At last, the true nature of Chamberlain's purpose was becoming more clear. But Eden, who had the most substantial influence on the Conservative back-benchers—much greater than Churchill's—would not express publicly his private consternation. Nonetheless, the alarm spread that a spectacular betrayal was at hand. A sense of impending humiliation reached out through the scattered Conservative Party. The French, also, were alarmed, and sought—and received—a British military guarantee for the 'new' emasculated Czechoslovakia. Although the Berchtesgaden talks had achieved nothing, they had persuaded Chamberlain that Hitler must be given a higher offer. Runciman had recommended the immediate transfer of all frontier districts where the Germans were a substantial majority; Chamberlain now proposed the transfer of all areas where the Germans constituted more than half of the population. The French agreed, and the Czechs were handed a plain ultimatum by their ally. Bitterly, they had no choice but to agree. Thus, Chamberlain seemed to have won over his critics, and on September 22nd flew to Godesberg to tie up the details, only to be confronted with larger demands. Hitler wanted immediate occupation by German troops of the disputed territories. After an angry discussion, he agreed not to act before October 1st.

By now the mood in London had turned hostile to any more concessions. The Cabinet was shocked, and it was evident that opinion in the House of Commons—Labour as well as Conservative—had swung violently again and would not tolerate the Godesberg proposals. The French Government reacted similarly. Suddenly everyone was highly belligerent, even—although mutedly—*The Times*. The Fleet was mobilised by Duff Cooper—with Chamberlain's acquiescence—on September 27th. There were startling evidences of air-raid precautions in London parks, in the distribution of gas-masks, and in plans for evacuating children to the country. The silver balloon-barrages rose into the clear autumn skies. But the crisis had come so suddenly, without any governmental warning or explanation, and seemed not only alarming but unreal. To even the most ardent, the spectacle of puny slit-trenches and the hasty distribution of gas-masks seemed inadequate preparations for the aerial onslaught that all expected. 'When war comes', Nicolson mused on the 21st, 'it will be a terrible shock to the country. The bombing of London by itself will provoke panic and perhaps riots. All those of us who said "We must make a stand" will be branded as murderers.'[1] Thus, the exaggerated fears of devastation from the air, so sedulously argued both by anti- and pro-rearmers for years, now had their effect. This apprehension was certainly not diminished by Chamberlain's broadcast on the 27th, which was markedly egotistical, and which included the lugubrious words, uttered in a tone of numbed melancholy that was unforgettable:

How horrible, fantastic, incredible it is that we should be digging trenches and trying on gas-masks here because of a quarrel in a far-away country between people of whom we know nothing.

Was Czechoslovakia worth a war? This was not, of course, the real question. But it was the question posed to himself by Chamberlain, as it had been for months, and now to the public, and his answer was clear. Through Nevile Henderson he suggested renewed negotiations

[1] Nicolson, op. cit., 368.

with Hitler. Godesberg had distressed his usually supine colleagues, and the popular mood was highly uncertain. But Chamberlain had certainly never given up, and in Paris the Daladier Government was now wavering again. Both directly to Hitler, and to Mussolini, Chamberlain proposed a meeting of the leaders of the four powers.

On September 28th the House of Commons, called back from its recess, reassembled in a confused mood of perplexity and tension, looking for some kind of lead. There was no war-fever, nor defeatism, in its temper. The majority of Members, clearly representing the principal view of their constituents, were baffled by the ugly turn of events. What did it all mean? What was the Government going to do? Most Ministers were in the same quandary. This was the atmosphere when Chamberlain rose in a packed and uneasy House of Commons. He described the events of the past two weeks precisely and calmly, and with considerable skill; as he approached his culmination, which was unclear to Members, but which seemed to be an admission of the failure of negotiation and British solidarity with France and her Czechoslovak ally, there was a famous dramatic moment, described by Harold Nicolson that evening in a radio broadcast:

'Yesterday morning', began the Prime Minister, and we were all conscious that some revelation was approaching. He began to tell us of his final appeal to Herr Hitler and Signor Mussolini. I glanced at the clock. It was twelve minutes after four. The Prime Minister had been speaking for exactly an hour. I noticed that a sheet of Foreign Office paper was being rapidly passed along the Government bench. Sir John Simon interrupted the Prime Minister and there was a momentary hush. He adjusted his pince-nez and read the document that had been handed to him. His whole face, his whole body, seemed to change. He raised his face so that the light from the ceiling fell full upon it. All the lines of anxiety and weariness seemed suddenly to have been smoothed out; he appeared ten years younger and triumphant. 'Herr Hitler', he said, 'has just agreed to postpone his mobilisation for twenty-four hours and to meet me in conference with Signor Mussolini and Signor Daladier at Munich.'

That, I think, was one of the most dramatic moments which I have ever witnessed. For a second, the House was hushed in absolute silence. And then the whole House burst into a roar of cheering, since they knew that this might mean peace. That was the end of the Prime Minister's speech, and when he sat down the whole House rose as a man to pay tribute to his achievement.[1]

Chamberlain departed on his mission to Munich in a blur of excitement and undisguised self-satisfaction. He was seen off at the airport by his beaming Cabinet colleagues, present to a man, and leaving only a very small minority of deeply troubled men. At Munich he virtually ignored Daladier, and the miserable business of the destruction of Czechoslovakia did not take very long. The German occupation of the Sudeten territories would be spread over ten days, and the 'new' Czechoslovakia would be guaranteed by the Powers. Thus was the peace of Europe secured. On the following morning Chamberlain offered Hitler a statement that this agreement was 'symbolic of the desire of our two peoples never to go to war with one another again', which Hitler gladly signed. Chamberlain returned to London with this paper to frenzied applause. Daladier, who had expected, understandably, to be lynched, also rode into Paris in triumph, rather more bemused. Addressing the crowd in Downing Street from an upper window, Chamberlain, invoking Disraeli's return from the Congress of Berlin in 1878, declared that 'This is the second time that there has come back from Germany to Downing Street peace with honour. I believe it is peace for our time'. He stood with the King and Queen on the balcony of Buckingham Palace, amid tumultuous cheers. His friends and supporters have subsequently argued that he was very tired, that the Downing Street crowd had to be told something, and that Chamberlain almost immediately regretted his rash words. Other observers were more struck by his personal elation and by his conviction that he had achieved a major and enduring triumph. He reacted negatively to Halifax's proposal to bring Churchill and Eden into the Government. He told his colleagues and friends that he was confident that 'Hitler is a man of his word'.[2]

[1] Nicolson, op. cit., 370–1. Nicolson did not add in his broadcast that he had refused to join the ovation; nor did Churchill, Eden, Amery, and the Communist M.P., William Gallacher. But accounts of the scene vary considerably, and Nicolson's immediate version is the most vivid. It is still not clear whether the drama was deliberately contrived, and no hard evidence that it was, in Mowat's words, 'all but a put-up job'. (Mowat, op. cit., 616.)

[2] Staying at Chevening, the exquisite Kent home of Lord Stanhope, early in 1939 he gave this opinion to Lord Rosebery at breakfast. Rosebery found that he had entirely lost his appetite.

His vanity was certainly not unaffected by the extraordinary wave of emotion that the Munich Agreement aroused in Britain and France. Chamberlain had become the Peacemaker of Europe.

It is as well to remember that Chamberlain had never experienced popularity in the House of Commons or in the country. Nor, to be fair to him, had he ever courted it. In Birmingham he was respected both as a Chamberlain and as a devout son of the city, but he had never aroused anything comparable to the enthusiasm and adulation that his father and Austen had evoked. Now, he had eclipsed them both, and the gratitude and admiration was both intense and wide-spread. This was his hour. It was to be very brief.

The enthusiasm and relief which greeted Chamberlain on his return were genuine enough, but the Munich terms shocked, embittered, and humiliated a small but very vocal minority. The passions which the previous German demands had aroused had abated somewhat in the circle of Chamberlain's critics, but were still present. Duff Cooper was the only Minister who resigned—'the pioneer along the nation's way back from hysteria to reason', in Vyvyan Adams' words. Duff Cooper was a man who was beloved and excessively admired by his friends, but in the House of Commons—after one of the best maiden speeches in the post-war period—he had become generally regarded as a light-weight, and his antipathy towards Germany and love of France made many discount him as unbalanced in his attitudes. He had been successively Financial Secretary to the Treasury, Secretary of State for War, the First Lord of the Admiralty, and his tenure of these offices had not been very distinguished. His friends considered him brilliant, sensitive, and perceptive; his critics regarded him as opinion-ated, hot-tempered, emotional, and rather lazy. His resignation over Munich was the making of his career, and his resignation speech completely restored his faltering position. But he quickly found, as did the other Conservative opponents of Munich, that to oppose Cham-berlain at that time was not a popular move.[1] The Labour attacks on Munich provoked some Conservatives to talk eagerly of a General Election.

In these circumstances, the size and the calibre of the Conservative rebellion against Munich was remarkable. Churchill, in one of his greatest speeches, described the agreement as 'a total and unmitigated defeat', to the fury of the bulk of the Conservative Party, and thirty

[1] Duff Cooper, op. cit., 253.

Conservatives abstained in the post-Munich vote. These included Churchill, Eden, Amery, Cranborne, Duff Cooper, Sir Roger Keyes, Boothby, Macmillan, and J. P. L. Thomas. Several others voted for the Government only with heavy hearts, and their emotions were very similar to those of A. P. Herbert, who later wrote 'I voted sadly for Munich; and the whole thing made me ill',[1] and Victor Cazalet, who could only bring himself to accept it as 'a regrettable decision'.

The tests of public feeling about Munich were not conclusive. In November there was a vehement by-election at Oxford, where the Master of Balliol, A. D. Lindsay, stood against the official Conservative candidate Quintin Hogg (the son of Lord Hailsham) with Labour and anti-Government Conservative backing. Harold Macmillan campaigned for Lindsay, as did the young Edward Heath. It was a passionate affair, but when the result came in it was seen that although the Conservative majority had been reduced by 3,000 votes, the hopes of the opponents of the Government had been severely disappointed. At Bridgwater, however, Vernon Bartlett stood as an anti-Government Independent and won, but the excitement this caused was checked when the Duchess of Atholl resigned her seat in protest against the Government's foreign policy and stood in the resulting by-election as an Independent and lost.

But the indications of popular attitudes, although confused, are that Munich was accepted, even though the immediate euphoria was replaced by a more sober realisation of what had happened. 'At our almost daily conferences with our friends', Macmillan has written, 'we had the gloomiest forebodings. The tide was, at present, too strong and it was flowing against us.'[2] Churchill only narrowly won a motion of confidence in Epping, and other Government critics in the Conservative Party had a difficult winter. But it should be noted that these difficulties were principally with the party faithful, who are liable to be outraged by any serious opposition against party conformity.

But Chamberlain's personal popularity was unquestionable, and surprised even those close to him. Unlike Baldwin, this was never seriously harmed. His enemies put this down, then and later, to the fact that he had duped the people with a spurious peace. This does not explain, however, the continued respect and gratitude which he

[1] A. P. Herbert: *Independent Member*, 113.
[2] Harold Macmillan: op. cit., 567.

evoked. Some of his critics actively wanted war, and saw as its alternative an endless series of abject political defeats which would give Germany control of Europe and make her invincible. 'Better now' was their belief. The majority of the Government's critics regarded war as an inevitable necessity. But there is little evidence that the British public accepted either alternative at that time. Some observers noted a new grim fatalism abroad in the land in the winter of 1938-9, but others a genuine belief that Chamberlain had indeed brought peace in their time, and were overwhelmed with gratitude. It is not surprising that the politicians, trying to read the signs of the popular temper, came up with sharply contradictory impressions. The Government's position in the House of Commons had, however, been shaken by the Conservative defections and the unexpectedly critical attitude of the Opposition. The Labour Party's attitude to the European situation remained full of contradictions and contrasts, but the majority sentiment—particularly on the Front Bench—was becoming one of repugnance against the long catalogue of Government capitulations to the Dictators, and there was genuine outrage—well expressed by Attlee in one of the best speeches in the Munich debates —at the treatment of the Czechs. The universal Labour dislike for Chamberlain personally did not make them disposed to accept his claims.

Ministers comforted themselves with the fact that their Conservative critics were themselves divided. Churchill could count on only three supporters—the mysterious Brendan Bracken, Boothby, and his son-in-law Duncan Sandys—but although the bulk of the dissidents (derided by the Whips as 'the glamour boys') grouped around Eden, he gave little leadership and seemed highly reluctant to criticise Ministers strongly in public. Furthermore, as Munich receded, and Ministers struck highly optimistic notes about the heartening prospects in Europe, it seemed possible that Chamberlain really had been able to come to a deal with Hitler. But this remarkable House of Commons seemed impossible to placate, and sensitive on matters such as the abandonment of the 1936 proposal to partition Palestine and lack of assistance to European refugees. Not only the dissident Conservatives but the loyal ones passed an uneasy winter.

The turning-point came on March 15th, when the Germans annexed the rest of Czechoslovakia. Five days before, Chamberlain had declared that Europe was settling down to a period of tranquillity, and that the Government was contemplating the possibility of a general limitation of armaments. The Nazi occupation of Czechoslovakia left his policies in ruin, and a surge of anger rippled through the Conservative ranks. Urgently advised by the party managers, and for once his own composure shaken, Chamberlain made a hurried *volte-face*.

*

By no extension of charity can the conduct of British foreign and defence policies between 1933 and 1939 be described as distinguished, but most accounts have been seriously distorted by the emotional and often political commitment of successive historians and politicians, given their lead by Churchill, Lewis Namier, Wheeler-Bennett and G. M. Young. A. J. P. Taylor's *Origins of the Second World War*, published in 1961, may be open to challenge and criticism on several points, but it marked the moment at which historians started thinking of the 1930s in more detached and historical terms. As Mr. Taylor has written:

> Hitler, it seems to me, had no precise plans of aggression, only an intention, which he held in common with most Germans, to make Germany again the most powerful state in Europe and a readiness to take advantage of events. I am confident that the truth of this interpretation will be recognised once the problem is discussed in terms of detached historical curiosity, and not of political commitment.[1]

This judgement has been borne out by subsequent scholarship, but it does not give sufficient importance to the very peculiar and frightening aspects of Hitler's appetite, greed, and cruelty. He was not the insensate madman that he is often depicted; but nor was he the calculating yet opportunistic politician of some portraits. He was inconstant, emotionally unstable, mentally twisted, yet with a natural understanding of harsh power politics. He read Chamberlain very clearly, and became convinced that the British would not interrupt his Eastward ambitions. He had reckoned without the House of Commons. But, so had Chamberlain.

The central dilemma is whether Hitler was ever 'stoppable' short of war. It is the argument of many—and of which Churchill was the

[1] *English History 1914–45*, 424, footnote 1.

most vigorous—that he was, and that a policy of British firmness backed by strong European alliances and effective rearmament would have contained him, and would in all probability have led to his downfall at home. In this particular argument, the attitudes of senior German Army officers are cited as evidence of dislike and distrust of Hitler and of fear about the direction in which he was moving.

This commentator is doubtful of this argument. With some exceptions, the hostility to Hitler in the German Army seems to have been based partly on personal distaste but principally on the belief that he was moving too rapidly, rather than in the wrong direction. The claim that the Army could have toppled Hitler is doubtful after the S.S. was fully organised and the senior commanders had been quietly purged or persuaded of Hitler's strength; all the evidence suggests that any attempt at a coup was very improbable after 1934, and must have resulted not merely in civil war but in deep divisions within the German Army itself.

The British had no conception—and still have no conception—of what life under a modern, centralised, ruthless dictatorship is like. They do not recognise the devastating simplicity of the power of an all-pervasive police state, which rules less on terror than on the elementary principles of the sense of self-preservation and political apathy of the individual. Nor do they realise how easy it is to manipulate information, distort history, and remove from individuals the basic facts on which they can exercise their judgements. Today, we have a much clearer understanding of how easy it all is, and how complete can be its effects. In the 1930s, these things were only dimly realised, if they were realised at all, by the British. And the Nazis were geniuses at this new art, compared with which the Tsars and Stalin were incompetent butchers. They were masters of propaganda and staged show-pieces. Hitler's oratory may have sounded in turns turgid and comically hysterical to British ears, but it aroused some deep emotions in the German personality. The Nazis may have been a bunch of gangsters, but they raised gangsterism to a new level. Thus the British dream of a coup, both then and later, was based upon a complete misunderstanding of how a modern dictatorship operates at every level of a society, how total is its power, how intimidating its warnings, and how pernicious its influence on intelligent people.

Grotesque though many of the Nazi attitudes were, their appeal to German instincts was in many cases profound. In the character of the

German people—and in this they are not unique—there lies a belief that Germany's proper role is in the front rank. There also lay the conviction that Germany's position was always under threat, and had been under threat since 1870. They envied the British their island protection, their vast possessions, and their assumption of security. They could also point out that the virility of other European nations —principally Britain, France, Holland and Portugal—had been manifested in gigantic territorial expansion outside Europe. For reasons of history and geography, this opportunity had been denied to Germany, and for the whole of the life of the nation she had been surrounded with hostile alliances. On these emotions the Nazi leaders played with very great skill.

It should also be remembered that, of all the nations engaged in the Great War, Germany had proportionately suffered physically the least. She had been defeated—a fact which most Germans denied— but it had taken a vast Coalition to achieve this. As Churchill wrote at the end of *The World Crisis*:

> For four years Germany fought and defied the five continents of the world by land and sea and air. The German armies upheld her tottering confederates, intervened in every theatre with success, stood everywhere on conquered territory, and inflicted on their enemies more than twice the bloodshed they suffered themselves. To break their strength and science and curb their fury, it was necessary to bring all the greatest nations of mankind into the field against them. Overwhelming populations, unlimited resources, measureless sacrifice, the Sea Blockade, could not prevail for fifty months. Small states were trampled down in the struggle; a mighty Empire was battered into unrecognisable fragments; and nearly twenty million men perished or shed their blood before the sword was wrested from that terrible hand. Surely, Germans, for history it is enough!

Europe's tragedy was that it was not enough. Throughout the 1920s, while the Weimar Republic was struggling to achieve European stature, the plans were being laid for Germany's military renaissance. This does not mean that the intentions were aggressive at the time; armaments were a symbol of national regeneration, the mark of sovereignty, and escape from the shameful ignominy of Versailles. It was Hitler who gave the Wehrmacht its political direction.

The British failure to support the League actively, and to make it a central part of its European strategy, was the result of a deeper repugnance for foreign entanglements. Surges of emotion over Spain and Abyssinia were brief, and—particularly in the former case— confined to an articulate minority. The emphatic rejection of the Lloyd George Coalition's sabre-rattling over Chanak had been a significant episode. The British had had enough of this nonsense, and the cause of the failure of Churchill's career in the inter-war period was this revulsion from bellicosity and threatening rhetoric. And thus Britain withdrew herself physically and mentally from European affairs. 'We behaved as though we could play an effective part in international affairs as a kind of mediator or umpire without providing ourselves with the necessary arms and without entering into firm commitments', as Strang had commented. Churchill, in 1933, put the same point when he said that 'if we wish to detach ourselves and lead a life of independence from European entanglements, we have to be strong enough to defend our neutrality'. But the desire, in Churchill's words again, 'to live our life in our island without being again drawn into the perils of the continent of Europe' was a fatal chimera. The most important single factor in the collapse of Europe in the 1930s was British isolationism. But the question persists—even if Britain had been armed to the teeth for purely defensive purposes, how would this have checked Hitler's expansionism in *Europe*? Britain was not Hitler's main target.

As has been emphasised, the acceptance by many in Britain of the essential evilness of the Nazi regime did not carry with it the inevitable corollary that its policies meant a European war. It was against this particular scepticism that Churchill argued so long, and unavailingly. Indeed, as its internal outrages increased, there were those who urged with even greater insistence that a true nobility lay in accommodation with such men—as though a truly Christian stance was to shake hands with the dictators while holding one's nose. Margot Asquith wrote in March 1939:

There is only one way of preserving Peace in the world, and getting rid of the enemy, and that is to come to some sort of agreement with him—and the *viler* he is, the more you must fight him with the opposite weapons than his . . . The greatest enemy of mankind today is *Hate*.

Chamberlain wrote to his sister on July 30th, 1939:

My critics think that it would be a frightful thing to come to any agreement with Germany without giving her a thorough thrashing 'to larn her to be a toad'. But I don't share that view; let us convince her that the chances of winning a war without getting thoroughly exhausted in the process are too remote to make it worthwhile. But the corollary of that must be that she has a chance of getting fair and reasonable consideration and treatment from us and others if she will give up the idea that she can force it from us, and convince us that she has given it up.

It was the dogged retention of these attitudes even after March 1939 that precluded any chance of bringing Churchill into the Government. As Chamberlain wrote, 'Churchill's chances improve as war becomes more possible, and *vice versa*. If there is any possibility of easing the tension and getting back to normal relations with the dictators, I wouldn't risk it by what would certainly be regarded by them as a challenge.'

Mr. Michael Astor has written:

It is astonishing to think that people who were almost professionally high minded, who abhorred violence, and who were prepared to act with the courage of their convictions, could seriously believe that it was possible to come to any honourable arrangements with Hitler.

Yet, surely, it was not astonishing at all. The moral fervour and faith that lay behind a policy of accommodation was in some respects its most impressive feature. How, may it be asked, can you accommodate with gangsters? How can you make deals with a man like Hitler? But, it would be retorted, what is the alternative? The alternative was the polarisation of Europe, the acceleration of the arms race, and war, when their sons would suffer the fate of Wilfred Owen's 'Doomed Youth', for whom:

> *The pallor of the girls' brows shall be their pall;*
> *Their flowers the tenderness of silent minds,*
> *And each slow dusk a drawing-down of blinds.*

*

But, after the cynical occupation of Czechoslovakia on March 15th, 1939, Chamberlain was temporarily jolted out of his policies. Two days later, in Birmingham, he was drawn by the evident mood of the audience into an unprepared denunciation of the German action, which was wildly applauded. There were suddenly fears for Romania and Poland. At once, Churchill's depiction of a German grand strategy of calculated aggression and acquisition seemed only too real. It was clear to the party managers that the House of Commons, and particularly the Conservatives, were not prepared to accept any more Munichs. The Franco-British guarantee to Poland of March 31st was a hastily-considered absurdity, and only makes sense in the context of a sudden desperation and desire to appear resolute. Harold Nicolson's account of this event should not be omitted:

> Chamberlain comes into the House looking gaunt and ill. The skin above his high cheekbones is parchment yellow. He drops wearily into his place. David Margesson proposes the Adjournment and the P.M. rises. He begins by saying that we believe in negotiation and do not trust in rumours. He then gets to the centre of his statement, namely that if Poland is attacked we shall declare war. That is greeted with cheers from every side. He reads his statement very slowly with a bent grey head. It is most impressive.[1]

The concomitant steps towards an Anglo-Russian agreement were dismally half-hearted. The once-confident Government was being stampeded into new alliances for which it had no enthusiasm and which were in their view impracticable and unnecessary. 'I must confess to the most profound distrust of Russia', Chamberlain wrote at the end of March. Outside the Labour Party it was widely shared. But this was one of those occasions when Governments are not masters of their own destinies. The Polish Guarantee was a case in point.

Halifax had been one of the first to realise that the Munich mood could not last, and after Prague there was a sharp reaction away from any further conciliation, a fact that was signified by the startling public restoration of Churchill's position. Few people could remember any of his individual speeches, but his persistent reiteration of the German menace had got through. The realisation, however vague, that he had been 'right' when virtually everyone else had been 'wrong' over-simplified the matter, but was certainly not unjustified. Personal abuse directed against him by the German leaders did him no harm at all. His stock rose rapidly in the House of Commons. A letter urging his

[1] Nicolson, op. cit., 393.

recall to the Government signed by a number of prominent people was published in the *Daily Telegraph* (after being rejected by *The Times*). He was being hailed by the *Daily Mirror* as 'Britain's most trusted statesman', and there were many other indications of his suddenly changed status.

Thus, in the early summer of 1939 Chamberlain was being forced by the evident feeling in the House of Commons into a reluctant belligerent posture while still believing that peace could be maintained. The introduction of military conscription—strongly opposed by Labour—was not a true indication of British resolve. The Government also announced in April the appointment of a Minister of Supply; the Minister himself was not appointed until July. The conscription was not immediate, and was limited to six months' preparatory training. The new Minister turned out to be Leslie Burgin, another Inskip. In May came the announcement of the 'Pact of Steel' alliance between Italy and Germany. The Anglo-Russian discussions were the touchstone of the British resolve towards Poland. Seldom has a matter of such importance been handled with such lethargy. The dispersal of the House of Commons on August 2nd was the occasion for angry scenes, in which pro-Chamberlain Conservatives shouted angrily at those who urged that Parliament should not adjourn.

Chamberlain stated that he would regard a vote on the matter as one of confidence, and the temperature rose rapidly. Forty Conservatives abstained, nonetheless, and Parliament adjourned in a sulphurous atmosphere. On August 22nd the thunderclap of the Nazi-Soviet Pact was announced, and Parliament was hastily summoned. 'The P.M. was dignified and calm', Nicolson wrote on the 24th, 'but without one word which could inspire anybody. He was exactly like a coroner summing up a case of murder. I see mighty little chance of peace.'

Some Ministers, however, still clutched at the hope that war might be averted. On September 1st Germany invaded Poland, but no British declaration of war followed. The House of Commons met in agitation, and received no clear indication of the Government's policy. Desperate efforts to avert the inevitable continued, but the mood of the House of Commons was no longer amenable to these endeavours. On the evening of September 2nd, Chamberlain's statement to the House was so equivocal that when Arthur Greenwood (deputising for Attlee, who was unwell) rose from the Front Opposition bench he was greeted with a bitter cry from Leo Amery, 'Speak for England!' In that instant the accumulated tensions of months exploded memorably. 'It was an astonishing demonstration', as Nicolson recorded. 'Greenwood almost staggered with surprise. When it subsided he had to speak and did so better than I expected. He began to say what an embarrassing task had been imposed on him. He had wanted to support, and was obliged to criticise. Why this delay? We had promised to help Poland "at once". She was being bombed and attacked. We had vacillated for 34 hours. What did this mean? He was resoundingly cheered. Then tension became more acute, since here were the P.M.'s most ardent supporters cheering his opponent with all their lungs. The front bench looked as if they had been struck in the face . . .'.[1] Chamberlain intervened lamely, and the House adjourned in 'great confusion and indignation', in Nicolson's words.

Immediately after the House rose, there was an even more unexpected revolt, this time from within the Government. Ministers decided upon immediate and direct action. The Minister of Agriculture—Sir Reginald Dorman-Smith—has related that:

> reports are quite wrong about stormy scenes. This was a plain *diktat* from the Cabinet . . . I remember that the P.M. was calm, even icy cold, all the time . . . The climax came most dramatically. The P.M. said quietly: 'Right, gentlemen, this means war.' Hardly had he said it when there was the most enormous clap of thunder, and the whole Cabinet Room was lit up by a blinding flash of lightning.

The most vehement single group against the impending war was Mosley's Fascists, declaring that 'The War on Want is The War We Want', and endeavouring to create a Peace Front. It was a motley collection of the good, the bad, the enlightened and the idiotic, bound together with the inextricable links of irrelevance. Dean Inge and Lord Alfred Douglas gave their full support. A vast rally—attended by some 20,000 people—had taken place at Earls Court on July 16th, at which Mosley excoriated the major parties and the Jews. 'We fight for Britain, yes, but a million Britons shall never die in your Jews' quarrel.' Mosley's arguments were in fact more subtle and realistic than his oratory would imply, but he had once again fatally misunderstood the mood of the times. It was to be his last misunderstanding. The political career that had opened so brilliantly and excitingly,

---

[1] Nicolson, op. cit., 419.

and which had shown such genuine promise, collapsed in derision and contempt.

There was no possible escape for Chamberlain short of resignation, and the British ultimatum to Germany was dispatched. It expired at 11 o'clock on the morning of September 3rd. At 11.15 Chamberlain spoke to the nation, in terms of melancholy acceptance which were strangely moving. The House of Commons was due to meet at noon, but was delayed by a false air-raid warning. The evening and night of September 2nd had been wild and stormy, but September 3rd was a perfect late-summer day. The House of Commons met in a strange atmosphere of calm, as if a prolonged and agonised nightmare had been concluded. Churchill had been invited to join the Government on September 1st, but had heard nothing since then, and was still on the back benches, from which he rose to make his last speech from the political wilderness. Later he recorded:

> As I sat in my place, listening to the speeches, a very strong sense of calm came over me, after the intense passions and excitements of the past few days. I felt a security of mind, and was conscious of a kind of uplifted detachment from human and personal affairs. The glory of Old England, peace-loving and ill-prepared as she was, but instant and fearless at the call of honour, thrilled my being and seemed to lift our fate to those spheres far removed from earthly facts and physical sensation.[1]

Not all enjoyed this sense of comfort and relief. Chamberlain spoke in terms of anguish. 'Everything I have worked for, everything that I have hoped for, everything that I have believed in during my public life, has crashed in ruins.' The mood was not one of exaltation, but of grim resignation. The euphoria and exhilaration of 1914 were gone, yet there was a remarkable lack of realisation of the scale and extent of the task which lay before the British people, and certainly little comprehension of the dangers which confronted them. But the British, like the Chamberlain Government, went reluctantly to war. 'At 1.50', Nicolson wrote in his diary for September 3rd, 'I motor down with Victor Cazalet to Sissinghurst. There are many army lorries passing along the road and a few pathetic trucks evacuating East End refugees. In one of those there is an elderly woman who shakes her fist at us and shouts that it is all the fault of the rich.'[2]

[1] Churchill, op. cit., 320.   [2] Nicolson, op. cit., 422.

RETROSPECT

PRESIDENT WILSON DECLARED in December 1918 that 'I believe that . . . men are beginning to see, not perhaps the golden age, but an age which at any rate is brightening from decade to decade, and will lead us some time to an elevation from which we can see the things for which the heart of mankind is longing'. The story of the inter-war years is how that vision quickly faded, then returned, only to be destroyed for ever.

It is easy for the historian, many years later, to point morals and deliver judgements. It is always important to remember that, to the contemporary, matters are always confused, and that it is always difficult to distinguish the meaningful from the irrelevant, the great issues from the small, the significant portent from the passing transient phenomenon. Consistency may be the hobgoblin of little minds; it is also a perilous attitude in an always changing situation.

It may also be a pleasant pastime for the historian to select his politicians and his parties and to impose upon them the policies and attitudes which he, with his subsequent wisdom, may deem to have been the most appropriate. The post-war Lloyd George Coalition should have striven to create and maintain the Weimar Republic in Germany and create a viable European order in the League. It should have entered into immediate negotiations for a settlement of the Irish Question. It should have addressed itself most seriously to industrial relations at home. It should have made use of the experience of the Great War in managing and developing a national economy. It should have pursued a mildly inflationary policy, invested heavily in the new industries while enabling the older ones to rehabilitate themselves. It should have eschewed romantic dreams of Free Trade, laissez-faire, and the return to gold. It should have recognised the fact of Soviet Russia, and the enormous potentialities of the United States. It should not have disarmed so quickly and completely.

But the Coalition was a liaison of individuals and parties that had had its origins in the darker period of the War. It was subject to the strong tides of electoral opinion. It was composed of men whose political lives and experiences had been well advanced before that war began. The policies that that Government followed were compounded of the respective attitudes, experiences, and prejudices of its members, and necessarily reflected their political background in the pre-war years. Victorians all, the experience of the war had confirmed them in their conviction that the foundations of that victory had been laid in the previous decades. The desire to return to 'normalcy' was accordingly a reactionary attitude in the best—if also the most disastrous—sense of the word. But, as we have seen, this essential conservatism did not apply to the Coalition leaders alone. The leaders of the nascent Labour and dying Liberal parties were also children of the Victorian era.

It was the misfortune of the Coalition leaders that they were the first to discover, the hard way, that so much had changed. The privileged and unchallenged dominance of the old political classes was itself fading. In 1918 Britain had taken a giant step towards becoming a full democracy, a process that was completed ten years later. It was significant that Churchill, in *My Early Life* (1930), looked back with such nostalgia to the good old days when 'we had a real political democracy, led by the hierachy of statesmen, and not a fluid mass distracted by newspapers. There was a structure in which statesmen, electors and the Press all played their part . . . All this was before the liquefaction of the British political system had set in.' By 1934 he was denouncing the British political system as 'a timid Caesarism refreshing itself by occasional plebiscites', and was declaring that 'all experience goes to show that once the vote has been given to everyone, and what is called full democracy has been achieved, the whole [political] system is very speedily broken up and swept away'.

In fact, the structure of British politics had been affected in more subtle manners than this gloomy diagnosis would suggest. The glittering personages of the Lloyd George Coalition—their manner, their style, their assumptions, their arrogant acceptance of authority —parade before us as characteristic figures of a political era that had gone. It is doubtful if any of them fully realised the true cause of their downfall, which was simply that they were out of date. At this distance of time it is possible to form a less severe judgement upon the Coalition and to appreciate more fully the magnitude of the burdens that it endured, than many contemporaries had been prepared to concede. But, if people expected too much, it may be remarked that they had been led to expect too much. Justice, in politics, usually is somewhat rough, but it is difficult to deny that the Coalition did receive justice.

It was unfortunate that power fell from the hands of one type of pre-war politician to another. Baldwin emerges as the most sensitive and sensible of the major inter-war political figures, to whom belated justice must be given for much wisdom and perceptiveness, yet his vision of a Britain in which Master and Worker lived in harmony and mutual respect was in many ways as unreal, as romantic, and as historically false as were the Imperial dreams of Churchill and Amery, and MacDonald's respectable, Utopian, socialism. Snowden's tenacious seizure of the Holy Grail of Free Trade ensured that the advent of Labour, far from heralding revolution and change, marked a decisive step backwards into nineteenth-century Radicalism. The claims of Mosley, Keynes, and Hubert Henderson to have found the cures for Britain's industrial and economic ailments may be viewed with some scepticism, but their remedies offered infinitely more hope than the essentially reactionary and unimaginative attitudes of Ministers, officials, and orthodox advisers in the 1920s and even in the 1930s.

One may notice the continuance of many of the problems and dilemmas in other fields from the pre-1914 era, often in a more acute form. Home Rule was at last conceded to Southern Ireland, but only after the British had been compelled to seek negotiations—and not the least of the significant features of this episode was the fact that it was British public opinion, for so long hostile to Irish ambitions, that was the decisive factor. The long struggle over Ireland ended with a virtual war in which the British resorted to methods that appalled decent opinion everywhere, and was followed by a Civil War that cost Ireland the lives of many of the men who could have made the new nation operate successfully in its formative years.

In Imperial matters we can see the development of the relationship of the self-governing Dominions carried to its logical conclusion in the definition of Dominion Status and the Statute of Westminster. The attempts of successive British Ministers and believers in Empire to bind the Empire into a more formal relationship failed, and the continued failure to achieve co-operation in Defence matters emphasised the fundamental separatist tendencies of the new nations. The existence of this separatism was covered up by phrases and formulae, and by the genuine mutual affection and regard that existed between the Dominions and Britain. But, as the Chanak Crisis of 1922 and the Imperial Conference of 1937 demonstrated once again—if further evidence had been required—British policy was becoming more dominated by Dominion attitudes than the other way around. In her continued faith in Empire, Britain had become imprisoned by it, and had become grossly over-extended in military and economic terms.

British Governments had not lost their interest in Imperial affairs. But, at the top, the emphasis was now on maintaining what existed rather than engaging in any serious attempt to change the *status quo*, and far less to extend British Imperial commitments. The revised terms of association with Egypt may be seen to be particularly significant. The dismissal of Lord Lloyd and the abandonment of the Cromer–Milner approach marked a new attitude and, some might say, a new realisation, however dimly perceived, that national interests could be preserved without the apparatus and authority of virtual complete rule.

Elsewhere—and India is the most conspicuous example—we can see the further development of ideas of association that were the logical conclusion of previous measures and attitudes. But here we can also see a failure to realise that the pace, particularly in the East, had sharply accelerated, and that what was offered was too little and, above all, too late. In the debates on the Government of India Act we can clearly see three distinct attitudes emerging—that represented by Churchill and his associates; that espoused by men like Amery, who believed in the future of the Empire as a world confederation of vast significance in which nationalism and supra-nationalism could dwell together; and that put forward by a minority in Parliament, but by a not derisory minority, to the effect that the movement must be towards complete independence and, if necessary, separatism. This may be said to represent a return to the Radical attitudes towards Empire of the first half of the nineteenth century. Had not the Second World War vastly increased the pace of the desire for independence, this development might have taken longer to achieve. It is difficult, however, to believe that it could have been averted. The pattern had been established in the case of the 'white' Dominions, and the illogicality of denying it to other peoples was clearly exposed in the lengthy debates on the 1935 Act. And the minority that argued thus in the early 1930s was to find itself in a majority after 1945. The Indians, as had the Irish, learned that their battle was to be won in England and that Disraeli had been right when he declared that 'the keys of India are in London'.

Nevertheless, we shall note that a sharp differentiation still existed between the African and non-African states. The unscrambling of Africa was to be essentially a post-Second World War phenomenon.

In British domestic politics the outstanding feature of this period, and most particularly of the inter-war years, was the dominance of the Conservative Party. This unique federation, constantly changing yet with its essential characteristics unchanged, survived all others in the years 1886 to 1939. Only in the years 1906–14 was it seriously out of office. For the rest, the history of these years is that of almost complete Conservative rule, with occasional and very fleeting interludes of Opposition. The fundamental reason for this remarkable durability lies in the development into unspoken doctrine of the Disraelian philosophy that change must come, but that it must be change conducted on the terms of the propertied classes. The Reform Acts had widened the franchise, but had still concentrated it upon a minority—and a minority with a profound stake in cautious, ordered, change. When Labour emerged in 1917–18, it, too, was dominated by this approach, and could not compete on level terms with the Conservative experience and ruthlessness in this particular limited political market.

Between the two, the Liberals were crushed into extinction. They could not command the mass of cautious conservatism which exists in all classes in Britain and which serves as the bed-rock of the Conservative Party. They were detached from the new masses which progressed from active trade unionism into dedicated support for the Labour Party. The Liberals accordingly drifted into a middle ground between two powerful combinations, each of which had a substantial unwavering constituency and the capacity to appeal to the uncommitted. It could be argued that Liberalism as a general philosophy had not died, and that its tenets had been accepted and appropriated by the other parties. But the schism of 1916 and the Asquith–Lloyd George feud had been more significant than issues of ideology. Its bold programme of 1928–9 was the last burst of energy from a party whose intellectual and practical contribution had transformed the political and social character of the nation. But it had become divided and irrelevant, and it perished.

The Conservatives certainly moved to the Left between 1919 and 1939. In essentials, this tendency was not more marked than that between the 1860s and the beginning of the Great War, but in most respects—and particularly in domestic reform—it was more coherent and better based. The eager social-reform Conservatives who came into politics from the trenches were disillusioned and disappointed by what was achieved, but their contribution had been significant. In particular, the nascent battle with trade unions had been averted in the 1920s, and the general approach of the Conservatives in the 1930s had been one of tolerance and reform. The overwhelming rejection of extreme policies, both in Dominion and home affairs, was of real historical significance in heralding the final decline of the 'two nations'. It was here that Baldwin's personal contribution was of such importance, and his defeats of his right-wing critics so fundamental to the continued relevance of his party. This was Baldwin's supreme achievement; like Disraeli, he 'educated' his party, and it was his misfortune that power came to him again in 1935 in circumstances in which neither he nor the nation had sufficient time for gradual change.

Labour had not presented an impressive picture in office. It lacked experience, leadership, and a real philosophy. Suddenly projected into prominence and office, it never enjoyed power. The roots of the Parliamentary Party lay deep in Victorian Liberalism, and the passionate craving for respectability and acceptability dominated its fevered and distracted counsels. Both in 1924 and in 1929–31 it demonstrated these characteristics with sad clarity. In some spheres— and not least in foreign affairs—Labour often had the right attitudes, but these were not accompanied with either practical experience or profound thinking. Labour's real chance came in 1940; war was to provide it with the experience and the stature and the freedom to operate which had always been denied to it before. But the lessons of the 1920s and the 1930s were to be of even greater importance in the establishment of the Labour Party as the natural and unchallengeable successor to the Liberal Party. Out of the tumults, the errors, the agonies and the heart-searchings of this formative period the modern Labour Party was born.

*

This narrative opened in 1880. The flaring gas-jets above the great glass ceiling of the House of Commons—that ceiling which had been built over the bitter objections of Sir Charles Barry—had, in 1880, flickered and illuminated Gladstone, Joseph Chamberlain, Parnell, Lord Randolph Churchill, Arthur Balfour, Harcourt and Hartington. In the same Chamber, on September 3rd, 1939, the sons of Joseph Chamberlain and Lord Randolph Churchill were prominent, the one white, tense, and temporarily crushed, the other pink-faced, determined, and grimly elated. On the Conservative benches there sat Leo Amery, who had fought his first election in 1906; opposite, there was Lloyd George, his hair now a shock of white mane, but his eyes still clear and crisp, first elected in 1890. Baldwin was in retirement, MacDonald, Balfour, Asquith and Campbell-Bannerman were dead. Yet in that tawny chamber, soon to be destroyed for ever, where Disraeli and Gladstone had debated, where Lord Randolph Churchill had risen and fallen, where the young Lloyd George had denounced the South African War and the even younger Winston Churchill had seen his party walk out contemptuously as he addressed the House in 1904, where Campbell-Bannerman had swept Balfour aside and Asquith had been howled down in the tempests of the 1911 Constitutional Crisis, a mysterious sense of continuity still existed. And it was this indefinable element, this incalculable sentiment of history and of fundamental justice, which was to bring the British Parliament and people through an ordeal unparalleled in the long annals of their turbulent history. The Britain of 1939 was very different from that of 1880. A vast, almost silent, revolution had been accomplished. Much more remained to be done, and many more injustices to be resolved. But the Britain of 1939 was in almost every respect a better nation, a more equitable nation, and a more united nation, than it had been when the gas-lights flared upon the House of Commons seventy years before.

Of course, the history of a people is not a stable, fixed, thing. The achievements of one generation may easily be lost by the next. There is little pattern in the past, few hints of what tomorrow may bring. But if the British can point to their survival as their principal achievement in the twentieth century, this is, in itself, no idle or unworthy claim. And it is in this spirit and resilience that we may find the answer to the quandary of how the British were to survive two World Wars, the loss of much of their wealth, the disappearance of their Empire, a reduction to minor status among the world powers, the continued follies of their leaders, and their manifest inadequacies in material possessions and economic systems when compared with other nations. How this was achieved must be the theme of a subsequent volume. But even in 1939, after these seventy years of triumph, tragedy, change and revolution, the British people could console themselves with Aeschylus' dictum:

Why repine at Fortune's frowns? The gain hath the advantage, and the loss does not bear down the scale.

And thus, on September 3rd, 1939, with none of the excitement of August 1914, and with grim forebodings, this remarkable, perplexing, and defiant people entered another stage of their curious, many-faceted, and unfinished odyssey.

SELECT BIBLIOGRAPHY

As this book is designed primarily for the general rather than the specialised reader, this Bibliography does not claim to be exhaustive, nor to include all the books and articles that have been consulted in its preparation.

GENERAL

The best brief book on the period is A. F. Havighurst: *Twentieth Century Britain* (1962), although H. Pelling: *Modern Britain, 1885–1955* (1960) runs it close. The best general studies are C. L. Mowat: *Britain Between The Wars, 1918–1940* (1955) and W. N. Medlicott: *Contemporary England, 1914–1964* (1967), but as both were written before the official archives were available some of their judgements require revision. The same applies to A. J. P. Taylor: *English History 1914–1945* (1965), which may fairly be described as brilliant but erratic. C. Barnett: *The Collapse of British Power* (1972) is a bitter denunciation of many villains, some of which seem to this author to have been harshly treated. S. Beer: *Modern British Politics* (1965) is excellent, as is D. Thomson's brief *England In The Twentieth Century* (1965). E. H. Carr: *The Twenty Years Crisis* (1939) is of considerable value, despite the correctives necessarily needed in the light of later knowledge; the same caution applies to W. McElwee: *Britain's Locust Years, 1918–1940* (1962), but which has tended to be underestimated by historians. G. H. Le May: *British Government 1914–1953; Select Documents* (1955) is invaluable, as is P. and G. Ford: *A Breviate of Parliamentary Papers 1917–1939* (1951). There is, alas, no Parliamentary commentator in the period comparable to H. W. Lucy or the younger A. G. Gardiner, but Lord Winterton: *Orders Of the Day* (1953), Harold Nicolson's diaries, volume one (1961), and those of Sir Henry Channon (1967) provide interesting sidelights on the House of Commons. On the general scene, to be recommended are M. Muggeridge: *The Thirties* (1940), R. Graves and A. Hodge: *The Long Week-End* (1940), and P. Quennell: *Life In Britain Between The Wars* (1970). The appropriate chapters of G. D. H. Cole and Raymond Postgate: *The Common People, 1746–1946* (1955), E. Shinwell: *Conflict Without Malice* (1955), W. Citrine: *Men and Work* (1964), A. Bullock: *Ernest Bevin*, Vol. I (1960), *Herbert Morrison: An Autobiography* (1960), and the diaries of Hugh Dalton *Call Back Yesterday* (1953) and *The Fateful Years* (1957) give a darker aspect to life in the period.

On economic matters, particularly recommended are A. J. Youngson: *The British Economy 1920–1957* (1960), H. Henderson: *The Inter-War Years and Other Papers* (1955), R. S. Sayers: *A History of Economic Change in England, 1880–1939* (1967), U. K. Hicks: *British Public Finances, 1880–1952* (1954), R. F. Harrod: *John Maynard Keynes* (1951) and R. Skidelsky: *Politicians and the Slump* (1967), which rightly goes farther and deeper than its account of the collapse of the 1929–31 Labour Government. W.

Ashworth: *Economic History of Modern England, 1870–1939* (1960) is perhaps the best single book of all.

On foreign affairs the massive *Documents on British Foreign Policy* provides vital basic material for much of the period. F. S. Northedge: *The Troubled Giant* (1966), W. N. Medlicott: *British Foreign Policy Since Versailles* (second edition, 1968), and P. A. Reynolds: *British Foreign Policy In The Inter-War Years* (1954) are good, but would benefit from revision to take account of new information from the Cabinet and Foreign Office archives. Winston Churchill's *The Gathering Storm* (1948) is an overwhelmingly convincing personal view of the inter-war years, and should, accordingly, be treated with great caution. Lord Avon: *Facing the Dictators* (1962), Lord Templewood: *Nine Troubled Years* (1954), Lord Vansittart: *The Mist Procession* (1958), I. Colvin: *Vansittart In Office* (1965), Lord Simon: *Retrospect* (1952), Duff Cooper: *Old Men Forget* (1953) also give points of view that are highly personal. Lloyd George's *War Memoirs* (6 volumes, 1933–6) are heavy going, and unreliable. Churchill's *The World Crisis* (5 volumes, 1923–9) is a classic of literature and also of personal vindication that does not totally convince all historians. A. J. P. Taylor: *The Origins of the Second World War* (revised edition, 1963) caused a highly satisfying sensation when it first appeared in 1961; it can now be seen as a most valuable and stimulating corrective to the then general thesis of Hitler's saturnine and calculated policies of aggression, and is now almost respectable. M. Howard: *The Continental Commitment* (1970) and R. K. Middlemas: *Diplomacy of Illusion* (1972) are two excellent recent additions to the literature, and D. C. Watt: *Personalities and Policies* (1965) remains fresh, invigorating, and shrewd. A. Bullock: *Hitler, A Study in Tyranny* (revised edition, 1964) still stands up remarkably well in spite of the torrent of books on Hitler since then. Dennis Mack Smith's biography of Mussolini (1976) is a comparably remarkable achievement. M. Gilbert: *The Roots of Appeasement* (1966) argues a thesis ably but not, in this author's view, convincingly. Hugh Thomas: *The Spanish Civil War* (1961) is an outstanding history. L. S. Amery: *My Political Life*, Volumes II and III (1953, 1955) is particularly useful on Commonwealth and Colonial matters in the 1920s, when he was in office, and Harold Nicolson: *Curzon, The Last Phase* (1934) is a dramatic and very sympathetic account of the negotiations leading to the Treaty of Lausanne. K. Young's biography of Balfour (1963) is not very strong on the final part of Balfour's remarkable career; R. K. Middlemas and J. Barnes put up a valiant defence of Baldwin (1969) which is marred by excessive length and detail, and perhaps protests too much. It is, however, a much-needed corrective to Churchill, G. M. Young, and Beaverbrook.

Mention should also be made to C. Thorne: *The Approach of War, 1938–9* (1967). K. Feiling: *Neville Chamberlain* (1946) remains the best biography of this controversial man; Iain Macleod's biography (1961) was a deep disappointment, and not least to the author. For all the mass of studies of foreign policy in the 1930s, no single volume as yet masters the complexities nor fully escapes the charge of emotional involvement.

BIOGRAPHIES AND MEMOIRS

In addition to those already mentioned, particular attention must be paid to M. Gilbert's continuing marathon biography of Winston Churchill, of which volume V (1976) takes the story up to 1939. It is such a remarkable personal achievement that it seems unkind to comment that it is in fact so long and so massively documented that the immense complexities and fascination of Churchill's extraordinary personality have become somewhat submerged. H. Pelling's single-volume biography (1974) is rather uncritical. R. Rhodes James: *Churchill, A Study In Failure 1900–1939* (1970) endeavoured to treat Churchill as a fallible, erratic, human being of immense ability but uneven judgement. Later discoveries have tended to confirm the validity of this then revolutionary approach to a post-1939 national idol.

R. Jenkins' admiring biography of Asquith (1964) has now been supplemented by a cooler perspective from S. Koss (1976). Lloyd George's later career still lacks its historian, and there is nothing to compare with J. Grigg's study of the early period. R. Blake: *The Unknown Prime Minister* (1955) is superb on Bonar Law, and H. Nicolson and Lady Donaldson have written admirable biographies of King George V (1952) and King Edward VIII (1974) respectively, although the latter cannot be called an official or authorised biography—perhaps the better for that. In R. Rhodes James: *Memoirs of a Conservative* (1968) the obscure but important J. C. C. Davidson gives his account of the 1920s, with some important insights and documents. Also of value are B. H. Liddell Hart: *Memoirs* (1965 and 1966), S. Roskill: *Hankey, Man of Secrets* (three volumes, 1970, 1972, and 1975), R. J. Minney: *The Private Papers of Hore-Belisha* (1960), H. Macmillan: *Winds of Change* (1966), R. Boothby: *I Fight To Live* (1947), P. J. Grigg: *Prejudice and Judgement* (1948), C. Addison: *Politics From Within* (1924), Mary Hamilton: *Remembering My Good Friends* (1944), T. Jones: *Diary With Letters* (1954) and his *Whitehall Diary*, edited by R. K. Middlemas in three volumes (1969–71). These are all, of course, personal views of men and events, but each is of use. Lord E. Percy: *Some Memories* (1958), Lord Swinton: *I Remember* (1948) and *Sixty Years of Power* (1966), and Lord Butler: *The Art of the Possible* (1971) are far above the average standard of politicians' memoirs, although none quite reaches the standard of Duff Cooper's.

It cannot be pretended that the period has yet produced biographies of the exceptional quality of the previous one. There is certainly none to compare with Morley on Gladstone, Monypenny and Buckle, and R. Blake, on Disraeli, Churchill and Rosebery on Lord Randolph Churchill, R. Barry O'Brien and Conor Cruise O'Brien on Parnell, or Lady Gwendolen Cecil on Salisbury. This does not mean that the standard is low. Of particular merit are A. J. P. Taylor: *Beaverbrook* (1972), H. Thomas: *John Strachey* (1973), Bullock on Ernest Bevin, M. Foot on Aneurin Bevan (Volume I, 1966), R. Skidelsky on Mosley (1975), and R. W. Clark: *Tizard* (1965). Also of value are Lord Birkenhead's biographies of Halifax (1964), his own father, F. E. Smith (1959), Walter Monckton (1969), and Lindemann (*The Prof in Two Worlds* (1964)). R. F. Harrod also wrote an interesting personal memoir of this strange man (1959). Randolph Churchill's *Lord Derby, King of Lancashire* (1959) contains some important raw material. Also recommended are C. Cross: *Philip Snowden* (1966), L. Mosley: *Curzon, The End of an Epoch* (1960), J. R. M. Butler: *Lord Lothian* (1960), M. Hamilton: *Arthur Henderson* (1938), Sir Charles Petrie's second volume of his biography of Austen Chamberlain (1940), and R. Rhodes James: *Victor Cazalet* (1976).

MISCELLANEOUS

The literature on the Great War is primarily military; the best brief study is that by C. Falls (1960), but the general standard is very high. On the political side, in addition to the titles already mentioned, Hankey's *The Supreme Command* (1961) has now been superseded by Roskill's biography, but remains of value. Beaverbrook's entrancing volumes (*Politicians and the War* (1928), *Men And Power* (1956), and *The*

Decline And Fall of Lloyd George (1963)) should be read and enjoyed, but with Taylor's biography close to hand to pour cold water on some of the better stories. R. Blake: *The Private Papers of Douglas Haig* (1953), Sir William Robertson's *Soldiers and Statesmen* (1926), and V. Bonham-Carter's biography of Robertson, *Soldier True* (1963) are essentially political rather than military sources. C. Hazlehurst: *Politicians At War, 1914–15* is a belligerent book, at times unnecessarily so, but based on solid research. T. Wilson: *The Downfall of the Liberal Party 1914–1935* is valuable on the war-time schisms, and there are useful contributions to the history of war-time politics in A. J. P. Taylor: *Politics in Wartime* (1964). There is, as yet, no single satisfying study of war-time politics, but the material is rapidly building up in biographies and special studies.

GENERAL POLITICAL

Finally, particular mention should be made of certain books that deal with specific aspects or periods. M. Cowling: *The Impact of Labour* (1971) hammers an important and valuable thesis almost into the ground, but is essential—if difficult—reading. His *The Impact of Hitler* (1974) also contains a mass of new material, but is also rather hard going. R. Blake: *The Conservative Party From Peel to Churchill* (1970) is fluent and perceptive, but is not the history of the Party that is so needed. Roy Douglas's *History of the Liberal Party 1895–1970* is not particularly informative. One of the best books on inter-war Labour politics is R. K. Middlemas: *The Clydesiders*, but its scope is necessarily limited. H. Pelling: *A Short History of the Labour Party* (1961) is excellent, but does not probe deeply. Of considerable use are C. A. Cline: *Recruits To Labour, 1914–1931*, R. W. Lyman: *The First Labour Government, 1924* (1957), R. Bassett: *1931— Political Crisis* (1958), and S. R. Graubard: *British Labour and the Russian Revolution* (1956). C. Cross: *The Fascists in Britain* (1961) and H. Pelling: *The Communist Party* (1958) deal rather unsatisfactorily with these fringe, but not insignificant, elements in inter-war poltics.

INDEX